11th Edition

How to Get a Green Card

Ilona Bray, J.D., and
Loida Nicolas Lewis, J.D.
Updated by Attorney Kristina Gasson

Eleventh Edition	JULY 2014
Editor	ILONA BRAY
Cover Design	SUSAN PUTNEY
Book Design	COLLEEN CAIN
Proofreading	IRENE BARNARD
Index	UNGER INDEXING
Printing	BANG PRINTING

ISSN: 2371-9885 (print)
ISSN: 2371-9915 (online)
ISBN: 978-1-4133-1961-3 (pbk)
ISBN: 978-1-4133-1962-0 (epub ebook)

This book covers only United States law, unless it specifically states otherwise.

Please note

We believe accurate, plain-English legal information should help you solve many of your own legal problems. But this text is not a substitute for personalized advice from a knowledgeable lawyer. If you want the help of a trained professional—and we'll always point out situations in which we think that's a good idea—consult an attorney licensed to practice in your state.

Acknowledgments

The original authors of this book were Loida Nicolas Lewis and Len Madlansacay. Nolo thanks them for their efforts in producing a work of such ambitious scope, and one that has endured for many years.

Of course, changes in immigration laws and practices have necessitated many rewrites and revisions of the original book.

For this edition we owe a tremendous debt of thanks to Kristina Gasson, a Massachusetts-based attorney, for thoroughly updating the contents and adding new tips and insights, particularly on the matters of Deferred Action for Childhood Arrivals (DACA) and U visas for victims of crime in the United States.

About the Authors

Ilona Bray came to the practice of immigration law through her long interest in international human rights issues. Before joining Nolo as legal editor in charge of immigration, she ran a solo law practice and worked for nonprofit immigration agencies including the International Institute of the East Bay (Oakland) and the Northwest Immigrant Rights Project (Seattle). Ms. Bray was also an intern in the legal office at Amnesty International's International Secretariat in London. She received her Bachelor's degree in philosophy from Bryn Mawr College, and her law degree and a Master's degree in East Asian (Chinese) Studies from the University of Washington. Ms. Bray is a member of the American Immigration Lawyers' Association (AILA). She has authored other books for Nolo, including *Fiancé & Marriage Visas: A Couple's Guide to U.S. Immigration* and *Becoming a U.S. Citizen: A Guide to the Law, Exam & Interview*.

Loida Nicolas Lewis is a former INS attorney with over 15 years' experience handling U.S. immigration matters. She practiced law in both New York and the Philippines.

Kristina Gasson (www.gassonlaw.com) assists clients with a number of immigration matters in her solo practice, including green card applications for spouses and other family members, fiancé visas, citizenship petitions, and employment-based green cards and visas. She has represented clients in removal proceedings and asylum hearings in Immigration Court. Ms. Gasson has also provided *pro bono* services for a number of legal clinics and nonprofit organizations and has interned for the Executive Office for Immigration Review (EOIR) and the U.S. Senate. She is a freelance writer and editor at Nolo, and has written content for a number of journals, practice manuals, newspapers, magazines, and online media. Ms. Gasson received her law degree from Temple University Beasley School of Law and her Bachelor's degree in political science from Brown University and is a member of the American Immigration Lawyers Association (AILA). She is licensed to practice law in Massachusetts and New York, but is able to represent immigration clients throughout the U.S. and internationally.

Table of Contents

Your Immigration Companion

Are you a foreign-born person who's interested in making your home in the United States? If so, this book may be just the ticket to finding out whether you're eligible for permanent U.S. residence, also known as a "green card." A green card gives you the right to live and work in the United States your whole life, travel in and out of the country without too much hassle, sponsor certain family members to join you, and, if all goes well for a few years, apply for U.S. citizenship.

This book will help you learn the application procedures, fill out the various forms, and pick up tips for dealing with often-difficult government officials. We try to give you a realistic view of your immigration possibilities and guide you along the path—which may be a long one—to reaching your goals. And unlike many government publications, we'll warn you about what could go wrong, and what steps to take to avoid delays and problems. Immigrants to the United States have to face a huge and often unfriendly government bureaucracy. Often, it's not the law itself that gives immigrants problems, but dealing with government delays, mistakes, and inattention. So, it helps to have a friend like this book by your side.

However, some people won't get the help they need from this book, so read this chapter carefully before you continue!

A. Types of Green Cards We Cover

This book was designed to help the "average" person—for example, someone who doesn't have a million dollars to invest, isn't internationally famous, and hasn't received a job offer from a U.S. employer. That's why we've focused our discussion on the following types of green card opportunities:

- family-based green cards, available to close relatives and adopted children of U.S. citizens and permanent residents

- political asylum and refugee status, available to people fleeing certain types of persecution
- the visa lottery ("diversity visa"), available to people with a certain level of education who win a random drawing, and
- opportunities for people who have lived in the United States for ten years or more and are in removal proceedings ("cancellation of removal").

This book does *not* cover green cards through employment, investment, the amnesty programs of the 1980s and the followup "NACARA" program, religious workers, or other, more obscure categories. Nor does it cover temporary visas (distinct from green cards in that they expire, usually in a few years). Examples of temporary visas include student, business visitor, H-1B specialty worker, and J-1 exchange visitor visas. (For a quick overview of these temporary visas, see Chapter 3.)

 CAUTION

Don't confuse green cards with U.S. citizenship. The highest status you can obtain under the U.S. immigration laws is citizenship. However, with only a very few exceptions, you must get a green card before you can apply for citizenship. For example, an immigrant who marries a U.S. citizen may gain the right to apply for a green card, but not yet to apply for U.S. citizenship.

B. How Much You Can Do Without a Lawyer

The advice given in this book is for simple, straightforward cases. In other words, it's for people who clearly meet the eligibility requirements laid out in this book and have the education and skills to understand and handle the application requirements.

Many tasks you can do yourself, such as filling in forms, collecting documents, and attending interviews. Still, even filling out immigration forms can be a challenge. You'll be dealing with a bureaucracy that loves paperwork, but isn't always friendly to someone who makes minor mistakes or submits inconsistent information. Hiring an attorney—who handles this type of paperwork every day and knows whom to call when things go wrong—can be well worth the expense, both for convenience and for your own peace of mind.

And if your case is more complex, you absolutely should hire a lawyer to advise or represent you. This may be the case if:

- you have been ordered to appear before an immigration judge for what are called "removal" proceedings because the immigration authorities do not believe that you have a legal reason to either enter or continue to stay in the United States
- you have a criminal record
- you have some other problems with your immigration paperwork, for example, you have submitted forged documents, or
- the paperwork and technical requirements are too heavy; for example, you must apply for political asylum and you'll need to assemble a lot of evidence about conditions in your home country, or you are appealing some decision made in your case by immigration authorities.

Of course, the key is to get a really good, experienced attorney. See Chapter 24 for guidance in hiring and working with a lawyer.

C. Using This Book

You need not read every chapter in this book—only those helpful to your specific situation. Here is some guidance.

Read **Chapter 1** if you're interested in a summary of immigration trends and laws throughout history.

Everyone should read **Chapters 2, 3, and 4.** They describe the basic requirements for obtaining legal permission to stay in the United States.

Everyone should also read **Chapter 5.** It explains the general forms and procedures required for obtaining a green card and the annual numbered limits or quotas that may apply.

 TIP

This book doesn't provide blank forms, for good reason. All the application forms you'll need—and we'll tell you exactly which ones they are—are either readily available for free (www.uscis.gov or www.state.gov) or will be mailed to you by the immigration authorities when the time is right. Some can even be filled out online. The forms get revised frequently, so it's best for you to obtain the most up-to-date form when you're ready to use it. We have, however, provided sample filled-in forms to illustrate our advice and show you what the form will look like.

Now you can choose and read the specific chapters that concern you. Look over the chapter headings for **Chapters 6 through 15, as well as 18 and 19**—and read the ones that make the most sense in your specific situation. For example, if you believe that you might qualify for a green card because you will be marrying or are already married to a U.S. citizen, read **Chapter 7.** It may refer you to other chapters you should read to get a more complete picture.

Each chapter contains samples of most of the forms you'll need to complete.

After reading about the various rules for specific types of immigrants, if you decide that you qualify to file for yourself or another person, read **Chapters 21 and 22.** These chapters will help you with filling out the necessary forms and getting them into the right hands.

If you lose your green card or need to renew or replace it, read **Chapter 23** to find out how to do so.

Some people will find that they don't qualify for U.S. immigration at all, or at least not yet—it's a complicated and narrow system. But the good news is that approximately one million people receive U.S. green cards every year.

 CAUTION

Green cards come with certain limitations. It's not a completely secure status. For example, you can lose your right to your green card if you:

- commit a crime
- don't make your primary home in the United States
- forget to report your change of address to the immigration authorities
- involve yourself in terrorist or subversive activities, or
- otherwise violate the immigration laws.

Steps You Must Take to Keep Up to Date

This book was as up-to-date as we could make it on the day it was printed. However, immigration laws change frequently, and USCIS changes its fees, rules, forms, and procedures even more often—at times without telling anyone.

That's why you must take certain steps on your own to protect your rights and interests. In particular, be sure to do the following:

- Check the USCIS website before turning in any application. Click the "Forms" tab. Make sure the form you filled out is still the most up to date, and that the fee hasn't gone up.
- Check the companion page for this book at **www.nolo.com/back-of-book/GRN.html** Here you'll find legal updates, author blog postings, and other useful information. Also see whether we've published a later edition of this book, in which case you'll probably want to get that later edition.
- Listen to the news, particularly for changes by the U.S. Congress. But don't rush to USCIS to apply for something until you're sure it's final. A lot of laws in progress get reported on before the president has actually signed them.

Immigration Then and Now
America: A Nation of Immigrants

To understand current immigration policy, it helps to know how it came about.

A. America's Earliest Settlers

Long before Cristobal Colon—the Spanish name for Christopher Columbus—opened the Americas to the Europeans in 1492, the first inhabitants of what is now the United States were the Native American Indians, including the Eskimos. Other early settlers included the Vikings, in the northernmost part of North America, and the ancestors of today's Hawaiians.

From the 15th century onward, the continent became a magnet for explorers and colonists from Spain, Holland, France, and England. In 1620, the pilgrims landed in Massachusetts—although they intended to land in Virginia—where they founded their new Zion, free from the interference of the English government. Quakers settled in Pennsylvania. Maryland provided refuge for Catholics who had been persecuted in England.

Spanish Jews, who had settled in Brazil after being expelled from Spain, arrived in New York when the Portuguese took over the former Spanish colony and started the Brazilian inquisition. After the Scottish rebellion was crushed, people from Scotland left for the colonies.

Other immigrants came in groups and provided their special skills to the new cities and settlements: Austrians from Salzburg made silk; Poles and Germans made tar, glass, and tools, and built homes. Later, Italians came and raised grapes. New Jersey was settled by the Swedes; northern Pennsylvania attracted a large number of Germans.

1. Forced Migration

Not everyone who came to the New World did so of their own free will. Many crossed the ocean as indentured servants for landowners in the English colonies.

And as cotton became the most important product in the South, plantation owners turned to the inhuman trade of African people to create a huge and cheap workforce, while the businessmen of the North who conducted the slave trade found it highly profitable.

By the time the first census of the new republic was taken in 1790, two-thirds of its four million inhabitants were English-speaking, and the rest were from other nations. Of these, 698,000 were African Americans who lived in human bondage mostly in the South; another 59,000 were free.

Although the U.S. Congress amended the Constitution in 1808 to ban the importation of slaves, it took nearly half a century before the smuggling of human beings stopped.

2. European Exodus

Between 1820 and 1910, Europe experienced the greatest migration of people to the New World. During that time, at least 38 million Europeans arrived in the United States.

Several important events caused this great migration: the Napoleonic Wars; the political disturbances in Germany, Austria-Hungary, Greece, and Poland; the Potato Famine in Ireland; the religious persecutions of Protestants, Catholics, and Jews in Czarist Russia and other parts of Europe; and the Industrial Revolution, which produced thousands of unemployed workers and peasants.

3. Growth of the Continental U.S.

At the same time, the United States was expanding into the West and the Southwest all the way to the Pacific Coast. The country grew by purchase, such as the Louisiana Purchase from Napoleon I of France, which bought an expanse of land from the Mississippi to the Rocky Mountains, and the purchase of Florida from Spain. It grew by war, such as the one waged with Mexico for California and Texas, and the one with Britain in 1812, which ended with a treaty granting the United States parts of Canada. The nation grew by possession of Native Americans' ancestral lands, sometimes by treaty, sometimes by purchase, and sometimes by outright massacre.

B. Early Immigration Restrictions

In California, the Gold Rush of 1849 brought not only people from all over America but also the Chinese from across the Pacific Ocean. Chinese workers provided cheap labor for the construction of the Union Pacific Railroad. However, they were not granted the right to become American citizens.

By 1882, there were approximately 300,000 low-wage Chinese laborers in America. These new workers became targets to Americans for antagonism and racial hatred. As a result, the Chinese Exclusion Act was passed in 1882, completely banning non-citizen Chinese from immigrating to the United States. This law remained in effect until 1943.

The Japanese then took the place of the Chinese in agriculture, domestic work, lumber mills, and salmon fisheries. By 1920, approximately 200,000 Japanese immigrants were found on the East Coast and 100,000 more on the sugar plantations in Hawaii. These Japanese workers also were subjected to racial hatred. They were excluded from the United States in 1908 and prohibited from becoming U.S. citizens by the Immigration Act of 1924.

Also during this time, after America purchased the Philippines from Spain in 1898, Filipinos were able to immigrate. They were concentrated mostly on the East Coast and Hawaii as laborers on farms and sugar plantations, and in fish canneries and logging camps. These Filipinos were not spared the racial animosity that permeated American society—and they also were excluded from citizenship by the immigration laws passed in 1924.

This great influx of people in the late 19th and early 20th centuries brought the passage of several restrictive immigration laws. At various times,

the U.S. Congress forbade people it considered undesirable to enter—paupers, drunkards, anarchists, polygamists, and people of various specific national origins.

In 1917, Congress passed an Immigration Act to restrict the entry of immigrants, especially the flow of illiterate laborers from central and eastern Europe. No immigration was permitted to the United States from the Asiatic Barred Zone. In addition to China and Japan, this zone included India, Siam (Thailand), Indochina (Vietnam, Cambodia, and Laos), Afghanistan, parts of Siberia, Iran, and Arabia, and the islands of Java, Sumatra, Ceylon, Borneo, New Guinea, and Celebes.

After World War I, America faced economic depression and unemployment, and the immigrant became the scapegoat. In 1921, a tight national-origins quota system was enacted as a temporary measure. Total immigration was limited to about 350,000 per year. Immigration from each country in a given year was limited to 3% of all nationals from that country who were living in the United States during the 1910 census.

This system was made permanent when the U.S. Congress approved the National Origins Act of 1924. Its purpose was "to arrest a trend toward a change in the fundamental composition of the American stock." Based on the ethnic composition of the United States as recorded in the 1920 census, it limited the entry of aliens from any one country to 2% of the number of their people living in the United States. In one stroke, the law reduced the total immigration of aliens from all countries to 150,000 per year.

The object of the law was not simply to limit immigration but to favor certain kinds of immigrants and keep out others. More immigrants were permitted from western Europe and fewer from southern and eastern Europe. The law totally excluded Asians. It was intended mainly to prohibit Chinese, Japanese, and Filipinos from acquiring U.S. citizenship.

After World War II, however, the door to immigration would again open—this time, to a few carefully selected groups of immigrants. A new category of naturalized Americans was admitted: thousands of alien soldiers who had served with the U.S. armed forces overseas during the war.

Congress also passed the War Brides Act in 1945 to facilitate the reunion of 118,000 alien spouses and children with members of the U.S. armed forces who had fought and married overseas.

The Displaced Persons Act of 1948 allowed 400,000 refugees admission to the U.S. over the next two years. Most of them had been displaced from Poland, Romania, Hungary, the Baltic area, the Ukraine, and Yugoslavia, and had been living in refugee camps in Germany, Italy, and Austria.

When the Iron Curtain fell on Eastern Europe, the Refugee Relief Act of 1953 allowed 214,000 refugees from Communist countries to be admitted into the United States. The anti-Soviet fighters from Hungary, after the suppression of their revolution in 1956, were paroled into the United States—that is, allowed to enter without a visa.

C. Today's Immigration Laws

When the Immigration and Nationality Act was passed in 1952, it wove all the existing immigration laws into one and formed a basic immigration law that's similar to the one we know now. (However, it was not until President Lyndon Johnson signed the 1965 amendments into law that the racially biased national origin quota was abolished.)

The amendments introduced two general ways of becoming an immigrant: by family relationship and by the employment needs of the United States. The legislation established a preference system— giving priority to some groups of immigrants over others. For example, spouses and children of U.S. citizens had higher priority than their brothers and sisters. The law also provided a separate category for refugees.

Where to Find the Immigration Laws

The entire set of immigration laws is now available online and at law libraries, in Title 8 of the U.S. Code. One way to look up code sections online is to go to www.nolo.com/legal-research, then click the heading "Federal Law Resources," then "U.S. Code," and then enter "8" in the first box ("Title") and the section number in the second. Occasionally in this book, we'll tell you where you can read a certain piece of the immigration laws by referring to the code section—for example, 8 U.S.C. § 1101.

However, immigration lawyers and government officials tend to use a separate numbering system for the same codes, preceded by the letters I.N.A., for "Immigration and Nationality Act," so when we include citations here we'll also give you the I.N.A. section reference. The I.N.A. is available on the USCIS website (www.uscis.gov) under "Laws."

---

1. Preference for Skilled Workers

In 1965, the laws were amended to allow skilled workers to move more easily to the United States. The departure of doctors, lawyers, engineers, scientists, teachers, accountants, nurses, and other professionals caused a "brain drain" not only in Europe, but also in Asia, the Pacific Rim, and developing countries.

This preference for skilled workers remains in effect. Although the laws allow a few unskilled workers to immigrate, the numbers are so limited that the category is useless for many people.

2. Refugees and Political Asylum

The end of the Vietnam War resulted in a flow of refugees from the Indochinese peninsula.

In 1980, Fidel Castro declared that the Port of Mariel was open to anyone who wanted to leave. Cuban refugees arrived on the shores of Florida by the thousands. These included some criminals and mentally ill people who had been forced by Castro to leave the jails and mental hospitals.

In response, the U.S. Congress passed the Refugee Act of 1980, which defined a "refugee" as someone who fears persecution in his or her home country because of religious or political beliefs, race, national origin, or ethnic identity. Based on this law, the U.S. admits tens of thousands of refugees annually, and grants asylum to many who have fled persecution and made it to the U.S. on their own.

3. Amnesty for Undocumented Workers in the 1980s

The Immigration Reform and Control Act of 1986, more commonly known as the "Amnesty Law," benefited a large number of Mexicans and other aliens. Those who had entered and were living without legal status in the United States since January 1, 1982—more than two million aliens—were granted legal residency. Their spouses and children were also entitled to become permanent residents.

At the same time, the Amnesty Law attempted to control the future influx of undocumented aliens into the United States—and those controls still exist today. Any employer who hires or recruits an alien or who, for a fee, refers an alien to another employer without first verifying the alien's immigration status, is subject to a fine ranging from $200 to $10,000 for each undocumented alien employed.

4. Immigration Acts From 1990 to the Present

With the Immigration Act of 1990, the U.S. Congress approved its most comprehensive overhaul of immigration law since 1965.

This act provided for a huge increase of immigrants, up to 675,000 from 1995 forward. It aimed to attract immigrants who have the education, skills, or money to enhance the economic life of the country, while at the same time maintaining the immigration policy of family reunification. The law therefore makes it easier for scientists, engineers, inventors, and other highly skilled professionals to enter the United States. Millionaire entrepreneurs have their own immigrant classification.

Under the act, citizens of nations that have had little immigration to the United States for the past five years were allocated 50,000 immigrant visas yearly under the "lottery" system. Temporary protections were added for people fleeing war or natural disasters, such as earthquakes. Refugees from the civil war in El Salvador were the first beneficiaries.

Such provisions made the Immigration Act of 1990 the most humane legislation for immigrants in the past century. However, more recent changes again closed America's doors to many immigrants. These changes included 1996's Antiterrorism and Effective Death Penalty Act (AEDPA) and Illegal Immigration Reform and Immigrant Responsibility Act (IIRIRA).

A variety of legislative and regulatory changes have also been added since the terrorist attacks of September 11, 2001, tightening controls on would-be immigrants as well as those who are already here.

The most notable of these were the USA Patriot Act of 2002, which expanded the definition of terrorism and increased the government's authority to detain and deport immigrants, and the November 2002 legislation establishing the new Department of Homeland Security (DHS), which broke the Immigration and Naturalization Service (INS) into three agencies under the DHS's power. These three new agencies include U.S. Citizenship and Immigration Services (USCIS), which took over the most public INS functions, such as deciding on applications for immigration benefits; Immigration and Customs Enforcement (ICE), which now handles enforcement of the immigration laws within the U.S. borders; and Customs and Border Protection (CBP), which handles U.S. border enforcement (including at land borders, airports, and seaports). These changes further illustrate that the immigration policy of the United States constantly shifts according to its needs and political will.

D. Looking Forward

Immigration law policies are a subject of ongoing congressional scrutiny, change, and then reverse change. With every shift in the U.S. economy and sense of security (or insecurity), public attitudes toward immigrants shift as well.

At the time this book went to print, Congress was hotly debating the matter of whether to overhaul the U.S. immigration laws. The proposals on the table would not, if passed, make many changes to the matters described in this book—and we'll tell you in cases where they would.

The opening lines of the Declaration of Independence of the United States of America, so eloquently written by Thomas Jefferson some 200 years ago, remain both an inspiration and a challenge:

We hold these truths to be self-evident, that all men are created equal, that they are endowed by their Creator with certain unalienable Rights, that among these are Life, Liberty, and the pursuit of Happiness.

All Ways to Get a Green Card

The official name for the green card is the Alien Registration Receipt Card. It has been called a green card because, when it was first introduced in the 1940s, the color of the plastic identification card with the alien's photo, registration number, date of birth, and date and port of entry was green.

Over the years, the card's color has been, at various times, blue, white, and pink, but now it is green again.

Front of Green Card

Back of Green Card

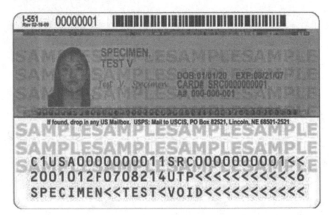

There are several ways a person can obtain a green card—that is, become a lawful permanent resident. The most popular ones are through family and work. The other ways include proving that you're fleeing from persecution, making large investments, and a few more obscure bases.

This book covers the green card categories most readily available to ordinary people, with an emphasis on family categories. However, this chapter will tell you a little about the other major green card categories, and where to go next if you're interested in them.

A. Family-Based Relationships

Recognizing that the family is important in the life of the nation, the U.S. Congress created ways for family members to be reunited with their relatives who are U.S. citizens or lawful permanent residents.

1. Related or Engaged to a U.S. Citizen

If you are the spouse (opposite-sex or same-sex), child, brother, sister, or parent of, or are engaged to be married to, a U.S. citizen, you can become a lawful permanent resident. The person to whom you're related or engaged must start the process by filing a petition with USCIS or the U.S. embassy in your country of residence.

If you are the widow or widower of a U.S. citizen and it was a good-faith marriage (not a sham to get a green card), you can petition for a green card for yourself, provided you file the application (Form I-360) within two years of the death of your spouse (unless your spouse had already filed a Form I-130 for you), you weren't legally separated at the time of death, and you haven't remarried.

2. Related to a Lawful Permanent Resident

If you are the spouse or unmarried child of a lawful permanent resident, you can obtain a green card—someday. First, the relative who has the green card must file a petition with USCIS. But you'll have to wait several years, until you reach the top of a waiting list, to apply for the actual green card.

3. Other Relatives

If you are the aunt, uncle, niece, nephew, cousin, grandmother, or grandfather of a U.S. citizen, or if you are the brother, sister, parent, or fiancé of someone who holds a green card, you do not qualify for a green card based on a "family relationship." Understandably, the U.S. Congress had to draw the line on what constitutes a family for the purpose of immigration.

 NEXT STEP

If you believe you qualify for a family-based green card, or are helping someone who does, here's where to go next: Readers who are engaged to U.S. citizens, see Chapter 6. Readers who are married to U.S. citizens or permanent residents, see Chapter 7. Readers who are parents of U.S. citizens, see Chapter 8. Readers who are children of U.S. citizens or permanent residents, see Chapter 9. For how to bring in an orphan child, see Chapter 10. Readers who are brothers or sisters of U.S. citizens, see Chapter 12.

B. Employment-Based Relationships

If you do not have a close family member who is a U.S. citizen or who holds a green card, you may be able to obtain a green card through a job offer from an employer in the United States—as either a priority or a non-priority worker.

1. Priority Workers

Priority workers are people with extraordinary ability (such as an internationally known artist), outstanding professors and researchers, and multinational executives and managers. Another name for this category is "employment first preference."

Such highly skilled people have a relatively easy immigration process. Some do not even need a job offer, and none are required to go through the difficult labor certification process that other immigrating workers must pass, in which the Department of Labor determines that there are no qualified U.S. workers available and willing to do the same job.

2. Other Workers

Applicants who have been offered jobs that require graduate degrees in the arts or sciences or a profession (such as a law degree), or a master's degree in business administration (MBA), or a bachelor's degree plus five years of specialized experience are eligible for immigrant visas. This category is known as "employment second preference."

These applicants will first need certification from the Department of Labor saying that no qualified U.S. worker is available, willing, and able to do the job.

Also, ordinary professionals (without graduate degrees) and skilled or unskilled workers (factory workers, plumbers, domestic workers, carpenters, and the like) may apply for labor certification and a green card on the basis of a job offer. This category is known as "employment third preference."

 SEE AN EXPERT

If you believe you qualify for any of these employment-based green cards, consult an experienced immigration attorney. As explained earlier, this book doesn't cover employment-based immigration. The employer who has offered you a job (and you must have a job offer in almost all categories described above) may have an attorney it works with regularly. The employer may even be willing to pay the attorneys' fees.

Be Ready to Wait

It may take you a long time to become a permanent resident under some of the immigrant visa categories described in this chapter. Once you file the first petition form to set the process in motion, however, it may become very difficult for you to come to the United States as a tourist or other nonimmigrant, or to have your status as a nonimmigrant extended. That's because, in order to obtain most non-immigrant visas, you have to prove that you plan to return to your home country after your stay on the visa—and it's hard to prove permanent ties to your home country if you're simultaneously planning to leave it behind and get a U.S. green card.

The only groups who need not be concerned with this warning are diplomats (A visas), employees of international organizations (G visas), intracompany transferees (L-1 or L-2 visas), and workers in specialty occupations that require a bachelor's degree or its equivalent (H-1B visas).

C. Special Immigrants

Certain categories of people may obtain a green card by special laws—in addition to certain provisions of the Immigration Act of 1990—intended to benefit limited groups. These include, for example:

- priests, nuns, pastors, ministers, rabbis, imams, and other workers of recognized religious denominations
- former employees of the U.S. government, commended by the U.S. Secretary of State for having performed outstanding service to the government for at least 15 years
- medical doctors who have been licensed in the United States and have worked and lived in the United States since January 1978
- former employees of the Panama Canal Zone

- retired officers or employees of certain international organizations who have lived in the United States for a certain time, plus their spouses and unmarried children
- foreign workers who have been employees of the U.S. consulate in Hong Kong for at least three years
- foreign children who have been declared dependent in juvenile courts in the United States, and
- international broadcasting employees.

All these people fall into a green card category known as "employment-based fourth preference."

SEE AN EXPERT

If you believe you fit one of these categories, consult an experienced immigration attorney. Special immigrants are not covered in this book. Your employer may be willing to hire an attorney for you.

D. Entrepreneur Immigrants

An alien entrepreneur from any country who invests at least one million dollars in a business (or $500,000 if the business is in an economically depressed area) and who employs at least ten U.S. citizens or lawful permanent residents is eligible for a green card. Each year, 10,000 immigrant visas are set aside for this millionaire immigrant category, which is designed to create employment. This category is also known as "employment-based fifth preference" or "EB-5."

SEE AN EXPERT

Are you financially able to qualify for a green card based on investment? If so, it's well worth hiring an experienced immigration attorney to help.

E. Asylum and Refugee Status

People who can prove that they fled their country based on past persecution or out of fear of future persecution owing to their race, religion, nationality, membership in a particular social group, or political opinion may apply for legal status as refugees (if they're outside the U.S.) or asylees (if they're already inside the U.S.).

A person who gains U.S. government approval as a refugee or asylee can apply for permanent residence status later (more specifically, one year after being admitted to the United States as a refugee or one year after asylee status is granted).

> **NEXT STEP**
> **For more information on applying for refugee or asylee status, see Chapter 13.**

F. Diversity Visa Lottery

The Immigration Act of 1990 created a green card category to benefit people from countries that in recent years have sent the fewest numbers of immigrants to the United States. You can enter the lottery if you are a native of one of those countries and meet certain educational and other requirements. Because the winners are selected through a random drawing, the program is popularly known as the green card lottery. Its official name is the Diversity Immigrant Visa Lottery.

There are 50,000 winners selected each year. They are chosen by dividing the world into regions and allocating no more than 7% of the total green cards to each region.

However, even if you win the lottery, you still have to make it through the green card application process—and many people fail, because they're inadmissible or the government can't process their application by the deadlines set by law.

> **NEXT STEP**
> **For more information on applying for the visa lottery, and what to do if you win, see Chapter 11.**

G. Amnesties

Once in a while, Congress gives blanket green card eligibility to people who have been living in the United States illegally.

The most recent amnesty was offered in the early 1980s. Although anti-immigrant commentators regularly complain that every new law that benefits immigrants is an "amnesty," there has been no actual amnesty offered since that time.

Immigration reform was proposed in Congress in 2013, and some of its provisions actually offered an amnesty-like path to a green card. No reform efforts had, however, been finalized by the time this book went to print in 2014. If and when comprehensive immigration reform does pass, it will not likely go into effect for several months thereafter. Keep your eyes on the news and the Nolo website for updates, and beware of the many scammers urging immigrants to pay to submit an application when no such application yet exists.

> **NEXT STEP**
> **Interested in learning more about a past or upcoming amnesty?** Consult an experienced immigration attorney or a local nonprofit. Do not go to a USCIS office unless you want to risk deportation.

H. Private Bills

You may have heard of people who became permanent residents by means of a private bill passed by the U.S. Congress. However, such cases are rare. You must have very special circumstances—and very strong political ties—to get a private bill passed.

Look into the possibility of a private bill where the law is against you but your case has strong humanitarian factors. Private bills succeed when an injustice can be corrected only by a special act of the U.S. Congress.

1. What Is a Private Bill?

A private bill is the last resort of a desperate alien facing removal (deportation)—a special urging by high-level U.S. politicians to allow you to stay in the U.S. legally. Currently, very few private bills are filed on behalf of aliens. Fewer than 100 private bills have been successful during each of the past several years.

The successful ones tend to be people in unusually tragic situations, such as a family that came to the U.S. seeking cancer treatment for a child, only to have the father and mother of the child killed in a car wreck.

2. How a Private Bill Is Passed

A private bill must be sponsored by one or more members of the House of Representatives and one or more members of the Senate who urge that one individual be given special consideration in being allowed to become a permanent resident or get citizenship.

Like a law, a private bill has to be introduced in both houses of Congress. It then has to be recommended favorably by the Judiciary Committee to which it has been assigned in both houses, after having been favorably reported on by the Subcommittee on Immigration of both houses.

Both houses of Congress must approve the bill during a regular session. The president of the United States must then sign it into law.

Thus, if you are an alien facing deportation, you will have to go through the eye of a needle before getting your private bill passed by Congress and signed by the president. In short, hiring the best immigration lawyer in town will likely give you a better chance to obtain a green card than will the private bill route.

Short-Term Alternatives to a Green Card

As you know, this book is only about green cards—or, in legal-speak, U.S. permanent residence. However, you probably also know that many people who want U.S. green cards will never be able to get one. The green card categories are very limited, and the application process is hard to get through successfully. That's why this chapter will briefly tell you about some other—sometimes easier—ways to come to the United States, even if it's for a shorter time.

RESOURCE

Want to learn more about the ways to stay temporarily in the United States? See *U.S. Immigration Made Easy,* by Ilona Bray (Nolo).

A. How Do Foreigners Enter the United States?

The basic rule is that most people may enter the United States only after receiving permission from the U.S. government, through the U.S. embassy or consulate in their own country. The permission or authority to enter the United States is called a "visa," and is stamped in your passport by the U.S. consul. A major exception is if you are eligible to enter under the Visa Waiver Program; see discussion in Section C, below.

If you enter the United States without permission, without a visa or a visa waiver, and without being examined by the immigration authorities, you are called an "undocumented alien" within the immigration laws and an "illegal alien" by the general public.

B. Types of Visas

There are two kinds of visas an alien can receive from the U.S. embassy or consulate: an immigrant visa and a nonimmigrant visa.

1. Immigrant Visas

Just to avoid confusion, we should mention that even those people who are in the process of getting a green card, as discussed in the rest of this book, must get a physical visa first if they'll be arriving from another country. They receive what is called an "immigrant visa." They receive the actual green card only after they have arrived in the United States and claimed their permanent residency. People who apply for their green cards from within the United States must also be allocated a visa number, although they'll never see or receive a physical visa.

2. Nonimmigrant Visas

Nonimmigrant visas are the main topic we'd like to introduce you to in this short chapter. A nonimmigrant visa gives you the ability to stay in the United States temporarily with limited rights. A visa that expires in a few years is probably your second choice, given that you're reading a book on green cards. However, a nonimmigrant visa might serve you in two different ways. First, it might allow you to legally visit the United States in order to decide whether you really want a green card, or to make a decision that will lead to your getting a green card. For example, a person might come to the U.S. on a tourist (B-2) visa to visit his or her U.S. citizen boyfriend or girlfriend, to find out whether getting married seems like a good idea.

Second, a nonimmigrant visa might be your only choice for the moment. If your research, using this book and other resources, leads you to believe that you don't qualify for a green card, then a nonimmigrant visa might allow you to at least live in the United States for a while, developing U.S. contacts or job skills, hoping that a green card opportunity will open up.

Unfortunately, nonimmigrant visas are not only short-term solutions, but they restrict your life in the United States in other ways. For example, a tourist visa (B-2) does not allow you to work. A student visa (F-1 or M-1) does not allow a student to stop studying in order to work. A temporary worker's visa (H-1B), given to a professional worker such as an accountant or engineer, does not authorize you to change employers without permission.

3. Nonimmigrant Visa Classifications

You will often hear visa classifications referred to in shorthand by a letter followed by a number. The following table summarizes the nonimmigrant visa classifications available.

Classification	Summary
A-1	Ambassadors, public ministers, consular officers, or career diplomats, and their immediate families
A-2	Other foreign government officials or employees, and their immediate families
A-3	Personal attendants, servants, or employees of A-1 and A-2 visa holders, and their immediate families
B-1	Temporary business visitors
B-2	Temporary pleasure visitors
C-1	Foreign travelers in immediate and continuous transit through the U.S.
D-1	Crewmembers (sea or air)
E-1	Treaty traders and their spouses or children
E-2	Treaty investors and their spouses or children
E-3	Australians who have at least a bachelor's degree or its equivalent, working in specialty occupations
F-1	Academic or language students
F-2	Spouses or children of F-1 visa holders
G-1	Designated principal resident representatives of foreign governments coming to the U.S. to work for an international organization, and their staff members and immediate families
G-2	Other representatives of foreign governments coming to the U.S. to work for an international organization, and their immediate families

Classification	Summary
G-3	Representatives of foreign governments and their immediate families, who would ordinarily qualify for G-1 or G-2 visas except that their governments are not members of an international organization
G-4	Officers or employees of international organizations, and their immediate families
G-5	Attendants, servants, and personal employees of G-1 through G-4 visa holders, and their immediate families
H-1B	Aliens working in specialty occupations requiring at least a bachelor's degree or its equivalent in on-the-job experience
H-2A	Temporary agricultural workers coming to the U.S. to fill positions for which a temporary shortage of American workers has been recognized by the U.S. Department of Agriculture
H-2B	Temporary workers of various kinds coming to the U.S. to perform temporary jobs for which there is a shortage of available qualified U.S. workers
H-3	Temporary trainees
H-4	Spouses or children of H-1A/B, H-2A/B, or H-3 visa holders
I	Representatives of the foreign press, coming to the U.S. to work solely in that capacity, and their immediate families
J-1	Exchange visitors coming to the U.S. to study, work, or train as part of an exchange program officially recognized by the U.S. Department of State
J-2	Spouses or children of J-1 visa holders
K-1	Fiancés and fiancées of U.S. citizens coming to the U.S. for the purpose of getting married
K-2	Children of K-1 visa holders
K-3	Spouses of U.S. citizens awaiting approval of their immigrant visa petition or the availability of a green card
K-4	Children of K-3 visa holders
L-1	Intracompany transferees who work as managers, executives, or persons with specialized knowledge

Classification	Summary
L-2	Spouses or children of L-1 visa holders
M-1	Vocational or other nonacademic students
M-2	Immediate families of M-1 visa holders
N	Children and parents of certain special immigrants
NATO-1	Principal permanent representatives of member states to NATO and its subsidiary bodies, who are residents in the U.S., and resident official staff members, secretaries general, assistant secretaries general, and executive secretaries of NATO, other permanent NATO officials of similar rank, or their immediate families
NATO-2	Other representatives to member states to NATO and its subsidiary bodies, including its advisers and technical experts of delegations, members of Immediate Article 3, 4 UST 1796 families; dependents of members of forces entering in accordance with the Status-of-Forces Agreement or in accordance with the Protocol on Status of International Military Headquarters; members of such a force if issued visas
NATO-3	Official clerical staff accompanying representatives of member states to NATO and its subsidiary bodies, and their immediate families
NATO-4	Officials of NATO other than those who can be classified as NATO-1, and their immediate families
NATO-5	Experts other than officials who can be classified as NATO-1, employed in missions on behalf of NATO, and their dependents
NATO-6	Members of civilian components accompanying forces entering in accordance with provisions of the NATO Status-of-Forces Agreement; members of civilian components attached to or employed by allied headquarters under the Protocol on Status of International Military Headquarters set up pursuant to the North Atlantic Treaty; and their dependents
NATO-7	Attendants, servants, or personal employees of NATO-1 through NATO-6 classes, and their immediate families

Classification	Summary
O-1	Aliens of extraordinary ability in the sciences, arts, education, business, or athletics
O-2	Support staff of O-1 visa holders
O-3	Spouses or children of O-1 or O-2 visa holders
P-1	Internationally recognized athletes and entertainers
P-2	Artists or entertainers in reciprocal exchange programs
P-3	Artists and entertainers coming to the U.S. to give culturally unique performances in a group
P-4	Spouses or children of P-1, P-2, or P-3 visa holders
Q-1	Participants in international cultural exchange programs
Q-2	Irish Peace Process Cultural and Training Program (Walsh Visas)
Q-3	Immediate family members of Q-1 visa holders
R-1	Aliens in religious occupations
R-2	Spouses or children of R-1 visa holders
S-5	Certain aliens supplying critical information relating to a criminal organization or enterprise
S-6	Certain aliens supplying critical information relating to terrorism
S-7	Immediate family members of S-5 and S-6 visa holders
T	Women and children who are in the United States because they are victims of trafficking, who are cooperating with law enforcement, and who fear extreme hardship (such as retribution) if returned home
TN	NAFTA professionals from Canada or Mexico
TD	Spouses and children of NAFTA professionals
U	Aliens who have been victims of crimes, have useful information about them, and have been helping U.S. law enforcement authorities with investigating and prosecuting these crimes.
V	Spouses and children of lawful permanent residents who have visa petitions that were filed for them prior to December 21, 2000, and who have been waiting for three years or more to qualify for a green card

4. Deferred Action for Childhood Arrivals

Another important short-term alternative to a green card comes not in the form of a visa, but as a special program to prevent deportation of people who came to the U.S. very young, and have attended school and otherwise made the U.S. their home. Because of its importance as a remedy, we cover it in this book, in Chapter 18.

5. Nonimmigrant U Visa Can Lead to a Green Card

One of the visas mentioned on our summary table bears further explanation. The U visa, for people who have been the victims of crimes in the U.S. and suffered as a result, and who are cooperating with law enforcement officials, can ultimately lead to a U.S. green card. For that reason, we cover it in Chapter 19 of this book.

C. Tourists Who Can Visit Without a Visa

The Visa Waiver Program (VWP) allows the citizens of certain countries—that the Department of State (DOS) chooses—to visit the United States for 90 days without first having a tourist visa stamped on their passports.

1. What You'll Need for VWP Travel

At the moment, 38 countries participate in the VWP. If you're from one of these countries, and wish to enter the U.S. without a tourist visa, you'll need to get these things first, before starting your trip:

- **A passport meeting U.S. government requirements.** This means either an electronic passport with an integrated chip (the e-passport) or a machine-readable passport (depending on the issuing country) that is valid for six months past your expected stay in the United States.

- **A ticket for both your arrival to and departure from the United States.** Your arrival ticket needs to be with an airline or boat company that is authorized to carry VWP passengers. The exception is if you'll be entering via Canada or Mexico, in which case no departure ticket is required.

- **Prior U.S. government authorization.** You'll do this through the Electronic System for Travel Authorization (ESTA), online at https://esta.cbp.dhs.gov. You can apply at any time prior to travel, and there is no fee. You'll probably get an answer immediately, although it sometimes takes up to three days. Authorizations are generally valid for up to two years, or until your passport expires, whichever comes first. If you don't receive authorization, you'll need to apply for a nonimmigrant visa at a U.S. embassy or consulate.

- **Fee.** Travelers arriving at a land border (from Canada or Mexico) will be required to pay an entry fee.

EXAMPLE: You want to visit the United States for two months. If you live in a country that is included in the VWP, you first make sure your passport meets U.S. requirements, then get authorization to travel by filling out the online ESTA application, and then buy your round-trip plane ticket to the United States. You do not need to visit a U.S. consulate to get a tourist visa. You may, however, upon arrival in the U.S., be asked to show your departure ticket as evidence that you are simply visiting and that you will return to your country within the 90-day limit.

2. VWP-Eligible Countries

Under the Visa Waiver Program, citizens of the following countries who can present a machine-readable passport are exempted from getting visas before entering the United States:

Andorra	Japan
Australia	Latvia
Austria	Liechtenstein
Belgium	Lithuania
Brunei	Luxembourg
Chile	Malta
Czech Republic	Monaco
Denmark	New Zealand
Estonia	Norway
Finland	Portugal
France	San Marino
Germany	Singapore
Great Britain (United Kingdom)	Slovakia
Greece	Slovenia
Holland (Netherlands)	South Korea
Hungary	Spain
Iceland	Sweden
Ireland	Switzerland
Italy	Taiwan

To be included in the Visa Waiver Program, the country must have:

- a very low rate of refusals of tourist visa applications, and
- few violations of U.S. immigration laws.

In short, countries whose citizens are least likely to stay too long or work illegally in the United States are most likely to be included in the Visa Waiver Program.

Disadvantages of Entering Without a Visa

There may be disadvantages to entering the U.S. under the Visa Waiver Program.

You cannot change your tourist status to another nonimmigrant status, such as that of student or temporary worker, nor can you request an extension of your 90-day stay.

With few exceptions, you also cannot change your status to a lawful permanent resident.

In addition, should the border officials deny you entry into the United States for any reason, you have no right to appeal. Political refugees who are fleeing persecution and who apply for asylum in the United States are the sole exception. (See Chapter 13.)

D. The Importance of Staying Legal

If you enter the United States as a tourist, student, temporary worker, entertainer, or any other nonimmigrant category, your chances at a future green card depend on your maintaining your legal status and not violating the conditions of your stay in the United States. Do not overstay the limits of your visa. Do not work when you are not authorized to work. Do not change schools or employers without first requesting and receiving permission from the immigration authorities.

The consequences for breaking the rules controlling immigration may be quite serious: You could be detained in an immigration jail; removal proceedings could be started against you; and, if deported, you could be barred from returning to the United States for the next five years or more.

Even if you are not deported, if you overstay by 180 days (around six months) and then leave the United States, you will have to stay outside for three years before being admitted again. If you overstay by 12 months and then leave, the waiting period is ten years before you will be allowed to return. (See Chapter 4.)

More to the point, by staying within the law, you can make use of almost all the ways enumerated in this book to stay in the United States, as long as your status is legal.

If you are running out of time on a permitted stay, one possibility is to apply to extend your stay (if you can show a good reason for needing more time) or change your status, for example from tourist to temporary worker. You can apply for extensions or changes of status only (in most cases) if your immigration status is legal, you are not an overstaying visitor, and you have not worked illegally.

If, instead, you overstay, your visa will be automatically void—even if it is a multiple entry, indefinite visa. You will then be required to apply for a new visa at the consulate in your home country, unless you can prove "exceptional circumstances."

If there is some question in your case, or if you need to change status, you should seek professional advice from an immigration support group, specialized clinic, or experienced immigration lawyer. (See Chapter 24.) Do not depend on advice from your friends or relatives.

E. How to Extend a Visitor Visa

Temporary business or tourist visitors—those who hold B-1 or B-2 visas—once admitted to the United States, can apply for an extension of stay. The basis can be business circumstances, family reasons, or any other good reason consistent with your visa.

For example, if a tourist decides to visit different locations or to spend more time with relatives, he or she can seek an extension. The application for extension must be mailed directly to the USCIS Service Center closest to where the applicant lives. (See the USCIS website at www.uscis.gov for contact details.)

The application must include the following:

- Form I-539, Application to Extend/Change Nonimmigrant Status
- a copy of your Form I-94, which you (unless you're one of the few people who received a paper I-94 card when entering the U.S.) will need to download from the U.S. Customs and Border Protection (CBP) website at www.cbp. gov (click "Travel" then "Arrival/Departure Forms: I-94 and I-94W")
- a filing fee (currently $290); either personal check or money order will be accepted
- a company letter or other supporting documentation stating the reason for the extension request—for example, more business consultations, ongoing medical reasons, extended family visit with a complete itinerary, or another reason
- evidence to show that the visit is temporary—particularly, evidence of continued overseas employment or residence and a return plane ticket, and
- evidence of financial support, such as a bank letter including amounts in accounts. You can also have a family member promise to support you, by filling out USCIS Form I-134, available at www.uscis.gov.

Also attach an itinerary or a letter explaining your reasons for requesting the extension.

The extension may not give you as much time as you'd like. Extensions of more than six months are rare. However, you are legally allowed to stay until USCIS makes a decision on your extension.

USCIS recommends that you file for an extension at least 45 days before the expiration date of your stay, which is shown on your Form I-94. If you are prone to procrastination, file the request for extension at least 15 days before the expiration date shown on your Form I-94.

F. Changing Your Reason for Staying

If you wish to request a change of status from one category to another or apply for a green card, be aware that applying for the change within the first two months after arriving in America may lead to USCIS denying your application based on the theory of "preconceived intent." Preconceived intent simply means that you lied about your reasons for coming to the United States.

For example, if you attempt to change your status from B-2 tourist to H-1B specialty worker soon after arriving in the United States, USCIS may conclude that you had the preconceived intent of working in the United States when you applied for a tourist visa from the U.S. embassy. Your failure to reveal your actual reason for going to the United States when you first requested a visa could be considered fraud.

A similar problem can arise for people who want to study in the U.S., but sensibly want to visit some schools and see whether they like them before going through the hassle of filling out application forms. You might think that the logical thing would be to come as a tourist and then, after choosing a school, apply for a change to student status.

However, logic and the immigration laws don't always match up. USCIS may deny this type of applicants' requests to change status, saying that the person lied about his or her intention to be a tourist (the person's real, secret intention was to become a student).

Fortunately, this is one of the few immigration law traps that you can get around with advance planning. If, when applying for your tourist visa, you tell the consular official that you may wish to change to student status after looking around, then you can have a "prospective student" notation made in your tourist visa. After that, you'll be free to apply to change status without worrying that it will look like you lied.

G. What to Do If Your Application Is Denied

If USCIS denies your request for an extension of your stay in the U.S., you could contest the denial. However, this will require help from an experienced immigration lawyer. (See Chapter 24.)

It might be easier to leave the U.S. and apply for a new visa from overseas. This is far safer than staying in the U.S. illegally.

H. Tips on Filling Out Form I-539

Most of Form I-539 is self-explanatory; see the sample below. However, on Part 4 of Form I-539, Additional Information, Questions 3a through 3g may act as time bombs if you answer "yes" to any one of them—that is, they may explode and prove fatal to your application. (In the case of 3g, however, you'll be okay if your employment was undertaken while you had a work permit (EAD) from USCIS.)

Do not lie and misrepresent your answer as no when the truthful answer is yes. But if you have to answer yes to any of these six questions, it is best to consult with an immigration lawyer or other experienced immigration professional.

> **EXAMPLE:** The first question on this part of the form is: Are you or any other person included in this application an applicant for an immigrant visa? Do not answer "no" if your U.S. citizen brother filed a relative visa petition for you, even if it was ten years ago, and your immigrant visa is still pending. In all probability, USCIS would find out your fraudulent answer, and you might never get your green card as a result.

Do Not Bring This Book With You

Because this book tells you how to stay and work legally in the United States, you should not have it—or any other book about immigrating to the U.S.—with you when you enter the United States on a tourist or other nonimmigrant visa.

If the border officials suspect that you are not a bona fide tourist, they may detain and question you at the airport or border about your purpose in coming to the United States.

For the same reason, you should not board the plane with a wedding dress, a stack of resumes, or letters from your Aunt Mary or cousin John stating that employment has been arranged for you as soon as you arrive in the United States. Should the border officials find such things when you land, you will not be admitted as a tourist; you may, in fact, be sent back to your home country without being allowed to set foot outside the airport or other port of entry in the United States.

If this happens, you will be unable to return to the U.S. for five years.

Sample Form I-539, Application to Extend/Change Nonimmigrant Status (page 1)

OMB No. 1615-0003; Expires 12/31/2015

Department of Homeland Security
U.S. Citizenship and Immigration Services

I-539, Application to Extend/Change Nonimmigrant Status

START HERE - Please type or print in blue or black ink

For USCIS Use Only

Part 1. Information About You

Family Name (Last Name)	Given Name (First Name)	Middle Name
Martino	Tony	Fernando

Address -
In care of -   Antero Martino

Street Number and Name		Apt. Number
3746 81st Street		2D

City	State	Zip Code	Daytime Phone Number
Jackson Heights	NY	11372	718-555-1212

Country of Birth	Country of Citizenship
Philippines	Philippines

Date of Birth (mm/dd/yyyy) 08/02/1975	U. S. Social Security # (if any) None	A-Number (if any) None

Date of Last Arrival Into the U.S. 02/05/2012	I-94 Number 33453908 03

Current Nonimmigrant Status B-2	Expires on (mm/dd/yyyy) 08/04/2014

For USCIS Use Only columns:

Returned

Date

Resubmitted

Date

Reloc Sent

Date

Reloc Rec'd

Date

Receipt

Part 2. Application Type *(See instructions for fee)*

1. I am applying for: *(Check one)*
   a. [X] An extension of stay in my current status.
   b. [ ] A change of status. The new status I am requesting is: _____
   c. [ ] Reinstatement to student status.

2. Number of people included in this application: *(Check one)*
   a. [ ] I am the only applicant.
   b. [X] Members of my family are filing this application with me.
       The total number of people (including me) in the application is: 2
       (Complete the supplement for each co-applicant.)

[ ] Applicant Interviewed on
_____ Date

[ ] *Extension Granted to (Date):*
_____

Change of Status/Extension Granted
New Class: From *(Date):* _____
               To *(Date):* _____

Part 3. Processing Information

1. I/We request that my/our current or requested status be extended until
   (mm/dd/yyyy):   01/15/2014

2. Is this application based on an extension or change of status already granted to your spouse, child, or parent?
   [X] No [ ] Yes. USCIS Receipt # _____

3. Is this application based on a separate petition or application to give your spouse, child, or parent an extension or change of status? [X] No [ ] Yes, filed with this I-539.

   [ ] Yes, filed previously and pending with USCIS. Receipt #: _____

4. If you answered "Yes" to Question 3, give the name of the petitioner or applicant: _____

   If the petition or application is pending with USCIS, also give the following data:

Office filed at	Filed on (mm/dd/yyyy)

If Denied:
[ ] Still within period of stay
[ ] S/D to: _____
[ ] Place under docket control

Remarks:

Action Block

Part 4. Additional Information

1. For applicant #1, provide passport information: Valid to: (mm/dd/yyyy)
   Country of Issuance: Philippines   01/16/2016

2. Foreign Address: Street Number and Name   Apt. Number
   66 Felix Manalo Street

City or Town	State or Province
Cubao, Quezon City	

Country	Zip/Postal Code
Philippines	1111

To Be Completed by Attorney or Representative, if any

[ ] Fill in box if G-28 is attached to represent the applicant.

ATTY State License # _____

Form I-539 (12/18/12) Y

Sample Form I-539 (page 2)

		Yes	No
3.	**Answer the following questions. If you answer "Yes" to any question, describe the circumstances in detail and explain on a separate sheet of paper.**		
a.	Are you, or any other person included on the application, an applicant for an immigrant visa?	☐	☒
b.	Has an immigrant petition ever been filed for you or for any other person included in this application?	☐	☒
c.	Has Form I-485, Application to Register Permanent Residence or Adjust Status, ever been filed by you or by any other person included in this application?	☐	☒
d. 1.	Have you, or any other person included in this application, ever been arrested or convicted of any criminal offense since last entering the United States?	☐	☒
d. 2.	Have you EVER ordered, incited, called for, commited, assisted, helped with, or otherwise participated in any of the following: (a) Acts involving torture or genocide? (b) Killing any person? (c) Intentionally and severely injuring any person? (d) Engaging in any kind of sexual contact or relations with any person who was being forced or threatened? (e) Limiting or denying any person's ability to exercise religious beliefs?	☐	☒
d. 3.	Have you EVER: (a) Served in, been a member of, assisted in, or participated in any military unit, paramilitary unit, police unit, self-defense unit, vigilante unit, rebel group, guerrilla group, militia, or insurgent organization? (b) Served in any prison, jail, prison camp, detention facility, labor camp, or any other situation that involved detaining persons?	☐	☒
d. 4.	Have you EVER been a member of, assisted in, or participated in any group, unit, or organization of any kind in which you or other persons used any type of weapon against any person or threatened to do so?	☐	☒
d. 5.	Have you EVER assisted or participated in selling or providing weapons to any person who to your knowledge used them against another person, or in transporting weapons to any person who to your knowledge used them against another person?	☐	☒
d. 6.	Have you EVER received any type of military, paramilitary, or weapons training?	☐	☒
e.	Have you, or any other person included in this application, done anything that violated the terms of the nonimmigrant status you now hold?	☐	☒
f.	Are you, or any other person included in this application, now in removal proceedings?	☐	☒
g.	Have you, or any other person included in this application, been employed in the United States since last admitted or granted an extension or change of status?	☐	☒

1. If you answered "Yes" to Question 3f, give the following information concerning the removal proceedings on the attached page entitled **"Part 4. Additional information. Page for answers to 3f and 3g."** Include the name of the person in removal proceedings and information on jurisdiction, date proceedings began, and status of proceedings.

2. If you answered "No" to Question 3g, fully describe how you are supporting yourself on the attached page entitled **"Part 4. Additional information. Page for answers to 3f and 3g."** Include the source, amount, and basis for any income.

3. If you answered "Yes" to Question 3g, fully describe the employment on the attached page entitled **"Part 4. Additional information. Page for answers to 3f and 3g."** Include the name of the person employed, name and address of the employer, weekly income, and whether the employment was specifically authorized by USCIS.

Form I-539 (12/18/12) Y Page 2

Sample Form I-539 (page 3)

	Yes	No
h. Are you currently or have you ever been a J-1 exchange visitor or a J-2 dependent of a J-1 exchange visitor?	☐	☒

If "Yes," you must provide the dates you maintained status as a J-1 exchange visitor or J-2 dependent. Willful failure to disclose this information (or other relevant information) can result in your application being denied. Also, provide proof of your J-1 or J-2 status, such as a copy of Form DS-2019, Certificate of Eligibility for Exchange Visitor Status, or a copy of your passport that includes the J visa stamp.

Part 5. Applicant's Statement and Signature *(Read the information on penalties in the instructions before completing this section. You must file this application while in the United States.)*

Applicant's Statement (Check One):

☒ I can read and understand English, and have read and understand each and every question and instruction on this form, as well as my answer to each question.

☐ Each and every question and instruction on this form, as well as my answer to each question, has been read to me by the person named below in _____, a language in which I am fluent. I understand each and every question and instruction on this form, as well as my answer to each question.

Applicant's Signature

I certify, under penalty of perjury under the laws of the United States of America, that this application and the evidence submitted with it is all true and correct. I authorize the release of any information from my records that U.S. Citizenship and Immigration Services needs to determine eligibility for the benefit I am seeking.

Signature *Tony F. Martino*	Print your Name Tony F. Martino	Date 06/29/2014
Daytime Telephone Number 718-555-1212	E-Mail Address tonytourist@hotmail.com	

NOTE: *If you do not completely fill out this form or fail to submit required documents listed in the instructions, you may not be found eligible for the requested benefit and this application may be denied.*

Part 6. Interpreter's Statement

Language used: _____

I certify that I am fluent in English and the above-mentioned language. I further certify that I have read each and every question and instruction on this form, as well as the answer to each question, to this applicant in the above-mentioned language, and the applicant has understood each and every instruction and question on the form, as well as the answer to each question.

Signature	Print Your Name	Date
Firm Name (if applicable)	Daytime Telephone Number *(Area Code and Number)*	
Address	Fax Number *(Area Code and Number)*	E-Mail Address

Sample Form I-539 (page 4)

Part 7. Signature of Person Preparing Form, if Other Than Above *(Sign Below)*

Signature	Print Your Name	Date
Firm Name (if applicable)	Daytime Telephone Number *(Area Code and Number)*	
Address	Fax Number *(Area Code and Number)*	E-Mail Address

I declare that I prepared this application at the request of the above person and it is based on all information of which I have knowledge.

Part 4. (Continued) Additional Information. (Page 2 for answers to 3f and 3g.)

If you answered "Yes" to Question 3f in Part 4 on Page 3 of this form, give the following information concerning the removal proceedings. Include the name of the person in removal proceedings and information on jurisdiction, date proceedings began, and status of proceedings.

If you answered "No" to Question 3g in Part 4 on Page 3 of this form, fully describe how you are supporting yourself. Include the source, amount and basis for any income.

My brother, Antero Martino, will provide my lodging and other support. See attached Form I-134, Affidavit of Support.

If you answered "Yes" to Question 3g in Part 4 on Page 3 of this form, fully describe the employment. Include the name of the person employed, name and address of the employer, weekly income, and whether the employment was specifically authorized by USCIS.

Sample Form I-539 (page 5)

Supplement -1
Attach to Form I-539 when more than one person is included in the petition or application.
(List each person separately. Do not include the person named in Form I-539.)

Family Name (Last Name)	Given Name (First Name)	Middle Name	Date of Birth (mm/dd/yyyy)	
Martino	Eduardo	Lorenzo	12/01/99	
Country of Birth	Country of Citizenship	U.S. Social Security # (if any)	A-Number (if any)	
Philippines	Philippines	None	None	
Date of Arrival (mm/dd/yyyy) 02/05/14			I-94 Number 334 533 909 03	
Current Nonimmigrant Status: B-2			Expires on (mm/dd/yyyy) 08/04/2014	
Country Where Passport Issued Philippines			Expiration Date (mm/dd/yyyy) 03/08/2016	

Family Name (Last Name)	Given Name (First Name)	Middle Name	Date of Birth (mm/dd/yyyy)	
Martino	Miranda	C.	04/02/1973	
Country of Birth	Country of Citizenship	U.S. Social Security # (if any)	A-Number (if any)	
Philippines	Philippines	None	None	
Date of Arrival (mm/dd/yyyy) 02/05/14			I-94 Number 334 533 910 03	
Current Nonimmigrant Status: B-2			Expires on (mm/dd/yyyy) 08/04/2014	
Country Where Passport Issued Philippines			Expiration Date (mm/dd/yyyy) 01/16/2015	

Family Name (Last Name)	Given Name (First Name)	Middle Name	Date of Birth (mm/dd/yyyy)	
Country of Birth	Country of Citizenship	U.S. Social Security # (if any)	A-Number (if any)	
Date of Arrival (mm/dd/yyyy)			I-94 Number	
Current Nonimmigrant Status:			Expires on (mm/dd/yyyy)	
Country Where Passport Issued			Expiration Date (mm/dd/yyyy)	

Family Name (Last Name)	Given Name (First Name)	Middle Name	Date of Birth (mm/dd/yyyy)	
Country of Birth	Country of Citizenship	U.S. Social Security # (if any)	A-Number (if any)	
Date of Arrival (mm/dd/yyyy)			I-94 Number	
Current Nonimmigrant Status:			Expires on (mm/dd/yyyy)	
Country Where Passport Issued			Expiration Date (mm/dd/yyyy)	

Family Name (Last Name)	Given Name (First Name)	Middle Name	Date of Birth (mm/dd/yyyy)	
Country of Birth	Country of Citizenship	U.S. Social Security # (if any)	A-Number (if any)	
Date of Arrival (mm/dd/yyyy)			I-94 Number	
Current Nonimmigrant Status:			Expires on (mm/dd/yyyy)	
Country Where Passport Issued			Expiration Date (mm/dd/yyyy)	

If you need additional space, attach a separate sheet of paper.
Place your name, A-Number, if any, date of birth, form number, and application date at the top of the sheet of paper.

Form I-539 (12/18/12) Y Page 5

Will Inadmissibility Bar You
From Getting a Green Card?

The U.S. government has decided that people with certain histories or conditions are a risk to others and therefore should not be allowed to enter the country. These people are called "inadmissible." Inadmissibility creates problems in green card applications. This chapter explains the conditions that make a person inadmissible—and whether there is any way under the bar of inadmissibility.

A. What Is Inadmissibility?

The U.S. government keeps a list of reasons that make a person unwelcome in the United States. The list includes affliction with various physical and mental disorders, commission of crimes, participation in terrorist or subversive activity, and more.

You may be judged inadmissible any time after you have filed an application for a green card, nonimmigrant visa, or other immigration status. Even a permanent resident who departs the United States for more than 180 days may be found inadmissible upon return.

If you are found inadmissible, your immigration application will probably be denied. The notice of denial will be issued in the same manner as denials for any other reason. Even if you manage to hide your inadmissibility long enough to receive a green card or visa and be admitted into the U.S., if the problem is discovered later—perhaps when you apply for U.S. citizenship—you can be removed or deported.

B. The Possibility of Waiving Inadmissibility

Not everyone who falls into one of the categories of inadmissibility is absolutely barred from getting a green card or otherwise entering the United States. Some grounds of inadmissibility may be legally excused, or "waived." Others may not.

Below is a chart summarizing all the grounds of inadmissibility, whether or not a waiver is available,

and the special conditions you must meet to get a waiver. For more details, see I.N.A. § 212, 8 U.S.C. § 1182.

C. Most Troublesome Grounds of Inadmissibility

The 1996 Immigration Reform law made many changes to the immigration code, most of them restrictive. Although it's been several years since their passage, these continue to be among the most troublesome of the grounds of inadmissibility for many immigrants. Some of the grounds that have the most significant impact are summarized here.

1. Being Unable to Show Family Financial Support

All family-based immigrants seeking permanent residence must include an Affidavit of Support, on either Form I-864 or I-864-EZ. This form helps satisfy the requirement that an immigrant show he or she is not likely to become a public charge (in other words, receive government assistance or welfare). (But even with this form, you can still be found inadmissible on public charge grounds.)

By filling out the form and attaching various documents, the petitioning U.S. citizen or permanent resident shows his or her earnings and savings, and promises to use that money to support the immigrant or to pay back any government agency that supplies need-based support to the immigrant.

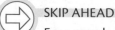 **SKIP AHEAD**

For a sample filled out Form I-864, see Chapter 17 of this book.

The I-864-EZ is a shorter, easier version of the form, which can be used only if you are the only person your petitioner is sponsoring, and your petitioner can meet the sponsorship requirements based solely upon his or her income (and nobody else's).

Inadmissibility Summary		
Ground of Inadmissibility	**Waiver Available**	**Conditions of Waiver and/or Exceptions**
Health Problems		
Communicable diseases, particularly tuberculosis. Note: HIV (AIDS) was once specifically listed as a ground of inadmissibility. However, in 2009, the Centers for Disease Control took it off the list of "communicable diseases of public health significance."	Yes	A waiver is available to a person who is an asylee or is the spouse, unmarried son or daughter, or the unmarried minor lawfully adopted child of a U.S. citizen or permanent resident, or of an alien who has been issued an immigrant visa; or to an individual who has a son or daughter who is a U.S. citizen; or to a permanent resident or an alien issued an immigrant visa, upon compliance with USCIS's terms and regulations.
Physical or mental disorders that threaten the property, welfare, or safety of the applicant or others.	Yes	Special conditions required by USCIS, at its discretion.
Drug abusers or addicts.	No	
Failure to show that the applicant has been vaccinated against certain vaccine-preventable diseases.	Yes	The applicant must show either that he or she subsequently received the vaccine, that the vaccine is medically inappropriate as certified by a civil surgeon, or that having the vaccine administered is contrary to the applicant's religious beliefs or moral convictions.
Criminal and Related Violations		
Commission of crimes involving moral turpitude.	Yes	Waivers are not available for commission of crimes such as attempted murder or conspiracy to commit murder, or for murder, torture, or drug crimes, or for people previously admitted as permanent residents, if they have been convicted of aggravated felony since such admission or if they have fewer than seven years of lawful continuous residence before deportation proceedings are initiated against them. Waivers for all other offenses are available only if the applicant is a spouse, parent, or child of a U.S. citizen or green cardholder; or the only criminal activity was prostitution; or the actions occurred more than 15 years before the application for a visa or green card is filed, and the alien shows that he or she is rehabilitated and is not a threat to U.S. security.
Convictions for two or more crimes.	Yes	
Prostitutes or procurers of prostitutes.	Yes	
Diplomats or others involved in serious criminal activity who have received immunity from prosecution.	Yes	
Human traffickers and their adult family members who benefited financially from trafficking in persons.	No	
Money launderers.	No	
Drug offenders.	No	However, there may be an exception for a first and only offense or for juvenile offenders. There's also a waiver for simple possession of less than 30 grams of marijuana.
Drug traffickers.	No	

Inadmissibility Summary (continued)		
Ground of Inadmissibility	**Waiver Available**	**Conditions of Waiver and/or Exceptions**
Immediate family members of drug traffickers who knowingly benefited from their illicit money within the last five years.	No	But note that the problem "washes out" after five years.
National Security and Human Rights Related Violations		
Spies, governmental saboteurs, violators of export or technology transfer laws.	No	
People intending to overthrow the U.S. government.	No	
Terrorists and members or representatives of foreign terrorist organizations.	No	
People whose entry would have adverse consequences for U.S. foreign policy.	No	But exceptions exist if the applicant is an official of a foreign government, or the applicant's activities or beliefs would normally be lawful in the U.S., under the Constitution.
Foreign government officials who carried out particularly severe violations of religious freedom.	No	
Involvement in population control policies including forced abortion or sterilization.	Yes	Does not apply to heads of state, heads of government, or cabinet level ministers. Waiver available if important to the U.S. national interest, with written notification and justification to Congress.
Involvement with coercive transplantation of human organs or bodily tissue, unless the foreign national has discontinued his or her involvement with, and support for, such practices.	Yes	Does not apply to heads of state, heads of government, or cabinet level ministers. Waiver available if important to the U.S. national interest, with written notification and justification to Congress.
Members of totalitarian parties.	Yes	An exception is made if the membership was involuntary, or is or was when the applicant was under 16 years old, by operation of law, or for purposes of obtaining employment, food rations, or other "essentials" of living. An exception is also possible for past membership if the membership ended at least two years prior to the application (five years if the party in control of a foreign state is considered a totalitarian dictatorship). If neither applies, a waiver is available for an immigrant who is the parent, spouse, son, daughter, brother, or sister of a U.S. citizen, or a spouse, son, or daughter of a permanent resident.
Participants in Nazi persecution, genocide, torture, extrajudicial killings, or the recruitment or use of child soldiers.	No	

Inadmissibility Summary (continued)		
Ground of Inadmissibility	**Waiver Available**	**Conditions of Waiver and/or Exceptions**
Economic Grounds		
Any person who, in the opinion of a USCIS or a border or consular official, is likely to become a "public charge," that is, receive public assistance or welfare in the United States. The official can consider factors such as the person's age, health, family and work history, and previous use of public benefits.	No	However, the applicant may cure the ground of inadmissibility by overcoming the reasons for it or obtaining an Affidavit of Support from a family member or friend. Also, there's an exception for refugees/asylees adjusting status. (See I.N.A. § 209.)
Family-sponsored immigrants and employment-sponsored immigrants where a family member is the employment sponsor (or such a family member owns 5% of the petitioning business) and the sponsor has not executed an Affidavit of Support (Form I-864).	No	But an applicant may cure the ground of inadmissibility by subsequently satisfying affidavit of support requirements.
Nonimmigrant public benefit recipients (where the individual came as nonimmigrant and applied for benefits without being eligible or through fraud). Five-year bar to admissibility.	No	But ground of inadmissibility expires after five years.
Labor Certifications & Employment Qualifications		
People without approved labor certifications, if one is required in the category under which the green card application is made.	No	
Graduates of unaccredited medical schools, whether inside or outside of the U.S., immigrating to the U.S. in a second or third preference category based on their profession, who have not both passed the foreign medical graduates exam and shown proficiency in English.	No	Physicians qualifying as special immigrants who have been practicing medicine in the U.S. with a license since January 9, 1978, are not subject to this rule.
Uncertified foreign health care workers seeking entry based on clinical employment in their field (but not including physicians).	No	But applicant may show qualifications by submitting a certificate from the Commission on Graduates of Foreign Nursing Schools or the equivalent.
Immigration Violators		
People who entered in the U.S. without inspection by U.S. border authorities.	Yes	Available for certain battered women and children who came to the U.S. escaping such battery or who qualify as self-petitioners. Also available for some individuals who had visa petitions or labor certifications on file before January 14, 1998 or before April 30, 2001 if they were in the U.S. on December 21, 2000 ($1,000 penalty required for latter waiver). Does not apply to applicants outside of the U.S.; or to refugees and asylees adjusting status (see I.N.A. § 209).
People who were deported after a removal hearing and seek admission within ten years.	Yes	Discretionary with USCIS.

Inadmissibility Summary (continued)		
Ground of Inadmissibility	**Waiver Available**	**Conditions of Waiver and/or Exceptions**
People who have failed to attend removal (deportation) proceedings (unless they had reasonable cause for doing so). Five-year bar to reentry.	Yes	Discretionary with USCIS.
People who have been summarily excluded from the U.S. and again attempt to enter within five years.	Yes	Advance permission to apply for readmission. Discretionary with USCIS.
People who made misrepresentations during the immigration process.	Yes	The applicant must be the spouse or child of a U.S. citizen or green card holder. A waiver will be granted if the refusal of admission would cause extreme hardship to that relative. Discretionary with USCIS.
People who made a false claim to U.S. citizenship.	No	
Individuals subject to a final removal (deportation) order under the Immigration and Naturalization Act § 274C (Civil Document Fraud Proceedings).	Yes	Available to permanent residents who voluntarily left the U.S., and to those applying for permanent residence as immediate relatives or other family-based petitions if the fraud was committed solely to assist the person's spouse or child and provided that no fine was imposed as part of the previous civil proceeding.
Student visa abusers (persons who improperly obtain F-1 status to attend a public elementary school or adult education program, or transfer from a private to a public program except as permitted). Five-year bar to admissibility.	No	
Certain individuals twice removed (deported) or removed after aggravated felony. Twenty-year bar to admissibility for those twice deported.	Yes	Discretionary with USCIS (advance permission to apply for readmission).
Individuals unlawfully present (time counted only after April 1, 1997 and after the age of 18). Presence for 180–364 days results in three-year bar to admissibility. Presence for 365 or more days creates ten-year bar to admissibility. Bars kick in only when the individual departs the U.S. and seeks reentry.	Yes	A waiver is provided for an immigrant who has a U.S. citizen or permanent resident spouse or parent to whom refusal of the application would cause extreme hardship. There is also a complex body of law concerning when a person's presence will be considered "lawful," for example, if one has certain applications awaiting decisions by USCIS or is protected by battered spouse/child provisions of the immigration laws.
Individuals unlawfully present after previous immigration violations. (Applies to persons who were in the U.S. unlawfully for an aggregate period over one year, who subsequently reenter without being properly admitted. Also applies to anyone ordered removed who subsequently attempts entry without admission.)	No	A permanent ground of inadmissibility. However, after being gone for ten years, an applicant can apply for permission to reapply for admission.

Inadmissibility Summary (continued)		
Ground of Inadmissibility	**Waiver Available**	**Conditions of Waiver and/or Exceptions**
Stowaways.	No	
Smugglers of illegal aliens.	Yes	Waivable if the applicant was smuggling in people who were immediate family members at the time, and either is a permanent resident or is immigrating under a family-based visa petition as an immediate relative; the unmarried son or daughter of a U.S. citizen or permanent resident; or the spouse of a U.S. permanent resident.
Document Violations		
People without required current passports or visas.	No	Except limited circumstance waivers. Under new "summary removal" procedures, border officials may quickly deport people for five years who arrive without proper documents or make misrepresentations during the inspection process.
Draft Evasion and Ineligibility for Citizenship		
People who are permanently ineligible for U.S. citizenship.	No	
People who are draft evaders, unless they were U.S. citizens at the time of evasion or desertion.	No	
Miscellaneous Grounds		
Practicing polygamists.	No	
Guardians accompanying excludable aliens.	No	
International child abductors. (The exclusion does not apply if the applicant is a national of a country that signed the Hague Convention on International Child Abduction.)	No	
Unlawful voters (voting in violation of any federal, state, or local law or regulation).	No	
Former U.S. citizens who renounced citizenship to avoid taxation.	No	

Exceptions. There are, however, limited exceptions to this requirement. If you, the immigrant, will qualify for automatic U.S. citizenship upon becoming a permanent resident (discussed in Chapter 9), the I-864 is not necessary. Also, if the immigrant has already worked in the U.S. for 40 or more work quarters as defined by Social Security (about ten years), Form I-864 is not required. Moreover, the immigrant can count time worked by either a parent, while the immigrant was under the age of 18, or by a U.S. petitioning spouse, toward these 40 quarters.

Others who don't need to submit a Form I-864 include self-petitioning widows or widowers of U.S. citizens, and self-petitioning battered spouses or children (explained in later chapters).

If you're exempt from the Affidavit of Support requirement due to one of these exceptions, you should fill out Form I-864W instead of the regular Form I-864.

Sponsor's responsibilities. The government can rely on the I-864 to hold the sponsor responsible if the immigrant receives public benefits. And it is also enforceable by the immigrant family member against the sponsor for support.

Finally, it requires that the sponsor show income for a similar household size (including family and dependents) that is at least 125% of the federal Poverty Guidelines level. These Poverty Guidelines are revised annually; see the table below. They show, for example, that in 2014, the sponsor would have to prove an income of $29,812 or more in order to support a family of four. (We don't just mean four immigrants—they ask you to count up everyone who is living in the house and depending on the sponsor for support.)

Your sponsor's income will need to meet the guidelines for the year when your Affidavit of Support is filed. Don't worry if the required income levels get raised later, it probably won't affect you. Your sponsor should include a copy of the current Poverty Guidelines with your Affidavit, in order to remind the immigration authorities of the then-current income requirements. Also, be aware that one exception exists: If more than a year passes since the Affidavit was submitted, the immigration authorities can ask for proof of the sponsor's current income, in which case they will judge it based on the most recent Poverty Guidelines.

The immigrant's income can also be added to the mix to help reach the Poverty Guidelines minimum, if the immigrant is already living with the petitioner in the U.S. and working legally at a job that will continue after getting the green card.

Who fills out the form. Family-based immigrants who file adjustment of status or immigrant visa applications are required to have Form I-864 filed by the person who is sponsoring their immigrant petition. However, if that family petitioner's income isn't high enough, another person—a joint sponsor—may add income if he or she meets the 125% income requirement for the household and is:

- a U.S. legal permanent resident or citizen
- over 18 years old
- living in the United States, and
- willing to be jointly liable.

The joint sponsor files a separate Affidavit of Support. The principal immigrant can have only one joint sponsor. However, if the joint sponsor's income is not sufficient to cover all the derivative beneficiaries (such as children), a second joint sponsor may be added. Two joint sponsors is the limit, however.

What if the primary petitioner can't find a joint sponsor to make up for an insufficient income and assets? Other people who live in the U.S. petitioner's household may also join their income to that of the primary sponsor to help reach the 125% level, but only if they are age 18 or older, and agree to be jointly liable by filing Form I-864A, Contract Between Sponsor and Household Member. This is different than being a joint sponsor. It means that the person is literally living in the same house—perhaps is an older child or a parent—and is willing to have his or her income counted toward the household total and support the immigrants.

Poverty Guidelines Chart for Immigrants

2014 HHS Poverty Guidelines for Affidavit of Support
Department of Homeland Security
U.S. Citizenship and Immigration Services

USCIS
Form I-864P
Supplement

2014 HHS Poverty Guidelines*
Minimum Income Requirements for Use in Completing Form I-864

For the 48 Contiguous States, the District of Columbia, Puerto Rico, the U.S. Virgin Islands, Guam, and the Commonwealth of the Northern Mariana Islands:

Sponsor's Household Size	100% of HHS Poverty Guidelines* *For sponsors on active duty in the U.S. Armed Forces who are petitioning for their spouse or child*	125% of HHS Poverty Guidelines* *For all other sponsors*
2	$15,730	$19,662
3	$19,790	$24,737
4	$23,850	$29,812
5	$27,910	$34,887
6	$31,970	$39,962
7	$36,030	$45,037
8	$40,090	$50,112
	Add $4,060 for each additional person.	Add $5,075 for each additional person.

For Alaska:		
Sponsor's Household Size	100% of HHS Poverty Guidelines* *For sponsors on active duty in the U.S. Armed Forces who are petitioning for their spouse or child*	125% of HHS Poverty Guidelines* *For all other sponsors*
2	$19,660	$24,575
3	$24,740	$30,925
4	$29,820	$37,275
5	$34,900	$43,625
6	$39,980	$49,975
7	$45,060	$56,325
8	$50,140	$62,675
	Add $5,080 for each additional person.	Add $6,350 for each additional person.

For Hawaii:		
Sponsor's Household Size	100% of HHS Poverty Guidelines* *For sponsors on active duty in the U.S. Armed Forces who are petitioning for their spouse or child*	125% of HHS Poverty Guidelines* *For all other sponsors*
2	$18,090	$22,612
3	$22,760	$28,450
4	$27,430	$34,287
5	$32,100	$40,125
6	$36,770	$45,962
7	$41,440	$51,800
8	$46,110	$57,637
	Add $4,670 for each additional person.	Add $5,837 for each additional person.

Means - Tested Public Benefits

Federal Means-Tested Public Benefits. To date, Federal agencies administering benefit programs have determined that Federal means-tested public benefits include Food Stamps, Medicaid, Supplemental Security Income (SSI), Temporary Assistance for Needy Families (TANF), and the State Child Health Insurance Program (SCHIP).

State Means-Tested Public Benefits. Each State will determine which, if any, of its public benefits are means-tested. If a State determines that it has programs which meet this definition, it is encouraged to provide notice to the public on which programs are included. Check with the State public assistance office to determine which, if any, State assistance programs have been determined to be State means-tested public benefits.

Programs Not Included: The following Federal and State programs are **not** included as means-tested benefits: emergency Medicaid; short-term, non-cash emergency relief; services provided under the National School Lunch and Child Nutrition Acts; immunizations and testing and treatment for communicable diseases; student assistance under the Higher Education Act and the Public Health Service Act; certain forms of foster-care or adoption assistance under the Social Security Act; Head Start Programs; means-tested programs under the Elementary and Secondary Education Act; and Job Training Partnership Act programs.

* These poverty guidelines remain in effect for use with Form I-864, Affidavit of Support, from March 1, 2014 until new guidelines go into effect in 2015.

Form I-864P   03/01/14   N

Page 1 of 1

Using assets to meet the requirements. Personal assets of either the sponsor or the immigrant—such as property, bank account deposits, and personal property such as automobiles (minus any outstanding debts)—may also be used to supplement the sponsor's income if the primary sponsor's actual income does not add up to 125% of the federal Poverty Guidelines income levels.

The sponsor or immigrant must show assets worth five times the difference between the Poverty Guidelines level and actual household income (or three times the difference for immediate relatives, for example husband and wife). The assets must be readily convertible to cash within one year. If using assets owned by the sponsor's household members or the immigrant, those people must submit a Form I-864A.

Immigrant's Story: Compensating for a Low Salary

Here is how Daniel, a U.S. citizen, dealt with his low income in sponsoring his Norwegian wife, Liv, and her twin boys from a previous marriage.

Daniel works as a youth counselor at a nonprofit, earning $21,000 a year. However, according to the 2014 Poverty Guidelines, Daniel will need an income of $29,812 or more to support a family of four—meaning he's $8,812 short. Liv plans to work in the U.S., but she is currently living in Norway, so that doesn't help.

Daniel could pick up a weekend job, to raise his income until Liv gets her green card (at which time no one would stop him from quitting). However, an easier solution is for him to declare his assets when filling out Form I-864. Because the value of assets must be divided by three for U.S. citizens sponsoring their spouses, Daniel will need $26,436 in assets to make up the shortfall.

Fortunately, Daniel has $28,000 in a money market account, so declaring this on his Form I-864 will be enough to help Liv and her children get approved for a green card. He'll need to remember to include a copy of a bank statement showing how much is in the account when he prepares the Form I-864.

SEE AN EXPERT

The requirements and paperwork burden of the Affidavit are complicated and substantial. If you have questions about your eligibility or the scope of your legal responsibility, consult an experienced immigration attorney.

2. Being Stopped at the Border

Another law that has a drastic impact on individuals requesting to enter the United States is the summary exclusion law. This law empowers an inspector at the airport to exclude and deport you at your attempted entry to the U.S. if:

- the inspector thinks you are making a misrepresentation (lying) about practically anything connected to your right to enter the U.S.—such as your purpose in coming, intent to return, prior immigration history, or use of false documents, or
- you do not have the proper documentation to support your entry to the U.S. in the category you are requesting.

If the inspector excludes you, you may not request entry for five years, unless a special waiver is granted. For this reason, it is extremely important to understand the terms of your requested status and not make any misrepresentations.

If the inspector looks likely to summarily exclude you, you may request withdrawing your application to enter the U.S., which will prevent having the five-year order on your record. The inspector may allow you to do this in some cases.

3. Being Barred From Returning After Past Unlawful U.S. Presence

Fairly new grounds of inadmissibility apply to people who were unlawfully present in the United States for 180 days (approximately six months) after April 1, 1997, who subsequently left, and who now seek admission, for example through adjustment of status or by applying for an immigrant or nonimmigrant visa. Such people are subject to a three-year waiting period; the period is ten years if they were unlawfully present for 365 days after April 1, 1997. A waiver is available, as described in Section D4, below.

Some important exceptions apply. For example, as long as you were under 18, your time in the U.S. doesn't count as unlawful presence. And the presence of people who have a bona fide pending asylum application or a pending application for adjustment of status is perfectly lawful. Also, battered spouses and children can get around the bars, if they can show a substantial connection between their unlawful presence and the abuse.

The worst-case scenario is for people who have lived in the United States illegally for more than one year and who then left or were deported but returned to the United States illegally (or were caught trying to). They can never get a green card. This is usually referred to as the "permanent bar." (Check with a lawyer before concluding that you're subject to the permanent bar, however—recent case law has carved out a few exceptions.) No waiver is available to the permanent bar for the first ten years.

4. Limitations on Who Can Adjust Status

The rules concerning adjustment of status—or getting your green card in the U.S. rather than at a U.S. consulate—are somewhat complicated. In general, if you entered the U.S. properly—by being inspected by a border official—and maintained your nonimmigrant status, you can probably get your green card without leaving the United States.

In addition, a "grandfather clause" helps a few people who happened to be in the United States when certain laws were changed (in particular, a law known as § 245(i)). Under the old laws, practically everyone had the right to stay in the United States to adjust their status, simply by paying a $1,000 penalty fee. But under the newer laws, paying this fee is no longer an option except for those few people who are grandfathered in (see Chapter 16 for details).

That means that many people who are just becoming eligible for green cards are in a trap. If they stay in the United States, the fact that they entered illegally or committed certain other violations means that they're not allowed to adjust their status to permanent resident within the United States. But if they leave the United States and attempt to apply for their green card through an overseas consulate, they may well face a three- or ten-year bar to returning to the United States, as punishment for their unlawful stay.

If you believe you're in this trap, consult a lawyer to make sure and to see if you might qualify for a waiver of the three- or ten-year bar. As of 2013, a new "stateside" or "provisional" waiver was allowing some people to avoid the trap by submitting a waiver application and receiving an answer BEFORE leaving the U.S. for their consular interview. However, only a few classes of applicants are eligible to submit this application (as described in Section D5 of this chapter). The provisional waiver cannot, therefore, be counted on as a solution, and will definitely need a lawyer's guidance.

Note: All refugees or political asylees can stay in the U.S. to adjust status.

5. Having Committed Crimes Involving Alcohol or Drugs

Criminal grounds of inadmissibility are the number one factor making temporary visa applicants inadmissible, and they affect a lot of green card applicants, too. If you've committed any sort of crime, you may be found inadmissible, and should consult an experienced immigration attorney. Some attorneys specialize in analyzing the significance of criminal convictions in the immigration context.

However, if you've been convicted of a crime involving alcohol, you've got double trouble. Even if the crime itself doesn't make you inadmissible, USCIS can, and often does, argue that it's a sign that you have a physical or mental disorder associated with harmful behavior—in other words, that you're inadmissible on health, rather than criminal, grounds.

This is most often a problem for people with convictions for DUI or DWI (Driving Under the Influence or Driving While Intoxicated). One DUI alone won't always create a problem, unless there were additional factors, such as someone having been injured, your license having been suspended, or your state treating the crime as a felony. But if USCIS sees a "significant criminal record of alcohol-related driving incidents," it will take a closer look. You may be required to undergo an additional examination by the doctor who filled out your medical report, or by more specialized doctors or psychiatrists.

DUIs aren't the only crime that can lead USCIS to find you inadmissible on health grounds. Crimes such as assaults or domestic violence where alcohol or drugs were contributing factors can lead to the same result. Again, see an attorney if this is an issue in your case—and remember that trying to hide crimes on your green card application will only get you in bigger trouble, after the fingerprint or police report reveals them.

6. Suspected of Terrorist Activity

No one will be surprised to hear that the U.S. forbids people who are linked to terrorism to enter the country, and takes an extra hard look at applications from anyone whose government is thought to support terrorism. (The U.S.'s top four suspected countries are Cuba, Iran, Sudan, and Syria.) However, the terrorism-based inadmissibility grounds are broader than you might expect, and have the potential to exclude some people who wouldn't ordinarily be thought of as terrorists.

The inadmissibility grounds cover being a member of a terrorist organization, inciting others to participate in terrorism, persuading others to support terrorism, endorsing terrorism, raising funds for an organization that the U.S. considers terrorist in nature, and more. The support and fundraising prohibitions can be especially problematic for some people who have given money to organizations that serve a mix of purposes or that have become

established political parties despite a terrorist or guerrilla past.

No hard proof or court conviction is necessary— the U.S. government can exclude someone based on having "reasonable grounds to believe" that the person falls into one of the categories described above.

Also, the spouse or child of any immigrant found inadmissible based on the above provisions can be excluded if the immigrant's activities took place within the last five years. To get around this, the spouse or child will need to show that they were not aware of, nor could reasonably have been expected to know of, the activity.

D. Reversing an Inadmissibility Finding

There are five ways to get past a finding that you are inadmissible. Each of them is discussed in some detail below. However, you'll most likely need an attorney's help.

- In the case of physical or mental illness only, you may be able to correct the condition.
- You can prove that you really don't fall into the category of inadmissibility USCIS believes you do.
- You can prove that the accusations of inadmissibility against you are false.
- You can apply for a waiver of inadmissibility.
- You can "wait out" the time period required by USCIS before reentering the U.S.

1. Correcting Grounds of Inadmissibility

If you have had a physical or mental illness that is a ground of inadmissibility and you have been cured of the condition by the time you submit your green card application, or at least by the time a decision is made on it, you will no longer be considered inadmissible for that reason. If the condition is not cured by the time you apply, with certain illnesses you can still get a waiver of inadmissibility.

2. Proving That Inadmissibility Does Not Apply

Proving that inadmissibility does not apply in your case is a method used mainly to overcome criminal and ideological grounds of inadmissibility. When dealing with criminal grounds of inadmissibility, the immigration authorities will consider both the type of crime committed and the nature of the punishment to see whether your criminal activity constitutes a ground of inadmissibility.

For example, with some criminal activity, only actual convictions are grounds of inadmissibility. If you have been charged with a crime and the charges were then dropped, you may not be inadmissible.

Another example involves crimes of moral turpitude. Crimes of moral turpitude are those showing dishonesty or basically immoral conduct. Committing an act that is considered a crime of moral turpitude can make you inadmissible, even if you have not been convicted.

Crimes with no element of moral turpitude, however, are often not considered grounds of inadmissibility. Opinions may differ on which crimes are considered to involve moral turpitude and which are not.

Other factors that may work to your benefit are:

- expungement laws that remove the crime from your record (but don't assume this will take care of the problem)
- the length of the prison term
- how long ago the crime was committed
- the number of convictions in your background
- conditions of plea bargaining, and
- available pardons.

Sometimes, a conviction can be erased or vacated if you can show it was unlawfully obtained or you were not advised of its immigration consequences.

Proving that a criminal ground of inadmissibility does not apply in your case is a complicated business. You need to have a firm grasp not only of immigration law, but also the technicalities of criminal law. If you have a criminal problem in your past, you may still be able to get a green card, but not without the help of an experienced immigration lawyer. (See Chapter 24.)

3. Proving That an Inadmissibility Finding Is Incorrect

If your green card or nonimmigrant visa application is denied because you are found inadmissible, you can try to prove that the finding of inadmissibility is incorrect. For example, if a USCIS medical examination shows that you have certain medical problems, you can present reports from other doctors stating that the first diagnosis was wrong and that you are free of the problem condition. If you are accused of lying on a visa application, you can present evidence proving you told the truth, or that any false statements were made unintentionally.

4. Applying for a Waiver

In many circumstances, you may be able to get a waiver of inadmissibility. By obtaining a waiver, you don't eliminate or disprove the ground of inadmissibility. Instead, you ask USCIS to overlook the problem and give you a green card or visa anyway.

For example, you can apply for a waiver if you can show that your being prevented from reentering the United States based on your 180 days or more of unlawful presence would cause extreme hardship to your U.S. citizen or permanent resident spouse or parent. (Note that having U.S. citizen children won't help here.)

The classic case of extreme hardship is if your spouse or parent is very ill, needs your care, and would suffer medically by joining you outside the United States. Note, however, that extreme hardship to you, the immigrant, does not count in this analysis.

All green card and visa application forms ask questions designed to find out whether any grounds of inadmissibility apply in your case. When the answers to the questions on these forms clearly show that you are inadmissible, you may be authorized to begin applying for a waiver immediately on filing your application. In most cases, however, the consulate or USCIS office insists on having your final visa or green card interview before ruling that you are inadmissible. If the USCIS office or consulate handling your case decides to wait until your final interview before finding you inadmissible, this will delay your ability to file for a waiver. This may delay your getting a green card or visa; waivers can take many months to process.

Once it is determined that a waiver is necessary, you will need to complete Form I-601 and pay a filing fee (currently $585). Note that if you file this with a U.S. consulate abroad, you will have to wait for the consulate to send your application to a USCIS office. The consulate cannot approve the waiver.

Once again, there are many technical factors that control whether or not a waiver of inadmissibility is granted. If you want to get one approved, you stand the best chance of success by hiring a good immigration lawyer.

5. New, Stateside Provisional Waiver for Applicants Facing Three- or Ten-Year Bar

As of March 4, 2013, green-card seekers who were not eligible to adjust status in the U.S. and were afraid to leave for their consular interview because their past unlawful presence might block their return gained a new procedural option. Some of them can now submit a "provisional waiver" (or "stateside waiver") application, and hopefully have it approved, before leaving the United States. We'll provide detailed information here on what's involved—but because of the complexities of the process and the high rate of USCIS denials so far, we urge you to get an attorney's help with this task.

a. Who Is Eligible to Submit a Provisional/Stateside Waiver Application

Not everyone is eligible to use this new option. Applicants must be:

- **Immediate relatives of U.S. citizens.** This includes a spouse, parent, or unmarried child under age 21. Note that this leaves out various other categories of family-based green card applicants, such as spouses and children of permanent residents, siblings of U.S. citizens, and adult or married children of U.S. citizens.
- **At least 17 years of age.** This doesn't really hurt anyone, because you cannot accrue unlawful presence in the U.S., and therefore don't need a waiver, until you're at least 18).
- **Physically present in the U.S. at the time of applying.**
- **Otherwise admissible to the United States.** In other words, you cannot separately ask for a waiver of any criminal, fraud, or other grounds of inadmissibility. In fact, if USCIS has any reason to believe that you are inadmissible on some ground other than unlawful presence, it will deny the provisional waiver. Furthermore, if the consular officer at your visa interview decides that you are otherwise inadmissible or are ineligible for the visa on some basis other than unlawful presence, the USCIS-approved provisional waiver will be automatically revoked.
- **Still awaiting a consular interview date.** Once that date has been set, too little time will remain for USCIS to make a decision on the provisional waiver.
- **Able to prove that, if not granted the waiver, their qualifying U.S. relatives will suffer extreme hardship as a result.** The list of qualifying relatives is shorter than for the regular waiver, in that it does NOT include permanent resident relatives—only a U.S. citizen's spouse or parents.

The benefits of this new procedure are potentially huge—though in practice, it is helping fewer people than was originally hoped. The main issue has been the high rate of denials in cases where applicants had even the most minor of blots on their criminal record. In response to expressions of protest by immigrant advocates, USCIS at last issued the following guidance to its officers, in a January, 2014 memo:

> *If, based on all evidence in the record, it appears that the applicant's criminal offense: (1) falls within the "petty offense" or "youthful offender" exception under INA section 212(a)(2) (A)(ii) at the time of the I-601A adjudication, or (2) is not a CIMT under INA section 212(a) (2)(A)(i)(I) that would render the applicant inadmissible, then USCIS officers should not find a reason to believe that the individual may be subject to inadmissibility under INA section 212(a)(2)(A)(i)(I) at the time of the immigrant visa interview solely on account of that criminal offense. The USCIS officer should continue with the adjudication . . . .*

(Note that "CIMT," used above, refers to a crime of moral turpitude.) Hopefully this, and the ever-increasing experience of USCIS officers handling this new application, will take care of the problem.

b. Timing of Filing Your Provisional, Stateside Waiver Application

If the U.S. petitioner hasn't already submitted the Form I-130 visa petition that starts the immigration process for a family member, he or she should indicate in Question 22 that the immigrant will apply for an immigrant visa at a U.S. consulate abroad rather than adjusting status in the United States. (If the immigrant were legally allowed to adjust status in the U.S., you wouldn't have to bother with the provisional waiver in the first place.)

By filling Question 22 out in this way, you will alert USCIS that it needs to, upon approving the I-130, transfer the file to the National Visa Center (NVC) for further action and for transfer to the consulate. If the petitioner were to say on the I-130 that the immigrant will apply for adjustment of status in the U.S., you would then have to take extra steps to have the file transferred to the NVC. (This includes filing a Form I-824 and paying a filing fee, then waiting many months for action on the request.)

Only after USCIS approves the I-130 can you file your Provisional Waiver Application (on USCIS Form I-601A, available at www.uscis. gov/i-601a). You cannot submit the visa petition at the same time as ("concurrently" with) the waiver application.

In addition, you will need to notify the National Visa Center (NVC) of your plans, after paying your immigrant visa processing fee. This is the agency that handles the case after USCIS approves the I-130. Contact it via email at NVCi601a@state.gov.

By doing this, you will ensure that the NVC schedules your immigrant visa interview only after USCIS has made a decision on your provisional stateside waiver application. Failing to notify NVC could result in your case being scheduled for interview at a U.S. embassy or consulate abroad before you are ready. If NVC has already scheduled your visa appointment before you have a chance to contact it, you must quickly notify the consulate at which your appointment is scheduled to let it know you'll be applying for the provisional waiver and to ask that your interview be postponed until you get back in touch to say that USCIS has made a decision on your application.

The DOS tries to schedule applicants for an immigrant visa interview within about two or three months of USCIS approving the stateside waiver request and the applicant filing all the necessary visa forms and documents. Applicants can remain in the U.S. during this time period.

c. Fee for Provisional Waiver Application

DHS has set the fee for Form I-601A at $585 (the same as for a regular Application for Waiver of Ground of Inadmissibility on Form I-601). In addition, applicants under the age of 79 will need to pay the biometrics (fingerprinting) fee, currently $85. No fee waiver requests will be considered.

The biometrics requirement means the immigrant will be fingerprinted and the name and prints run through an FBI database to check for a criminal and immigration enforcement record. If there's a chance this will turn up negative information, consult a lawyer before going any further. There's no indication that DHS will use this as simply a way to find and arrest undocumented immigrants who haven't committed crimes, however—their current enforcement priorities are geared toward removing people without close family members, or who are national security risks or public safety threats.

d. What to File for a Provisional Stateside Waiver Request

In addition to Form I-601A and the fee, you will need to provide proof of your eligibility, and documents showing that you merit the waiver as a matter of discretion. USCIS requires that you provide:

☐ a copy of the USCIS approval notice of your Form I-130 visa petition

☐ EOIR Administrative Closure order (if applicable because your case was in removal proceedings)

☐ proof of the U.S. citizen status of your qualifying relative IF it is not the same person who filed the immigrant visa petition for you

☐ proof of your relationship to your qualifying relative IF it is not the same person who filed the immigrant visa petition for you

☐ documents showing that your qualifying relative (U.S. spouse or parent) would suffer extreme hardship if you were denied the U.S. visa, and

☐ receipt showing that you have paid the DOS-required immigrant visa processing fee.

Wondering what extreme hardship is? You might find the following DHS statement interesting: "extreme hardship is not a definable term and elements to establish extreme hardship are dependent upon the facts and circumstances of each case." In any such waiver application, however, you will need to prove that the hardship that your qualifying family members would suffer if you were denied that visa is greater than the suffering that any family member would naturally feel upon being separated or forced to move to a foreign country.

USCIS will not, in most cases, call applicants in for an interview on their stateside waiver request, since it would then have to transfer the file from its National Benefits Center to a local office.

e. If USCIS Deems Your Waiver Application Incomplete

USCIS will not necessarily deny a stateside waiver application that's missing some materials. Instead, it routinely send out Requests for Evidence (RFEs) for applications that lack critical information related to issues like the qualifying relatives' extreme hardship, whether the applicant merits a favorable exercise of discretion, or on some other relevant topic. But USCIS can also simply deny an application outright, so do your best to submit a complete application the first time around.

Also, if you don't pay the correct fee, sign your application, or provide certain key bits of eligibility information, USCIS will return your entire application to you and you will have to refile.

f. Options After Denial of Provisional Waiver

Although you cannot appeal USCIS's denial of your stateside waiver request, you have a couple of options in this situation.

You can file a new I-601A and waiver application with USCIS, during the time that your case is still pending with the DOS. Of course, there is little point in doing this if you don't provide new or extra information to overcome USCIS's original reason for the denial. If you aren't already using an attorney, this would definitely be the time to consult one.

Another option is to go ahead and attend your consular interview, and then file the traditional waiver request on Form I-601 ("Application for Waiver of Grounds of Inadmissibility") with USCIS. This, of course, risks your being unable to return to the U.S. for three or ten years if USCIS once again denies your waiver application, though it will be handled by a different USCIS officer this time around.

Also, you shouldn't worry that DHS agents will come knocking on your door in the U.S. to arrest you after an I-601A denial. According to U.S. government statements, "DHS also does not envision initiating removal proceedings against aliens whose Form I-601As are denied or withdrawn prior to final adjudication"—unless, that is, the person "has a criminal history, has committed fraud, or otherwise poses a threat to national security or public safety."

6. Remaining Outside the U.S. for the Required Amount of Time

If you're subject to a penalty requiring you to remain outside the U.S. for three or ten years before reentering—most likely because you stayed in the U.S. unlawfully—you don't have to wait for an immigration authority to tell you you're subject to the penalty to start the clock ticking on your time away.

For example, if you overstayed your tourist visa by more than one day but less than six months during a past visit to the U.S., you'll eventually be penalized by having to wait outside the U.S. for three years before reentering on any kind of visa. If you stay in the U.S. and wait to receive your visa interview notice before you leave—and then at your interview, the consulate denies your request for a waiver of your unlawful stay—you'll be stuck outside the U.S. for three years following your interview. That's why some immigrants prefer to leave the U.S. sooner, in order to start counting up the three years as soon as possible.

How Long You'll Have to Wait

Among the most common questions immigrants ask their attorneys are ones concerning how long the immigration process takes, such as:

- "As a U.S. citizen, I filed the papers for my brother five years ago. Why is it taking so long for the U.S. Embassy in India to give him his immigrant visa?"
- "My ten-year-old daughter was born in Hawaii, where I was a graduate student at the University of Hawaii. Since she is a U.S. citizen, when can I get a green card by having her claim me as her mother?"
- "Three years ago, based on my green card, I sponsored my wife, who comes from Mexico. She is still waiting for her green card. What is the problem?"

Such questions are often asked by people who may have expected some delay in getting their green cards, but who can't believe how many years it's taking.

There are numerous causes of common immigration delays. The first type of delay no one can escape. It's the operation of U.S. immigration law, defining when you become eligible for a green card. In the example of the mother of the U.S. citizen born in Hawaii, above, she'll need to wait until her child turns 21 to so much as start the immigration process.

Another common source of delay is simply the bureaucratic backup caused by an overworked government agency trying to deal with many thousands of applications every year. Even the amount of time you spend waiting for a decision on one application can be shocking—many months or years is normal. And a fair number of people wait months only to discover that their application got misplaced or lost in the paperwork shuffle. Although USCIS is perpetually launching efforts to fix these problems, no one expects miracles. See Chapters 21 and 22 for tips on preventing and dealing with these delays.

Another type of delay is the security checks and double checks your name and fingerprints will be run through, sometimes more than once, during the application process. Although security checks were always part of the application process, they've become more rigorous since the terrorist attacks of September 11, 2001. For people with common names, this can create particular problems. Of course, if you've had any arrests or other history that you believe will raise questions in the immigration process, you should consult an attorney.

Then there is a type of delay that applies only to applicants in green card categories that have a yearly limit on how many are given out. For example, spouses of U.S. citizens don't have to worry, because as immediate relatives, the government can grant unlimited numbers of green cards to them, no matter how many apply. But spouses of U.S. permanent residents are less lucky. Their annual limit is 87,934, and far more spouses than that apply every year. Spouses of permanent residents have to wait, usually five years or more, until all the people who applied before them have gotten their green cards. After that, in technical terms, a "visa number" is said to become available, and they can continue their application for a green card.

TIP

"Visa" and "green card" can have similar meanings. When we're talking about numbers and quotas, the immigration laws always refer to "visas" rather than "green cards," for technical reasons. Part of the reason is that if you come from overseas, you don't become a permanent resident (green card holder) until you receive an "immigrant visa" and use it to enter the United States. But even if you're applying within the United States, you can't become a permanent resident until a "visa number" is allotted to you. So, when you hear about numbers and limits on "visas" in this discussion, assume it means your right to a green card, no matter where you're coming from or whether you use an actual, physical, entry visa.

You'll face delays based on limited numbers of visas if you apply for a green card in any of the so-called "preference" categories (which we'll explain below). All the preference categories come with limits, or "quotas," on how many visas or green cards can be passed out in a year. And in every family preference category, the demand for green cards always seems to exceed the supply.

To make matters more complicated, no country is allowed to send more than 7% of all preference immigrants (or 25,620 people) to the United States in a year. That means that for certain countries with high rates of immigration to the United States—like Mexico, India, China, and the Philippines—the U.S. government sometimes has to start a separate—and longer—waiting list. This isn't discrimination so much as it is mathematics.

A. Immediate Relatives of U.S. Citizens: No Waiting

Immigrant visas are immediately available for one group of eligible aliens: immediate relatives of U.S. citizens. They have the highest priority in immigration law because of the congressional intent to encourage families of U.S. citizens to live together and stay together.

Members of this group have to wait only for as long as it takes various government offices to handle their applications. This averages from two to twelve months, depending on various factors such as whether the immigrant is coming from another country or already lives legally in the United States, and how backed up the office serving his or her region is.

For purposes of immigration law, you are an immediate relative and eligible for an immigrant visa without waiting if you are:

- the husband or wife of a U.S. citizen
- the parent of a U.S. citizen, if the citizen is at least 21 years of age
- the unmarried child under 21 years of age (including stepchildren and children adopted before they reach the age of 16) of a U.S. citizen, or
- the widow or widower of a U.S. citizen (assuming you weren't legally separated at the time of death and haven't remarried since).

Although children of U.S. citizens must remain unmarried until they receive their visa, those approaching 21 do get some protection from a law called the Child Status Protection Act. As long as the visa petition was filed for them when they were under 21 years old, these immediate relative children never "age out," or lose their eligibility based on being too old. Previously, once an immediate relative child turned 21, he or she would automatically move into the less favored preference category. Now, the child's age is frozen at whatever it was when the visa petition was filed, so the child stays in the immediate relative category.

> **EXAMPLE:** The U.S. citizen father of Yasmeen, a 20-year-old girl, files a visa petition for her along with an application for adjustment of status to permanent resident. By the time of the interview, however, Yasmeen is 22 years old. Fortunately, under the CSPA, Yasmeen's age of 20 years old was permanently frozen or "locked in" when the visa petition was filed, so she is considered 20 years old for as long as it takes USCIS to approve her green card.

B. Relatives in Preference Categories: Longer Waits

In all family-based preference categories, petitions from U.S. citizens generally have higher priority than those of lawful permanent residents.

Family first preference: unmarried sons or daughters of U.S. citizens. This category is for children who are 21 years old or older and not married—meaning either single, divorced, or widowed. (A son or daughter who is under 21 years old and not married would be classified as an immediate relative.) A maximum of 23,400 immigrant visas are now available worldwide for the family first preference category. The current waiting period is approximately seven years, but 20 years if you're from Mexico and 22 years from the Philippines.

Family second preference: spouses and unmarried children of permanent residents. This category is divided into two parts, including:

- husbands and wives of lawful permanent residents and their unmarried children who are under 21 years old (category 2A), and
- unmarried (meaning single, divorced, or widowed) sons or daughters (over 21 years old) of a lawful permanent resident (category 2B, which waits somewhat longer than category 2A).

A total of 114,200 immigrant visas worldwide are given to second preference immigrants. However, 77% (87,934) of the total is intended for the spouses and minor children of green cardholders (2As), while 23% (26,266) of the total is meant for the unmarried children over 21 years of age (2Bs).

The typical wait in category 2A is approximately three years, though the category became "current" in 2013 and has had record-breaking short waits since then. In category 2B, the current wait is approximately seven years, except that applicants from Mexico wait about 19 years and applicants from the Philippines wait about 11 years.

Family third preference: married sons and daughters of U.S. citizens. What if a U.S. citizen's unmarried son or daughter (in the family first preference category) gets married before entering the U.S. as a lawful permanent resident? Or what if he or she is married already? Either way, the third preference category provides a solution, although the waits tend to be long. Only 23,400 visas worldwide are made available every year for married sons and daughters of U.S. citizens.

The current wait in the third preference category is approximately ten years, except that applicants from Mexico and the Philippines wait as many as 20 years.

Family fourth preference: brothers and sisters of U.S. citizens. The brother or sister of a U.S. citizen has to wait until the U.S. sibling turns 21 years of age before a petition can be filed for the alien brother or sister. A total of 65,000 visas worldwide are available each year for this category. The waiting list is always very long, from 12 to 24 years.

C. Dealing With the Wait

If you belong to a preference category in which there are many hopeful immigrants waiting—for example, in Mexico, there are well over 60,000 brothers and sisters of U.S. citizens on file—you may have to wait several years for your immigrant visa number.

If, during these years, you want to come to the United States as a nonimmigrant—as a tourist, businessperson, student, or other category—be prepared for it to be more difficult for you to get that visa. Once a visa petition has been filed for you by a family member, the U.S. government figures you intend to come to the U.S. and stay permanently— which disqualifies you from most short-term visas.

You may be able to convince the U.S. consul that you will not remain illegally in the United States waiting for your immigrant visa to come up by demonstrating your ties to your home country. You are more likely to be able to show that you will not remain in the U.S. illegally if you are in a category requiring a wait of ten years or more, rather than one or two.

There are only a few exceptions to the general rule that nonimmigrants must convince the U.S. consul that they do not intend to stay permanently in the U.S. One is for people who qualify for certain temporary work statuses (H and L visas). Although they may have an approved visa petition by reason of their U.S. citizen spouse, child, parent, brother, or sister, or a lawful permanent resident spouse or parent, the U.S. embassy is supposed to issue them an H or L visa if they qualify for that nonimmigrant visa while waiting for a visa number to become available. Another is for spouses of U.S. citizens who may qualify for the newly expanded K visa (see Chapter 7).

D. Can You Predict How Long You'll Wait?

No one can tell you for certain how long you'll wait for a visa or green card. If you're an immediate relative, you'll get your best estimate from asking people who work in the office you're dealing with what the current expected application processing times are. Processing times for certain applications are also posted on USCIS's website at www.uscis. gov. Click "Check Your Case Status," then go to "Processing Times" and choose the office at which your case is pending. You'll be given a list of what types of petitions and applications the office handles and either a number of months or the date of the oldest pending case of a particular type at that office.

If you are not in the immediate relative category, you must start by tracking how long you're likely to spend on the waiting listing. Pay special attention to the Priority Date and the cutoff date that apply to your visa application.

1. The Priority Date

The Priority Date is the date on which your relative began the process by filing a petition for you with USCIS (or INS, as it was formerly called).

The first notification of your Priority Date will be on the receipt notice that your relative gets, showing the date the petition was received and the fee paid to USCIS. That date will also be shown on your approval notice, which is the next piece of paper your relative will get from USCIS—and which is even more important to keep while you wait for your Priority Date to become current.

> **CAUTION**
>
> **Your relative may wait several years for an answer on the initial visa petition.** In 2004, USCIS announced a new policy on handling approvals and denials of Form I-130 visa petitions. Instead of reviewing all petitions in the order received, they began prioritizing

those filed on behalf of people whose visas will be available sooner. That means that if you're in a category with long waits, your U.S. citizen or resident relative could receive a receipt notice one year and the approval notice several years later, when it's almost time for you to immigrate. This practice won't add any delays to your overall wait—it's like having two sources of delay going on simultaneously. It will, however, add uncertainty to your life, since you won't know until the last minute whether the initial visa petition will be approved or denied.

The Department of State keeps careful count of how many immigrant visas are issued for each country in each preference category. If the quota has been reached in one category before the fiscal year is over (in October), the department will not issue any immigrant visas in that category for the rest of the fiscal year and will, in addition, state that visas are temporarily unavailable for that category, either for a particular country or worldwide.

October 1 of each year marks the beginning of another fiscal year for the federal government—and the count of the immigrant visas issued begins all over again for each country in each preference category.

2. Tracking Your Progress: Visa Cutoff Date

Each month, the Department of State issues a *Visa Bulletin*, which sets out the immigrant visa cutoff date of each visa preference. See the sample below.

The cutoff date simply announces which Priority Dates in each category are receiving attention from the Department of State because people holding those numbers have become eligible for an immigrant visa. All applicants whose Priority Date falls before this cutoff date will be given an appointment within a few months if they're overseas, or will be allowed to submit the next part of their application if they're in the U.S. and eligible to adjust status there. Anyone whose priority date falls after the cutoff date will have to wait.

Excerpt from *Visa Bulletin* for March 2014					
Family Sponsored	All Chargeability Areas Except Those Listed	CHINA-mainland born	INDIA	MEXICO	PHILIPPINES
F1	01FEB07	01FEB07	01FEB07	15OCT93	15AUG01
F2A	08SEP13	08SEP13	08SEP13	15APR12	08SEP13
F2B	01SEP06	01SEP06	01SEP06	01MAY93	08JUN03
F3	15JUN03	15JUN03	15JUN03	08JUN93	15FEB93
F4	08NOV01	08NOV01	08NOV01	15NOV96	01SEP90

EXAMPLE: You were born in Poland. Your brother, who is a naturalized U.S. citizen, filed a petition for you on February 1, 2001, which becomes your Priority Date.

You are in the fourth preference category. The *Visa Bulletin* of March 2014 says the State Department is processing siblings with a Priority Date on or before November 8, 2001. Your appointment for your immigrant visa is currently available. It doesn't matter that the dates don't match exactly. The point is that people whose visa petitions were filed later than yours are receiving visas, so you should too.

However, if you were from another country, the waiting period could be longer, as you can see in the chart above.

The cutoff dates announced in the *Visa Bulletin* may not change much from one month to the next—sometimes one week for one preference and two weeks for another preference. Or the date may not move at all for several months in your category. Be prepared to wait.

The *Visa Bulletin* is normally available in each embassy or consulate, or in USCIS offices. You can also call the Department of State in Washington, DC, at 202-485-7699 for a tape-recorded message that gives the cutoff dates for each preference category being processed that month. Or, visit the State Department website at www.travel.state.gov. Click "Immigrate" then "Visa Bulletins." You can even

subscribe to an email service that will automatically send you the latest *Visa Bulletin* every month as it becomes available. Details about how to do this can be found at the bottom of the bulletin itself.

3. Some People Can Switch Preference Categories

A special rule applies to family-based immigrant visas, allowing you to hang onto your Priority Date if you change from one preference category to another.

If you belong to one family preference, and some event (marriage, divorce, death of spouse, or the simple passage of time) places you in a different preference category, your original Priority Date may remain unchanged. That means you won't lose much ground, because your place on the new waiting list will reflect the fact that your petition was filed long before many other people's.

The types of situations in which a family-based beneficiary who has undergone a change of circumstance can convert to another category without losing the original Priority Date include:

- Marriage of the son or daughter (over 21 years old) of U.S. citizen—moves down from first to third preference.
- Marriage of child (under 21 years old) of U.S. citizen—moves down from immediate relative to third preference.

- Divorce of child or adult son or daughter—moves up from third preference to immediate relative or first preference, depending on child's age at divorce.
- Naturalization of legal resident petitioner—2A spouse and unmarried children under 21 move up from second preference to immediate relative and children age 21 or older move to first preference from category 2B.
- Child of lawful permanent resident reaching age 21 before Priority Date becomes current—drops from category 2A to category 2B of the second preference. However, if the child reaches age 21 after his or her Priority Date has become current but before actual approval for permanent residency, the child can retain 2A status as long as he or she applies within one year of the Priority Date having become current. (This represents a change in the law, as of 2002—formerly such children would have also dropped into category 2B, simply by virtue of not having received their approval on time, and therefore had to wait longer.)

! CAUTION

Some life changes make you ineligible for any visa at all. Not everyone who marries, divorces, or whose petitioning family member dies can switch to another preference category. You can switch only if, at the time, an existing category fits your new situation. So, for example, the child of a U.S. citizen who marries can switch to the third preference category. But the child of a lawful permanent resident who marries is out of luck, because there's no category for married children of permanent residents. Such issues are explained further in Section E, below.

4. Advise USCIS If You Can Upgrade

If you can switch to a better (faster) visa category—most likely because the person petitioning for you has gone from being a permanent resident to being a U.S. citizen—you'll need to let USCIS know.

How you do that depends first on where your file is located at the time of change. If, for example, your Form I-130 visa petition is still pending at a USCIS service center, you'll want to send a letter titled "I-130 UPGRADE REQUEST" identifying you and the petitioner and explaining the situation (see the sample below). Also be sure to include a copy (not the original) of the petitioner's signed naturalization certificate.

Sample Request for Upgrade to USCIS

123 Central Avenue
Treesbird, VT 14235
April 14, 2014

Department of Homeland Security
U.S. Citizenship and Immigration Services
P.O. Box 648005
Lee's Summit, MO 64064

RE: I-130 UPGRADE REQUEST
     Petitioner: Samuel Thornburgh
     Beneficiary: Junyi Cho

Dear Sir/Madam:

I filed an I-130 visa petition for the above-named beneficiary on February 11, 2014, during which time I was a U.S. permanent resident. That petition is still pending.

Since filing the petition, however, I have become a naturalized U.S. citizen. A copy of my naturalization certificate is attached.

Please continue processing this case, but as an immediate relative petition. Thank you for your attention to this matter.

Very truly yours,
Samuel Thornburgh

Enclosed: copy of naturalization certificate

If the I-130 visa petition has already been approved, and the beneficiary is living outside the U.S., you'll need to send a similar letter along with a copy of the visa petition approval notice (Form I-797) from USCIS, to:

National Visa Center

31 Rochester Avenue, Suite 100

Portsmouth, NH 03801-2915

And if the beneficiary is living in the U.S. and is eligible to adjust status, you don't need to send a letter anywhere. You simply submit the full adjustment of status application (Form I-485, with supporting documents and fees) with a copy of the I-130 approval and the naturalization certificate.

These rules may sound hard to follow, but because they can make a big difference in how quickly your application is processed, it is worth your time to understand which rules apply to your situation.

Situations Where Children Are Protected From Switching Categories

The Child Status Protection Act of 2002 allows certain children of U.S. citizens and permanent residents to retain their original visa eligibility even if they turn 21 while they're waiting for the process to finish up. (Formerly, turning 21 would have automatically dropped them into a lower preference category and caused them to have to wait longer for their visa or green card.) Those who benefit include:

- Children of U.S. citizens—will retain immediate relative status even if they turn 21 at any time after a visa petition has been filed on their behalf.

- Children of lawful permanent residents—will retain 2A status if they turn 21 after their Priority Date has become current, so long as they file for a green card within one year of becoming current. (Technically, by filing for the green card the child "locks in" his or her age at 21 minus the number of days it took USCIS to approve the initial I-130 visa petition. However, given USCIS delays, that almost always shaves off enough months to keep the child's age, for immigration purposes, at less than 21.)

Immigrant Story: Uniting the Family

Here is how the quota system affected Giti and Meena, two young sisters from Afghanistan:

After waiting for more than ten years, their father was about to get a green card through his U.S. citizen brother. He planned to bring his wife and two children with him, as is allowed in this visa category (family fourth preference). What the family did not realize, however, was how their plans would be affected if either of the sisters married or turned 21 years old before they entered the U.S.

Just before the visa interview, Giti, who was 19 years old, married a man from their town in Afghanistan. Her eligibility for the green card was destroyed.

Meena, on the other hand, was unmarried but 21 years and 6 months old at the time of the family's interview. Her eligibility was not destroyed, because legal protections provided by the Child Status Protection Act allow her (and other children in the preference categories) to subtract from her age the amount of time it took USCIS to approve the visa petition. In this particular case, it had taken USCIS nine months to approve the petition (and then the family waited another ten years for the Priority Date to become current). So Meena is considered to have another three months before "aging out." Once her visa is approved, she needs to be sure that she enters the U.S. before she "ages out."

What should the family do about Giti? Although it will take a long time, Giti's best bet is for one or both of her parents to learn English and become a U.S. citizen as soon as possible (this will normally take at least five years). Next, the parents will need to petition for her and her husband under the family third preference category. They'll wait approximately seven years before being allowed to immigrate to the United States.

Giti's father wonders whether Giti shouldn't just divorce the young man. However, that would be considered immigration fraud if done just to allow her to get a green card. If the immigration authorities found out about the fraud, it would destroy her eligibility for any green card in any category.

E. Revocation of a Petition or Application

Here is a bit of scary information, but it's better to know it than not to know: After a petition or application has been filed on behalf of an alien, it can be revoked or canceled—even if it has already been approved by the INS or USCIS.

One reason for revocation would be the would-be immigrant's unintended "failure to prosecute" the petition. This can happen when your relative, the petitioner, has not informed USCIS about address changes, and so does not get notification that USCIS is ready for further processing of your case. If USCIS gets no response after repeated attempts to contact the petitioner, it will assume that you are no longer interested in going forward on the petition. USCIS then can revoke and cancel the petition! To avoid this, make sure USCIS always has the petitioner's updated address, and sign up for USCIS's automatic email/text alerts.

Another reason for revocation is a change in your circumstances that makes you no longer eligible for the visa. It can also be based on a discovery that you committed fraud, for example by pretending to be someone's relation when you really weren't.

USCIS will normally revoke a petition if, for example:

- the person who filed the petition decides to withdraw it and informs USCIS of this decision
- the person who filed the petition dies; however, USCIS may decide not to revoke the petition if the law allows you to self petition (as it does for widows/widowers of U.S. citizens) or if it is convinced that there are "humanitarian reasons" not to do so
- in a marriage case, the couple divorces or the marriage is annulled before the green card is approved, or
- in a family second preference case, the unmarried son or daughter gets married before the green card is approved.

> **Special Rules for Widows and Widowers**
>
> If the beneficiary is the spouse of a U.S. citizen, the petition will be granted as long as the widowed beneficiary was not legally separated or divorced from the citizen at the time of death, applies within two years of the spouse's death, and has not remarried.

Consider this scenario: A permanent resident mother has brought all her children to the United States except her eldest son, who marries before she could petition for him. After five years, she becomes a U.S. citizen and immediately files a petition for her married son, still living in the foreign country. The petition is approved, but before the son and his family come to the United States, the mother dies. The petition is automatically revoked, and the son remains separated from his brothers and sisters, who have been living in the United States since their mother received her green card.

That application of the regulations seems cruel. It is precisely for such cases that the regulations have been somewhat liberalized. The beneficiary of a petition filed by a U.S. citizen or by a permanent resident who dies before the alien beneficiary could come to the United States is no longer in an entirely hopeless situation.

With a lawyer's help, you may be able to show the immigration authorities that for "humanitarian reasons" revocation would be inappropriate. There is, however, a catch: Because every immigrant to the United States must have a financial sponsor— that is, someone who promises to support the immigrant if he or she is unable to support him- or herself—you will need to find a substitute sponsor for the person who died. Only certain people can fill this substitute role, including your spouse, parent, mother-in-law, father-in-law, sibling, son, daughter, son-in-law, or daughter-in-law. As in the case of other sponsors, your sponsor must maintain an annual income equal to at least 125% of the federal Poverty Guidelines.

Fiancé and Fiancée Visas

The fiancé visa (K-1) was designed to allow people who've become engaged to but haven't yet married a U.S. citizen to travel to the U.S. for the wedding. Unfortunately, it isn't available to the fiancés of U.S. permanent residents (green card holders). Your minor children can go with you to the U.S. If you marry within 90 days, you and your children can apply for a green card. Otherwise, you must leave the U.S. before the date indicated on your passport.

A. Who Qualifies for a Fiancé Visa

To qualify for a fiancé visa, you must:

- intend to marry a U.S. citizen (see Section 1, below)
- have met your intended spouse in person within the last two years (though this can be waived based on cultural customs or extreme hardship; see Section 2, below), and
- be legally able to marry (see Section 3, below).

It's important to realize that a fiancé visa is not a green card. It's only a temporary, 90-day right to be in the United States. However, it's included in this book because it's an important first step towards getting a green card. After the immigrant has arrived in the United States and gotten married, he or she can file for a green card—through a process called "adjustment of status"—at a U.S.-based USCIS office. (Or, if the immigrant has no desire for a U.S. green card, he or she can simply return home before the fiancé visa runs out.)

1. You Must Intend to Marry a U.S. Citizen

Of course you want to get married—but how do you plan to prove that to the U.S. government? As part of your application, you'll have to supply documents that show your intention to get married. We'll talk more about this in the sections that discuss paperwork.

TIP

Make your wedding plans flexible. You can't know exactly how long it will take to get a fiancé visa, but you'll have to hold your wedding within 90 days of entering the United States. Before you sign any contracts for catering, photographic, or other services, discuss the situation with the service providers and build some flexibility into your contracts or agreements in case the date needs to change.

The person you plan to marry must be a citizen, not a permanent resident, of the United States. A U.S. citizen is someone who was either:

- born in the United States or its territories
- became a citizen through a process of application and testing (called "naturalization"), or
- acquired or derived citizenship through a family member (for more information, see Nolo's website at www.nolo.com; look for the article entitled "U.S. Citizenship by Birth or Through Parents").

2. You Must Have Met in Person Within the Last Two Years

To protect against sham marriages, the law requires that you and your fiancé have met in person within the last two years. Even a brief meeting may be enough. Perhaps the immigrant can visit the United States on a tourist visa. However, getting approval for a tourist visa may be difficult, because the U.S. consulate may believe that the immigrant actually intends to get married and apply for the green card right away—which would be a misuse of the tourist visa, and could amount to visa fraud. It will probably be easier for the U. S. citizen to visit the immigrant overseas.

If, however, you're from a country where prospective husbands and wives don't meet before the wedding, for religious or cultural reasons, this meeting will obviously be a greater hardship. In such cases, you can ask the immigration authorities to "waive" (overlook) the meeting requirement.

You'll need letters from your religious leader, parents, or other relevant people, and other proof of the normal practices in your culture, to succeed with your request. Getting a lawyer's help would be a good idea here.

U.S. Citizen Petitioners Must Now Disclose Criminal Records

Recently Congress became concerned that immigrating fiancés were particularly susceptible to domestic violence and abuse—particularly those whose engagements were arranged through a marriage broker (sometimes called "mail order brides"). In response, Congress passed the International Marriage Brokers Regulation Act of 2005 (IMBRA). As a result of IMBRA, the fiancé visa petition (Form I-129F) now asks *all* U.S. citizen petitioners whether they have a history of violent crime and crime relating to alcohol or controlled-substance abuse. In addition, Form I-129F now asks whether you and your fiancé or spouse met through an international marriage broker. If you did, the immigrant will be asked, at the visa interview, whether the broker complied with new legal requirements to collect information on the U.S. fiancé or spouse's criminal record and pass it to the immigrant.

---

3. You Must Be Legally Able to Marry

For most people, the requirement that you be legally able to marry won't pose any problems. However, if one of you is already married or too young to legally marry in the state or country where you plan to perform the wedding, or if the two of you are close relatives, such as cousins, and forbidden to marry in the state or country where you plan to hold the wedding, you may not qualify for a fiancé visa.

Same-sex couples may face additional obstacles, as a minority of states permit same-sex marriage. You will, if you're in a same-sex relationship, need to make sure the fiancé lives in, or you can make

plans to travel to, a state that recognizes same-sex marriage. A civil union or domestic partnership won't work for immigration purposes.

If possible, take steps to correct the problem—for example, obtain a divorce, figure out a different place to marry, or wait until you're older.

B. Quick View of the Fiancé Visa Application Process

Here's what to plan for on your path to a fiancé visa:
1. The U.S. citizen submits a fiancé visa petition to USCIS (on Form I-129F).
2. USCIS sends the U.S. citizen a receipt notice, after confirming that the application is complete, then (within several weeks or more often months) a notice of its decision, hopefully approving the petition. (Occasionally, USCIS will call in the U.S. citizen petitioner for an interview before deciding on the petition.)
3. USCIS will transfer the file to an intermediary called the National Visa Center (NVC), which then transfers it to the U.S. consulate serving the immigrant's country. The consulate will instruct the immigrating fiancé on what documents to prepare.
4. The immigrating fiancé attends the interview, and if all goes well, is approved for a fiancé visa. The visa will usually need to be picked up on a separate day. The immigrant must use it to enter the U.S. within six months.

C. Detailed Instructions for the Fiancé Visa Application Process

All the immigration forms required and prohibitions explained here are very unromantic. But because the immigration laws have been abused by people who used marriage simply to obtain a green card, romance takes a backseat. Obtaining a fiancé visa—also called a K-1 visa—requires time, patience, and paperwork.

1. Documents Required for Fiancé Visa Petition

To start the process, the U.S. citizen must prepare the following:

☐ Form I-129F, Petition for Alien Fiancé(e). (See the sample at the end of this chapter, done for the immigrant.)

☐ Separate passport-style color photographs of the U.S. citizen and the alien fiancé.

☐ Form G-325A, Biographic Information, one for each person. (See the sample at the end of this chapter.)

☐ Form G-1145 (optional, but useful so that you'll receive an email or text notification from USCIS when it has gotten your application)

☐ Proof of your U.S. fiancé's U.S. citizenship, such as a copy of a passport, birth certificate, or naturalization certificate (see Chapter 21, Section D3 for details).

☐ Proof that any previous marriages have been terminated by death, divorce, or annulment.

☐ Written affidavit from the U.S. citizen stating how the couple met, how they decided to get married, and the plans for the marriage and the honeymoon (see the sample at the end of this chapter).

☐ Written affidavit from the immigrating fiancé also discussing their relationship and their intention to marry.

☐ Proof that the U.S. citizen and the foreign-born fiancé have met each other within the past two years: photographs, plane tickets, letters, etc. This evidence will also help show that your relationship is genuine.

☐ If the U.S. citizen has ever been convicted of any violent crime, or a crime involving domestic violence or substance abuse (a more complete list is provided in the instructions to Form I-129F), certified copies of all police and court records showing the outcome (get a lawyer's help in this instance).

Immigrant Story: Proving They'd Met

Doug, from Ireland, and Carol, a U.S. citizen, met online and exchanged emails for over a year before they decided to get married. However, Carol was living with her parents in Philadelphia while she finished her Ph.D. in medieval history, and her family was extremely protective. She knew they would have panicked at the idea of her so much as corresponding with a stranger online, much less marrying him.

So although Carol definitely wanted to meet Doug before the wedding, she decided a secret meeting would be best. When a history conference took her to Newark, New Jersey, she suggested to Doug that he meet her there. They stayed with friends of Carol's, had a great time, and reaffirmed their intention to marry.

Then came time to prove that they'd met the meeting requirement. Carol suddenly realized she had almost no proof of their meeting. She'd driven to Newark, hadn't paid for a hotel room, and eaten either conference food or in her friends' kitchen the whole time. But after thinking harder, she realized she'd paid for gas with a credit card while in New Jersey, and had a registration form proving that she'd been at the conference. She also asked her friends to sign a sworn statement explaining that she and Doug had stayed with them. This, plus proof of Doug's plane ticket, was enough to satisfy the meeting requirement, and Doug was granted a fiancé visa.

☐ Proof that the two of you intend to marry within 90 days after the alien fiancé arrives in the United States: for example, letters, long-distance telephone bills, letter from the religious or civil authority who will officiate at the wedding, letter from the place where the reception will be held, receipts or contracts for wedding expenses, and engagement or wedding announcement or invitation.

☐ Filing fee (currently $340), payable to the U.S. Department of Homeland Security, in the form of a money order or bank check. (You do not, however, have to pay the fee if you're already married and filing Form I-129F after filing a Form I-130 in order to obtain a K-3 visa, as described in Chapter 7.)

2. Where and How to Send the Fiancé Visa Petition

Once the U.S. citizen petitioner has prepared everything on the above list, he or she should make two complete photocopies of everything, including the check or money order. This will be extremely important in the all-too-common event that USCIS misplaces the petition. Send one copy to the immigrating fiancé, for his or her records. The U.S. citizen should assemble the original package neatly, and preferably write a cover letter that lists, in bullet points, everything inside.

The petitioner should send the completed visa petition by certified mail, return receipt requested, to the appropriate USCIS lockbox. (See the USCIS website for contact details. As of this book's print date, all I-129F petitions were to be mailed to the Dallas, Texas lockbox.) You *cannot* just walk the form into your local USCIS office.

It is also a good idea to file Form G-1145, asking USCIS to send you an email and/or text notification when your application has been accepted. (See sample at the end of this chapter.)

Once you have a receipt from USCIS, you can use the receipt number to sign up to receive automatic email updates that let you know whenever mail is sent regarding your application. Go to the USCIS website at www.uscis.gov and enter your receipt number in the box on the left hand side of the page that says "Case Status." Enter your receipt number. Click "Check status." On this page, you can register for automatic case status updates by email and text message, by clicking on "creating an account."

3. Visa Petition Interviews

Although it does not happen often, it is possible that the U.S. citizen petitioner will be called in for an interview by a USCIS officer. He or she should bring all original documents to the interview. If the documents and the interview convince USCIS that true romance is behind the planned marriage, the petition will be approved and a Notice of Action, Form I-797, will be mailed to the U.S. citizen. The form will contain instructions for the next step to take—and may include a request for additional information or documentation.

4. U.S. Consulate Notified of Approval

After USCIS approves the Form I-129F visa petition, it will advise a processing unit called the National Visa Center (NVC). The NVC will send you, the immigrating fiancé, a receipt number as well information on what to do next.

As of October 2013, an online DS-160 form has replaced many of the older paper forms that K visa applicants once needed to fill out (namely DS-230 Part I, DS-156, and DS-156K).

DS-160 is a fairly straightforward application, but you will need access to the Internet and at least a limited command of the English language. There is no paper version of the form (for which reason we do not supply a sample in this book.)

By setting your location and nationality on the Bureau of Consular Affairs website, you can get the questions and guidance translated into your native language. You will, however, need to answer all questions in English. Each applicant for a K visa (including any accompanying children) will need to complete a separate Form DS-160, though you can complete the form for any of your children under age 16.

Make sure you record the Application ID that you are given once you first begin the online form. This will allow you to retrieve a saved DS-160 if you do not complete it or if the application "times out" due to issues such as a poor Internet connection.

What You'll Need for Your Consular Interview

It's never too early to begin gathering the necessary documents to bring with you to your scheduled interview at the U.S. embassy or consulate:

☐ confirmation page and bar code, showing that you (and any accompanying family members) completed an online Form DS-160

☐ a current passport for yourself and for all of your unmarried children under 21 years of age, if they are coming with you or following you to the United States

☐ divorce or death certificates for any previous spouses of either you or the U.S. citizen, with English translations

☐ police clearance from all places you have lived for more than six months (except from the United States, where USCIS gathers the information)

☐ originals of all documents, copies of which were submitted by your U.S. citizen fiancé with Form I-129F (see the sample at the end of this chapter) to confirm your relationship and show your eligibility for the visa

☐ two passport-style photographs of yourself and each of any children applying with you for a visa (see Chapter 21, Section E for detailed photo requirements)

☐ report of your own medical examination and those of all children over 14 years of age to verify that you've had all your vaccinations and no one has a communicable disease. You will need to get this medical exam from a designated panel physician. For a list of panel physicians near you, visit http://travel.state. gov and click "Immigrate" then "Learn About Immigrating to the United States" then (on the flow chart), "Prepare for the Interview," then "Medical Examination."

☐ Form I-134, Affidavit of Support, filled out by your U.S. citizen fiancé. (See the sample at the end of this chapter.)

You will be asked for personal information such as any names used, date and place of birth, address, phone number and email, any national identification or other numbers, and passport information.

Also, you will need a recent and clear digital photograph of yourself to upload, and information on your U.S. travel plans. You will be asked for your expected date of U.S. arrival, names of any travel companions, previous U.S. travel history and contacts, family information, and work and educational history.

Although you don't need to print the application for submission, it's a good idea to keep a copy for your records. You WILL need a copy of the DS-160 confirmation page and bar code to bring to your interview at the U.S. embassy or consulate, which will allow the consular officer to upload your application.

The next step is to schedule an interview at the U.S. embassy or consulate nearest you. This is another new development, as the consulate used to send visa applicants an interview notice. Now you must schedule your own appointment using your receipt number and DS-160 bar code number. Do so by locating your consulate at www.usembassy.gov and following its instructions for scheduling nonimmigrant or K visa interviews.

If you live far away from the consulate, you may want to arrive a couple of days before your actual interview. This will give you time to have the medical exam done and receive the results (if no doctors closer to your home were on the consulate's list). Also, check out the situation around the consulate itself. Often, there are long lines, so you'll need to arrive well before your appointment time and expect to be let in long after. Many prospective immigrants who have applied for a visa at a local consulate have posted their experiences online, so it's worth doing your homework beforehand.

5. Interview at the Embassy

The U.S. embassy or consulate will schedule the immigrating fiancé for an interview. You should bring all the forms and documents listed in the consulate's instructions and under "What You'll Need for Your Consular Interview," above. There will be an application fee of $240 per person.

Form I-134. This form, called an Affidavit of Support, is used to show that you will not become a public charge (dependent on government support) while in the U.S., because your petitioner/sponsor has sufficient income and/or assets to support you. See the sample Form I-134 toward the end of this chapter. Note that at one time, it was necessary to sign this form in front of a notary public, but no longer.

It's important to realize, however, that you'll need to prove you won't become a public charge once again, after you marry and apply for the green card in the United States. At that time, you will need to submit a new Affidavit of Support on a different form, Form I-864, which comes with more demanding income requirements. Form I-134 sponsors need only show that their income is at least 100% of the federal Poverty Guidelines, while I-864 sponsors must show that it reaches 125%. In support of this form, the citizen should add copies (as appropriate) of his or her:

- ☐ bank statements
- ☐ recent tax returns and W-2s
- ☐ employment verification (make this an original letter from the employer detailing salary, hours, and whether the position is temporary or permanent), and

- ☐ if necessary to bring the citizen's income above the Poverty Guidelines levels, documents showing the value of any of the following property, if owned: bonds and stocks, real estate, and mortgage information or life insurance.

Medical exam. The immigrating fiancé will also need to have a medical exam done. The fiancé can't just go to the family doctor, but will have to go to a clinic specified by the consulate. The doctor will do an exam, ask questions about medical history and drug and alcohol use, take X-rays, and withdraw blood. Although vaccinations are not required for K visa issuance, they will be required when you adjust your status to permanent resident. Embassies therefore encourage fiancés to fulfill the vaccination requirements at the time of the fiancé medical examination. The cost (including vaccines) is usually around $300.

Forms for children. Most of the forms and documents must be separately filled out for you and for any minor children who will also be going to the United States.

Security checks. Because of new and increased security procedures, it is unlikely that you will receive your visa on the same day as you attend your interview. It can take several weeks for the consulate to run security checks on you—and even longer if you come from a country that the United States suspects of supporting terrorism.

Approval. If the U.S. consular official is ultimately convinced that you and your U.S. citizen fiancé are truly engaged to be married and will marry upon your arrival in the United States, and that you aren't barred from entry for any of the reasons described in Chapter 4, your passport will be stamped with the K-1 visa. The passports of your accompanying minor children will be stamped with the K-2 visa, meaning that they are dependent upon you for their immigration status.

Questions to Expect at K-1 Visa Interview

At your interview, the consular officer will ask a few basic questions about you and your fiancé and about five to ten additional questions to test the validity of your relationship. On average, the entire K-1 visa interview takes 15 to 30 minutes.

Be prepared for questions about any previous marriages and about your or your fiancé's children. Make sure you know basic information about your fiancé including occupation, hometown, birthday, and names of close family members. Other sample questions about your relationship might include:

☐ "How long did you date before you got engaged?"

☐ "What types of activities do you like to do together?"

☐ "How many times have you met in person? Where and when?"

☐ "How are you communicating during the long-distance relationship? Is it difficult being apart?"

☐ "Have you met your fiancé's family? Has he or she met yours?"

☐ "When and where will the wedding be held?"

☐ "Do you have any plans for a honeymoon?"

TIP

If you're already married but are applying for a K-3 fiancé visa, most of the advice in this section regarding the visa interview applies to you, too. However, you won't have to worry about convincing anyone that you plan to get married. Your main task will simply be to show that your paperwork is in order, with the understanding that you will complete the green card application after you've arrived in the United States.

The fiancé visa is considered a nonimmigrant visa because you are simply promising to marry a U.S. citizen. You are not yet an immigrant.

6. At the Border

Once you receive your fiancé visa, you'll have six months to use it to enter the United States. At the U.S. port of entry, the border officer will examine the contents of your visa envelope and ask you a few questions. Be careful with this—if the officer spots a reason that you should not have been given the fiancé visa, he or she has the power to deny your entry right there. You would have no choice but to find a flight or other means of transport home. And you might not be allowed back for five years (unless the officer allows you to withdraw the application before it's officially denied, which is entirely at the officer's discretion).

Assuming all goes well, the border officer will stamp your passport with your K-1 fiancé visa status, and indicate in your passport the 90-day duration of your status.

7. Permission to Work in the U.S.

When you arrive in the United States, you can apply at once for an Employment Authorization card that will enable you to work legally. The proper paperwork to complete for this is Form I-765. (See the USCIS website, www.uscis.gov/i-765.)

However, you'll have to submit your application to a USCIS Service Center, and the service centers are famous for delays of many months. Submitting this application may not be worth the effort since the maximum time the work permit will be good for is three months (based on the length of your fiancé visa). You may be better off getting married, then submitting your green card application together with an application for a work permit. This allows you more time to work before the card expires (it will last for approximately one year).

D. How to Bring Your Children on a Fiancé Visa

Your unmarried children under age 21 are eligible to accompany you on your fiancé visa and apply for green cards after you're in the United States and you have gotten married. This includes biological as well as adopted children. All you have to do at the beginning of the fiancé visa application process is to include your children's names in Part 2 of the fiancé visa petition (Form I-129F). You, as the parent, can complete a Form DS-160 for any accompanying child under age 16.

Your children will probably be asked to attend your consular interview with you, although some consulates let younger children stay home. The technical name of their visa will be K-2. For the visa interview, they'll normally be asked to bring:

- ☐ DS-160 confirmation recipt
- ☐ birth certificate (original and photocopy, with English translation)
- ☐ police record (if the child is over age 16)
- ☐ passport (unless your country permits the child to be included on your passport)
- ☐ two photos, and
- ☐ medical exam results.

Even if your children don't accompany you when you first enter the U.S. as a fiancé, they can join you under the same visa for a year after yours was approved. Just make sure they remain unmarried and under the age of 21. They'll need to complete Forms DS-160 and schedule an interview. If they don't plan to immigrate with you, but want to attend your wedding, their other option is a visitor visa.

When it comes time to apply for green cards, you and your children will each have to submit a separate application, before each of your visas expires.

TIP

Don't let anyone tell you that your child needs to have been under 18 when you were married. Some USCIS officers get confused when dealing with K-2 applicants for adjustment of status, and expect them to meet the standards for stepchildren that apply to certain other applicants. The confusion is common enough that USCIS sent out a general reminder memo to all of its offices in 2007. The bottom line: So long as your K-2 child is under 21 (and unmarried), and you've gotten married to your U.S. citizen petitioner, the child can apply to adjust status and get a green card.

E. Marriage and After

It's a good idea to marry as soon as possible after you arrive. That will give you enough time to prepare and submit your application for adjustment of status before your fiancé visa expires, so that you remain in lawful fiancé status the whole time. (See Chapter 16 for more information about submitting your application for adjustment of status.) There may be delays in preparing the application that are out of your control. For example, your local government office may take several weeks to issue your official marriage certificate, which is a required document in your adjustment of status package—USCIS will not accept your application with just the initial "souvenir" certificate issued by civil and religious authorities.

You should definitely try to marry within 90 days of entering the U.S., that is, before your fiancé visa expires. You can wait until after the 90 days to submit your adjustment of status application, but you will be without any legal status from the time the 90 days expires until USCIS receives your application.

If something happens and you miss the 90-day deadline for getting married, you and your fiancé can still go ahead and get married and file for your adjustment of status. The difference is that you will have to also submit a Form I-130 (visa petition) along with its filing fee, currently $420.

> **CAUTION**
>
> **What if, after coming to the U.S., you change your mind and decide not to get married?** In that case, you should leave the U.S. before your 90 days on the fiancé visa are up.

If you fail to marry your U.S. citizen fiancé at all, USCIS can start removal (deportation) proceedings against you and all children who came with you on a fiancé visa.

If you enter the U.S. on a fiancé visa, you can adjust your status to permanent resident only if you marry your fiancé. If you marry someone else, you cannot adjust your status based on that other marriage—although you might be able to get a green card through consular processing. (Check Chapter 4 to see whether any grounds of inadmissibility might apply if you try to consular process, particularly the bar that is triggered if you were in the U.S. for more than 180 days after the expiration of your fiancé status.)

If you do marry your U.S. citizen fiancé within 90 days, there is one more important step you must take in order to get a green card. You must file for adjustment of status (see Chapter 16), for yourself and all your minor children who came on the fiancé visa.

> **CAUTION**
>
> **Beware of the two-year time limit.** Going through the adjustment of status procedure will give you and your minor children conditional permanent residence status, and you will acquire a green card that is valid for only two years. To make it a permanent green card after the two years, follow the procedures for conditional permanent residents, laid out in Chapter 7.

e-Notification of Application/Petition Acceptance

Department of Homeland Security
U.S. Citizenship and Immigration Services

USCIS
Form G-1145
OMB No. 1615-0109
Expires 09/30/2014

What Is the Purpose of This Form?

Use this form to request an electronic notification (e-Notification) when U.S. Citizenship and Immigration Services accepts your immigration application. This service is available for applications filed at a USCIS Lockbox facility.

General Information

Complete the information below and clip this form to the first page of your application package. You will receive one e-mail and/or text message for each form you are filing.

We will send the e-Notification within 24 hours after we accept your application. Domestic customers will receive an e-mail and/or text message; overseas customers will only receive an e-mail. Undeliverable e-Notifications cannot be resent.

The e-mail or text message will display your receipt number and tell you how to get updated case status information. It will not include any personal information. The e-Notification does not grant any type of status or benefit; rather it is provided as a convenience to customers.

USCIS will also mail you a receipt notice (I-797C), which you will receive within 10 days after your application has been accepted; use this notice as proof of your pending application or petition.

USCIS Privacy Act Statement

AUTHORITIES: The information requested on this form, and the associated evidence, is collected under the Immigration and Nationality Act, section 101, et seq.

PURPOSE: The primary purpose for providing the requested information on this form is to determine if you have established eligibility for the immigration benefit for which you are filing. The information you provide will be used to grant or deny the benefit sought.

DISCLOSURE: The information you provide is voluntary. However, failure to provide the requested information, and any requested evidence, may delay a final decision or result in denial of your form.

ROUTINE USES: The information you provide on this form may be shared with other Federal, State, local, and foreign government agencies and authorized organizations following approved routine uses described in the associated published system of records notices [DHS-USCIS-007 - Benefits Information System and DHS-USCIS-001 - Alien File, Index, and National File Tracking System of Records, which can be found at **www.dhs.gov/privacy**]. The information may also be made available, as appropriate, for law enforcement purposes or in the interest of national security.

Paperwork Reduction Act

An agency may not conduct or sponsor an information collection and a person is not required to respond to a collection of information unless it displays a currently valid OMB control number. The public reporting burden for this collection of information is estimated at 3 minutes per response, including the time for reviewing instructions and completing and submitting the form. Send comments regarding this burden estimate or any other aspect of this collection of information, including suggestions for reducing this burden, to: U.S. Citizenship and Immigration Services, Regulatory Coordination Division, Office of Policy and Strategy, 20 Massachusetts Avenue, NW, Washington, DC 20529-2140. OMB No. 1615-0109. **Do not mail your completed Form G-1145 to this address.**

Complete this form and clip it on top of the first page of your immigration form(s).

Applicant/Petitioner Full Last Name	Applicant/Petitioner Full First Name	Applicant/Petitioner Full Middle Name
BEACH	Sandra	Leah

E-mail Address	Mobile Phone Number (Text Message)
sandrab@email.com	212-555-1313

Form G-1145 02/28/13

Page 1 of 1

Sample Form I-129F, Petition for Alien Fiancé(e) (page 1)

Petition for Alien Fiancé(e)
Department of Homeland Security
U.S. Citizenship and Immigration Services

USCIS
Form I-129F
OMB No. 1615-0001
Expires 06/30/2016

For USCIS Use Only	Fee Stamp	Action Block
Case ID Number		
A-Number		
G-28 Number		

☐ The petition is approved for status under Section 101(a)(5)(k). It is valid for 4 months from the date of action. _____	**Extraordinary Circumstances Waiver** ☐ Approved Reason _____ ☐ Denied _____

General Waiver	Mandatory Waiver	AMCON: _____
☐ Approved Reason _____ ☐ Denied _____	☐ Approved Reason _____ ☐ Denied _____	☐ Personal Interview ☐ Previously Forwarded ☐ Document Check ☐ Field Investigation

Initial Receipt	Relocated	Completed	Remarks	IMBRA Applies?
	Received	Approved		☐ Yes *(DOS disclosure to*
Resubmitted	Sent	Returned		*the beneficiary required)* ☐ No

▶ **START HERE - Type or print in black ink.**

Part 1. Information About You

1.a Family Name *(Last Name)* BEACH

1.b Given Name *(First Name)* Sandra

1.c Middle Name Leah

Your Mailing Address

2.a In Care of Name

2.b Street Number and Name 114 Fulton St.

2.c Apt. ☒   Ste. ☐   Flr. ☐   6E

2.d City or Town New York

2.e State NY   **2.f** Zip Code 10038

2.g Postal Code

2.h Province

2.i Country U.S.A.

3 Alien Registration Number (A-Number)
▶ A-

4 City/Town/Village of Birth
Horseheads, NY

5 Country of Birth
U.S.A.

6 Date of Birth *(mm/dd/yyyy)* ▶ 12/20/1988

7 Gender ☐ Male   ☒ Female

8 Marital Status
☐ Married   ☐ Widowed   ☒ Single   ☐ Divorced

Other Names Used

9.a Family Name *(Last Name)* (None)

9.b Given Name *(First Name)*

9.c Middle Name

10 U.S. Social Security Number *(if any)*
▶ 1 2 3 4 5 6 7 8 9

Name of Prior Spouse 1

11.a Family Name *(Last Name)* (None)

11.b Given Name *(First Name)*

11.c Middle Name

11.d Date Marriage Ended
(mm/dd/yyyy) ▶

Name of Prior Spouse 2

12.a Family Name *(Last Name)*

12.b Given Name *(First Name)*

Sample Form I-129F, Petition for Alien Fiancé(e) (page 2)

Part 1. Information About You *(continued)*

12.c. Middle Name

12.d. Date Marriage Ended
(mm/dd/yyyy) ▶

My citizenship was acquired through (Select **only one** box):

13.a. ☒ Birth in the United States

13.b. ☐ Naturalization

13.c. ☐ Parents

13.d. Have you obtained a Certificate of Naturalization or a Certificate of Citizenship in your name? ☐ Yes ☒ No

If "Yes," complete the following:

13.d.1. Certificate Number

13.d.2. Place of Issuance

13.d.3. Date of Issuance
(mm/dd/yyyy) ▶

14. Have you ever filed for this or any other alien fiancé(e) or husband/wife before?
☐ Yes ☒ No

If you answered "**Yes**," provide the following for each alien *(attach additional sheets as necessary)*

14.a. Alien Registration Number (A-Number)
▶ A- ☐☐☐☐☐☐☐☐☐

14.b. Family Name *(Last Name)*

14.c. Given Name *(First Name)*

14.d. Middle Name

14.e. Date of Filing *(mm/dd/yyyy)* ▶

14.f. City or Town

14.g. State

14.h. Result

Part 2. Information About Your Alien Fiancé(e)

1. Identify the classification sought for your beneficiary *(select one):*

☒ K-1 Fiancé

☐ K-3 Spouse

2.a. Family Name *(Last Name)*   HOLLIS

2.b. Given Name *(First Name)*   Nigel

2.c. Middle Name   Ian

Alien Fiancé(e)'s Mailing Address

3.a. In Care of Name

3.b. Street Number and Name   123 Limestone Way

3.c. Apt. ☒ Ste. ☐ Flr ☐   7

3.d. City or Town   Penzance

3.e. State ☐   **3.f.** Zip Code   TR197NL

3.g. Postal Code

3.h. Province   Cornwall

3.i. Country   U.K.

Other Information About Your Alien Fiancé(e)

4. City/Town/Village of Birth
Port Navas

5. Country of Birth
U.K.

6. Date of Birth *(mm/dd/yyyy)* ▶   8/17/1986

7. Country of Citizenship
U.K.

8. Gender   ☒ Male   ☐ Female

9. Marital Status
☐ Married ☐ Widowed ☐ Single ☒ Divorced

Other Names Used (Including Maiden Name)

10.a. Family Name *(Last Name)*   (None)

10.b. Given Name *(First Name)*

10.c. Middle Name

11. Alien Registration Number (A-Number)
▶ A- ☐☐☐☐☐☐☐☐☐

Sample Form I-129F, Petition for Alien Fiancé(e) (page 3)

Part 2. Information About Your Alien Fiancé(e) *(continued)*

12. U.S. Social Security Number *(if any)*

▶ [ ][ ][ ][ ][ ][ ][ ][ ][ ]

Name of Prior Spouse 1

13.a. Family Name
(Last Name) — SIMPSON

13.b. Given Name
(First Name) — Jane

13.c. Middle Name — Ellyn

13.d. Date Marriage Ended

(mm/dd/yyyy) ▶ 05/20/2011

Name of Prior Spouse 2

14.a. Family Name
(Last Name)

14.b. Given Name
(First Name)

14.c. Middle Name

14.d. Date Marriage Ended

(mm/dd/yyyy) ▶

15. Has your fiancé(e) ever been in
the United States? ☒ Yes ☐ No

**If your fiancé(e) is currently in the United States, complete
the following:**

15.a. **He or she last arrived as a:** *(visitor, student, exchange
alien, crewman, stowaway, temporary worker, without
inspection, etc.)*

15.b. I-94 Arrival/Departure Record Number

▶ [ ][ ][ ][ ][ ][ ][ ][ ][ ][ ][ ]

15.c. Date of Arrival *(mm/dd/yyyy)* ▶

15.d. Date authorized stay expired or will expire as shown on
I-94 or I-95. *(mm/dd/yyyy)* ▶

15.e. Passport Number

15.f. Travel Document Number

15.g. Country of Issuance for Passport or Travel Document

15.h. Expiration Date for Passport or Travel Document

(mm/dd/yyyy) ▶

Complete the following for all children of your alien
fiancé(e) *(if any)*.

Child 1 of Alien Fiancé(e)

16.a. Family Name
(Last Name)

16.b. Given Name
(First Name)

16.c. Middle Name

17. Country of Birth

18. Date of Birth *(mm/dd/yyyy)* ▶

19.a. Street Number
and Name

19.b. Apt. ☐ Ste. ☐ Flr. ☐

19.c. City or Town

19.d. State [ ] **19.e.** Zip Code

19.f. Postal Code

19.g. Province

19.h. Country

Child 2 of Alien Fiancé(e)

20.a. Family Name
(Last Name)

20.b. Given Name
(First Name)

20.c. Middle Name

21. Country of Birth

22. Date of Birth *(mm/dd/yyyy)* ▶

23.a. Street Number
and Name

23.b. Apt. ☐ Ste. ☐ Flr. ☐

23.c. City or Town

23.d. State [ ] **23.e.** Zip Code

23.f. Postal Code

23.g. Province

23.h. Country

Sample Form I-129F, Petition for Alien Fiancé(e) (page 4)

Part 2. Information About Your Alien Fiancé(e) *(continued)*

Child 3 of Alien Fiancé(e)

24.a. Family Name
(Last Name)

24.b. Given Name
(First Name)

24.c. Middle Name

25. Country of Birth

26. Date of Birth *(mm/dd/yyyy)* ▶

27.a. Street Number
and Name

27.b. Apt. ☐ Ste. ☐ Flr. ☐

27.c. City or Town

27.d. State   **27.e.** Zip Code

27.f. Postal Code

27.g. Province

27.h. Country

Address in the United States where your fiancé(e) intends to live.

28.a. Street Number
and Name   114 Fulton St.

28.b. Apt. ☒ Ste. ☐ Flr. ☐   6E

28.c. City or Town   New York

28.d. State   NY   **28.e.** Zip Code   10030

Your fiancé(e)'s address abroad.

29.a. Street Number
and Name   123 Limestone Way

29.b. Apt. ☒ Ste. ☐ Flr. ☐   7

29.c. City or Town   Penzance

29.d. Postal Code   TR197NL

29.e. Province   Cornwall

29.f. Country   U.K.

30. Daytime Phone Number   Extension

1234-123456

If your fiancé(e)'s native alphabet uses other than Roman letters, write his or her name and address abroad in the native alphabet.

31.a. Family Name
(Last Name)

31.b. Given Name
(First Name)

31.c. Middle Name

Your fiancé(e)'s address abroad. *(Native Alphabet)*

32.a. Street Number
and Name

32.b. Apt. ☐ Ste. ☐ Flr. ☐

32.c. City or Town

32.d. Postal Code

32.e. Province

32.f. Country

33. Is your fiancé(e) related to you?   ☐ Yes ☒ No

33.a. If you are related, state the nature and degree of relationship, e.g., third cousin or maternal uncle, etc.

34. Has your fiancé(e) met and seen you within the 2-year period immediately preceding the filing of this petition?
☒ Yes ☐ No

34.a. Describe the circumstances under which you met. If you have not personally met each other, explain how the relationship was established. If you met your fiancé(e) or spouse though an international marriage broker, please explain those circumstances in number **35.a**. Explain in detail any reasons you may have for requesting that the requirement that you and your fiancé(e) must have met should not apply to you.

See attached statement

35. Did you meet your fiancé(e) or spouse through the services of an international marriage broker?
☐ Yes ☒ No

35.a. If you answered "Yes," provide the Internet and/or Street Address below. In additional, attach a copy of the signed, written consent form the IMB obtained from your beneficiary authorizing the release of your beneficiary's personal contact information to you. If additional space is needed, attach a separate sheet of paper.

Sample Form I-129F, Petition for Alien Fiancé(e) (page 5)

Part 2. Information About Your Alien Fiancé(e) *(continued)*

Your fiancé(e) will apply for a visa abroad at the American embassy or consulate at:

36.a. City or Town

> London

36.b. Country

> England

NOTE: Designation of a U.S. embassy or consulate outside the country of your fiancé(e)'s last residence does not guarantee acceptance for processing by that foreign post. Acceptance is at the discretion of the designated embassy or consulate.

Part 3. Other Information

1. If you are serving overseas in the Armed Forces of the United States, please answer the following:

I presently reside or am stationed overseas and my current mailing address is:

1.a. Street Number and Name

1.b. Apt. ☐ Ste. ☐ Flr. ☐

1.c. City or Town

1.d. State [ ] **1.e.** Zip Code

1.f. Postal Code

1.g. Province

1.h. Country

2. Have you ever been convicted by a court of law (civil or criminal) or court martialed by a military tribunal for any of the following crimes:

2.a. Domestic violence, sexual assault, child abuse and neglect, dating violence, elder abuse or stalking? (Please refer to Page 3 of the instructions for the full definition of the term "domestic violence"). ☐ Yes ☒ No

2.b. Homicide, murder, manslaughter, rape, abusive sexual contact, sexual exploitation, incest, torture, trafficking, peonage, holding hostage, involuntary servitude, slave trade, kidnapping, abduction, unlawful criminal restraint, false imprisonment or an attempt to commit any of these crimes? ☐ Yes ☒ No

2.c. Three or more convictions for crimes relating to a controlled substance or alcohol not arising from a single act? ☐ Yes ☒ No

These questions must be answered even if your records were sealed or otherwise cleared or if anyone, including a judge, law enforcement officer, or attorney, told you that you no longer have a record. Using a separate sheet(s) of paper, provide information relating to the conviction(s), such as crime involved, date of conviction and sentence.

3. If you have provided information about a conviction for a crime listed above and you were being battered or subjected to extreme cruelty by your spouse, parent, or adult child at the time of your conviction, check all of the following that apply to you:

3.a. ☐ I was acting in self-defense.

3.b. ☐ I violated a protection order issued for my own protection.

3.c. ☐ I committed, was arrested for, was convicted of, or plead guilty to committing a crime that did not result in serious bodily injury, and there was a connection between the crime committed and my having been battered or subjected to extreme cruelty.

If your beneficiary is your fiancé(e) and: (a) this is the third (or more) Form I-129F petition that you have filed; or (b) this is the third (or more) Form I-129F petition you have filed and your first Form I-129F petition was approved within the last 2 years, then your petition cannot be approved unless a waiver of the multiple filing restriction is granted. Attach a signed and dated letter, requesting the waiver and explaining why a waiver is appropriate under your circumstances, together with any evidence in support of the waiver request.

4. Indicate which waiver applies:

☐ Multiple Filer, No Disqualifying Convictions **(General Waiver)**

☐ Multiple Filer, Prior Criminal Conviction for Specified Offenses **(Extraordinary Circumstances Waiver)**

☐ Multiple Filer, Prior Criminal Convictions Resulting from Domestic Violence **(Mandatory Waiver)**

☐ Not applicable, beneficiary is my spouse

NOTE: See Page 3, question 3.b. of the filing instructions.

Sample Form I-129F, Petition for Alien Fiancé(e) (page 6)

Part 4. Signature of Petitioner

Penalties

You may by law be imprisoned for not more than 5 years, or fined $250,000, or both, for entering into a marriage contract for the purpose of evading any provision of the immigration laws, and you may be fined up to $10,000 or imprisoned upon to five years, or both, for knowingly and willfully falsifying or concealing a material fact or using any false document in submitting this petition.

Your Certification

I certify that I am legally able to and intend to marry my alien fiancé(e) within 90 days of his or her arrival in the United States. I certify, under penalty of perjury under the laws of the United States of America, that the foregoing is true and correct. Furthermore, I authorize the release of any information from my records that U.S. Citizenship and Immigration Services needs to determine eligibility for the benefit that I am seeking.

Moreover, I understand that this petition, including any criminal conviction information that I am required to provide with this petition, as well as any related criminal background information pertaining to me that U.S. Citizenship and Immigration Services may discover independently in adjudicating this petition will be disclosed to the beneficiary of this petition.

1.a. Signature of Petitioner

Sandra L. Beach

1.b. Date of Signature *(mm/dd/yyyy)* ► 08/02/2014

2. Daytime Phone Number   212-555-1212

3. Mobile Phone Number   212-555-1313

4. E-mail Address *(if any)*

sandrab@email.com

Part 5. Signature of Person Preparing This Petition, If Other Than the Petitioner

NOTE: If you are an attorney or representative, you must submit a completed Form G-28, Notice of Entry of Appearance as Attorney or Accredited Representative, along with this Petition.

☐ Form G-28 submitted with this Petition.

G-28 ID Number _____

Preparer's Full Name

1.a. Preparer's Family Name *(Last Name)*

1.b. Preparer's Given Name *(First Name)*

2. Preparer's Business or Organization Name

Preparer's Contact Information

3. Preparer's Daytime Phone Number   Extension

4. Preparer's E-mail Address *(if any)*

Preparer's Mailing Address

5.a. Street Number and Name

5.b. Apt. ☐ Ste. ☐ Flr. ☐

5.c. City or Town

5.d. State ____   **5.e.** Zip Code

5.f. Postal Code

5.g. Province

5.h. Country

Declaration

To be completed by all preparers, including attorneys and authorized representatives: I declare that I prepared this benefit request at the request of the Petitioner, that it is based on all the information of which I have knowledge, and that the information is true to the best of my knowledge.

6.a. Signature of Preparer

6.b. Date of Signature *(mm/dd/yyyy)* ►

Sample Fiancé Meeting Statement—Attachment to Form I-129F

Filed by Sandra Beach on Behalf of Nigel Hollis

Question 18

I met my fiancé 18 months ago, while visiting a college friend who has settled in England. My friend Carrie had been telling me for months that she wanted to introduce me to Nigel, because of our offbeat senses of humor and shared interest in long-distance swimming. I've had bad experiences with friends trying to set me up before, so I didn't take it very seriously. But when vacation plans took me to England, I let her arrange for me and Nigel to meet over lunch at a pub.

To my amazement, we clicked right away. We had a lot to talk about—he had completed an English Channel swim a few months before, and I'm hoping to swim the Channel next year. Both of us have built our lives around swimming, which sometimes leaves little time for other things, including relationships. We compared notes on training techniques, equipment, dealing with cold water, rip tides, and more.

Our lunch lasted all afternoon and into the evening. By the end of that evening, I considered Nigel a friend, and someone I could very easily fall in love with.

Nigel and I spent almost all my remaining week's vacation together. Poor Carrie joked that her plan had backfired, because I spent embarrassingly little time at her house. By the end of the week, we both knew this was headed toward a serious relationship.

Since then, Nigel and I have corresponded almost constantly by email, and call each other twice a week. During one long phone call, we decided to get married.

It was difficult deciding where we would live after marrying—Nigel has a beautiful cottage in Cornwall, and I could happily live in England. However, my mother is in poor health, and ever since my father passed away last year, she has relied on my help, so we agreed to make our home in New York.

As proof that Nigel and I are in love and plan to marry, I am attaching copies of his plane tickets to New York; photos of the two of us together; copies of our telephone bills and some of our emails; copies of catering and other contracts showing that the two of us plan to marry in July; and copies of our travel itinerary for New Zealand, where we will honeymoon.

Signed: _Sandra L. Beach_
Sandra L. Beach

Date: _8/2/14_

Sample Form G-325A, Biographic Information

Department of Homeland Security U.S. Citizenship and Immigration Services					OMB No. 1615 0008; Expires 02/28/2015 **G-325A, Biographic Information**		

Family Name	First Name	Middle Name	[X] Male [ ] Female	Date of Birth (mm/dd/yyyy)	Citizenship/Nationality	File Number
HOLLIS	Nigel	Ian		08/17/1988	Great Britain	A None

All Other Names Used (include names by previous marriages)		City and Country of Birth	U.S. Social Security No. (if any)

	Family Name	First Name	Date of Birth (mm/dd/yyyy)	City, and Country of Birth (if known)	City and Country of Residence
Father	Hollis	Kevin	01/12/1959	York, England	York, England
Mother (Maiden Name)	Chumley	Sarah	04/17/1963	York, England	York, England

Current Husband or Wife (If none, so state) Family Name (For wife, give maiden name)	First Name	Date of Birth (mm/dd/yyyy)	City and Country of Birth	Date of Marriage	Place of Marriage
None					

Former Husbands or Wives (If none, so state) Family Name (For wife, give maiden name)	First Name	Date of Birth (mm/dd/yyyy)	Date and Place of Marriage	Date and Place of Termination of Marriage
Simpson	Jane	10/31/1986	06/10/2008 London, England	05/20/2011 London, England

Applicant's residence last five years. List present address first.

Street Name and Number	City	Province or State	Country	From Month	From Year	To Month	To Year
123 Limestone Way #7	Penzance	Cornwall	England	07	2003	Present Time	

Applicant's last address outside the United States of more than 1 year.

Street Name and Number	City	Province or State	Country	From Month	From Year	To Month	To Year
None							

Applicant's employment last five years. (If none, so state.) List present employment first.

Full Name and Address of Employer	Occupation (Specify)	From Month	From Year	To Month	To Year
Outbound Design, Inc., 222 Heather Lane Penzance, Cornwall TR198NI	Sportswear Designer	08	2006	Present Time	

Last occupation abroad if not shown above. (Include all information requested above.)

This form is submitted in connection with an application for: [ ] Naturalization [X] Other (Specify): Fiance Visa (K-1) [ ] Status as Permanent Resident	Signature of Applicant *Nigel I. Hollis*	Date 11/20/2014

If your native alphabet is in other than Roman letters, write your name in your native alphabet below:

Penalties: Severe penalties are provided by law for knowingly and willfully falsifying or concealing a material fact.

Applicant: Print your name and Alien Registration Number in the box outlined by heavy border below.

Complete This Box (Family Name)	(Given Name)	(Middle Name)	(Alien Registration Number)
HOLLIS	Nigel	Ian	A

Sample Form I-134, Affidavit of Support (page 1)

OMB No. 1615-0014; Expires 02/29/2016

Department of Homeland Security
U.S. Citizenship and Immigration Services

Form I-134, Affidavit of Support

(Answer all items. Type or print in black ink.)

I, Sandra Leah Beach , residing at 114 Fulton Street, Apt. 6E
(Name) (Street Number and Name)

New York NY 10038 - U.S.A.
(City) (State) (Zip Code if in U.S.) (Country)

certify under penalty of perjury under U.S. law, that:

1. I was born on 12/20/1988 in Horseheads , NY , U.S.A.
(Date [*mm/dd/yyyy*]) (City) (State) (Country)

If you are not a U.S. citizen based on your birth in the United States, or a non-citizen U.S. national based on your birth in American Samoa (including Swains Island), answer the following as appropriate:

    a. If a U.S.citizen through naturalization, give Certificate of Naturalization number _____

    b. If a U.S. citizen through parent(s) or marriage, give Certificate of Citizenship number _____

    c. If U.S. citizenship was derived by some other method, *attach a statement of explanation.*

    d. If a Lawful Permanent Resident of the United States, give A-Number _____

    e. If a lawfully admitted nonimmigrant, give Form I-94, Arrival-Departure Record, number _____

2. I am 25 years of age and have resided in the United States since birth
(Date [*mm/dd/yyyy*])

3. This affidavit is executed on behalf of the following person:

Name (Family Name)	(First Name)	(Middle Name)	Gender	Age
Hollis	Nigel	Ian	M	27

Citizen of (Country)		Marital Status	Relationship to Sponsor	
United Kingdom		Divorced	Fiancé	

Presently resides at (Street Number and Name)	(City)		(State)	(Country)
123 Limestone Way #7	Penzance		Cornwall	U.K.

Name of spouse and children accompanying or following to join person:

Spouse	Gender	Age	Child		Gender	Age
Child	Gender	Age	Child		Gender	Age
Child	Gender	Age	Child		Gender	Age

4. This affidavit is made by me for the purpose of assuring the U.S. Government that the person(s) named in **item (3)** will not become a public charge in the United States.

5. I am willing and able to receive, maintain, and support the person(s) named in **item 3**. I am ready and willing to deposit a bond, if necessary, to guarantee that such person(s) will not become a public charge during his or her stay in the United States, or to guarantee that the above named person(s) will maintain his or her nonimmigrant status, if admitted temporarily, and will depart prior to the expiration of his or her authorized stay in the United States.

6. I understand that:

    a. Form I-134 is an "undertaking" under section 213 of the Immigration and Nationality Act, and I may be sued if the person(s) named in **item 3** becomes a public charge after admission to the United States;

    b. Form I-134 may be made available to any Federal, State, or local agency that may receive an application from the person(s) named in **item 3** for Food Stamps, Supplemental Security Income, or Temporary Assistance to Needy Families; and

    c. If the person(s) named in **item 3** does apply for Food Stamps, Supplemental Security Income, or Temporary Assistance for Needy Families, my own income and assets may be considered in deciding the person's application. How long my income and assets may be attributed to the person(s) named in **item 3** is determined under the statutes and rules governing each specific program.

Sample Form I-134, Affidavit of Support (page 2)

7. I am employed as or engaged in the business of _____ Executive Assistant _____ with _____ Helport Foundation _____
(Type of Business)   (Name of Concern)

at _____ 87 West 57th Street _____, _____ New York _____ _____ NY _____ 10039 - _____
(Street Number and Name)   (City)   (State)   (Zip Code)

I derive an annual income of: *(If self-employed, I have attached a copy of my last income tax return or report of commercial rating concern which I certify to be true and correct to the best of my knowledge and belief. See instructions for nature of evidence of net worth to be submitted.)* $ _____ 45,000 _____

I have on deposit in savings banks in the United States: $ _____ 8,000 _____

I have other personal property, the reasonable value of which is: $ _____ 7,500 _____

I have stocks and bonds with the following market value, as indicated on the attached list, which I certify to be true and correct to the best of my knowledge and belief: $ _____ 0 _____

I have life insurance in the sum of: $ _____ 0 _____

With a cash surrender value of: $ _____

I own real estate valued at: $ _____ 0 _____

With mortgage(s) or other encumbrance(s) thereon amounting to: $ _____

Which is located at: _____, _____ _____ -
(Street Number and Name)   (City)   (State)   (Zip Code)

8. The following persons are dependent upon me for support: *(Check the box in the appropriate column to indicate whether the person named is **wholly** or **partially** dependent upon you for support.)*

Name of Person	Wholly Dependent	Partially Dependent	Age	Relationship to Me
None	☐	☐		
	☐	☐		
	☐	☐		

9. I have previously submitted affidavit(s) of support for the following person(s). If none, state "None".

Name of Person	Date submitted
None	

10. I have submitted a visa petition(s) to U.S. Citizenship and Immigration Services on behalf of the following person(s). If none, state "None".

Name of Person	Relationship	Date submitted
Nigel Ian Hollis	Fiancé	08/02/2012

11. I ☐ intend ☒ do not intend to make specific contributions to the support of the person(s) named in **item 3**.

(If you check "intend," indicate the exact nature and duration of the contributions. For example, if you intend to furnish room and board, state for how long and, if money, state the amount in U.S. dollars and whether it is to be given in a lump sum, weekly or monthly, and for how long.

_____
_____
_____

Oath or Affirmation of Sponsor

I acknowledge that I have read "Sponsor and Alien Liability" on Page 2 of the instructions for this form, and am aware of my responsibilities as a sponsor under the Social Security Act, as amended, and the Food Stamp Act, as amended.

I certify under penalty of perjury under United States law that I know the contents of this affidavit signed by me and that the statements are true and correct.

Signature of Sponsor _Sandra L. Beach_ _____ **Date** 08/02/2014 _____

Green Cards Through Marriage

Every year, thousands of immigrants fall in love with U.S. citizens or permanent residents. Some couples meet overseas, others meet when the foreigner is studying or traveling in the United States. In a few cases, both members of the couple are foreign born, but one becomes a U.S. citizen or permanent resident. No matter how it came about, your topmost priority right now may be to join up in the U.S. as soon as possible. This chapter will lay out the possibilities and help you decide the easiest, fastest way to achieve this.

![CAUTION icon] **CAUTION**

We're assuming that you plan to live in the United States. If not, there's no point in applying for a green card now. You won't get one if the U.S. citizen or permanent resident can't show that he or she is, or soon will be, living and earning income in the U.S., and you'll lose the green card if you don't make the U.S. your home. If you're going to be living overseas for a while, wait until your plans change to apply for the green card.

A. Who Qualifies

You are eligible for a green card if you have entered into a bona fide (genuine), legal marriage with a U.S. citizen or lawful permanent resident. Bona fide means that the marriage is based on your desire to create a life together with your new spouse, not merely on your desire to obtain a green card. Legal means that it is valid and recognized by the laws of the state or country in which you live. It doesn't matter whether you hold the marriage ceremony in the United States or overseas, but you do need to abide by local laws—and obtain a document, such as a marriage certificate, to prove that you've done so.

- **Marriage to a U.S. citizen** makes you an immediate relative and eligible to receive a green card just as soon as you can get through the application process.

- **Marriage to a U.S. permanent resident,** unfortunately, will not yield such fast results. Your new spouse can file a visa petition for you right away, but then you'll be placed in category 2A of the family visa preferences and have to wait, probably several years, before a green card becomes available to you. Only after that waiting period is over and you've applied for your green card will you be legally permitted to live in the United States.

The Inconveniences of Marriages of Convenience

In the early 1980s, the U.S. government came to believe that as many as half the petitions based on marriage were fraudulent—in other words, entered into solely for the purpose of obtaining a green card. In 1986, the U.S. Congress passed a law called the Immigration Marriage Fraud Amendments, to eliminate as many "paper marriages" as possible.

U.S. citizens, permanent residents, and aliens who evade immigration laws by means of a fraudulent marriage can be charged with a federal crime. Those found guilty can be imprisoned for up to five years, fined up to $250,000, or both. In addition, permanent residents can be deported, as can those who are undocumented.

If you are even entertaining the idea of entering into a sham marriage, consider the following:

- Do you want to live with the possibility of being blackmailed emotionally, psychologically, and financially?
- Do you want to be prosecuted for a federal crime with a penalty of five years in prison, a fine of up to $250,000, or both?

If USCIS discovers that you have entered into a marriage or even helped someone else enter into a marriage to evade the immigration laws—or if you have submitted papers to USCIS based on such a marriage—you will almost certainly forever lose the possibility of getting a green card, no matter what relationships you may have in the future.

!CAUTION

If the U.S. petitioner has a criminal record, see an attorney. Under the Adam Walsh Child Protection and Safety Act of 2006, U.S. citizens and lawful permanent residents who have been convicted of any "specified offense against a minor" are prohibited from filing a family-based immigrant petition on behalf of any beneficiary (whether a child or not). USCIS will run security checks on all petitions and may call the petitioner in for fingerprinting. If the petitioner has a conviction for one of the specified offenses against a minor, then the petition will not be approved unless USCIS determines that the U.S. petitioner poses no risk to the beneficiary.

B. Special Rules in Court Proceedings

Suppose that removal—formerly called deportation or exclusion—proceedings have been started against you, perhaps because the immigration authorities have found that you are out of status or that you entered the U.S. without the proper documentation. While the proceedings are pending, you marry a U.S. citizen. You are now potentially eligible to file your marriage-based petition and the application for adjustment of status with the judge.

However, because you married while removal proceedings were going on, your marital status is suspect. After all, you did get married with the "shotgun" of a possible removal order facing you. You, the newly married alien, will have to provide clear and convincing evidence showing that the marriage was entered into in good faith and not solely for the purpose of getting a green card, and that no fee or financial arrangements were given for filing the petition. (Don't worry about the money you might have paid an attorney or other person to help you, which doesn't count.)

You will have to clearly establish that you married to establish a life together—for love and with a real commitment—not simply to avoid removal from the United States. See Section D4, below, for more guidance on gathering this kind of evidence. Also seek help from an experienced immigration attorney.

Same-Sex Couples Are Now Able to Obtain Green Cards Through Marriage

On June 26, 2013, the U.S. Supreme Court in *U.S. v. Windsor* struck down major portions of the federal Defense of Marriage Act (DOMA). This law once blocked individuals in same-sex marriages from receiving the federal benefits afforded to those in opposite-sex marriages, such as tax breaks and yes, immigration rights. Now, U.S. citizens and U.S. permanent residents can finally file a green card petition for their same-sex spouses.

The procedures for applying for immigration benefits for your same-sex spouse are exactly the same as described in this chapter and the rest of this book. Just remember that your marriage must be legally recognized in either the state or the foreign country where the marriage was performed. And marriage is the key word: civil unions and domestic partnerships won't count for immigration purposes.

So if you're not legally married, you will need to marry in order to obtain a green card for the foreign spouse. That might seem impossible if the foreign spouse's country does not recognize same-sex marriage or if international travel to the U.S. or another country is difficult or expensive.

A good way to get around this is to use the K-1 fiancé visa to bring your partner to the U.S. for the purpose of getting married (see Chapter 6 for information on fiancé visas). Keep in mind that this option will work only for the partners of U.S. citizens, as the fiancés of U.S. permanent residents are not eligible for K-1 visas.

C. Quick View of the Marriage-Based Green Card Application Process

Let's start with the general concept: To get a marriage-based green card, the U.S. citizen or permanent resident spouse must begin the process by submitting (by mail) a "visa petition" (Form I-130). (You can't just walk this form into your local USCIS office.) This form serves to prove to the immigration authorities that you're legally married. After that petition is approved, you, the immigrant, complete your half of the process by submitting a green card application and attending an interview, usually with your spouse. Your application serves to prove not only that your marriage is technically legal, but that it's the "real thing," and that you're otherwise eligible for U.S. permanent residence.

However, the details of when and how all this happens depend on several things: first, whether you, the immigrant, are living overseas or in the United States; and second, whether your spouse is a U.S. citizen or a permanent resident. We'll briefly describe each possible situation separately. It will also depend on the procedures, practices, and scheduling backup at the embassy where you'll be receiving your visa eventually.

Immigrant living overseas, married to a U.S. citizen, option 1 (immigrant visa). Under the traditional methods, the U.S. citizen mails the I-130 visa petition to a USCIS office (unless the citizen also lives overseas, in which case some consulates will accept the visa petition directly). After USCIS approves the visa petition, the immigrant goes through consular processing (fully described in Chapter 17), which involves sending in fees and paperwork and ultimately attending a visa interview at a U.S. consulate in the immigrant's home country. At the interview (which only the immigrant is required to attend), the immigrant is approved for a visa. He or she must then use the visa to enter the United States within six months to claim his or her permanent residence (or "conditional" residence, if you've been married

less than two years at this time; see Section F for details). The entire process usually takes up to a year.

Immigrant living overseas, married to a U.S. citizen, option 2 (K-3 visa). Several years ago, obtaining a visa overseas based on marriage was taking almost two years, while obtaining a fiancé visa was taking about nine months. The discrepancy was due to the amount of time that it took USCIS to make a decision on the initial petitions (the I-130 and the I-129F). To address this unfair situation, a method was devised to allow the long-waiting spouses of U.S. citizens to enter the U.S. within the same time frame as a fiancé, by allowing spouses to enter the U.S. on a kind of fiancé visa for married people, called a K-3 visa.

More recently, USCIS has begun processing the I-130s and the I-129Fs in the same amount of time, so it often makes no sense for married people to use the fiancé visa (which adds steps and expense to the process). To check the current processing times so you will know whether using the K-3 visa will speed things up for you, go to the USCIS website (www.uscis.gov), click "Check Your Case Status," and compare your local Service Center's processing times for I-129Fs (the line indicating "K-3s") to its processing times for I-130s (spouses of U.S. citizens). Make sure you are looking at the processing times for the correct Service Center, based on where you live. If the processing time for K-3 visas is many months less than that for I-130s, then you can speed up your U.S. entry by using the K-3 method. If the processing times are roughly the same, it will not help you to use the K-3 method.

If you decide to use the K-3 method, the U.S. citizen starts the process by mailing a visa petition (on Form I-130) to USCIS. However, as soon as the U.S. citizen receives a receipt notice from USCIS, he or she can submit a separate, fiancé visa petition (on Form I-129F) to USCIS.

After USCIS approves the fiancé visa petition, the immigrant goes through consular processing (described later in this chapter), and attends an interview at a U.S. consulate. The consulate approves the immigrant for a K-3, or fiancé, visa. This does not mean that the immigrant has been approved for a green card; the K-3 visa simply allows the immigrant to enter the United States in order to apply for the green card there.

After entering the U.S., the immigrant can prepare and mail an adjustment of status application to USCIS. After several months, the immigrant and his or her spouse must attend an interview, at which the immigrant will be approved for permanent residence (or conditional residence if they've been married for less than two years at that time; see Section F for details).

> CAUTION
> **The traditional marriage visa procedure is certainly cheaper.** Adjustment of status fees in the United States are now over $1,000 per person, and if you use a K-3 fiancé visa to enter the U.S., the last stage of your application will be to adjust status in the United States. By contrast, if you immigrate as a regular spouse, you'll do all your visa processing overseas, and pay $492 in filing fees per person for the corresponding final stages of the process.

Immigrant living overseas, married to a U.S. permanent resident. The U.S. permanent resident mails the visa petition to USCIS. It will stay there until close to the time the immigrant's Priority Date is current (see Chapter 5 for a discussion of Priority Dates). After it's approved, it will be sent to the National Visa Center for further processing, before being forwarded to the U.S. consulate where the immigrant will attend his or her interview.

At the interview at a U.S. consulate, (which only the immigrant is required to attend), the immigrant is approved for a visa, and must then enter the United States within six months to claim permanent residence.

Immigrant living in the United States, married to a U.S. citizen. Ideally, the U.S. citizen mails the visa petition together with the immigrant's green

Immigrant Story: Dealing With Entry Without Inspection

Carmela, from Costa Rica, won the green card lottery one year, and moved to San Diego, California. Her boyfriend Jorge, who missed Carmela terribly, made his way to Mexico and then crossed the border to join her. Jorge was unable to get a visa or other document allowing him to enter the U.S. legally, so he and some friends crossed the border at an unguarded spot—in immigration law lingo, without being "inspected and admitted."

Jorge and Carmela got married seven months later, and picked up a copy of this book. Carmela then filed a form I-130 visa petition on Jorge's behalf. However, they also realized that Jorge would be ineligible to adjust status in the United States after his Priority Date became current (which they expected to take a few years).

What's more, Jorge realized, when it came time to get his green card at a U.S. consulate, he could be barred from returning for three years, because he'd already stayed in the U.S. unlawfully for more than 180 days—and that if he stayed another five months, he would be barred from returning for a whole ten years. (A waiver based on extreme hardship to family helps some people avoid this ten-year bar, but Jorge's situation presents no such extraordinary circumstances.)

Jorge decides to leave the United States before his unlawful presence has added up to one year. The good news is, he can work off the three-year bar on reentering as soon as he's out of the U.S. and while he's waiting for his Priority Date to become current. In fact, he's likely to have to wait another two years after working off his three-year bar until his Priority Date is current (in the category for spouses of permanent residents or "2A," average waits have been about five years lately).

card application (adjustment of status packet complete with forms, photos, and the results of a medical exam) to USCIS. The immigrant is sent a fingerprint appointment notice and later an interview appointment notice. Both husband and wife must attend the interview, which will be held at a local USCIS district office. At the interview, the immigrant is approved for permanent residence (or conditional residence, if they've been married less than two years at this time; see Section F for details). However, not all immigrants are eligible to use the adjustment of status procedure—in particular, those whose last entry into the U.S. was made without inspection and admission by a border official cannot. See Chapter 16 for details.

Immigrant living in the United States, married to a U.S. permanent resident. The U.S. permanent resident mails the visa petition to USCIS. It will stay there until close to the time the immigrant's Priority Date (discussed in Chapter 5) is current. After it's approved, however, things can get complicated. The only way the immigrant can remain in the United States to adjust status (submit a green card application) is if he or she has either been living legally in the United States during all the intervening years (in which case the immigrant can adjust status as described in this book) or started the process when previous laws were in effect. (See Chapter 16 for details on who can adjust status.) The immigrant's alternative is to continue with the case at an overseas U.S. consulate, but if the immigrant has been living illegally in the U.S., this could result in a three- or ten-year bar on reentry (as explained in Chapter 4). See an attorney for a full personal analysis.

CAUTION

Entering the U.S. without inspection causes problems. Except in rare circumstances (described in Chapter 16), people who entered the United States surreptitiously (for example, by crossing the border away from an inspection point) do not have the right to adjust status—that is, apply for a green card—in the United States. Attempting to turn your application in to USCIS could get you deported. Your best course is to get help from an experienced immigration attorney in evaluating and completing your application.

D. Detailed Instructions for the Marriage-Based Green Card Application Process

Now we'll break the application process down into individual procedures, some of which will be covered here and others in the next chapters—we'll tell you exactly where to turn to for your situation. We'll start by discussing the visa petition, which all couples must prepare to begin the process.

Note: The legal term for the U.S. citizen or permanent resident who is signing immigration papers for an alien spouse is "petitioner." The legal term for the immigrating spouse is "beneficiary."

1. Beginning the Process: The Visa Petition

No matter what the circumstances, the U.S. citizen or permanent resident must prepare and collect the following items that make up the visa petition:

☐ Form I-130, Petition for Alien Relative. (See the sample at the end of this chapter. However, if you're also planning to apply for a fiancé visa for entry into the United States, there's one important change to the usual procedures for filling out the form: On Question 22, the U.S. spouse should write "Applicant plans to obtain a K-3 visa abroad and adjust status in the United States," then fill in the lines regarding which city the immigrant plans to adjust status in, and which consulate he or she would return to, if necessary, as a backup.) This form must be signed by the U.S. citizen or permanent resident spouse. It gives information about both the husband and the wife.

☐ Two copies of Form G-325A, Biographic Information—one for the husband and the other for the wife. Each person must fill out a separate form and sign it. (See the sample at the end of this chapter.) The form contains information about the parents, places of residence, employers of both spouses during the past five years, and any previous foreign residences. Both of these forms can be used for checking on the alien spouse's background.

☐ Form G-1145. This is optional, but filing it is a good idea, so that you'll receive an email and/or text notification from USCIS when your application has been accepted. Once USCIS sends you a receipt number, you can use that number to sign up to receive automatic email updates letting you know whenever mail is sent regarding your application.

TIP

Here's how to sign up for automatic email updates: Go to www.uscis.gov and click "Check your Case Status" on the home page, then, click "Sign-up for Case Updates." Enter your email address or mobile phone number in order to receive updates from USCIS on your case.

☐ Photos of the immigrant and the spouse (one each). These must be passport-style, in color, and taken within 30 days before the filing. See Chapter 21 for more detailed photo requirements. Write your name in pencil on the back of the photo, in case it gets separated from your file.

☐ Proof that the American half of the couple (the "petitioner") is either a U.S. citizen or permanent resident. If a citizen, the petitioner should provide a copy of his or her passport, birth certificate, naturalization certificate (don't worry, it's legal to photocopy it for this purpose), or copy of Form FS-20 (Report of Birth Abroad of a Citizen of the United States, issued by a U.S. consulate).

If a permanent resident, the person should provide a copy of his or her green card (front and back), passport stamp, or USCIS approval notice.

☐ Documents to prove that there is a valid marriage, including copies of the documents listed below.

- **Marriage certificate.** Submit the civil registry certificate and not the marriage license or the church certificate, unless your country accepts a church marriage certificate as an official document. Marriage by proxy, a cultural practice in certain countries, is not acceptable to the immigration authorities.

- **Previous marriages.** If either of you was previously married, attach proof of the termination of the previous marriage—a divorce decree, annulment decree, or death certificate. Some foreign divorces may not be recognized by USCIS. The law provides that at least one of the parties must be living in the place where the divorce was granted. In addition, if the divorcing pair is living in the U.S., they should obtain a divorce in a local court, not at their embassy.

☐ Filing fee (currently $420) in the form of a check, money order, or certified check payable to the U.S. Department of Homeland Security.

See Chapter 21 for more detailed instructions on preparing these documents.

When you've completed and assembled all these items, make two complete copies of the entire packet for yourself and your spouse. What you'll do with it next depends on where you are living, how you entered the U.S. and whether you're eligible to adjust status here, your spouse's status, and where your spouse is living, as detailed on the summary chart below. Look under "Where to Mail the Application," below.

2. Option for Overseas Spouses of U.S. Citizens: The Fiancé Visa Petition (K-3)

If you've elected to use the fiancé visa option to get you into the United States in order to adjust status there, the U.S. citizen will also need to submit a separate visa petition, consisting of:

- ☐ Form I-129F, Petition for Alien Fiancé(e). (See the sample for married couples at the end of this chapter.) The most important thing to realize about this form is that it's usually used for people who haven't yet gotten married—who are, in fact, fiancés. Don't be thrown off by instructions or questions directed at people who aren't yet married.

- ☐ Proof that the U.S. half of the couple (the petitioner) is a U.S. citizen, such as a copy of his or her passport, birth certificate, naturalization certificate (don't worry, it's legal to photocopy it for this purpose), or copy of Form FS-20 (Report of Birth Abroad of a Citizen of the United States, issued by a U.S. consulate).

- ☐ Proof that the U.S. citizen spouse has already filed Form I-130, Petition for Alien Relative, with USCIS. Wait until USCIS sends a Form I-797 receipt notice, then photocopy this and send the copy.

- ☐ Photos of the immigrant and the spouse (one each). These must be in color, passport-style, and taken within the 30 days before the filing.

Because you're a K-3 applicant, your petitioner need not pay the usual fee for this petition.

When you've completed and assembled all these items, make two complete copies for each of your records. Then mail the completed package to the USCIS lockbox shown on the Form I-129F instructions.

3. Moving the Process Forward

After the U.S. citizen or permanent resident spouse has submitted Form I-130 (and possibly Form I-129F or an adjustment of status packet) to USCIS, it's time to start playing the waiting game. You'll probably wait longer than you'd like for a decision on your application, particularly if you're the spouse of a U.S. permanent resident.

See Chapter 5 for a full explanation of how long you're likely to wait, and why. Spouses of U.S. permanent residents should understand that years-long waits are caused by limitations on the number of green cards given out in their category every year.

The sooner the permanent resident spouses can apply for U.S. citizenship, the better. Once they become citizens, the immigrating spouses automatically become immediate relatives, and can proceed with the application for a green card. (You don't even have to file a new I-130 visa petition—it's enough to advise USCIS that the petitioner has become a citizen, by sending a letter, including a copy of his or her naturalization certificate, to the last USCIS office you corresponded with. See Chapter 5 for a sample letter.)

If you will be consular processing, and if your spouse is a U.S. citizen, the current (mid-2014) processing time for a decision on the Form I-130 is approximately nine months.

If you will not be consular processing, but instead will be filing to adjust status in the U.S., then as long as you send your I-485 and other documents for adjustment of status along with your I-130, you may get a decision sooner, because it will be handled by the same USCIS office as will handle your interview.

Check current processing times by going to www.uscis.gov. Click "Check your Case Status" and then "Check Processing Times." If you're proceeding with the consular processing method, select the Service Center where your I-130 is being processed (shown on your receipt notice). If using adjustment of status, select the Field Office where you will be interviewed and then check on the processing time for the I-485 application (since

Summary Chart: From Visa Petition To Green Card Application		
Your situation	**Where to mail the application**	**What's next**
You're living overseas, and your spouse is a U.S. citizen living in the United States.	**Option 1: Standard procedure.** The petitioner sends the I-130 visa petition via certified mail with a return receipt requested to the USCIS lockbox in either Chicago or Phoenix, depending on where you live. This office will forward it to the Service Center that serves your spouse's geographic region. Find the correct address and post office box on the USCIS website at www.uscis.gov/i-130-addresses.	**Option 1: Standard procedure.** As soon as the visa petition is approved, you'll be able to apply for your immigrant visa and green card through an overseas U.S. consulate. (See Chapter 17.)
	Option 2: K-3 visa. Although you're married, you're allowed to use a special type of fiancé visa to get you into the United States, after which you must apply to adjust status in order to become a permanent resident. To take advantage of this option, send Form I-130 as detailed above, but as soon as you can prove that USCIS received it, also send Form I-129F to the USCIS office where the I-130 is pending.	**Option 2: K-3 fiancé visa procedure.** As soon as USCIS approves the Form I-129F fiancé visa petition, you will be able to apply for a nonimmigrant visa at an overseas consulate (see Chapter 6, Section A5 for instructions). (If your Form I-130 is approved before your consular interview for the K-3 visa, the consulate will prefer to continue processing your case so that you can enter the U.S. as a permanent resident rather than as a fiancé. You may need to make sure that the I-130 approval is forwarded to the consulate. After you enter the United States, it's time to apply for a green card through USCIS (see Chapter 16 for instructions on the adjustment of status application). To avoid USCIS confusion, you should, as soon as possible after entering the U.S., send a letter to the service center processing the Form I-130 saying that you are here and will be adjusting status. (Without such a letter, some service centers have been known to send the case to the overseas consulate for processing.)

Summary Chart: From Visa Petition To Green Card Application (continued)		
Your situation	**Where to mail the application**	**What's next**
You're living overseas, and your spouse is a U.S. lawful permanent resident living in the United States.	Send the I-130 visa petition via Priority Mail to the USCIS lockbox in Chicago or Phoenix, depending on where you live. This office will forward it to a USICS office that serves your spouse's geographic region. Find the correct address and post office box on the USCIS website at www.uscis.gov/i-130-addresses.	Approval of the visa petition will give you a Priority Date, but you'll have to wait until that date is current to apply for your green card. You'll need to wait overseas during that time, after which you'll apply for your immigrant visa and green card through a U.S. consulate. (See Chapter 17.)
You're presently in the U.S., and your spouse is a lawful permanent resident.	Send the I-130 visa petition via Priority Mail to the USCIS lockbox in Chicago or Phoenix, depending on where you live. This office will forward it to a USICS office that serves your spouse's geographic region. Find the correct address and post office box on the USCIS website at www.uscis.gov/i-130-addresses.	Approval of the visa petition will give you a Priority Date, but you'll have to wait until that date is current to apply for your green card. Unless you have a separate visa to remain in the U.S. for those years, or will be eligible to adjust status in the U.S (see Chapter 16), you may have to leave soon to avoid the three- and ten-year time bars for having lived in the U.S. illegally.
You're presently in the U.S., and your spouse is a U.S. citizen. **Situation one:** You entered the U.S. without inspection.	See an immigration attorney for help—you may not be able to apply for a green card without leaving the United States, which could expose you to a three- or ten-year bar on returning; or you might qualify for a provisional waiver of unlawful presence, allowing you to safely leave for a consular interview and return.	
Situation two: You entered legally (with a visa or on a visa waiver, no matter if your expiration date passed), but did not misuse your visa to enter in order to get a green card.	You are eligible to adjust status in the United States. Submit your I-130 visa petition in combination with the immigrant's adjustment of status application (Form I-485 and supporting documents, described in Chapter 16).	Await fingerprinting and, later, an interview at your local USCIS office.

your I-130 will be processed simultaneously with your I-485).

If your application seems to be held up due to a simple bureaucratic delay, see Chapter 21 for sample inquiry letters and other instructions on prodding the USCIS into taking action.

> **TIP**
>
> **What if the U.S. petitioner dies?** If your U.S. citizen spouse submitted an I-130 on your behalf but then died before it was approved, all you need to do is submit proof of the death to USCIS, and it will automatically convert the I-130 to an I-360 "self-petition." You will then be able to proceed with processing your case. If the U.S. citizen did not submit the I-130 before dying, you can "self-petition" by submitting Form I-360. The requirements for this are that you and your U.S. citizen spouse were married (and not legally separated) at the time of death, that you file the self-petition within two years of the death, and that you have not remarried.

For the next step in the process, see the "What's Next" column in the summary chart above. For most immigrants, the next step will involve either applying for a green card from outside the United States, through a process called consular processing (discussed in Chapter 17), or from inside the United States, through a process called adjustment of status (discussed in Chapter 16). However, a few unlucky immigrants will get stuck at this point, realizing that because of past illegal entries into the U.S. or other problems, their application cannot go forward. Such persons should consult with an experienced immigration attorney.

> **TIP**
>
> **Regardless of whether you will be completing your application overseas or in the United States, come back to this chapter for a discussion of materials that only married couples need to prepare in advance of their interview.** (See Section D, below.)

4. Advice for Spouses of Permanent Residents

You cannot apply for a green card as a second preference alien—that is, as the spouse of a green-card holder—until your Priority Date is current. In the recent past there were waits of five years or more for the 2A second preference category.

However, as of March 2014, the 2A category has had the shortest wait time of recent history—around five to six months—which is actually shorter than the nine- to ten-month processing time for spouses of U.S. citizens. This does not happen often, and in the past, many U.S. permanent residents were eager to naturalize as soon as possible in order to speed up green card processing for their spouses and children.

This is why it's important to pay close attention to the *Visa Bulletin* (see Chapter 5 for a discussion on the *Visa Bulletin* and Priority Dates) when deciding whether the U.S. petitioner spouse should apply for U.S. citizenship before filing or proceeding with a pending Form I-130.

However, despite the current favorable conditions for permanent resident spouses, keep in mind that if the date of your permitted stay in the U.S. expired or if you worked without authorization ("fell out of status"), you will not be able to apply for adjustment of status unless your U.S. spouse first becomes a U.S. citizen.

5. Advice for People Who Entered the U.S. Without Inspection

If you entered the U.S. without being met and inspected by an immigration officer ("EWI") you most likely won't be able to adjust status in the United States. There is a rare exception for people who are covered by an old law, the LIFE Act, which allowed otherwise ineligible applicants to adjust status by paying a $1,000 penalty. While most foreign citizens who EWI would love to simply pay a penalty to avoid leaving the U.S. and possibly facing a time bar before being allowed to return, it covers only people with a visa petition or labor certification on file before January 14, 1998; or those who were physically present in the U.S. on December 21, 2000 with a visa petition on file by April 30, 2001.

As time passes, fewer and fewer people are able to benefit from the provisions of the LIFE Act. The vast majority of people who EWI'd therefore cannot adjust status in the U.S. and will instead need to apply for a green card at a U.S. consulate abroad.

If you came to the U.S. as an EWI and your period of unlawful presence in the U.S. is less than 180 days, you should leave the U.S. immediately in order to avoid being barred from reentering for

three years. If it's already too late and you've been time-barred from applying for a U.S. immigration benefit, you may be able to benefit from a new waiver, the provisional waiver of unlawful presence. (For more on inadmissibility, and the provisional waiver, see Chapter 4.)

6. Documenting Your Bona Fide Marriage

Whether you are applying for adjustment of status or for an immigrant visa at a consulate abroad, start gathering documents for your green card interview. At the interview, you must present not only the

---

Immigrant Story: Provisional Stateside Waiver Provides Assurance That Spousal Visa Applicant Can Promptly Reenter U.S.

In 2008, Miguel, a citizen of Costa Rica, entered the U.S. at a remote point on the Mexican border, without being inspected by an immigration officer. He settled in the U.S. and began working without permission. In 2010, Miguel married Andrea, a U.S. citizen. In 2011, Andrea gave birth to their son, Paul.

When Miguel and Andrea married, they were surprised to learn that Miguel could not adjust status in the United States. Even worse, because Miguel had spent so much time in the U.S. illegally, he would not be eligible to apply for a green card at a consulate abroad until at least ten years after departing the U.S. unless he was granted a waiver based on extreme hardship to his qualifying relatives.

In 2012, Andrea was severely injured in a car accident and was no longer able to work or provide full-time care for Paul. Miguel worked long hours in order to support the family. He consulted with an immigration attorney, who told him that based on these hardships he might qualify for a waiver, but that he would still need to return to Costa Rica in order to apply—and if denied, he could be stuck outside the U.S. for ten years before continuing with the green-card application. Miguel decided not to risk being separated from his family for so long.

In March 2013, USCIS announced that people who entered without inspection could apply for a provisional, "stateside" waiver of unlawful presence before leaving the United States. This means that Miguel could learn whether or not the waiver was approved before returning to Costa Rica for his consular interview.

Andrea filed Form I-130 and indicated that Miguel would apply for a green card using consular processing. After USCIS approved the I-130, Miguel enlisted the help of an immigration attorney and applied for the provisional waiver (using Form I-601A and including evidence of Andrea's injuries and her inability to work and care for their son full time). Miguel also included a letter from Andrea's doctor explaining that Andrea could not receive adequate medical treatment in Costa Rica and paystubs and tax returns showing that he was the sole earner in their family.

Miguel's provisional waiver application was approved. After submitting paperwork to the consulate in San Jose, Costa Rica, he received an interview date. At the interview, Miguel's immigrant visa was approved and about a week later, he received his passport and visa allowing him to reenter the U.S. as a legal permanent resident.

standard information that every immigrant does, but also separate documents showing that you have a real, valid marriage. These may include:

- [ ] birth certificates for all children born to you and your U.S. spouse
- [ ] leases on apartments that you two have occupied, together with rent receipts or canceled checks
- [ ] hospital cards, union books, insurance policies, pay vouchers, joint bank account statements, utility bills, or charge cards containing both your names
- [ ] federal income tax returns for the years that you have been married
- [ ] your wedding pictures, and
- [ ] any snapshots of the two of you together taken before the marriage and, more importantly, since the marriage, taken in different locations, and taken with different people or groups of people who may appear to know that the two of you are a couple.

Collect and make copies of as many of these documents as possible. If you and your spouse have married for love, you will eventually prevail. Nevertheless, you still have to present the required documentary proof.

E. Bringing Your Children

People immigrating through marriage are often allowed to bring their children with them, even if the children are from a previous marriage or relationship. For immigration purposes, your children must be unmarried and under the age of 21 to immigrate at the same time as you. (Options for older or married children are discussed in Chapter 9.)

However, the rules and procedures for having your children immigrate with you vary slightly depending on whether your U.S. spouse is a permanent resident or a citizen.

1. If You're Marrying a U.S. Citizen

If you're marrying a U.S. citizen, each of your children must separately qualify as an "immediate relative" of your spouse in order to immigrate with you.

To qualify as an immediate relative, your child can either be:

- the natural child of the U.S. citizen (if born out of wedlock to a U.S. citizen father, the father must have either legitimated the child while the child was under 18 and living in his custody, or demonstrated a bona fide relationship, through financial or other support), or
- the stepchild of the U.S. citizen, meaning it's legally your (the immigrant's) child, whether by birth or adoption, and you married the U.S. citizen before the child reached the age of 18.

Your spouse will need to submit a separate visa petition (Form I-130) for each one of these immediate-relative children, preferably in the same packet as the visa petition for you, the immigrant. (If you have no choice but to submit the visa petitions separately, write a letter to accompany the later petitions, explaining that you'd like the cases joined together.)

If you're also using a fiancé visa for U.S. entry, your spouse must additionally fill out a separate Form I-129F fiancé visa petition for each child.

2. If You're Marrying a U.S. Permanent Resident

If you're marrying a permanent resident, your children (natural or adopted) who are unmarried and under age 21 are considered "derivative beneficiaries." As a practical matter, this means that, at least at the beginning, your children won't need a separate initial visa petition in order to be included in your immigration process—your spouse must simply fill in the blanks on Form I-130 where it asks for the children's names. Unlike many other applicants, your children won't need to prove that your spouse is their parent or stepparent.

Your children will be given the same Priority Date as you, and most likely get a visa at the same time (provided they remain unmarried and under the age of 21). If they marry, they lose their chance to immigrate as beneficiaries. If they turn 21 before the Priority Date becomes current, they risk dropping into a separate visa category (2B) and having to wait longer for their Priority Date to become current in that category. Under the Child Status Protection Act, however, this situation is sometimes taken care of, because they get to subtract from their age the amount of time that they were waiting for USCIS to decide on the I-130.

> **EXAMPLE:** Maria was 17 years old when her mother, Luisa, married a U.S. permanent resident, who immediately filed a petition for Luisa (which included Maria). Because USCIS knew that it would be approximately five years before the Priority Date became current in that category, USCIS waited three years and seven months to approve the petition. Under the old law, if the Priority Date was still not current when Maria turned 21 (four years after the petition was submitted), she would "age out" and immediately fall into the 2B category with a longer wait. Under the Child Status Protection Act, however, Maria gets to take into account the three years and seven months that she waited for the I-130 to be approved, so Maria will not "age out" until she is 24 years and seven months old. If her Priority Date still is not current at that point, she will drop into the 2B category.

3. Final Phases of Children's Green Card Application

After the visa petition has been approved and you and your children are ready to submit your paperwork for your green cards, each child must submit his or her own application, whether to the U.S. consulate overseas or to a U.S. immigration office. These applications are discussed in Chapters 18 and 19.

As a practical matter, however, you can help your child fill out the forms, and even sign them if the child is too young (just write next to your signature, "by [*your name*], the child's [*mother or father*]."

F. If Your Marriage Is Less Than Two Years Old

If you become a U.S. resident within two years of the date you were married, whether you were granted your green card through adjustment of status or consular processing, your green card is only conditional—in other words, it expires in another two years. You are considered a "conditional permanent resident."

It seems contradictory to be both "permanent" and "conditional" at the same time, but it actually makes sense in this situation. This is because once you remove the conditional basis, your two years of conditional residence will count as unconditional or permanent residence for naturalization (citizenship) and other purposes.

To receive a green card without conditions that will be valid for more than two years, you could wait until you have been married at least two years before becoming a permanent resident. In fact, if you're overseas, this may mean delaying your date of entry to the United States—because even after you get your immigrant visa from the consulate, you're not a permanent resident until you go through a U.S. port of entry. If your marriage is already two years old at the time your permanent residence is granted, you are a full-fledged permanent resident and do not need to file papers to remove any conditions.

However, most people go ahead and become permanent residents, then wait two years minus 90 days and request the removal of the conditional status. Your foreign-born sons or daughters who may have been petitioned by your spouse must likewise apply for removal of their conditional statuses.

! CAUTION

The timing of your request is crucial. Mark on your calendar the third month before your second anniversary of becoming a conditional permanent resident, and get your application in before your residence expires. USCIS may send you a reminder, but keep track on your own, just in case (especially if you've changed addresses).

EXAMPLE: Your date of admission as a conditional permanent resident was December 7, 2010, the date printed on your conditional green card. The second anniversary of your conditional permanent residence is December 7, 2012. And 90 days (three months) before the second anniversary of December 7, 2012 is September 7, 2012. Therefore, you must file for the removal of the conditional status any time after September 7, 2012 and before December 7, 2012.

1. Forms Required for Removal of Conditions

Within the 90 days before the second anniversary of your conditional permanent residence, you must submit the following:

☐ Form I-751, Petition to Remove the Conditions on Residence, signed by both husband and wife (see the sample at the end of this chapter), or by the alien spouse alone, if seeking a waiver, and

☐ application fee (currently $590, which includes the biometrics fee) in the form of a money order or personal check, payable to U.S. Department of Homeland Security.

You must also present evidence of a true marriage. To do this, submit copies of as many of the following documents as possible (from within the past two years):

☐ your federal and state income taxes for the last two years (assuming they were filed as "married")

☐ title to house or condo or co-op, or any other real property showing joint ownership

☐ lease to your apartment showing joint tenancy since the time of marriage

☐ telephone or electric and gas bills showing both your names

☐ bank books or statements showing evidence of a joint checking or savings account; to prevent identity theft, you are allowed to partially black out the account numbers

☐ registration and title documents, with both names, of cars or any personal property

☐ insurance policies taken by husband or wife and showing the other as the beneficiary of any insurance benefits

☐ birth certificate of any child born of the marriage, showing both parents' names

☐ current letter from employer of both husband and wife, on the company letterhead, stating present job and salary and the name of a person to be notified in case of emergency, if that person is your spouse

☐ current will showing one spouse as the beneficiary of the other's estate, and

☐ a minimum of two sworn statements from people who know that you are married. The letter writer could be your friend, relative, coworker, neighbor, or anyone else who knows that you are married. The person should give his or her own contact information—address and telephone number—and explain how he or she knows the two of you, and knows that you have a real marriage. It's helpful if the person can mention specific times and places at which you appeared as a married couple.

These documents should be sent by Priority Mail to the USCIS Service Center serving your area. (See the USCIS website for the address and P.O. box.) You may receive a notice for an interview, or your petition may be approved without one. If you receive a notice for an interview, we recommend that you have an attorney review your case prior to the interview.

While you're waiting for a decision, however, the receipt notice that you get from the USCIS Service Center will be your only proof that you are legally in the United States. Your stay will remain legal until a decision is made on your Form I-751, but the receipt notice normally expires at one year. As long as your receipt notice has not expired, you can use it in combination with your expired green card to prove your right to work and to return from foreign travel. If you travel, however, the border officials will likely take your expired green card and put a stamp in your passport.

In any case, with or without an interview, your green card becomes permanent only when UCIS decides to approve your joint petition.

> **TIP**
>
> **What if one year has gone by and you still haven't gotten a USCIS decision on your I-751 application?** Although you're technically still legal, it will be hard to prove that to anyone. The best thing to do is make an InfoPass appointment at your local USCIS office. They may be able to find out what's happening, and should give you a stamp in your passport showing your conditional resident status.

2. If Your Spouse Does Not Sign the Joint Petition

If your spouse will not or cannot sign the joint petition, do not despair. Where certain circumstances are beyond your control, USCIS allows you, as the conditional permanent resident alien, to file without your spouse's signature.

You must fill out the same form, Form I-751, Petition to Remove the Conditions on Residence (see the sample at the end of this chapter), and mail it with the same fee. However, you must also request one of the waivers described on the form. These waivers cover situations where:

- your spouse died
- you were the victim of battery or domestic abuse
- your marriage was valid when it occurred but is now legally terminated (you divorced or got an annulment), or
- you would suffer extreme hardship if removed.

These waivers require the assistance of an experienced immigration attorney. (See Chapter 24 for tips on finding a good one.)

3. People Married Two Years or More

If the original date of your admission as a permanent resident is more than two years after your marriage, you are not considered a conditional permanent resident. You are a full-fledged permanent resident and not subject to the conditions on residence.

> **EXAMPLE:** You married a permanent resident on February 14, 2008, and a visa petition was filed on your behalf shortly thereafter in the second preference category. However, your visa number was not immediately available, and you had to wait a few years. You finally received your green card and were admitted as a permanent—not conditional—resident on July 4, 2012, more than two years after your date of marriage.

G. If You Marry Again

If your marriage ends in divorce or annulment after you receive your permanent green card, and then you marry another foreign-born person, it will be difficult for you to sponsor your new spouse for a green card.

To obtain permanent residence for your alien spouse during the first five years after you received your green card through marriage, you'll have to show by "clear and convincing evidence" that your first marriage—the one by which you got your green card—was not fraudulent and was entered into in good faith. (See I.N.A. § 204(a)(2)(A); 8 U.S.C. § 1154(a)(2)(A).) Again, this means showing you got married because you wanted to establish a life together, not just to get a green card.

In addition to the other proof required (see Section D, above), you will be asked to explain:

- why and when you got the previous divorce
- how long you lived with your first spouse
- how, when, and where you met your intended spouse, and
- facts about your courtship.

However, after you have been a green card holder for five years—the number of years required for naturalization—you can file a petition for your second spouse without providing such evidence.

Again, Congress provided this restriction because a number of alien couples had obtained green cards fraudulently. One of them would marry either a U.S. citizen or a permanent resident. After getting the immigrant visa, the marriage to the citizen or permanent resident would be ended by divorce or annulment. The immigrant, then in possession of a valid green card, would then marry the original boyfriend, girlfriend, or spouse to give that person a green card, too.

H. Common Questions About Marriage and Immigration

The answers to most immigration questions depend on timing and the specific history of those involved, so it is difficult to give one correct response in solving a problem. There are, however, a number of questions that are asked over and over.

1. Before Marriage

Q: My boyfriend, who is a U.S. citizen, is getting a divorce soon. Can he file a petition now for me to get a green card?

A: No—because he has not yet legally ended his previous marriage, he cannot marry you now.

He can marry you as soon as his previous divorce petition is finalized.

Q: I intend to marry a U.S. citizen, but because work obligations will require us to live in different states for a while, we will not be living together for the first six months or so after we're married. Can she file for me to get a green card?

A: Yes. But you will have to prove to the USCIS examiner that your marriage is true and not a sham. Good evidence of that would be ticket stubs from visits to one another; telephone bills showing frequent calls to one another; stubs from social events you attended together such as movies, theater performances, and meals; copies of joint bank accounts; and bills bearing both of your names.

2. After Marriage

Q: I entered the U.S. with another name. Now I am married to a U.S. citizen using my real name. Can I get my green card?

A: Yes. But you may need to request that the misrepresentation be waived, or forgiven, before USCIS will approve your case. You should see a lawyer in this case.

Q: I have a minor child living with me in the U.S. and two more young children now living outside the U.S. Can I get green cards for all of them?

A: Yes—if your U.S. citizen spouse files separate petitions for them. If your spouse is a permanent resident, not a citizen, he or she can simply include the children on your visa petition.

Q: What will happen if my marriage legally ends before the conditional status of my green card is removed?

A: A conditional resident can file an application for a waiver with USCIS. However, because there are complicated matters of proof, it is best to consult an experienced immigration lawyer for help.

Sample Form I-130, Petition for Alien Relative (page 1)

Department of Homeland Security
U.S. Citizenship and Immigration Services

OMB No. 1615-0012; Expires 12/31/2015

I-130, Petition for Alien Relative

DO NOT WRITE IN THIS BLOCK - FOR USCIS OFFICE ONLY

A#	Action Stamp	Fee Stamp

Section of Law/Visa Category
- [ ] 201(b) Spouse - IR-1/CR-1
- [ ] 201(b) Child - IR-2/CR-2
- [ ] 201(b) Parent - IR-5
- [ ] 203(a)(1) Unm. S or D - F1-1
- [ ] 203(a)(2)(A)Spouse - F2-1
- [ ] 203(a)(2)(A) Child - F2-2
- [ ] 203(a)(2)(B) Unm. S or D - F2-4
- [ ] 203(a)(3) Married S or D - F3-1
- [ ] 203(a)(4) Brother/Sister - F4-1

Petition was filed on: _____ (priority date)
- [ ] Personal Interview
- [ ] Pet. [ ] Ben. " A" File Reviewed
- [ ] Field Investigation
- [ ] 203(a)(2)(A) Resolved
- [ ] Previously Forwarded
- [ ] I-485 Filed Simultaneously
- [ ] 204(g) Resolved
- [ ] 203(g) Resolved

Remarks:

A. Relationship   You are the petitioner. Your relative is the beneficiary.

1. I am filing this petition for my:
- [X] Spouse [ ] Parent [ ] Brother/Sister [ ] Child

2. Are you related by adoption?
- [ ] Yes [X] No

3. Did you gain permanent residence through adoption?
- [ ] Yes [X] No

B. Information about you

1. Name (Family name in CAPS) (First) (Middle)

NGUYEN   Teo   Thanh

2. Address (Number and Street)   (Apt. No.)

1640 Lincoln Park

(Town or City)   (State/Country)   (Zip/Postal Code)

Beaverton   Oregon   97006

3. Place of Birth (Town or City)   (State/Country)

Portland   Oregon

4. Date of Birth **5. Gender** **6. Marital Status**

04/12/1988 [X] Male [ ] Female [X] Married [ ] Single [ ] Widowed [ ] Divorced

7. Other Names Used (including maiden name)

None

8. Date and Place of Present Marriage (if married)

05/22/2013—Salem, Oregon

9. U.S. Social Security Number (If any)   **10. Alien Registration Number**

756-91-0637

11. Name(s) of Prior Spouse(s)   **12. Date(s) Marriage(s) Ended**

None

13. If you are a U.S. citizen, complete the following:

My citizenship was acquired through (check one):
- [X] Birth in the U.S.
- [ ] Naturalization. Give certificate number and date and place of issuance.

_____
- [ ] Parents. Have you obtained a certificate of citizenship in your own name?
  - [X] Yes. Give certificate number, date and place of issuance. [ ] No

14. If you are a lawful permanent resident alien, complete the following:

Date and place of admission for or adjustment to lawful permanent residence and class of admission.

14b. Did you gain permanent resident status through marriage to a U.S. citizen or lawful permanent resident?
- [ ] Yes [X] No

C. Information about your relative

1. Name (Family name in CAPS) (First) (Middle)

NGUYEN   Lea   Nadres

2. Address (Number and Street)   (Apt. No.)

1640 Lincoln Park

(Town or City)   (State/Country)   (Zip/Postal Code)

Beaverton   Oregon   97006

3. Place of Birth (Town or City)   (State/Country)

Quezon City   Philippines

4. Date of Birth **5. Gender** **6. Marital Status**

07/18/1987 [ ] Male [X] Female [X] Married [ ] Single [ ] Widowed [ ] Divorced

7. Other Names Used (including maiden name)

Pebet

8. Date and Place of Present Marriage (if married)

05/22/2013—Salem, Oregon

9. U.S. Social Security Number (If any)   **10. Alien Registration Number**

11. Name(s) of Prior Spouse(s)   **12. Date(s) Marriage(s) Ended**

13. Has your relative ever been in the U.S.? [X] Yes [ ] No

14. If your relative is currently in the U.S., complete the following:

He or she arrived as a: Student
(visitor, student, stowaway, without inspection, etc.)

Arrival/Departure Record (I-94)   **Date arrived**

1 4 6 ▬ 0 7 7 1 2 2 1 0   12/23/2008

Date authorized stay expired, or will expire, as shown on Form I-94 or I-95

D/S

15. Name and address of present employer (if any)

Date this employment began

16. Has your relative ever been under immigration proceedings?
- [X] No [ ] Yes Where _____ When _____
- [ ] Removal [ ] Exclusion/Deportation [ ] Rescission [ ] Judicial Proceedings

INITIAL RECEIPT	RESUBMITTED	RELOCATED: Rec'd	Sent	COMPLETED: Appv'd	Denied	Ret'd

Form I-130 (12/18/12) Y

Sample Form I-130, Petition for Alien Relative (page 2)

C. Information about your relative (continued)

17. List spouse and all children of your relative.

(Name)	(Relationship)	(Date of Birth)	(Country of Birth)
N/A			

18. Address in the United States where your relative intends to live.

(Street Address)	(Town or City)	(State)
1640 Lincoln Park	Beaverton	Oregon

19. Your relative's address abroad. (Include street, city, province and country)   Phone Number (if any)

1678 Trout Chautoco Roxas District, Q.C., Philippines

20. If your relative's native alphabet is other than Roman letters, write his or her name and foreign address in the native alphabet.

(Name)   Address (Include street, city, province and country).

N/A

21. If filing for your spouse, give last address at which you lived together. (Include street, city, province, if any, and country):

		From:	To:
1640 Lincoln Park	Beaverton, Oregon	05/2013	Present

22. Complete the information below if your relative is in the United States and will apply for adjustment of status.

Your relative is in the United States and will apply for adjustment of status to that of a lawful permanent resident at the USCIS office in:

If your relative is not eligible for adjustment of status, he or she will apply for a visa abroad at the American consular post in:

Portland,	Oregon	Manila	Philippines
(City)	(State)	(City)	(Country)

NOTE: Designation of a U.S. embassy or consulate outside the country of your relative's last residence does not guarantee acceptance for processing by that post. Acceptance is at the discretion of the designated embassy or consulate.

D. Other information

1. If separate petitions are also being submitted for other relatives, give names of each and relationship.

2. Have you ever before filed a petition for this or any other alien? ☐ Yes ☒ No

If "Yes," give name, place and date of filing and result.

WARNING: USCIS investigates claimed relationships and verifies the validity of documents. USCIS seeks criminal prosecutions when family relationships are falsified to obtain visas.

PENALTIES: By law, you may be imprisoned for not more than five years or fined $250,000, or both, for entering into a marriage contract for the purpose of evading any provision of the immigration laws. In addition, you may be fined up to $10,000 and imprisoned for up to five years, or both, for knowingly and willfully falsifying or concealing a material fact or using any false document in submitting this petition.

YOUR CERTIFICATION: I certify, under penalty of perjury under the laws of the United States of America, that the foregoing is true and correct. Furthermore, I authorize the release of any information from my records that U.S. Citizenship and Immigration Services needs to determine eligiblity for the benefit that I am seeking.

E. Signature of petitioner

Teo Thanh Nguyen   Date June 11, 2014   Phone Number (503)730-1493

F. Signature of person preparing this form, if other than the petitioner

I declare that I prepared this document at the request of the person above and that it is based on all information of which I have any knowledge.

Print Name _____   Signature _____   Date _____

Address _____   G-28 ID or VOLAG Number, if any. _____

Sample Form I-129, Petition for Alien Fiancée (as used by married couple) (page 1)

Petition for Alien Fiancé(e)
Department of Homeland Security
U.S. Citizenship and Immigration Services

USCIS
Form I-129F
OMB No. 1615-0001
Expires 06/30/2016

For USCIS Use Only	Fee Stamp	Action Block
Case ID Number		
A-Number		
G-28 Number		

☐ The petition is approved for status under Section 101(a)(5)(k). It is valid for 4 months from the date of action. _____

Extraordinary Circumstances Waiver
☐ Approved   Reason _____
☐ Denied

General Waiver		**Mandatory Waiver**	
☐ Approved	Reason	☐ Approved	Reason
☐ Denied	_____	☐ Denied	_____

AMCON: _____
☐ Personal Interview   ☐ Previously Forwarded
☐ Document Check   ☐ Field Investigation

Initial Receipt	**Relocated**	**Completed**	**Remarks**
	Received	Approved	
Resubmitted	Sent	Returned	

IMBRA Applies?   ☐ Yes *(DOS disclosure to the beneficiary required)*   ☐ No

▶ **START HERE - Type or print in black ink.**

Part 1. Information About You

1.a Family Name *(Last Name)*   ANDERSON

1.b Given Name *(First Name)*   Christa

1.c Middle Name   Lee

Your Mailing Address

2.a In Care of Name

2.b Street Number and Name   123 4th Street

2.c Apt. ☒   Ste. ☐   Flr. ☐   2

2.d City or Town   San Diego

2.e State   CA   **2.f** Zip Code   92120

2.g Postal Code

2.h Province

2.i Country   USA

3. Alien Registration Number (A-Number)
▶ A-

4. City/Town/Village of Birth   Portland OR

5. Country of Birth   USA

6. Date of Birth   *(mm/dd/yyyy)* ▶   04/18/1987

7. Gender   ☐ Male   ☒ Female

8. Marital Status
☒ Married   ☐ Widowed   ☐ Single   ☐ Divorced

Other Names Used

9.a Family Name *(Last Name)*

9.b Given Name *(First Name)*

9.c Middle Name

10. U.S. Social Security Number *(if any)*
▶ 1 2 3 4 5 6 7 8 9

Name of Prior Spouse 1

11.a Family Name *(Last Name)*

11.b Given Name *(First Name)*

11.c Middle Name

11.d Date Marriage Ended   *(mm/dd/yyyy)* ▶

Name of Prior Spouse 2

12.a Family Name *(Last Name)*

12.b Given Name *(First Name)*

Sample Form I-129, Petition for Alien Fiancée (as used by married couple) (page 2)

Part 1. Information About You *(continued)*

12.c. Middle Name

12.d. Date Marriage Ended

(mm/dd/yyyy) ▶

My citizenship was acquired through (Select **only one** box):

13.a. [X] Birth in the United States

13.b. [ ] Naturalization

13.c. [ ] Parents

13.d. Have you obtained a Certificate of Naturalization or a Certificate of Citizenship in your name? [ ] Yes [ ] No

If "Yes," complete the following:

13.d.1. Certificate Number

13.d.2. Place of Issuance

13.d.3. Date of Issuance

(mm/dd/yyyy) ▶

14. Have you ever filed for this or any other alien fiancé(e) or husband/wife before? [ ] Yes [X] No

If you answered "**Yes**," provide the following for each alien *(attach additional sheets as necessary)*

14.a. Alien Registration Number (A-Number)

▶ A-

14.b. Family Name *(Last Name)*

14.c. Given Name *(First Name)*

14.d. Middle Name

14.e. Date of Filing *(mm/dd/yyyy)* ▶

14.f. City or Town

14.g. State

14.h. Result

Part 2. Information About Your Alien Fiancé(e)

1. Identify the classification sought for your beneficiary *(select one):*

[ ] K-1 Fiancé

[X] K-3 Spouse

2.a. Family Name *(Last Name)* CUEVAS

2.b. Given Name *(First Name)* Bernardo

2.c. Middle Name Cristobal

Alien Fiancé(e)'s Mailing Address

3.a. In Care of Name

3.b. Street Number and Name 123 Calle Centro

3.c. Apt. [X] Ste. [ ] Flr. [ ] 42

3.d. City or Town Bogota

3.e. State

3.f. Zip Code

3.g. Postal Code 123456

3.h. Province

3.i. Country Colombia

Other Information About Your Alien Fiancé(e)

4. City/Town/Village of Birth

Bucaramanga

5. Country of Birth

Colombia

6. Date of Birth *(mm/dd/yyyy)* ▶ 07/24/1986

7. Country of Citizenship

Colombia

8. Gender [X] Male [ ] Female

9. Marital Status

[X] Married [ ] Widowed [ ] Single [ ] Divorced

Other Names Used *(Including Maiden Name)*

10.a. Family Name *(Last Name)*

10.b. Given Name *(First Name)*

10.c. Middle Name

11. Alien Registration Number (A-Number)

▶ A-

Sample Form I-129, Petition for Alien Fiancée (as used by married couple) (page 3)

Part 2. Information About Your Alien Fiancé(e) *(continued)*

12. U.S. Social Security Number *(if any)*

▶ [ ][ ][ ][ ][ ][ ][ ][ ][ ]

Name of Prior Spouse 1

13.a. Family Name *(Last Name)* — Carcamo

13.b. Given Name *(First Name)* — Sonya

13.c. Middle Name

13.d. Date Marriage Ended
(mm/dd/yyyy) ▶ 11/02/2009

Name of Prior Spouse 2

14.a. Family Name *(Last Name)*

14.b. Given Name *(First Name)*

14.c. Middle Name

14.d. Date Marriage Ended
(mm/dd/yyyy) ▶

15. Has your fiancé(e) ever been in the United States? — [X] Yes [ ] No

If your fiancé(e) is currently in the United States, complete the following:

15.a. He or she last arrived as a: *(visitor, student, exchange alien, crewman, stowaway, temporary worker, without inspection, etc.)*

15.b. I-94 Arrival/Departure Record Number

▶ [ ][ ][ ][ ][ ][ ][ ][ ][ ][ ][ ]

15.c. Date of Arrival *(mm/dd/yyyy)* ▶

15.d. Date authorized stay expired or will expire as shown on I-94 or I-95. *(mm/dd/yyyy)* ▶

15.e. Passport Number

15.f. Travel Document Number

15.g. Country of Issuance for Passport or Travel Document

15.h. Expiration Date for Passport or Travel Document
(mm/dd/yyyy) ▶

Complete the following for all children of your alien fiancé(e) *(if any)*.

Child 1 of Alien Fiancé(e)

16.a. Family Name *(Last Name)* — Cuevas

16.b. Given Name *(First Name)* — Jorge

16.c. Middle Name — Carcamo

17. Country of Birth — Colombia

18. Date of Birth *(mm/dd/yyyy)* ▶ 02/21/2008

19.a. Street Number and Name — 100 Calle De Las Montanas

19.b. Apt. [ ] Ste. [ ] Flr. [ ]

19.c. City or Town — Bogota

19.d. State — **19.e.** Zip Code

19.f. Postal Code — 123456

19.g. Province

19.h. Country — Colombia

Child 2 of Alien Fiancé(e)

20.a. Family Name *(Last Name)*

20.b. Given Name *(First Name)*

20.c. Middle Name

21. Country of Birth

22. Date of Birth *(mm/dd/yyyy)* ▶

23.a. Street Number and Name

23.b. Apt. [ ] Ste. [ ] Flr. [ ]

23.c. City or Town

23.d. State — **23.e.** Zip Code

23.f. Postal Code

23.g. Province

23.h. Country

Sample Form I-129, Petition for Alien Fiancée (as used by married couple) (page 4)

Part 2. Information About Your Alien Fiancé(e) *(continued)*

Child 3 of Alien Fiancé(e)

24.a. Family Name *(Last Name)*

24.b. Given Name *(First Name)*

24.c. Middle Name

25. Country of Birth

26. Date of Birth *(mm/dd/yyyy)* ▶

27.a. Street Number and Name

27.b. Apt. ☐ Ste. ☐ Flr. ☐

27.c. City or Town

27.d. State ___   **27.e.** Zip Code

27.f. Postal Code

27.g. Province

27.h. Country

Address in the United States where your fiancé(e) intends to live.

28.a. Street Number and Name — 123 4th Street

28.b. Apt. ☒ Ste. ☐ Flr. ☐ — 2

28.c. City or Town — San Diego

28.d. State — CA   **28.e.** Zip Code — 92120

Your fiancé(e)'s address abroad.

29.a. Street Number and Name — 123 Calle Centro

29.b. Apt. ☒ Ste. ☐ Flr. ☐ — 42

29.c. City or Town — Bogota

29.d. Postal Code — 123456

29.e. Province

29.f. Country — Colombia

30. Daytime Phone Number — 571222333   Extension

If your fiancé(e)'s native alphabet uses other than Roman letters, write his or her name and address abroad in the native alphabet.

31.a. Family Name *(Last Name)*

31.b. Given Name *(First Name)*

31.c. Middle Name

Your fiancé(e)'s address abroad, *(Native Alphabet)*

32.a. Street Number and Name

32.b. Apt. ☐ Ste. ☐ Flr. ☐

32.c. City or Town

32.d. Postal Code

32.e. Province

32.f. Country

33. Is your fiancé(e) related to you? ☒ Yes ☐ No

33.a. If you are related, state the nature and degree of relationship, e.g., third cousin or maternal uncle, etc.

Married (not blood-related) K-3 visa

34. Has your fiancé(e) met and seen you within the 2-year period immediately preceding the filing of this petition? ☒ Yes ☐ No

34.a. Describe the circumstances under which you met. If you have not personally met each other, explain how the relationship was established. If you met your fiancé(e) or spouse though an international marriage broker, please explain those circumstances in number **35.a.** Explain in detail any reasons you may have for requesting that the requirement that you and your fiancé(e) must have met should not apply to you.

We met at a conference and were married in Colombia in 2012.

35. Did you meet your fiancé(e) or spouse through the services of an international marriage broker? ☐ Yes ☒ No

35.a. If you answered "Yes," provide the Internet and/or Street Address below. In additional, attach a copy of the signed, written consent form the IMB obtained from your beneficiary authorizing the release of your beneficiary's personal contact information to you. If additional space is needed, attach a separate sheet of paper.

Sample Form I-129, Petition for Alien Fiancée (as used by married couple) (page 5)

Part 2. Information About Your Alien Fiancé(e) *(continued)*

Your fiancé(e) will apply for a visa abroad at the American embassy or consulate at:

36.a. City or Town

> Bogota

36.b. Country

> Colombia

NOTE: Designation of a U.S. embassy or consulate outside the country of your fiancé(e)'s last residence does not guarantee acceptance for processing by that foreign post. Acceptance is at the discretion of the designated embassy or consulate.

Part 3. Other Information

1. If you are serving overseas in the Armed Forces of the United States, please answer the following:

I presently reside or am stationed overseas and my current mailing address is:

1.a. Street Number and Name

1.b. Apt. ☐ Ste. ☐ Flr. ☐

1.c. City or Town

1.d. State ☐ **1.e.** Zip Code

1.f. Postal Code

1.g. Province

1.h. Country

2. Have you ever been convicted by a court of law (civil or criminal) or court martialed by a military tribunal for any of the following crimes:

2.a. Domestic violence, sexual assault, child abuse and neglect, dating violence, elder abuse or stalking? (Please refer to Page 3 of the instructions for the full definition of the term "domestic violence").   ☐ Yes ☒ No

2.b. Homicide, murder, manslaughter, rape, abusive sexual contact, sexual exploitation, incest, torture, trafficking, peonage, holding hostage, involuntary servitude, slave trade, kidnapping, abduction, unlawful criminal restraint, false imprisonment or an attempt to commit any of these crimes?   ☐ Yes ☒ No

2.c. Three or more convictions for crimes relating to a controlled substance or alcohol not arising from a single act?   ☐ Yes ☒ No

These questions must be answered even if your records were sealed or otherwise cleared or if anyone, including a judge, law enforcement officer, or attorney, told you that you no longer have a record. Using a separate sheet(s) of paper, provide information relating to the conviction(s), such as crime involved, date of conviction and sentence.

3. If you have provided information about a conviction for a crime listed above and you were being battered or subjected to extreme cruelty by your spouse, parent, or adult child at the time of your conviction, check all of the following that apply to you:

3.a. ☐ I was acting in self-defense.

3.b. ☐ I violated a protection order issued for my own protection.

3.c. ☐ I committed, was arrested for, was convicted of, or plead guilty to committing a crime that did not result in serious bodily injury, and there was a connection between the crime committed and my having been battered or subjected to extreme cruelty.

If your beneficiary is your fiancé(e) and: (a) this is the third (or more) Form I-129F petition that you have filed; or (b) this is the third (or more) Form I-129F petition you have filed and your first Form I-129F petition was approved within the last 2 years, then your petition cannot be approved unless a waiver of the multiple filing restriction is granted. Attach a signed and dated letter, requesting the waiver and explaining why a waiver is appropriate under your circumstances, together with any evidence in support of the waiver request.

4.   Indicate which waiver applies:

☐ Multiple Filer, No Disqualifying Convictions **(General Waiver)**

☐ Multiple Filer, Prior Criminal Conviction for Specified Offenses **(Extraordinary Circumstances Waiver)**

☐ Multiple Filer, Prior Criminal Convictions Resulting from Domestic Violence **(Mandatory Waiver)**

☐ Not applicable, beneficiary is my spouse

NOTE: See Page 3, question 3.b. of the filing instructions.

Sample Form I-129, Petition for Alien Fiancée (as used by married couple) (page 6)

Part 4. Signature of Petitioner

Penalties

You may by law be imprisoned for not more than 5 years, or fined $250,000, or both, for entering into a marriage contract for the purpose of evading any provision of the immigration laws, and you may be fined up to $10,000 or imprisoned upon to five years, or both, for knowingly and willfully falsifying or concealing a material fact or using any false document in submitting this petition.

Your Certification

I certify that I am legally able to and intend to marry my alien fiancé(e) within 90 days of his or her arrival in the United States. I certify, under penalty of perjury under the laws of the United States of America, that the foregoing is true and correct. Furthermore, I authorize the release of any information from my records that U.S. Citizenship and Immigration Services needs to determine eligibility for the benefit that I am seeking.

Moreover, I understand that this petition, including any criminal conviction information that I am required to provide with this petition, as well as any related criminal background information pertaining to me that U.S. Citizenship and Immigration Services may discover independently in adjudicating this petition will be disclosed to the beneficiary of this petition.

1.a. Signature of Petitioner

Christa L. Anderson

1.b. Date of Signature *(mm/dd/yyyy)* ▶ 02/28/2014

2. Daytime Phone Number 8585551214

3. Mobile Phone Number 8584443434

4. E-mail Address *(if any)*

christa37@email.com

Part 5. Signature of Person Preparing This Petition, If Other Than the Petitioner

NOTE: If you are an attorney or representative, you must submit a completed Form G-28, Notice of Entry of Appearance as Attorney or Accredited Representative, along with this Petition.

☐ Form G-28 submitted with this Petition.

G-28 ID Number

Preparer's Full Name

1.a. Preparer's Family Name *(Last Name)*

1.b. Preparer's Given Name *(First Name)*

2. Preparer's Business or Organization Name

Preparer's Contact Information

3. Preparer's Daytime Phone Number   Extension

4. Preparer's E-mail Address *(if any)*

Preparer's Mailing Address

5.a. Street Number and Name

5.b. Apt. ☐ Ste. ☐ Flr. ☐

5.c. City or Town

5.d. State   **5.e.** Zip Code

5.f. Postal Code

5.g. Province

5.h. Country

Declaration

To be completed by all preparers, including attorneys and authorized representatives: I declare that I prepared this benefit request at the request of the Petitioner, that it is based on all the information of which I have knowledge, and that the information is true to the best of my knowledge.

6.a. Signature of Preparer

6.b. Date of Signature *(mm/dd/yyyy)* ▶

Sample Form I-751, Petition To Remove Conditions on Residence (page 1)

Petition to Remove Conditions on Residence
Department of Homeland Security
U.S. Citizenship and Immigration Services

USCIS
Form I-751
OMB No. 1615-0038
Expires 04/30/2015

For USCIS Use Only	Receipt	Action Block	Remarks

Reloc Sent Date ___/___/___   **Reloc Rec'd** Date ___/___/___

Date ___/___/___   Date ___/___/___

☐ Petitioner interviewed on _____

☐ Approved under INA 216(c)(4)(C) Battered Spouse/Child

To be completed by an Attorney or BIA-accredited Representative, if any

☐ Check the box if Form G-28 is attached to represent the petitioner

Attorney State License Number: _____

▶ **START HERE - Type or print in black ink.**

Part 1. Information About You, the Conditional Resident

1.a. Family Name *(Last Name)* — HOLLIS

1.b. Given Name *(First Name)* — Nigel

1.c. Middle Name — Ian

Other Names Used *(including maiden name)*

2.a. Family Name *(Last Name)*

2.b. Given Name *(First Name)*

2.c. Middle Name

3.a. Family Name *(Last Name)*

3.b. Given Name *(First Name)*

3.c. Middle Name

Other Information

4. Date of Birth *(mm/dd/yyyy)* ▶ 8/17/1986

5. Country of Birth — United Kingdom

6. Country of Citizenship — United Kingdom

7. Alien Registration Number *(A-Number)*
▶ A- 1 2 3 4 5 6 7 8 9

8. U.S. Social Security Number *(if any)*
▶ 8 8 8 1 1 8 8 8 8

Contact Information

9. Daytime Phone Number (212) 555 - 1212

10. E-Mail Address *(if any)*
nigelh@email.com

Marital Status

11. Marital Status   ☒ Married   ☐ Single
☐ Divorced   ☐ Widowed

12. Date of Marriage *(mm/dd/yyyy)* ▶ 11/05/2014

13. Place of Marriage
New York, NY

14. If the marriage through which you gained conditional residence has ended, give the date it ended *(date of divorce or date of death)* *(mm/dd/yyyy)* ▶

15. Conditional Residence Expires On *(mm/dd/yyyy)* ▶ 08/07/2016

Form I-751 04/11/13 N

Page 1 of 5

Sample Form I-751, Petition To Remove Conditions on Residence (page 2)

Part 1. Information About You, the Conditional Resident *(continued)*

Physical Address

16.a. In Care Of Name

16.b. Street Number and Name
114 Fulton Street

16.c. Apt. [X] Ste. [ ] Flr. [ ]
6E

16.d. City or Town
New York

16.e. State NY   **16.f.** Zip Code 10038

Mailing Address *(If different than Physical Address)*

17.a. In Care Of Name

17.b. Street Number and Name

17.c. Apt. [ ] Ste. [ ] Flr. [ ]

17.d. City or Town

17.e. State   **17.f.** Zip Code

Additional Information About You

18. Are you in removal, deportation, or rescission proceedings? [ ] Yes [X] No

19. Was a fee paid to anyone other than an attorney in connection with this petition? [ ] Yes [X] No

20. Have you ever been arrested, detained, charged, indicted, fined, or imprisoned for breaking or violating any law or ordinance (excluding traffic regulations), or committed any crime which you were not arrested in the United States or abroad? [ ] Yes [X] No

21. If you are married, is this a different marriage than the one through which conditional residence status was obtained? [ ] Yes [X] No

22. Have you resided at any other address since you became a permanent resident? *(If "Yes," attach a list of all addresses and dates.)* [ ] Yes [X] No

23. Is your spouse or parent's spouse currently serving with or employed by the U.S. Government and serving outside the United States? [ ] Yes [X] No

If you answered "Yes" to **Item Number 20.**, provide a detailed explanation on a separate sheet of paper and refer to the section entitled **"What Initial Evidence Is Required?"** to determine what criminal history document to include with your petition.

Part 2. Basis for Petition

Joint Filing

My conditional residence is based on my marriage or my parent's marriage to a U.S. citizen or permanent resident, and I am filing this joint petition together with:

1.a. [X] My spouse

1.b. [ ] My parent's spouse because I am unable to be included in a joint petition filed by my parent and my parent's spouse.

OR *(check all that apply)*

Waiver Request Filing

My conditional residence is based on my marriage or my parent's marriage to a U.S. citizen or permanent resident; I am unable to file a joint petition with my spouse or my parent's spouse and I request a hardship waiver because:

1.c. [ ] My spouse or my parent's spouse is deceased.

1.d. [ ] I or my parent entered the marriage in good faith, but the marriage was terminated through divorce or annulment.

1.e. [ ] I entered the marriage in good faith, and, during the marriage, I was battered, or was the subject of extreme cruelty, by my U.S. citizen or permanent resident spouse.

1.f. [ ] My parent entered the marriage in good faith and, during the marriage, I was battered, or was subjected to extreme cruelty, by my parent's U.S. citizen or permanent resident spouse or by my conditional resident parent.

1.g. [ ] The termination of my status and removal from the United States would result in an extreme hardship.

Sample Form I-751, Petition To Remove Conditions on Residence (page 3)

Part 3. Information About the Petitioning Spouse or, If Filing as a Child Separately, Information About the U.S. Citizen or LPR Stepparent Through Whom You Gained Your Conditional Residence

Relationship

1.a. ☒ Spouse or Former Spouse

1.b. ☐ Parent's Spouse or Former Spouse

2.a. Family Name *(Last Name)* Beach

2.b. Given Name *(First Name)* Sandra

2.c. Middle Name Leah

3. Date of Birth *(mm/dd/yyyy)* ▶ 12/20/1986

4. U.S. Social Security Number *(if any)*
▶ 1 2 3 4 5 6 7 8 9

5. Alien Registration Number *(A-Number)*
▶ A-

6.a. Street Number and Name 114 Fulton Street

6.b. Apt. ☒ Ste. ☐ Flr. ☐ 6E

6.c. City or Town New York

6.d. State NY 6.e. Zip Code 10038

6.f. Postal Code

6.g. Province

6.h. Country United States

Part 4. Information About Your Children

List All Your Children *(Attach other sheets if necessary).*

Child 1

1.a. Family Name *(Last Name)* Hollis

1.b. Given Name *(First Name)* Nadine

1.c. Middle Name Anne

2. Date of Birth *(mm/dd/yyyy)* ▶ 12/02/2015

3. Alien Registration Number *(A-Number)*
▶ A-

4.a. Street Number and Name 114 Fulton Street

4.b. Apt. ☒ Ste. ☐ Flr. ☐ 6E

4.c. City or Town New York

4.d. State or Province NY

4.e. Zip Code or Postal Code 10038

4.f. Country

5. Is child living with you? ☒ Yes ☐ No

6. Is child applying with you? ☐ Yes ☒ No

Child 2

7.a. Family Name *(Last Name)*

7.b. Given Name *(First Name)*

7.c. Middle Name

8. Date of Birth *(mm/dd/yyyy)* ▶

9. Alien Registration Number *(A-Number)*
▶ A-

10.a. Street Number and Name

10.b. Apt. ☐ Ste. ☐ Flr. ☐

10.c. City or Town

10.d. State or Province

10.e. Zip Code or Postal Code

10.f. Country

11. Is child living with you? ☐ Yes ☐ No

12. Is child applying with you? ☐ Yes ☐ No

Child 3

13.a. Family Name *(Last Name)*

13.b. Given Name *(First Name)*

13.c. Middle Name

14. Date of Birth *(mm/dd/yyyy)* ▶

15. Alien Registration Number *(A-Number)*
▶ A-

Sample Form I-751, Petition To Remove Conditions on Residence (page 4)

Part 4. Information About Your Children *(continued)*

16.a. Street Number and Name

16.b. Apt. ☐ Ste. ☐ Flr. ☐

16.c. City or Town

16.d. State or Province

16.e. Zip Code or Postal Code

16.f. Country

17. Is child living with you? ☐ Yes ☐ No

18. Is child applying with you? ☐ Yes ☐ No

Child 4

19.a. Family Name *(Last Name)*

19.b. Given Name *(First Name)*

19.c. Middle Name

20. Date of Birth *(mm/dd/yyyy)* ▶

21. Alien Registration Number *(A-Number)*
▶ A- ☐☐☐☐☐☐☐☐☐

22.a. Street Number and Name

22.b. Apt. ☐ Ste. ☐ Flr. ☐

22.c. City or Town

22.d. State or Province

22.e. Zip Code or Postal Code

22.f. Country

23. Is child living with you? ☐ Yes ☐ No

24. Is child applying with you? ☐ Yes ☐ No

Child 5

25.a. Family Name *(Last Name)*

25.b. Given Name *(First Name)*

25.c. Middle Name

26. Date of Birth *(mm/dd/yyyy)* ▶

27. Alien Registration Number *(A-Number)*
▶ A- ☐☐☐☐☐☐☐☐☐

28.a. Street Number and Name

28.b. Apt. ☐ Ste. ☐ Flr. ☐

28.c. City or Town

28.d. State or Province

28.e. Zip Code or Postal Code

28.f. Country

29. Is child living with you? ☐ Yes ☐ No

30. Is child applying with you? ☐ Yes ☐ No

Part 5. Accommodations for Individuals With Disabilities and Impairments *(Read the information in the instructions before completing this section.)*

I am requesting an accommodation:

1. Because of my disability(ies) and/or impairment(s).
☐ Yes ☒ No

2. For my spouse because of his or her disability(ies) and/or impairment(s).
☐ Yes ☒ No

3. For my included child(ren) because of his or her (their) disability(ies) and/or impairment(s).
☐ Yes ☒ No

If you answered "Yes," check any applicable box. Provide information on the disability(ies) and/or impairment(s) for each person:

4.a. ☐ Deaf or hard of hearing and request the following accommodation(s) (if requesting a sign-language interpreter, indicate which language (e.g., American Sign Language)):

_____

_____

_____

4.b. ☐ Blind or sight-impaired and request the following accommodation(s):

_____

_____

_____

Sample Form I-751, Petition To Remove Conditions on Residence (page 5)

Part 5. Accommodations for Individuals With Disabilities and Impairments *(continued)*

4.c. ☐ Other type of disability(ies) and/or impairment(s) (describe the nature of the disability(ies) and/or impairment(s) and accommodation(s) being requested):

_____

_____

_____

Part 6. Signature *(Read the information on penalties in the instructions before completing this section. If you checked Block 1.a. in Part 2, your spouse must also sign below. Signature of a conditional resident child under the age of 14 is not required; a parent may sign for the child).*

I certify, under penalty of perjury under the laws of the United States of America, that this petition and the evidence submitted with it is all true and correct. If conditional residence was based on a marriage, I further certify that the marriage was entered in accordance with the laws of the place where the marriage took place and was not for the purpose of procuring an immigration benefit. I also authorize the release of any information from my records that U.S. Citizenship and Immigration Services needs to determine eligibility for the benefit sought.

Signature of Conditional Resident

1.a. Signature of Conditional Resident

Nigel Ian Hollis

1.b. Printed Name of Conditional Resident

Nigel Ian Hollis

2. Date of Signature *(mm/dd/yyyy)* ▶ 06/01/2016

Signature of Spouse or Individual Listed In Part 3 *(if applicable)*

3.a. Signature of Spouse

Sandra Leah Beach

3.b. Printed Name of Spouse

Sandra Leah Beach

4. Date of Signature *(mm/dd/yyyy)* ▶ 06/01/2016

NOTE: If you do not completely fill out this form or fail to submit any required documents listed in the instructions, you may not be found eligible for the requested benefit and this petition may be denied.

Part 7. Signature and Contact Information of Person Preparing Form, If Other Than Above

I declare that I prepared this petition at the request of the above person, and it is based on all information of which I have knowledge.

1. Signature of Preparer

2. Date of Signature *(mm/dd/yyyy)* ▶

Preparer's Full Name

3.a. Preparer's Family Name *(Last Name)*

3.b. Preparer's Given Name *(First Name)*

4. Preparer's Business or Organization Name

Preparer's Mailing Address

5.a. Street Number and Name

5.b. Apt. ☐ Ste. ☐ Flr. ☐

5.c. City or Town

5.d. State   5.e. Zip Code

Preparer's Contact Information

6. Daytime Phone Number (   )   -

7. E-mail Address *(if any)*

Sample Form G-325A, Biographic Information

Department of Homeland Security
U.S. Citizenship and Immigration Services

OMB No. 1615-0008; Expires 02/28/2015

G-325A, Biographic Information

Family Name	First Name	Middle Name	☐ Male ☒ Female	Date of Birth (mm/dd/yyyy)	Citizenship/Nationality	File Number
SALONGA	Fe	Valdez		03/07/1971	Filipino	A

All Other Names Used (include names by previous marriages)	City and Country of Birth	U.S. Social Security No. (if any)
Fe Agnes Salonga	Manila, Philippines	210-76-9478

	Family Name	First Name	Date of Birth (mm/dd/yyyy)	City, and Country of Birth (if known)	City and Country of Residence
Father	SALONGA	Amando	06-09-1947	Manila, Philippines	Manila, Philippines
Mother (Maiden Name)	VALDEZ	Lourdes	12-05-1949	Manila, Philippines	-deceased

Current Husband or Wife (If none, so state) Family Name (For wife, give maiden name)	First Name	Date of Birth (mm/dd/yyyy)	City and Country of Birth	Date of Marriage	Place of Marriage
None					

Former Husbands or Wives (If none, so state) Family Name (For wife, give maiden name)	First Name	Date of Birth (mm/dd/yyyy)	Date and Place of Marriage	Date and Place of Termination of Marriage
None				

Applicant's residence last five years. List present address first.

Street Name and Number	City	Province or State	Country	From Month	From Year	To Month	To Year
741 12th Avenue	White Plains	NY	U.S.A.	09	2009	Present Time	
676 W. Houston Street	New York	NY	U.S.A.	08	2007	08	2007

Applicant's last address outside the United States of more than 1 year.

Street Name and Number	City	Province or State	Country	From Month	From Year	To Month	To Year
52-50 MBLA Court, Malaya St.	Marikina	Metro Manila	Philippines	since birth		08	2007

Applicant's employment last five years. (If none, so state.) List present employment first.

Full Name and Address of Employer	Occupation (Specify)	From Month	From Year	To Month	To Year
Griffith School, 560 Lexington Avenue, NY, NY 10118	Teacher	03	2004	Present Time	
Embassy of Japan, Buendia Ave., Makati, Metro Manila, Philippines	Secretary	05	2000	08	2007

Last occupation abroad if not shown above. (Include all information requested above.)

see above					

This form is submitted in connection with an application for:	Signature of Applicant	Date
☒ Naturalization ☐ Other (Specify): ☐ Status as Permanent Resident	*Fe Valdez Salonga*	02/26/2014

If your native alphabet is in other than Roman letters, write your name in your native alphabet below:

Penalties: Severe penalties are provided by law for knowingly and willfully falsifying or concealing a material fact.

Applicant: Print your name and Alien Registration Number in the box outlined by heavy border below.

Complete This Box (Family Name)	(Given Name)	(Middle Name)	(Alien Registration Number)
SALONGA	Fe	Valdez	A

Form G-325A (Rev. 02/07/13) Y

Your Parents as Immigrants

If you are a U.S. citizen age 21 or over, but your parents are citizens of another country, your parents are your "immediate relatives" and you may request U.S. green cards for them. They must separately meet the other criteria for green card approval, however.

Another important issue is whether your parents really want to come to the United States. Many are interested in family togetherness, but don't really want to permanently leave the life they've made for themselves elsewhere. Remember that a green card is not just an easy travel pass—unless your parents are ready to settle down in the U.S. permanently, they could lose the green card by spending too much time overseas (and all your hard work could go down the drain).

However, one reason that some parents agree to come is that they can help other family members get green cards; see "Family Immigration Strategies After Your Parents Get Green Cards," below.

A. Who Qualifies to Petition for Their Parents

To petition to get a green card for your parents, you must meet a couple of basic requirements.

> **CAUTION**
>
> **If the U.S. petitioner has a criminal record, see an attorney.** Under the Adam Walsh Child Protection and Safety Act of 2006, U.S. citizens and lawful permanent residents who have been convicted of any "specified offense against a minor" are prohibited from filing a family-based immigrant petition on behalf of any beneficiary (whether a child or not). USCIS will run security checks on all petitions and may call the petitioner in for fingerprinting. If the petitioner has a conviction for one of the specified offenses against a minor, then the petition will not be approved unless USCIS determines that the U.S. petitioner poses no risk to the beneficiary.

1. You Must Be a U.S. Citizen

You must be a U.S. citizen to file a petition on behalf of your parents. You are a citizen of the United States if you were:

- naturalized (after you applied and passed an exam)
- born in any of the 50 states of the United States or its territories—U.S. Virgin Islands, Puerto Rico, or Guam, or
- born outside the United States or its territories, if one of your parents was a U.S. citizen when you were born. See Chapter 20 for details or contact the U.S. Embassy; if you are not satisfied, consult a lawyer or other experienced naturalization professional. (See Chapter 24.)

2. You Must Be at Least 21 Years Old

As a U.S. citizen, you must be 21 years old or older to bestow the immigration benefit of a green card on your mother and your father as your immediate relatives.

If you were born in the United States to parents who live there illegally, 21 years will be a frustratingly long time to wait. In fact, because your parents may be ineligible to apply for green cards within the U.S. using the procedure called adjustment of status (see Chapter 16) but may instead have to leave the U.S. and apply through a U.S. consulate (see Chapter 17), your citizenship may turn out not to be much help to them.

The reason is that too much time spent in the U.S. illegally can result in bars on returning to the U.S. after they leave (for three or ten years, based on illegal stays of six months or one year or more).

In rare circumstances, your parents might benefit from the newer, "stateside" provisional waiver of unlawful presence, which would allow them to have their unlawful time in the U.S. forgiven before leaving the U.S. for their consular interview. The major difficulty, however, is that your parents will not be able to get a waiver based on any hardship their ban would cause to *you*, the child petitioner. They would need a "qualifying relative" who is either a U.S. citizen spouse or a parent, and who would suffer extreme hardship if they were denied the green card. This is a new and tricky area of law, so you'd do best to consult with an attorney before applying for a waiver. If your family is in this situation, see an experienced immigration attorney.

B. Who Qualifies As Your Parent

If you're from a traditional family—that is, you were born and raised by a married couple—you should have no problem petitioning for your parents to immigrate. However, the immigration law also recognizes some variations on the traditional family. Under certain circumstances, you can also petition for unmarried parents, stepparents, and adoptive parents, as described further below. You'll usually have to provide additional documents to prove the relationship, as also described below.

1. Natural Mother

If your mother was not married to your father when you were born, so that your mother's maiden name appears on your birth certificate, you can prove your relationship by presenting a copy of your birth certificate when you file the petition for your mother.

If your mother has changed her maiden name because she has married someone else, then also present her marriage certificate to show her change of name.

2. Natural Father

If your biological father did not marry your mother either before or after you were born, you can still petition for him as your immediate relative. You must also provide some evidence of your relationship.

- Make a copy of your birth certificate, baptismal certificate, or other religious records showing his name as your father. USCIS may

---

Family Immigration Strategies After Your Parents Get Green Cards

By becoming U.S. permanent residents, your parents can petition for of all their unmarried children—in family second preference category 2A or 2B. If they become naturalized U.S. citizens, they can petition even for their married children—in the family third preference category.

Although as a U.S. citizen you may have filed for your brothers and sisters (family fourth preference), your mother or father, after becoming U.S. citizens, could secure a green card for them more quickly. It's okay to file more than one visa petition for the same person at the same time. (You can wait to see which Priority Date becomes current first.)

However, your parents must be aware that getting a green card does not automatically mean that their children can get their own green cards. Your parents would also have to live (maintain residence) in the United States until their other children obtain their green cards, which will take years.

The rules on maintaining U.S. residency are complicated and require that the person make the United States his or her home. While the law allows travel overseas, most important family and business ties should be in the United States, and your parents should compile evidence of these, such as:

- a lease, rental agreement, or title to property in the United States
- utility bills
- a driver's license or car registration, or
- state and federal tax returns.

And that's just the minimum, for maintaining permanent resident status. The rules for amount of time spent in the U.S. before applying for U.S. citizenship are even stricter. If you or your parents have questions about whether you are properly maintaining permanent residence, consult an immigration attorney.

require both you and your father to take a blood test as proof of your relationship.

- If you and your father did not live together before you turned 18, you must present proof that, up to the time you turned 21 years of age, he maintained a father-child relationship with you by providing financial support, writing to you or your mother about your well-being, sending you birthday cards, holiday cards, and photographs, or perhaps naming you as a beneficiary to his life insurance.
- If you lived with your father before your 18th birthday, you must present proof that there was a father-child relationship, as evidenced by school records, photographs, letters, civil records, or written statements from friends and relatives.

If You, the Petitioner, Change Names

If you are a female U.S. citizen petitioning for your parents as immediate relatives, you may have changed your maiden name, which appears on your birth certificate. You may now be using your married name—that is, your husband's surname.

Therefore, in addition to your birth certificate to prove the parent-child relationship when you send the Petition for Alien Relative, Form I-130, for your mother or father, you must also attach your marriage certificate to show your change of name.

If you have changed your name by petitioning the court, you must attach a final court judgment as proof of that change.

---

3. Stepmother or Stepfather

If your father or mother marries somebody other than your biological parent before you turn 18 years of age, the person he or she marries becomes your stepmother or stepfather.

When you file a petition for your stepmother or stepfather as your immediate relative (by submitting the usual petition Form I-130), add to it the following documents:

- your birth certificate showing the name of your remarried parent, and
- the marriage certificate of your remarried parent to show the name of the new spouse (your stepparent).

For you to petition for your stepparent, the marriage must have occurred before your 18th birthday. If the marriage happened after your 18th birthday, then say, "I love you, but I cannot claim you as my immediate relative for immigration into the United States."

But all is not lost.

Your natural mother or father, after qualifying as your immediate relative and obtaining a green card, can petition for your stepparent who is now the spouse of a permanent resident—2A, the second preference beneficiary. Unfortunately, however, the stepparent may have to wait a few years until a visa becomes available in this category.

Immigrant Story: Petitioning for a Surviving Stepparent

Luzmaria, originally from El Salvador, married a U.S. citizen at age 25, and became a U.S. citizen herself at age 29. She then filed visa petitions for her father and for her stepmother, who her father married when Luzmaria was 14.

Sadly, Luzmaria's father died a few months later. Luzmaria was doubly heartbroken, thinking that now her stepmother would not be eligible to immigrate.

However, because the stepmother continues to fit the criteria for immediate relative of a U.S. citizen (having married Luzmaria's father when Luzmaria was under 18), she is able to continue with her application and eventually receive a U.S. green card.

4. Adoptive Mother and Father

Suppose you were adopted by a non-U.S. citizen before your 16th birthday. If you are a U.S. citizen and you are now 21 years or older, you can petition for your adoptive mother and father as your immediate relatives.

When you file the visa petition (Form I-130), you must also submit:

- the court decree of your adoption
- your birth certificate showing the name of your adopting parents as your father and mother, and
- a statement showing the dates and places you have lived together.

> ⚠ **CAUTION**
>
> **Adopted children cannot petition for their natural parents.** When you were adopted, your natural parents gave up all parental ties with you. Therefore, you will never be able to petition for your natural parents as your immediate relatives. The adoption decree cuts off all legal ties between you and your natural parents.

C. Quick View of the Application Process

To get a green card for your parent, you must begin the process by preparing a visa petition (Form I-130, together with certain documents). Form I-130 serves to prove to the immigration authorities that your parents are truly and legally yours. After that petition is approved (in most cases), your parents must complete their half of the process by submitting a green card application and attending an interview, sometimes but not always with you accompanying them. Their application serves to prove that not only do they qualify as parents of a U.S. citizen, but that they're otherwise eligible for U.S. permanent residence.

However, the details of when and how your parents complete their half of the process depend on whether your parents are living overseas or in the United States, as described next.

D. Detailed Instructions for the Application Process

Now we'll break the application process down into individual procedures, some of which will be covered in this chapter, and others in later chapters—we'll tell you exactly where to turn to for your situation.

1. The Visa Petition

Let's start by discussing the visa petition, which all people petitioning for their parents must prepare to begin the process. You'll need to assemble:

- ☐ Form I-130, Petition for Alien Relative (available at www.uscis.gov/i-130; see the sample at the end of this chapter)
- ☐ documents showing your U.S. citizenship
- ☐ a copy of your birth certificate, showing your name as well as your mother's name, if filing for your mother, and the names of both parents, if filing for your father
- ☐ a copy of the marriage certificate of your parents if you are filing for your father; your stepparents' marriage certificate, if you are filing for either stepparent
- ☐ a copy of your adoption decree, if you are filing for your adoptive parent
- ☐ the filing fee, currently $420 in a personal check or money order payable to the Department of Homeland Security. Don't send cash.
- ☐ Form G-1145. This is optional, but filing it is a good idea, so that you'll receive an email and/or text notification from USCIS when your application has been accepted. Once USCIS sends you a receipt number, you can use that number to sign up to receive automatic email updates letting you know whenever mail is sent regarding your application.

TIP

Here's how to sign up for automatic email updates: Go to www.uscis.gov and click "Check Your Case Status" then "Sign-up for Case Updates." Then you can register for automatic case status updates by email and text message by clicking "Register as an applicant customer."

Once you've assembled all these items, make a copy of everything (including the check or money order) for your records. It's also a good idea to write a cover letter, explaining what type of visa petition it is (for example, saying "I am a U.S. citizen, filing the enclosed visa petition on behalf of my mother"). The letter should include a bulleted list, much like the one above, of everything you're sending. This will help USCIS see that you're organized. It will help you, too, to make sure that nothing has been forgotten.

If your parents are not in the United States, mail all these documents and the fee by certified mail to the USCIS Chicago lockbox, which will forward it to the appropriate USCIS office. (See the USCIS website for contact details.) If your parents are in the United States, they may be able to file directly for adjustment of status (see Chapter 16) in which case, you may choose to mail the I-130 along with the forms and documents required for adjustment of status.

2. The Green Card Application

The next step in your parents' immigration process depends on where they're located. If they're in the United States, you need to start by figuring out whether they are eligible to adjust status (apply for their green card) here. See Chapter 16, Section A, to determine this. (If they entered on valid visas, then they are probably eligible, even if they remained in the U.S. past the date they were allowed to stay.)

CAUTION

Traveling outside the U.S. may trigger penalties. Even though remaining in the U.S. past the date allowed by USCIS will not prevent your parents' applications from being granted, if they travel outside the U.S. before that time—either with or without USCIS permission—they will trigger a penalty for their unlawful presence and may not be granted permanent residence for three to ten years, depending on the length of their unlawful stay.

Your parents should also know that if they obtained a tourist or other visa with the secret intention of applying for a green card after they got here, that could be visa fraud. They can be denied the green card based on this fraud.

 NEXT STEP

If your parents are allowed to adjust status in the U.S. You can mail the I-130 visa petition in combination with an adjustment of status application to a USCIS office, as also described in Chapter 16. Eventually they will be fingerprinted, called in for an interview at a local USCIS office, and hopefully approved for U.S. residency. In straightforward cases, where all required paperwork is properly submitted with the application, USCIS may opt to approve the application without an interview.

NEXT STEP

If your parents do not qualify to adjust status but are currently in the U.S. With limited exceptions, if your parents entered the U.S. without inspection, they are not eligible to apply for adjustment of status. If they leave the U.S., however, to apply for a visa at a U.S. consulate, their departure after unlawful presence could result in them being prevented from reentering for three or ten years, depending on the length of their unlawful stay. There is a new provisional waiver, known as the "stateside" waiver of unlawful presence, which allows certain immediate relatives who are in this situation to learn whether or not USCIS will grant them a waiver of the time bar BEFORE they leave the United States. (See Chapter 4 for more on this.) The provisional waiver is difficult to get, however, and they would need a qualifying U.S. citizen spouse or parent who would experience "extreme hardship," in order to apply. Seek the advice of an immigration attorney before applying.

NEXT STEP

If your parents still live in their home country. Their next step is to await USCIS approval of the Form I-130 visa petition and then go through consular processing, as described in Chapter 17. Eventually, they will be called in for an interview at their local U.S. consulate, at which time they will hopefully be approved for an immigrant visa to enter the United States and claim their permanent residency.

RELATED TOPIC

See Chapter 23 for important information on how your parents can protect their right to keep the green card.

Be Kind to the Elderly

If your mother or father is elderly, take some time to help them get acquainted with the customs and cultural habits of the country.

Introduce them to the senior citizen center located in their new neighborhood. Teach them how to use the public transportation system, including precautions to be taken if you live in a big city. Bring them to the cultural or popular entertainment activities available in your area.

It is unfair to make your parents mere babysitters for your young children. They have already done all the childrearing they were responsible for when they raised you. Pay them a decent amount if they take care of your children. Do not abuse their kindness by taking advantage of their presence in your home to do the work you should be doing.

Sample Form I-130, Petition for Alien Relative (as used for immigrating parents) (page 1)

OMB No. 1615-0012; Expires 12/31/2015

Department of Homeland Security
U.S. Citizenship and Immigration Services

I-130, Petition for Alien Relative

DO NOT WRITE IN THIS BLOCK - FOR USCIS OFFICE ONLY

A#	Action Stamp	Fee Stamp

Section of Law/Visa Category
- [ ] 201(b) Spouse - IR-1/CR-1
- [ ] 201(b) Child - IR-2/CR-2
- [ ] 201(b) Parent - IR-5
- [ ] 203(a)(1) Unm. S or D - F1-1
- [ ] 203(a)(2)(A)Spouse - F2-1
- [ ] 203(a)(2)(A) Child - F2-2
- [ ] 203(a)(2)(B) Unm. S or D - F2-4
- [ ] 203(a)(3) Married S or D - F3-1
- [ ] 203(a)(4) Brother/Sister - F4-1

Petition was filed on: _____ (priority date)
- [ ] Personal Interview   [ ] Previously Forwarded
- [ ] Pet. [ ] Ben. " A" File Reviewed   [ ] I-485 Filed Simultaneously
- [ ] Field Investigation   [ ] 204(g) Resolved
- [ ] 203(a)(2)(A) Resolved   [ ] 203(g) Resolved

Remarks:

A. Relationship   You are the petitioner. Your relative is the beneficiary.

1. I am filing this petition for my:
[ ] Spouse [X] Parent [ ] Brother/Sister [ ] Child

2. Are you related by adoption?
[ ] Yes [X] No

3. Did you gain permanent residence through adoption?
[ ] Yes [X] No

B. Information about you

1. Name (Family name in CAPS) (First) (Middle)
SOLOMOS   Evadne   Helia

2. Address (Number and Street) (Apt. No.)
121 3rd Street

(Town or City) (State/Country) (Zip/Postal Code)
Baton Rouge   LA/USA   70808

3. Place of Birth (Town or City) (State/Country)
Athens   Greece

4. Date of Birth
07/03/1980

5. Gender
[ ] Male [X] Female

6. Marital Status
[X] Married [ ] Single [ ] Widowed [ ] Divorced

7. Other Names Used (including maiden name)
Evadne Helia ADIMIDIS

8. Date and Place of Present Marriage (if married)
03/17/1999, New Orleans, LA

9. U.S. Social Security Number (If any)
111-22-3333

10. Alien Registration Number
n/a

11. Name(s) of Prior Spouse(s)

12. Date(s) Marriage(s) Ended

13. If you are a U.S. citizen, complete the following:

My citizenship was acquired through (check one):
- [ ] Birth in the U.S.
- [X] Naturalization. Give certificate number and date and place of issuance.
  321234, 12/03/2009, New Orleans
- [ ] Parents. Have you obtained a certificate of citizenship in your own name?
  - [ ] Yes. Give certificate number, date and place of issuance. [ ] No

14. If you are a lawful permanent resident alien, complete the following:
Date and place of admission for or adjustment to lawful permanent residence and class of admission.

14b. Did you gain permanent resident status through marriage to a U.S. citizen or lawful permanent resident?
[X] Yes [ ] No

C. Information about your relative

1. Name (Family name in CAPS) (First) (Middle)
ADIMIDIS   Halimeda   Madora

2. Address (Number and Street) (Apt. No.)
Galanou 25

(Town or City) (State/Country) (Zip/Postal Code)
Athens   Greece   105 53

3. Place of Birth (Town or City) (State/Country)
Santorini   Greece

4. Date of Birth
10/12/1962

5. Gender
[X] Male [X] Female

6. Marital Status
[ ] Married [ ] Single [X] Widowed [ ] Divorced

7. Other Names Used (including maiden name)
Halimeda Madora MAMALIS

8. Date and Place of Present Marriage (if married)

9. U.S. Social Security Number (If any)
None

10. Alien Registration Number
None

11. Name(s) of Prior Spouse(s)
Cyrus Danous ADIMIDIS

12. Date(s) Marriage(s) Ended
11/04/2007

13. Has your relative ever been in the U.S.?
[X] Yes [ ] No

14. If your relative is currently in the U.S., complete the following:
He or she arrived as a:
(visitor, student, stowaway, without inspection, etc.)

Arrival/Departure Record (I-94)   Date arrived

Date authorized stay expired, or will expire, as shown on Form I-94 or I-95

15. Name and address of present employer (if any)
None

Date this employment began

16. Has your relative ever been under immigration proceedings?
[X] No [ ] Yes Where _____ When _____
[ ] Removal [ ] Exclusion/Deportation [ ] Rescission [ ] Judicial Proceedings

INITIAL RECEIPT _____ RESUBMITTED _____ RELOCATED: Rec'd _____ Sent _____ COMPLETED: Appv'd _____ Denied _____ Ret'd _____

Form I-130 (12/18/12) Y

Sample Form I-130, Petition for Alien Relative (as used for immigrating parents) (page 2)

C. Information about your relative (continued)

17. List spouse and all children of your relative.

(Name)	(Relationship)	(Date of Birth)	(Country of Birth)
Kadmus ADIMIDIS	Son	08/07/1982	Greece

18. Address in the United States where your relative intends to live.

(Street Address)	(Town or City)	(State)
131 3rd Street	Baton Rouge	Louisiana

19. Your relative's address abroad. (Include street, city, province and country)   Phone Number (if any)

Galanou 25, 105 53 Athens, Greece

20. If your relative's native alphabet is other than Roman letters, write his or her name and foreign address in the native alphabet.

(Name)   Address (Include street, city, province and country):

21. If filing for your spouse, give last address at which you lived together. (Include street, city, province, if any, and country):

From: To:

22. Complete the information below if your relative is in the United States and will apply for adjustment of status.

Your relative is in the United States and will apply for adjustment of status to that of a lawful permanent resident at the USCIS office in: If your relative is not eligible for adjustment of status, he or she will apply for a visa abroad at the American consular post in:

(City)	(State)	(City)	(Country)

NOTE: Designation of a U.S. embassy or consulate outside the country of your relative's last residence does not guarantee acceptance for processing by that post. Acceptance is at the discretion of the designated embassy or consulate.

D. Other information

1 If separate petitions are also being submitted for other relatives, give names of each and relationship.

2. Have you ever before filed a petition for this or any other alien? ☐ Yes ☒ No

If "Yes," give name, place and date of filing and result.

WARNING: USCIS investigates claimed relationships and verifies the validity of documents. USCIS seeks criminal prosecutions when family relationships are falsified to obtain visas.

PENALTIES: By law, you may be imprisoned for not more than five years or fined $250,000, or both, for entering into a marriage contract for the purpose of evading any provision of the immigration laws. In addition, you may be fined up to $10,000 and imprisoned for up to five years, or both, for knowingly and willfully falsifying or concealing a material fact or using any false document in submitting this petition.

YOUR CERTIFICATION: I certify, under penalty of perjury under the laws of the United States of America, that the foregoing is true and correct. Furthermore, I authorize the release of any information from my records that U.S. Citizenship and Immigration Services needs to determine eligiblity for the benefit that I am seeking.

E. Signature of petitioner

Evadne H. Solomos   Date 7/9/2014   Phone Number (225) 555-1313

F. Signature of person preparing this form, if other than the petitioner

I declare that I prepared this document at the request of the person above and that it is based on all information of which I have any knowledge.

Print Name _____   Signature _____   Date _____

Address _____   G-28 ID or VOLAG Number, if any. _____

Child Immigrants

When Congress writes laws regulating immigration, it aims to keep families together. Foreign-born children of U.S. citizens or permanent residents are eligible to get a green card when a parent files a petition for them. However, you need to look carefully at who qualifies as a "child."

Note: This chapter addresses only children whose parents have already immigrated to the United States. The situation of children accompanying an immigrating parent is covered in other chapters of this book.

A. Who Qualifies

A person is eligible for a green card if he or she is the child of:

- a U.S. citizen, and is under 21 years of age (immediate relative)
- a U.S. citizen, if the child is over 21 and not married (family first preference category)
- a U.S. citizen, if the child is married (family third preference category)
- a lawful permanent resident, if the child is not married and is under 21 (family second 2A preference), or
- a lawful permanent resident, if the child is over 21 years old and not married (family second 2B preference). If the child was formerly married, but is now divorced or a widow or widower, or if the marriage has been annulled, the child can still immigrate in the 2B category.

> **CAUTION**
>
> **If the U.S. petitioner has a criminal record, see an attorney.** Under the Adam Walsh Child Protection and Safety Act of 2006, U.S. citizens and lawful permanent residents who have been convicted of any "specified offense against a minor" are prohibited from filing a family-based immigrant petition on behalf of any beneficiary (whether a child or not). USCIS will run security checks on all petitions and may call the petitioner in for fingerprinting. If the petitioner has a conviction for one of the specified offenses against a minor, then the petition will not be approved, unless USCIS determines that the U.S. petitioner poses no risk to the beneficiary.

Adult Children of Permanent Residents Wait Longer

Around 88,000 immigrant visas are allowed to be given out each year to the spouses and unmarried children under 21 years of age of green card holders. But only around 26,000 visas per year can go to their unmarried children over 21 years of age. The law places no time limits on processing the applications.

The current waiting period for a spouse and unmarried children under the age of 21 (category 2A) is a little less than two years. This is the lowest wait time in this category in recent history. Children over 21 (category 2B) should, however, be prepared to wait eight years or more for their immigrant visas.

The green card–holding parent or spouse may be able to hurry the process along by becoming a U.S. citizen.

> **CAUTION**
>
> **Caution for children who get married or turn 21 before receiving their green cards.** As a general rule, the visa categories described above must fit the children not only when the visa application process is begun, but at the very end. This end may be years later, when the child attends the interview at which he or she is approved for the green card, and also, if coming from overseas, when the child actually enters the United States.
>
> There are some exceptions to the general rule however. These exceptions were added by the Child Status Protection Act (CSPA). The exceptions work differently depending on whether the child is an immediate relative

or is in a preference category. For immediate relatives, as long as the visa petition was submitted when the child was less than 21 years old, that child remains an immediate relative child regardless of his or her age at the time of actual immigration. Children in the 2A preference category, however, only get to add to their age the time that it took USCIS to make a decision on their visa petition. For details, see Chapter 5. Although the CSPA exceptions will prevent some children from "aging out" after their 21st birthday, they won't protect children who marry. If, for example, the child of a permanent resident gets married, his or her green card eligibility will be destroyed (at least until the parent becomes a U.S. citizen and starts the petition process all over again). If you are a permanent resident, tell your children to consider not getting married if they want to protect their right to immigrate.

B. Definition of "Child"

Immigration law recognizes many different meanings of the word "child" as it relates to obtaining a green card. This definition is important because it determines what kind of documents USCIS will require when the visa petition is filed.

1. Child of Married Parents

When a child is born to a man and a woman who are married to each other, the child is, in legal terms, their legitimate child. If the mother will be filing the visa petition, the only document necessary to establish their relationship is the birth certificate showing the name of the mother and of the child.

If the father will be filing the visa petition, to show the relationship of father and child, two documents are necessary:

- the birth certificate, which shows the name of the father and the child, and
- the marriage certificate, which shows that the mother and the father were married before the birth of the child.

2. Child of Unmarried Parents

A woman and a man who conceive a child are that child's natural parents. Proving this relationship for immigration purposes requires extra steps if the woman and man are not married to one another.

Proving through mother. When a child is born of a woman who is not married to the child's father, the child is her natural child.

To establish the relationship of mother and child, the only document necessary is the birth certificate showing the name of the mother and the name of the child.

If the mother's maiden name as shown on the birth certificate of her child differs from her present name, the mother must present the document showing that her name was changed. Usually, she has changed her name after marrying. The marriage certificate will then verify that the mother named on the birth certificate and the mother on the immigration form are the same person.

Proving through father. Even if the father of the child is not married to the mother when the child is born, the father can petition for the child to immigrate into the United States.

But it may become complicated to prove the father-child relationship. First, the father must establish that he is really the biological father of the child. The birth certificate is the best proof, if his name appears as the father of the child.

If his name is not on the birth certificate, the father should apply to his civil registry requesting that his name be added to the birth certificate as the father of the child. He should do this before the child turns 18.

In some countries, the father may have to acknowledge before a civil court, government agency, or civil registry that he is the father of the child. Doing this "legitimates" the child for purposes of U.S. immigration law; acknowledgment occurs before the child turns 18 years old.

If none of this is available, a blood test, accompanied by an affidavit from the mother stating that the man is the father of the child, may be acceptable to prove paternity, although it doesn't "legitimate" the child.

In cases where the father did not legitimate the child before the child turned 18, the father must show that he was not simply the biological father, but that there was a father-child relationship in existence before the child turned 21. He must provide documents to prove that:

- the father and child lived together before the child turned 21, or
- there was a true father-child relationship before the child turned 21 or got married.

This relationship can be shown by letters written by one to the other; canceled checks or other proof of money sent regularly to support the child; photos of both of them together; school records showing the father's name; sworn statements from at least two people who know of the father-child relationship; U.S. income tax returns showing the child listed as a dependent; birthday cards; or Valentine, Christmas, or other holiday cards sent and received.

In short, almost any evidence may help show that the father did not abandon the child, but kept up paternal ties before the child turned 21 years old.

Some Countries Require No Proof

The governments in some countries, such as China, Haiti, Trinidad and Tobago, and Jamaica, have passed laws erasing the legal distinction between children born to parents who are married to one another and those whose parents are not married.

But if these laws were recently passed, the father has to show USCIS that the law was changed before the child turned 18 years of age. If he can show this, he need not submit all those letters, sworn statements, school records, and other proof mentioned above.

---

3. Legitimated Child of Recently Married Parents

When a child is born to a man and a woman who are not married to each other when the child was born but who marry each other before the child turned 18 years of age, the child is considered to be a legitimated child.

To prove the relationship of mother and child, only the birth certificate is necessary.

To prove the relationship of father and child, two documents are needed: the birth certificate and the marriage certificate.

4. Stepchild

When the mother or the father of a child marries a person who is not the biological parent of that child, a step-relationship is created between the new parent and the child.

For there to be any immigration benefit, the marriage between the child's parent and stepparent must occur before the child turns 18 years of age. A U.S. citizen or green card–holding spouse can petition for a foreign-born spouse's children (as his or her stepchildren) at any time, as long as the children were under 18 years of age at the time of the marriage.

In addition to the birth certificate of the child, a marriage certificate is necessary to show that the step-relationship was created by a marriage that occurred before the child's 18th birthday.

5. Adopted Child

The first thing to know about adopting an immigrant child is that the adoption usually must be finalized before the child turns 16 years of age. An adoption after the age of 16 may benefit the child in ways unrelated to immigration—for example, making inheritance simpler—but it will not usually help the child get a green card.

The next thing that you must know is whether that child lives in a country that has signed onto the

Hague Convention on the Protection of Children. You can find an up-to-date list of countries on the U.S. Department of State's adoption website at http://adoption.state.gov. Click "Hague Convention," and then "Convention Countries." At time of publication, 78 countries were listed.

When the child lives in a Hague Convention country. The Hague Convention entered into force in the U.S. in April of 2008, and has significantly changed the rules and procedures for immigrating adopted children. Each country that is a party to the Convention must have an officially designated central authority to safeguard the adoption process, which in the U.S. is the Department of State (DOS).

Only U.S. citizens may petition. The visa petition must be filed before the child's 16th birthday (no exceptions), and the child must be adopted abroad. One thing that is easier in Hague Convention cases is that, unlike in other cases, there's no requirement that you have two years legal custody of and joint residence with the child.

> ⚠ CAUTION
> **Adoptions from Hague Convention countries must be completed in the exact order specified by the Convention, step by step.** Even if you otherwise meet all the requirements, failing to meet them in the specified order can result in the child being unable to immigrate based upon the adoption.

Here are the basic steps for non-orphan adoptions of children from Hague Convention countries.

- **Choose an adoption service provider (ASP).** The ASP must be authorized to provide adoption services in connection with a Hague adoption, so ask about this before hiring or paying any money to a provider.
- **Obtain a home study report.** This must come from someone authorized to complete a Hague adoption home study.

- **File Form I-800A with USCIS.** This form must be filed before you are matched with the child to be adopted. To be eligible to file this form, you must be a U.S. citizen and habitually reside in the United States. If you are married, your spouse must also sign your Form I-800A and must also intend to adopt any child whom you adopt. If you are not married, you must be at least 24 years of age when you file your Form I-800A, and you must be at least 25 years of age when you later file Form I-800.
- **Once USCIS approves your Form I-800A, work with the ASP to obtain a proposed adoption placement.**
- **File Form I-800.** This serves to determine the child's eligibility as a Convention adoptee.
- **Adopt the child.** Or, you can obtain custody in order to adopt the child in the United States.
- **Obtain an immigrant visa for the child.**
- **Bring the child to the United States.**

The filing fee for Form I-800A is $720. An $85 fee for biometrics is also required, not only for the applicant but also for each person 18 years of age or older who is living with the applicant. There is no fee required for the first Form I-800 filed for a child on the basis of an approved Form I-800A. If more than one Form I-800 is filed during the approval period for different children, the fee is $720 for the second and each subsequent Form I-800, except that if the children were siblings before the adoption, no additional filing fee is required. See the form instructions for where to file.

Adopting a child from a Hague Convention country is complicated. We recommend that you consult an attorney who is experienced in immigration and adoptions before proceeding.

When the child does not live in a Hague Convention country. An adopted immigrant child from a non-Hague convention country will be considered the child (or adult son or daughter) of the adopting parent as long as there was a full and final adoption before the child's 16th birthday.

There is one exception to this age limit, which applies to a child between the ages of 16 and 18, if the older child is the natural sibling of a younger child you have already adopted or are adopting at the same time as the older one. "Natural sibling" means the children share at least one biological parent. Unlike an orphan child (discussed in Chapter 10), the adopted child is neither orphaned nor abandoned by his or her natural parents.

Additional requirements under this process are that the parent must have had legal and physical custody of the child for at least two years while the child was a minor, and the child must have lived with the adopting parents at least two years before the petition was filed.

When these two periods have occurred, either at the same time or one after the other, the immigrant petition can be filed.

Because of these requirements, the most practical way the adopted child can get an immigrant visa is, in most cases, for one or both of the adopting parents to live in the foreign country with the alien child. But this is, as a practical matter, impossible for lawful permanent resident parents, who must maintain their U.S. residences in order to keep their green cards.

What if you're a U.S. citizen and the child you want to adopt is already living in the United States? This gets complicated, and you'll probably want to get an immigration lawyer's help. But let's take a brief look at the three main possibilities, after first reviewing one bit of good news: A child under 18 can't rack up "unlawful presence" in the U.S., and therefore you probably won't have to worry about the three- and ten-year bars (described in Chapter 4) being used to block the child from returning to the U.S. if, for example, he or she needs to leave and have a visa interview at a U.S. consulate. (But watch the timing carefully if you're adopting a child who's already close to 16.) However, a child who is staying in the U.S. without a visa or other permission from the immigration authorities can

still be arrested and removed (deported)—though in practice, USCIS would rarely do that unless the child committed a serious crime.

The child entered the U.S. illegally. If the child entered illegally, you can petition a court for legal custody, but that just makes you the rightful parent. It doesn't make the child's U.S. stay legal for immigration purposes. At the end of the two years of legal custody and having the child live with you, you can file the visa petition, but will ultimately have to take the child to a U.S. consulate abroad for the visa interview (which completes the green card application process).

The child entered the U.S. legally but has overstayed. If the child originally came to the U.S. on a visa, but has stayed past the expiration date on his or her I-94 card (either a small white card tucked into the passport or, if the child entered in 2013 or later, the online version of Form I-94), you can petition a court for legal custody. However, being granted custody just makes you the rightful parent. It doesn't make the child's U.S. stay legal for immigration purposes. At the end of the two years' custody and residence, you can file a visa petition and an adjustment of status application with USCIS. (Note that this is a different procedure than for the child who entered illegally; the combination of your U.S. citizenship and the child's legal entry saves this child from having to do part of the green card application through a U.S. consulate in another country). However, don't interpret this section to mean that you should go to another country, adopt a child, then use a tourist visa to bring the child back to the U.S. in hopes of completing the application process here. That could probably be interpreted as visa fraud, and destroy the child's chances of immigrating.

The child entered the U.S. legally and is still legal. If the child originally came to the U.S. on a visa, and the expiration date on his or her I-94 card (either a small white card tucked into the passport or, if the child entered in 2013 or later, the online version of Form I-94), hasn't passed, you're in relatively good shape. You can petition a court for legal custody, making you the child's rightful parent. Then the question becomes, when does the I-94 run out? If the child is on a student visa, it might easily run for the two years you'll need before submitting the visa petition and green card application (without leaving the U.S.). If not, see the paragraph above this one—and talk to a lawyer. Though certain visa stays can be extended, you wouldn't want to ruin the entire plan by lying about the reasons for the extension.

Another alternative may be to process the immigration papers required for an orphan child. (See Chapter 10.)

C. Quick View of the Application Process

With the exception of children adopted from Hague Convention countries, the standard process for someone to get a green card as a child is as follows. The U.S. citizen or permanent resident parent must begin the process by mailing what's called a "visa petition" (using Form I-130) to USCIS. We're going to assume that the person reading this is the parent.

Form I-130 serves to prove to the immigration authorities that your children are truly and legally yours. After that petition is approved (in most cases), your children complete their half of the process (with your help, of course) by submitting a green card application and attending an interview, most likely with you accompanying them. Their application serves to prove that not only do they qualify as children of a U.S. citizen or permanent resident, but that they're otherwise eligible for U.S. permanent residence.

However, the details of when and how your children complete their half of the process depend on whether they are living overseas or in the United States, as described next.

D. Detailed Instructions for the Application Process

Now we'll break the application process down into individual procedures, some of which will be covered in this chapter, and others in later chapters—we'll tell you exactly where to turn to for your situation.

1. Preparing the Form I-130 Visa Petition

We'll start by discussing the visa petition, which all parents of immigrating children must prepare to begin the process. You'll need to assemble:

- ☐ Form I-130, Petition for Alien Relative (available at www.uscis.gov/i-130; see sample at the end of this chapter)
- ☐ Form G-325A, Biographic Information (signed by child; see sample at end of chapter)
- ☐ birth certificate of child
- ☐ parents' marriage certificate
- ☐ documents proving the parent's U.S. citizenship or permanent residence (see Chapter 20)
- ☐ filing fee for Form I-130, currently $420, payable by check or money order to the U.S. Department of Homeland Security, and
- ☐ Form G-1145. This is optional, but filing it is a good idea, so that you'll receive an email and/or text notification from USCIS when your petition has been accepted. Once USCIS sends you a receipt number, you can use that number to sign up to receive automatic email updates letting you know whenever mail is sent regarding your case.

TIP
Here's how to sign up for automatic email updates: Go to www.uscis.gov. Click "Check Your Case Status," then "Sign-up for Case Updates." Then, you can register for automatic case status updates by email and text message by clicking "Register as an Applicant Consumer."

In cases where the child is adopted from a non–Hague Convention country, the following documents must also be presented (remember that if the child is from a Hague Convention country, Forms I-800A and I-800 are used instead of Form I-130, and that the legal and procedural requirements are different):

- ☐ the adoption decree showing adoption prior to 16 years of age
- ☐ documents showing legal custody for at least two years
- ☐ documents proving that the adopted child has resided with the adopting parent or parents for at least two years (such as school and medical records)
- ☐ a birth certificate of the child showing the adopting parent as mother or father by reason of the adoption decree, and
- ☐ documents showing the marital status of the petitioning parent.

Once you've assembled all these items, make a copy for your records. It's also a good idea to write a cover letter, explaining what type of visa petition it is (for example, saying "I am a U.S. citizen, filing the enclosed visa petition on behalf of my married daughter."). The letter should include a bulleted list, much like the one above, of everything you're sending. This will help USCIS see that you're organized. It will help you, too, to make sure that nothing has been forgotten.

2. Where to Submit the I-130 Visa Petition

Once you've assembled and copied everything, your next step, including where to send the visa petition, depends on which visa category your child will be applying in and where the child is now, as detailed below.

NEXT STEP

Next step for unmarried children under age 21 of U.S. citizens (immediate relatives) if the children live overseas. The parent should mail the visa petition to USCIS's Chicago or Phoenix lockbox (depending on where he or she lives). The lockbox facility will forward it to a USCIS office appropriate for the parent's geographical area. Soon after the visa petition is approved, the U.S. consulate serving the country where the child lives will take over. The child will apply for the immigrant visa and green card through consular processing, described in Chapter 17.

Immigrant Story: Children Nearing Age 21

Rajiv, a U.S. permanent resident, petitioned for his wife and three children to come to the United States from India. When he first filed the I-130 petition, the children were teenagers. But with people in category 2A having to wait about four years for their Priority Dates to become current, the family rightly worried that the children would "age out" before they could be issued their green cards.

When the Priority Date finally became current, the oldest child, Sandip, was already 22 years old and eight months. The middle child, Ayanna, turned 21 years old that month, and the youngest child, Iqbal, was then 19 years old.

Can Sandip and Ayanna immigrate to the U.S. even though they're both now over 21? Under the Child Status Protection Act, the children get to subtract from their age the amount of time it took USCIS to approve the I-130. Although the family waited four years for the Priority Date to become current, they waited only eight months for USCIS to approve the I-130. Unfortunately, eight months is not enough to help Sandip. Eight months will help Ayanna, however, by making her—for purposes of getting a visa—20 years and three months old. To take advantage of this protection, Ayanna will have to file her green card application within one year of the Priority Date becoming current. So long as she acts soon, she doesn't have to worry about turning 21.

The last child, Iqbal, is still only 19 years old, so does not need to worry (unless he ruins his eligibility by getting married).

NEXT STEP

Next step for unmarried children under age 21 of U.S. citizens (immediate relatives) if the children live in the United States. If the child is eligible for adjustment of status (as explained in Chapter 16), then the parent shouldn't file the visa petition by itself, but should combine it with the adjustment of status application, and then mail it according to the instructions in Chapter 16. If, however, the child is not eligible to adjust status, and has spent any time in the U.S. illegally or out of status, consult an experienced immigration attorney.

NEXT STEP

Next step for all children of U.S. permanent residents, and married or over-21 children of U.S. citizens (preference relatives) if the children live overseas. The parent should mail the visa petition to USCIS's Chicago or Phoenix lockbox (depending on where he or she lives). The lockbox facility will forward it to the USCIS office appropriate for the parent's geographical area. After the visa petition is approved, the child will be put on a waiting list, based on his or her Priority Date. When the Priority Date becomes "current," the U.S. consulate serving the country where the child lives will take over. The child will apply for the immigrant visa and green card through consular processing, described in Chapter 17.

NEXT STEP

Next step for all children of U.S. permanent residents and married or over-21 children of U.S. citizens (preference relatives) if the children live in the United States. The parent should mail the visa petition to USCIS's Chicago or Phoenix lockbox (depending on where he or she lives). The lockbox facility will forward it to the appropriate USCIS office for the parent's geographical area. After the visa petition is approved, the child will be put on a waiting list, based on his or her Priority Date. It may be many years before the Priority Date becomes current, during which time the mere filing of a visa petition gives the child no rights to remain in the United States (though many do, illegally). After the child's Priority Date becomes current, then:

- If the child is still living in the U.S. and is eligible for adjustment of status (unlikely), see Chapter 16 for instructions.
- If the child is living in the U.S. and is not eligible for adjustment of status, or has left the U.S. but spent more than six months here illegally before leaving, see an experienced immigration attorney for help.
- If the child left the U.S. without having spent too much time there illegally, you can safely continue the process, and the U.S. consulate serving the country where the child lives will take over. The child will apply for the immigrant visa and green card through consular processing, described in Chapter 17.

E. Automatic Citizenship for Some Children

In 2000, Congress passed important new legislation allowing many children living in the U.S. with green cards to become citizens automatically if they have at least one U.S. citizen parent. Natural-born as well as adopted children can benefit from these new laws.

The law is slightly less helpful for children living overseas, who must go through an application process in order to claim their U.S. citizenship.

1. Children Living in the United States

For natural-born children to qualify for automatic citizenship, one parent needs to be a U.S. citizen, the child must have a green card and be living in the legal and physical custody of the U.S. citizen parent, and the child must still be under age 18 when all of these conditions are fulfilled.

For adopted children to qualify, one of the parents must be a U.S. citizen, a full and final adoption must have occurred, the child must be living in the United States after having entered on an immigrant visa (meaning the child is a green card holder), and the child must still be under age 18 at the time that all these things become true.

Though the process is automatic—and USCIS tries to send such children certificates of citizenship within six weeks of when they get their green cards—it's an excellent idea for such children to also apply for U.S. passports as proof of their U.S. citizen status.

> **EXAMPLE:** Lorna is 16 years old and living in Mexico. Some years ago, her father, a U.S. permanent resident, petitioned for her to immigrate. Even before her Priority Date became current, however, he became a U.S. citizen, so the process was speeded up. Lorna successfully applies for an immigrant visa through consular processing, and enters the United States to live with her father.
>
> Almost as soon as Lorna enters the U.S., she automatically becomes a U.S. citizen, because she (1) has a U.S. citizen parent, (2) has a green card, (3) is living in the citizen parent's legal and physical custody, and (4) was still under 18 when the first three things became true. USCIS should, recognizing her status, automatically send her a citizenship certificate. (Note: If Lorna's father had become a citizen after she got her green card and came to the U.S., but before she turned 18, USCIS wouldn't realize she'd become an automatic citizen, and Lorna would have to request a certificate to prove it.)

Children living in the U.S. can also, if USCIS fails to send a certificate, file for a certificate of citizenship on Form N-600. This form is used for biological and adopted children. For further instructions, see the USCIS website at www.uscis.gov/n-600.

2. Children Living Overseas

For children who are living overseas, the process is somewhat more complex. Either natural-born or adopted children may qualify for automatic citizenship, but they need to have one U.S. citizen parent; that parent or the parent's parent must have been physically present in the U.S. for five years, two of which were after the age of 14; the child must be visiting the U.S. on a temporary visa or other lawful means of entry; the child must live in the legal and physical custody of the U.S. citizen parent in their overseas home; and the child must remain under the age of 18 and in valid visa status until USCIS makes its decision on the citizenship application.

In practice, these conditions are very hard to meet. You might wish to consult with a lawyer. The application is made on Form N-600K for biological and adopted children. For a sample of Form N-600K, see the end of the chapter. For further instructions, see the USCIS website at www.uscis.gov/n-600K.

Sample Form I-130, Petition for Alien Relative (as used for immigrating children) (page 1)

Department of Homeland Security
U.S. Citizenship and Immigration Services

OMB No. 1615-0012; Expires 12/31/2015

I-130, Petition for Alien Relative

DO NOT WRITE IN THIS BLOCK - FOR USCIS OFFICE ONLY

A#	Action Stamp	Fee Stamp

Section of Law/Visa Category
- [ ] 201(b) Spouse - IR-1/CR-1
- [ ] 201(b) Child - IR-2/CR-2
- [ ] 201(b) Parent - IR-5
- [ ] 203(a)(1) Unm. S or D - F1-1
- [ ] 203(a)(2)(A)Spouse - F2-1
- [ ] 203(a)(2)(A) Child - F2-2
- [ ] 203(a)(2)(B) Unm. S or D - F2-4
- [ ] 203(a)(3) Married S or D - F3-1
- [ ] 203(a)(4) Brother/Sister - F4-1

Petition was filed on: _____ (priority date)
- [ ] Personal Interview
- [ ] Previously Forwarded
- [ ] Pet. [ ] Ben. " A" File Reviewed
- [ ] I-485 Filed Simultaneously
- [ ] Field Investigation
- [ ] 204(g) Resolved
- [ ] 203(a)(2)(A) Resolved
- [ ] 203(g) Resolved

Remarks:

A. Relationship   You are the petitioner.   Your relative is the beneficiary.

1. I am filing this petition for my:
[ ] Spouse [ ] Parent [ ] Brother/Sister [X] Child

2. Are you related by adoption?
[ ] Yes [X] No

3. Did you gain permanent residence through adoption?
[ ] Yes [X] No

B. Information about you

1. Name (Family name in CAPS) (First) (Middle)
CARLTON   Derek   Andrew

2. Address (Number and Street) (Apt. No.)
575 7th St.

(Town or City) (State/Country) (Zip/Postal Code)
Champaign   IL/USA   61820

3. Place of Birth (Town or City) (State/Country)
Chicago   IL/USA

4. Date of Birth 06/18/1980
5. Gender [X] Male [ ] Female
6. Marital Status [X] Married [ ] Single [ ] Widowed [ ] Divorced

7. Other Names Used (including maiden name)

8. Date and Place of Present Marriage (if married)
04/12/2012

9. U.S. Social Security Number (If any)
656-56-5656
10. Alien Registration Number
None

11. Name(s) of Prior Spouse(s)
None
12. Date(s) Marriage(s) Ended

13. If you are a U.S. citizen, complete the following:
My citizenship was acquired through (check one):
[X] Birth in the U.S.
[ ] Naturalization. Give certificate number and date and place of issuance.
_____
[ ] Parents. Have you obtained a certificate of citizenship in your own name?
[ ] Yes. Give certificate number, date and place of issuance. [ ] No

14. If you are a lawful permanent resident alien, complete the following:
Date and place of admission for or adjustment to lawful permanent residence and class of admission.

14b. Did you gain permanent resident status through marriage to a U.S. citizen or lawful permanent resident?
[ ] Yes [ ] No

C. Information about your relative

1. Name (Family name in CAPS) (First) (Middle)
SRISAI   Kanya   Lawan

2. Address (Number and Street) (Apt. No.)
14 Sri Ayudayha Road

(Town or City) (State/Country) (Zip/Postal Code)
Bangkok   Thailand

3. Place of Birth (Town or City) (State/Country)
Saraburi   Thailand

4. Date of Birth 02/02/2014
5. Gender [ ] Male [X] Female
6. Marital Status [ ] Married [ ] Single [ ] Widowed [ ] Divorced

7. Other Names Used (including maiden name)
none

8. Date and Place of Present Marriage (if married)
N/A

9. U.S. Social Security Number (If any)
None
10. Alien Registration Number
None

11. Name(s) of Prior Spouse(s)
None
12. Date(s) Marriage(s) Ended

13. Has your relative ever been in the U.S.? [ ] Yes [X] No

14. If your relative is currently in the U.S., complete the following:
He or she arrived as a:
(visitor, student, stowaway, without inspection, etc.)

Arrival/Departure Record (I-94)   Date arrived
| | | | ▬ | | | | | | | | |

Date authorized stay expired, or will expire, as shown on Form I-94 or I-95

15. Name and address of present employer (if any)
None
Date this employment began

16. Has your relative ever been under immigration proceedings?
[X] No [ ] Yes Where _____ When _____
[ ] Removal [ ] Exclusion/Deportation [ ] Rescission [ ] Judicial Proceedings

INITIAL RECEIPT	RESUBMITTED	RELOCATED: Rec'd	Sent	COMPLETED: Appv'd	Denied	Ret'd

Form I-130 (12/18/12) Y

Sample Form I-130, Petition for Alien Relative (as used for immigrating children) (page 2)

C. Information about your relative (continued)

17. List spouse and all children of your relative.

(Name)	(Relationship)	(Date of Birth)	(Country of Birth)
None			

18. Address in the United States where your relative intends to live.

(Street Address)	(Town or City)	(State)
575 7th St.	Champaign	Illinois

19. Your relative's address abroad. (Include street, city, province and country)   Phone Number (if any)

14 Sri Ayudayha Road, Bangkok, Thailand   None

20. If your relative's native alphabet is other than Roman letters, write his or her name and foreign address in the native alphabet.

(Name)   Address (Include street, city, province and country):

21. If filing for your spouse, give last address at which you lived together. (Include street, city, province, if any, and country):

From: To:

22. Complete the information below if your relative is in the United States and will apply for adjustment of status.

Your relative is in the United States and will apply for adjustment of status to that of a lawful permanent resident at the USCIS office in:

If your relative is not eligible for adjustment of status, he or she will apply for a visa abroad at the American consular post in:

(City)	(State)	(City)	(Country)

NOTE: Designation of a U.S. embassy or consulate outside the country of your relative's last residence does not guarantee acceptance for processing by that post. Acceptance is at the discretion of the designated embassy or consulate.

D. Other information

1. If separate petitions are also being submitted for other relatives, give names of each and relationship.

Chosita Chanakarn SRISAI, wife

2. Have you ever before filed a petition for this or any other alien? ☐ Yes ☒ No

If "Yes," give name, place and date of filing and result.

WARNING: USCIS investigates claimed relationships and verifies the validity of documents. USCIS seeks criminal prosecutions when family relationships are falsified to obtain visas.

PENALTIES: By law, you may be imprisoned for not more than five years or fined $250,000, or both, for entering into a marriage contract for the purpose of evading any provision of the immigration laws. In addition, you may be fined up to $10,000 and imprisoned for up to five years, or both, for knowingly and willfully falsifying or concealing a material fact or using any false document in submitting this petition.

YOUR CERTIFICATION: I certify, under penalty of perjury under the laws of the United States of America, that the foregoing is true and correct. Furthermore, I authorize the release of any information from my records that U.S. Citizenship and Immigration Services needs to determine eligiblity for the benefit that I am seeking.

E. Signature of petitioner

Derek A. Carlton   Date 8/19/2014   Phone Number (217) 555-1313

F. Signature of person preparing this form, if other than the petitioner

I declare that I prepared this document at the request of the person above and that it is based on all information of which I have any knowledge.

Print Name _____   Signature _____   Date _____

Address _____   G-28 ID or VOLAG Number, if any. _____

Form I-130 (12/18/12) Y Page 2

Sample Form G-325A, Biographic Information (page 1)

OMB No. 1615-0008; Expires 02/28/2015

Department of Homeland Security
U.S. Citizenship and Immigration Services

G-325A, Biographic Information

Family Name	First Name	Middle Name	☐ Male ☒ Female	Date of Birth (mm/dd/yyyy)	Citizenship/Nationality	File Number
SRISAI	Kanya	Lawan		02/02/2014	Thai	A

All Other Names Used (Include names by previous marriages)	City and Country of Birth	U.S. Social Security No. (if any)
None	Saraburi, Thailand	None

	Family Name	First Name	Date of Birth (mm/dd/yyyy)	City, and Country of Birth (if known)	City and Country of Residence
Father	Kantawong	Kiet	12/07/1991	Saraburi, Thailand	Tak, Thailand
Mother (Maiden Name)	Srisai	Chosita	09/08/1990	Saraburi, Thailand	Bangkok, Thailand

Current Husband or Wife (If none, so state) Family Name (For wife, give maiden name)	First Name	Date of Birth (mm/dd/yyyy)	City and Country of Birth	Date of Marriage	Place of Marriage
None					

Former Husbands or Wives (If none, so state) Family Name (For wife, give maiden name)	First Name	Date of Birth (mm/dd/yyyy)	Date and Place of Marriage	Date and Place of Termination of Marriage
None				

Applicant's residence last five years. List present address first.

Street Name and Number	City	Province or State	Country	From Month	Year	To Month	Year
14 Sri Ayadayha Road	Bangkok	Bangkok	Thailand	02	2014	Present Time	

Applicant's last address outside the United States of more than 1 year.

Street Name and Number	City	Province or State	Country	From Month	Year	To Month	Year
14 Sri Ayadayha Road	Bangkok	Bangkok	Thailand	02	2014		

Applicant's employment last five years. (If none, so state.) List present employment first.

Full Name and Address of Employer	Occupation (Specify)	From Month	Year	To Month	Year
n/a				Present Time	

Last occupation abroad if not shown above. (Include all information requested above.)

This form is submitted in connection with an application for:	Signature of Applicant	Date
☐ Naturalization ☐ Other (Specify): ☒ Status as Permanent Resident	Kanya Srisai (by Chosita Srisai, mother)	08/17/2014

If your native alphabet is in other than Roman letters, write your name in your native alphabet below:

Penalties: Severe penalties are provided by law for knowingly and willfully falsifying or concealing a material fact.

Applicant: Print your name and Alien Registration Number in the box outlined by heavy border below.

Complete This Box (Family Name)	(Given Name)	(Middle Name)	(Alien Registration Number)
SRISAI	Kanya	Lawan	A

Form G-325A (Rev. 02/07/13) Y

Sample Form N-600K, Application for Citizen and Issuance of Certificate Under Section 322 (page 1)

OMB No. 1615-0087; Expires 05/31/2015

Department of Homeland Security
U. S. Citizenship and Immigration Services

**Form N-600K, Application for Citizenship and
Issuance of Certificate Under Section 322**

Print or type your answers fully and accurately in black ink. Write "N/A" if an item is not applicable. Write "None" if the answer is none. Failure to answer all of the questions may delay your Form N-600K.

Part 1. Information About Your Eligibility *(check only one box)*	**Your A-Number:**
	A _____ - _____ - _____

The application is being filed on your behalf. You are under 18 years of age and:

1. ☒ The BIOLOGICAL child of a qualifying U.S. citizen (USC) parent filing this form.

2. ◯ The ADOPTED child of a qualifying USC parent filing this form.

3. ◯ The grandchild of a qualifying USC grandparent or the child ward of a USC legal guardian filing this form within 5 years of the death of my USC parent.

For USCIS Use Only

Bar Code	Date Stamp

Remarks

Action

Part 2. Information About You, the Child *(for whom this application is being filed)*

1. Current Legal Name *(do **not** provide a nickname)*

Family Name *(last name)*

Rosi

Given Name *(first name)*

Adriana

Middle Name *(if applicable)*

Suzetta

2. Name exactly as it appears on your Permanent Resident Card *(if applicable)*

Family Name *(last name)*

Rosi

Given Name *(first name)*

Adriana

Middle Name *(if applicable)*

Suzetta

3. Other name(s) you have used since birth *(if applicable. Include nicknames.)*

Family Name *(last name)*	Given Name *(first name)*	Middle Name *(if applicable)*

4. U.S. Social Security Number *(if applicable)*

None

5. Date of Birth *(mm/dd/yyyy)*

02/01/2002

6. Country of Birth

Italy

7. Country of Citizenship/Nationality

Italy

8. Gender

◯ Male ☒ Female

9. Height

Feet 4 Inches 11

10. Home Address

Street Number and Name *(do **not** provide a P.O. Box in this space unless it is your **ONLY** address.)*

Viale Europa 22

Apartment Number

City

Roma

State

ZIP Code

Province *(foreign address only)*

RM

Country *(foreign address only)*

Italy

Postal Code *(foreign address only)*

00144

Form N-600K (Rev. 05/03/13) N

Sample Form N-600K, Application for Citizen and Issuance of Certificate Under Section 322 (page 2)

Part 2. Information About You, the Child *(continued)*	A _____ - _____ - _____

11. Mailing Address

C/O *(in care of name)*

Street Number and Name: Viale Europa 22   Apartment Number:

City: Roma   State: ZIP Code:

Province *(foreign address only)*: RM   Country *(foreign address only)*: Italy   Postal Code *(foreign address only)*: 00144

12. Daytime Phone Number: (033) 12011290   Work Phone Number *(if any)*: ( )   Evening Phone Number: (033) 1201770

Mobile Phone Number *(if any)*: (033) 1201771   **13. E-Mail Address** *(if any)*: adrianar@email.com

14. Marital Status

☒ Single, Never Married   ◯ Married   ◯ Divorced   ◯ Widowed

◯ Marriage Annulled   ◯ Other *(explain)*: _____

15. Information about your admission into the United States and current immigration status

(Do NOT complete this section. The USCIS officer will complete it with you during the interview.)

You arrived in the following manner:

Port of Entry *(City/State)*   Date of Entry *(mm/dd/yyyy)*   Current Immigration Status

Exact Name Used at Time of Entry

16. Do you know of any prior application for citizenship or for a U.S. passport?   ◯ Yes   ☒ No

17. Were you adopted?   ◯ Yes   ☒ No

Date of Adoption *(mm/dd/yyyy)*   Date Legal Custody Began *(mm/dd/yyyy)*   Date Physical Custody Began *(mm/dd/yyyy)*

18. Were your parents married to each other when you were born (or adopted)?   ☒ Yes   ◯ No

Part 3. Information About Your U.S. Citizen Biological or Adoptive Parent *(Provide information about yourself below if you are a U.S. citizen father or mother applying on behalf of your eligible child. Provide information about the child's U.S. citizen parent in the sections noted if you are the U.S. citizen grandparent or legal guardian.)*

1. Current legal name of U.S. citizen father or mother submitting this Form N-600K.

Family Name *(last name)*: Smith   Given Name *(first name)*: Johanna   Middle Name *(if applicable)*: Darling

Sample Form N-600K, Application for Citizen and Issuance of Certificate Under Section 322 (page 3)

| Part 3. Information About Your U.S. Citizen Biological or Adoptive Parent *(continued)* | A ____ - ___ - ____ |

2. Date of Birth *(mm/dd/yyyy)*
02/28/1967

3. Country of Birth
United States

4. U.S. Social Security Number *(if applicable)*
123-45-6789

5. Home Address

Street Number and Name *(do **not** provide a P.O. Box in this space)*
Viale Europa 22

Apartment Number

City
Roma

State

ZIP Code

Province *(foreign address only)*
RM

Country *(foreign address only)*
Italy

Postal Code *(foreign address only)*
00144

6. Daytime Phone Number
(033)12011290

Work Phone Number *(if any)*
(033)1201773

Evening Phone Number
(033)1201770

Mobile Phone Number *(if any)*
(033)12022290

7. E-Mail Address *(if any)*
josmith@email.com

8. Your parent is a U.S. citizen by:

☒ Birth in the United States
☐ Acquisition after birth through naturalization of alien parent(s)
☐ Birth abroad to U.S. citizen parent(s)

Certificate of Citizenship Number

A-Number *(if known)*

☐ Naturalization

Date of Naturalization *(mm/dd/yyyy)*

Place of Naturalization *(name of court and City/State or USCIS office location)*

Certificate of Naturalization Number

A-Number *(if known)*

9. Has your U.S. citizen father or mother ever lost U.S. citizenship or taken any action that would cause loss of U.S. citizenship?

☐ Yes *(provide full explanation on an additional sheet(s) of paper.)*   ☒ No

10. Marital History

A. How many times has your U.S. citizen father or mother been married *(including annulled marriages and marriage(s) to the same person)*? 1

B. What is your U.S. citizen father or mother's current marital status?

☐ Single, Never Married   ☒ Married   ☐ Separated   ☐ Divorced   ☐ Widowed

☐ Marriage Annulled   ☐ Other *(explain)*:

C. Information about your U.S. citizen father's or mother's **current spouse:**

Family Name *(last name)*
Rossi

Given Name *(first name)*
Amerigo

Middle Name *(if applicable)*
Benito

Date of Birth *(mm/dd/yyyy)*
10/15/1952

Country of Birth
Italy

Country of Citizenship/Nationality
Italy

Sample Form N-600K, Application for Citizen and Issuance of Certificate Under Section 322 (page 4)

Part 3. Information About Your U.S. Citizen Biological or Adoptive Parent *(continued)*	A _ _ _ - _ _ - _ _ _ _

Spouse's Home Address

Street Number and Name *(do **not** provide a P.O. Box in this space)*

Viale Europa 22

Apartment Number

City

Roma

State

ZIP Code

Province *(foreign address only)*

RM

Country *(foreign address only)*

Italy

Postal Code *(foreign address only)*

00144

Date of Marriage *(mm/dd/yyyy)*

02/14/1994

Place of Marriage *(City/State or Country)*

Columbus, Ohio   USA

Spouse's Immigration Status

○ U.S. Citizen   ○ Permanent Resident   ○ Other *(explain)*: _____

D. Is your U.S. citizen father's or mother's current spouse also your biological (or adopted) parent?   ☒ Yes   ○ No

11. Member of U.S. Armed Forces

A. Is the sponsoring U.S. citizen parent a member of the U.S. Armed Forces?   ○ Yes   ☒ No

B. If you answered yes, then are you are on official orders authorizing you to accompany and reside with your sponsoring U.S. citizen parent who is a member of the U.S. Armed Forces?   ○ Yes   ○ No

---

NOTE: If your U.S. citizen biological or adoptive parent is filing this application AND has the required physical presence in the United States, skip Part 4 and go directly to Part 5.

Part 4. Information About Your Qualifying U.S. Citizen Grandparent *(complete this part **only** if your U.S. citizen parent (or adoptive parent), grandparent, or legal guardian is applying for citizenship for you, and the U.S. citizen parent **has not** been physically present in the United States for 5 years; 2 years of which were after the age of 14.)*

1. Current legal name of U.S. citizen grandfather or grandmother submitting this Form N-600K.

Family Name *(last name)*

Given Name *(first name)*

Middle Name *(if applicable)*

2. Date of Birth *(mm/dd/yyyy)*   **3.** Country of Birth   **4.** U.S. Social Security Number *(if applicable)*

5. Home Address

Street Number and Name *(do **not** provide a P.O. Box in this space)*

Apartment Number

City

State

ZIP Code

Province *(foreign address only)*

Country *(foreign address only)*

Postal Code *(foreign address only)*

Sample Form N-600K, Application for Citizen and Issuance of Certificate Under Section 322 (page 5)

Part 4. Information About Your Qualifying U.S. Citizen Grandparent *(continued)*	A ____ - ____ - ____

6. Daytime Phone Number   **Work Phone Number** *(if any)*   **Evening Phone Number**

( )   ( )   ( )

Mobile Phone Number *(if any)*   **7. E-Mail Address** *(if any)*

( )

8. My grandparent is a U.S. citizen by:

○ Birth in the United States

○ Acquisition after birth through naturalization of alien parent(s)

○ Birth abroad to U.S. citizen parent(s)

    Certificate of Citizenship Number   A-Number *(if known)*

○ Naturalization

    Date of Naturalization *(mm/dd/yyyy)*   Place of Naturalization *(name of court and City/State or USCIS office location)*

    Certificate of Naturalization Number   A-Number *(if known)*

9. Has your grandparent ever lost U.S. citizenship or taken any action that would cause loss of U.S. citizenship?

    ○ Yes *(provide full explanation on an additional sheet(s) of paper)*   ○ No

---

Part 5. Physical Presence in the United States From Birth Until Filing of Form N-600K *(Provide the dates that your U.S. citizen parent or grandparent was present in the United States. If your U.S. citizen parent **has not** been physically present in the United States for 5 years, 2 years of which were after the age of 14, then you must use the physical presence of your U.S. citizen grandparent.)*

Indicate whether this information relates to your U.S. citizen parent or to your qualifying grandparent   ☐ U.S. Citizen Parent   ☐ U.S. Citizen Grandparent

Physical Presence in the United States *(mm/dd/yyyy)*					
From	02/28/1967	Until	06/14/1996	From		Until	
From		Until		From		Until	
From		Until		From		Until	
From		Until		From		Until	
From		Until		From		Until	
From		Until		From		Until	
From		Until		From		Until	
From		Until		From		Until	
From		Until		From		Until	

NOTE: If your U.S. citizen biological/adoptive parent is filing this application, skip Part 6 and go directly to Part 7.

Sample Form N-600K, Application for Citizen and Issuance of Certificate Under Section 322 (page 6)

Part 6. Information About Your Legal Guardian *(complete this part only if your legal guardian is filing this application in lieu of a deceased U.S. citizen parent)*

A ___ - ____ - ____

1. Current legal name of U.S. citizen father or mother submitting this Form N-600K.

Family Name *(last name)*

Given Name *(first name)*

Middle Name *(if applicable)*

2. Date of Birth *(mm/dd/yyyy)*   **3. Country of Birth**   **4. U.S. Social Security Number** *(if applicable)*

5. Home Address

Street Number and Name *(do **not** provide a P.O. Box in this space)*   Apartment Number

City   State   ZIP Code

Province *(foreign address only)*   Country *(foreign address only)*   Postal Code *(foreign address only)*

6. Daytime Phone Number   **Work Phone Number** *(if any)*   **Evening Phone Number**

( )   ( )   ( )

Mobile Phone Number *(if any)*   **7. E-Mail Address** *(if any)*

( )

8. My legal guardian is a U.S. citizen by:

○ Birth in the United States

○ Acquisition after birth through naturalization of alien parent(s)

○ Birth abroad to U.S. citizen parent(s)

Certificate of Citizenship Number   A-Number *(if known)*

○ Naturalization

Date of Naturalization *(mm/dd/yyyy)*   Place of Naturalization *(name of court and City/State or USCIS office location)*

Certificate of Naturalization Number   A-Number *(if known)*

9. Date of Legal Guardianship *(mm/dd/yyyy)*   **10. Name of Authority that Granted Legal Guardianship**

11. Address of Authority that Granted Legal Guardianship

Part 7. Preferred Location and Date for Interview

1. Location *(USCIS Office, City, or State)*   **2. Preferred Date** *(mm/dd/yyyy)*

New York, NY   02/15/2015

USCIS will attempt to accommodate your preferences.

NOTE: Interview date should be at least 90 days <u>after</u> filing Form N-600K and before your (the child's) 18th birthday.

Sample Form N-600K, Application for Citizen and Issuance of Certificate Under Section 322 (page 7)

Part 8. Your Signature *(USCIS will reject your Form N-600K if it is not signed.)*

A _____ - _____ - _____

I certify, under penalty of perjury under the laws of the United States, that this application, and the evidence submitted with it, is all true and correct. I authorize the release of any information from my records that U.S. Citizenship and Immigration Services needs to determine eligibility for the benefit I am seeking.

Your Signature

Adriana Rossi

Date *(mm/dd/yyyy)*

12/11/2014

Part 9. Signature of Person Who Prepared This Form For You *(if applicable)*

I declare that I prepared this application at the request of the above person. The answers provided are based on information of which I have personal knowledge and/or were provided to me by the above-named person in response to the questions contained on this application.

Preparer's Printed Name

Preparer's Signature

Date *(mm/dd/yyyy)*

Preparer's Firm or Organization Name *(if applicable)*

Preparer's Daytime Phone Number
(   )

Preparer's Fax Number
(   )

Preparer's Email Address

Preparer's Address

Street Number and Name *(do **not** provide a P.O. Box in this space)*

City

State

ZIP Code

Province *(foreign address only)*

Country *(foreign address only)*

Postal Code *(foreign address only)*

> **NOTE: Do not complete the part below until the USCIS officer instructs you to do so at the interview.**

Part 10. Affidavit

I, the parent/grandparent/legal guardian, _____ do swear or affirm, under penalty of perjury under

the laws of the United States, that I know and understand the contents of this application signed by me, and the attached

supplementary pages number (_____) to (_____) inclusive, that the same are true and correct to the best of my knowledge, and

that corrections number (_____) to (_____) were made by me or at my request.

Applicant, Parent or Legal Guardian's Signature

Date *(mm/dd/yyyy)*

Subscribed and sworn or affirmed before me upon examination of the applicant and U.S. citizen parent/grandparent/legal guardian on

_____ at _____ .

Interviewing USCIS Officer's Name and Title

Interviewing USCIS Officer's Signature

Sample Form N-600K, Application for Citizen and Issuance of Certificate Under Section 322 (page 8)

| Part 11. USCIS Officer Report and Recommendation | A ___ - __ - ____ |

On the basis of the documents, records and the testimony of person examined, and the identification upon personal appearance of the underage beneficiary, I find that all the facts and conclusions set forth under oath in this application are:

1. ☐ true and correct;

2. ☐ The applicant derived or acquired U.S. citizenship on _____
(mm/dd/yyyy)

3. The applicant derived or acquired U.S. citizenship through *(check the box next to the appropriate section of law or, if the section of law is not reflected, write the applicable section of law in the space next to "Other")*

☐ Section 322(a)(2)(A) of the INA *(Parent residence)*;

☐ Section 322(a)(2)(B) of the INA *(Grandparent residence)*; **or**

☐ Other _____

I recommend that this Form N-600K be: ☐ Approved ☐ Denied

Issue Certificate of Citizenship in the Name of

USCIS Officer's Name and Title	**USCIS Officer's Signature**	**Date** *(mm/dd/yyyy)*

I do _____ do not _____ concur with the USCIS officer's recommendation of the Form N-600K.

USCIS Field Office Director's Signature	**Date** *(mm/dd/yyyy)*

Orphan Immigrants in Non-Hague Convention Countries

If you're considering adopting a child, and that child might be an orphan, you may not need to read this chapter—it depends entirely on what country the child is from. That's because of the recent change in immigration law, based on the Hague Convention on the Protection of Children and Cooperation in Respect of Intercountry Adoption having taken effect in the United States on April 1, 2008. If you plan to adopt from a country that has signed onto the Hague Convention, it doesn't matter whether the child is an orphan or not—the procedures will essentially be the same, and are covered in Chapter 9, not this one.

If, however, you plan to adopt from a country that has not signed onto the Hague Convention (or you began this process before April 1, 2008, either by adopting the child or by filing either a Form I-600 or I-600A before that date), keep reading. This chapter describes the special process for adopting orphans who live in countries that have not signed the Hague Convention.

For the list of countries that are parties to the Hague Convention, go to the Department of State's adoption website at http://adoption.state.gov. This website also provides information about each country's individual requirements, regardless of whether the country is a party to the Hague Convention.

The requirements for adopting and immigrating a non-Hague orphan child are less difficult than the requirements for adopting and immigrating a non-Hague non-orphan. Most important is that there is no requirement that you live with the child for two years before the adoption. That is why many of the U.S. citizens who have adopted from overseas in the past adopted orphans.

There are two types of orphan immigrant visas:

- an IR-3 visa classification, for orphans who have met the parents and whose adoptions were completed abroad, and
- an IR-4 classification, for orphans who, although in the legal custody of the U.S.

citizen parent or parents, still need to be legally adopted after reaching the United States, or who need to be readopted because the U.S. parents haven't yet seen the child.

In either case, the application process includes a number of complexities.

Because of these complexities, most Americans who adopt from overseas use an agency that specializes in international adoptions, although direct adoption is also possible. Even with an agency, expect the process to take at least six to twelve months. Although we can't provide you with a list of reputable agencies, two California-based groups that Nolo lawyers have had good experiences with are Adopt International, at 415-934-0300, www.adoptinter.org; and Adoption Connection, at 415-359-2494, www.adoptionconnection.org.

Be selective in choosing an adoption agency—look for one that has been doing adoptions for a number of years, successfully completes a comparatively large number per year, serves the countries in which you're interested, and is happy to show you evidence that it's licensed and comes with good references.

CAUTION

If the U.S. petitioner has a criminal record, see an attorney. Under the Adam Walsh Child Protection and Safety Act of 2006, U.S. citizens and lawful permanent residents who have been convicted of any "specified offense against a minor" are prohibited from filing a family-based immigrant petition on behalf of any beneficiary (whether a child or not). USCIS will run security checks on all petitions and may call the petitioner in for fingerprinting. If the petitioner has a conviction for one of the specified offenses against a minor, then the petition will not be approved unless USCIS determines that the U.S. petitioner poses no risk to the beneficiary.

CAUTION

You'll also need to follow the rules of the country you're adopting from. Not every country allows international adoptions, and those that do usually impose various requirements on the parents. For example, some countries refuse to allow single-parent adoptions, or require that adopting parents be of a certain age. This chapter covers only the U.S. requirements; you'll need to research the international requirements with the help of your adoption agency or by going to the DOS website at http://adoption.state.gov, which provides information about each country's special requirements.

A. Who Qualifies as an Orphan Child

A child under 16 years of age (or under 18, if he or she is being adopted along with a brother or sister under 16) is considered an orphan if the child meets any of the following conditions:

- both parents have died or have disappeared
- the sole or surviving parent is incapable of providing the proper child care and has, in writing, released the child for adoption and emigration, or
- both father and mother have abandoned the child, or have become separated or lost from the child—and the legal authorities in the child's country, recognizing the child as abandoned, have granted legal custody of the child to an orphanage.

However, if the child has been placed with other people, or temporarily in the orphanage, or if one or both parents continue to maintain contact—for example, sending gifts, writing letters, or showing that they have not ended their parental obligations to the child—the child will not be considered an orphan by the U.S. government. You also can't get around the requirements by having the overseas parent or parents "abandon" the child into the hands of the adopting U.S. couple or person.

B. Who Can Petition for an Orphan Child

Only U.S. citizens are allowed to file a visa petition for an orphan child; lawful permanent residents may not do so. A number of other regulations also apply.

- If a married couple is adopting, only one of them need be a U.S. citizen (but both have to be age 21 or over and sign the petition).
- If the U.S. citizen is not married, then he or she must be at least 25 years of age before filing the petition. In addition, if the citizen was under 25 when the foreign adoption took place, the adoption will be considered invalid, and the citizen will have to readopt the child after the child reaches the United States (if allowed in his or her state of residence).
- The orphan child must be less than 16 years of age when the petition is filed (or under 18, if the parents are also petitioning for the child's brother or sister who is under 16).
- The adopting married couple, or single person, must have completed certain pre-adoption requirements, such as a home study, before filing the petition. (See Section C, below.)
- The adopting married couple, or single person, must have seen the child in the orphan's country before or during the adoption proceedings, or show that they'll be able to "readopt" the child in the United States.

CAUTION

Beware of the lawbreakers. In some developing countries, kidnapping poor children and then selling them for adoption to childless couples in the United States and Europe has become scandalously rampant.

Your search for a child of your own should not cause the kidnapping or sale of another person's child. Before you sign up with any adoption organization, check its references with friends who have worked with the organization—or ask for the names of some former clients, and then call them. Above all, avoid direct arrangements with the surviving parent or private individuals acting as brokers for a fee.

International Adoption for Lesbians and Gays

Only a handful of countries allow adoption by same-sex couples, and many countries prohibit adoption by an openly gay person. Most countries strongly prefer that the adopting parents be married, which effectively discriminates against many same-sex couples, who have been denied the right to marry, as well as lesbian and gay individuals.

At least one country (China) is so determined not to grant adoptions to lesbians and gays that it requires adoptive parents to sign an affidavit swearing that they are heterosexual. Apparently undeterred, a large number of same-sex couples have successfully adopted Chinese girls who were being raised in orphanages.

If you are proceeding with a foreign adoption, you may opt to keep your sexual orientation—and your relationship with your partner—hidden from the host country. It is a judgment call whether or not you tell the agency helping you with the adoption. Many agencies operate on a wink-and-nod basis—they are fully aware of the nature of your relationship with your partner, but refer to the partner as a "roommate" in their reports to the host country, and simply ignore the issue of sexual orientation.

For more about adoption and parenting for same-sex couples, check out *A Legal Guide for Lesbian & Gay Couples*, by Denis Clifford, Frederick Hertz, and Emily Doskow (Nolo).

C. Pre-Adoption Requirements

To protect the child and to ensure that the adopting parent or parents will care for the child properly, the immigration laws require what's called a "home study" before an adoption decree is finalized or before a petition for an orphan child will be approved. Many couples take care of this first, as part of an advance processing application, described below in Section D1.

The purpose of the home study is to allow the state agency handling adoptions to investigate the future home of the child (and any adult living in it) and verify whether the adopting couple, or the single person, is psychologically and economically fit to adopt a child. Most home studies take about three months.

The home study must result in a favorable report recommending the proposed adoption. The report must be signed by an official of a state agency, or an agency licensed by the state in which the child will live with the adopting parent or parents. The home study should be submitted to USCIS within six months of the date it is completed.

This report must contain the following information:

- the financial ability of the parent or parents to raise and educate the child
- a discussion of possible negative factors, such as a history of substance abuse, child abuse, sexual abuse, domestic violence, criminal behavior, or past denials of adoptions or unfavorable home study reports
- a detailed description of the living accommodations, including special accommodations for a child with disabilities or medical issues, and
- a factual evaluation of the physical, mental, and moral ability of the adopting parent or parents, including observations made during personal interviews.

In addition to the home study, other pre-adoption conditions may be required by some states before an adoption petition may be filed with local courts. Therefore, if you are planning to adopt the orphan child in the United States, you must first comply with these state rules.

In every state, there is one main agency that oversees adoptions. To contact the local representative of your state agency, check your state government website or look in the telephone book under Adoption, Child Welfare, or Social Services.

D. Starting the Adoption Process

The first steps toward adoption depend in part on whether or not the orphan child has been identified (chosen).

1. When the Child Is Not Yet Identified

If a particular child has not yet been singled out and the parents are going abroad to locate an orphan child for adoption, or for adoption after arrival in the United States, they should file an advance processing application, as follows:

- ☐ Form I-600A, Application for Advance Processing of Orphan Petition, signed by the U.S. citizen and, if married, the spouse. (See sample at end of this chapter.)
- ☐ Proof of petitioner's U.S. citizenship. (See Chapter 21.)
- ☐ If married, evidence of the spouse's U.S. citizenship or lawful legal status in the United States.
- ☐ Marriage certificate, divorce or annulment decree, or death certificate, as evidence of present and previous marital status.
- ☐ Fees of $85 each for fingerprints of the U.S. citizen and, if married, of the spouse. You can pay by check or money order, made out to the U.S. Department of Homeland Security. Also, all adults aged 18 years or older who live in the household must be fingerprinted. (See Chapter 21, Section F.)
- ☐ Evidence of petitioner's age, if unmarried.

- ☐ A favorable home study report. If the home study report is not yet available, it must be submitted within one year from the date of filing the advance application. Otherwise, the application will be considered to have been abandoned.
- ☐ Proof of compliance with any pre-adoption requirements of the state in which the child will live if the adoption is to be completed in the United States (see Section C).
- ☐ A filing fee (currently $720).

After the advance processing application has been approved by USCIS, you have 18 months in which to locate an orphan child and continue with the application process. If you're not having any luck finding an orphan child within one year, you can ask USCIS for a onetime extension. Do so within the 90 days before the USCIS approval notice expires—don't wait until it has already expired. You must make the request in writing, to the same office that approved your Form I-600A. With your letter, you must include an updated or amended home study report. You'll probably also need to request a onetime re-fingerprinting (without charge), since the original fingerprints are valid for only 15 months.

If you miss the deadline to ask for an extension, or you still can't find a child even after an extension, you basically need to start over. That means you'll have to submit a new advance processing application (with a new filing fee) if the child has not yet been identified, or a petition as described below (which also requires the filing fee of $720) if the child has been identified.

When you look at the sample I-600A, you'll notice that it assumes you've already figured out which country you plan to adopt a child from, and asks questions about your travel plans. But what if you end up being unable to find a child in that country? If you're still within the 18-month approval period, you can request a onetime change of country, at no extra charge. To do so, you'll need to send a letter to the same USCIS office that approved the I-600A petition. However, if you later want to change the country of adoption a second time, you'll need to file USCIS Form I-824, Application for Action on an Approved Application or Petition, along with a filing fee (currently $405). The reason for all this paperwork is that by now, USCIS will have notified the U.S. consulate in the country you originally planned to adopt from, and now needs to notify a different consulate instead (you'll specify which one in Part 2 of Form I-824).

Can You Bring the Child to the U.S. First?

It's frustrating for parents eager to bring an orphan child into their home to have to wait for all the immigration procedures to be completed. In light of this, the U.S. government tries to give high priority to orphan petitions. However, the government doesn't smile upon efforts by parents to get around the U.S. immigration laws, for example by bringing the child in on a tourist or student visa, and attempting to complete the adoption and immigration processes afterward. Basically, this won't work. In rare cases, however, USCIS will grant humanitarian parole to allow an orphan into the U.S. even before the immigration procedures have been finished—most often because of a medical or similar emergency. You're best off consulting an experienced immigration attorney for help in requesting humanitarian parole.

---

2. When the Child Is Identified

When the adopting parent or parents have identified the orphan child they wish to adopt, they can immediately file a petition for the child at the appropriate USCIS Service Center. (See the USCIS website at www.uscis.gov for the exact address.) Or, if the U.S. citizen will be overseas to adopt or locate the orphan, you can file the petition with the U.S. consulate in the country of the child's residence.

This can be done even if the advance processing application has not yet been approved or has not yet been filed. If the advance processing application has been filed but not approved, include a copy of the filing receipt with the petition. If it has already been approved, include a copy of the approval notice.

You must file all the documents listed in Section D1 above (except Form I-600A), as well as:

☐ Form I-600, Petition to Classify Orphan as an Immediate Relative

☐ the birth certificate of the orphan child, who must be under 16 years of age when the petition is filed

☐ death certificates of the parents of the child or proof of legal abandonment by both the father and mother

☐ the adoption decree or evidence that you have legal custody of the orphan and are working toward adoption, and

☐ filing fee (currently $720) unless you're filing based on an approved I-600A filed within the previous 18 months, in which case you don't need to pay the fee.

E. After the Petition Is Approved

If the petition is filed and approved by USCIS in the United States, the entire file is sent to the U.S. consulate in the country in which the child lives.

The consular officer then investigates the child. This may take either a few days or several months. The investigation aims to confirm that the child:

• meets the legal definition of an orphan, and

• does not have an illness or disability that was not described in the orphan petition.

A long delay in the adoption process of an orphan child can cause would-be parents much anxiety. However, keep in mind that the investigation is performed as a service to protect adopting parents from the heartbreaking situation that could develop if the child later proved not to be available for adoption.

Meeting Face-to-Face

The American individual or couple who wishes to adopt need not have seen the child personally before filing the visa petition if the adoption is to be done in the United States. However, if you are going to adopt a child to raise as your own for the rest of your life, you will likely want to find out what the child looks like, how you react to each other, what the child's physical condition is, and other imperceptible factors that only a face-to-face encounter can provide. Most people prefer to visit the child abroad before beginning adoption proceedings.

F. Filing for a Visa

When the petition is approved, the case will be transferred to the U.S. consulate in the orphan child's country of residence, for immigrant visa processing. (See Chapter 17 for advice and instructions on consular processing.)

In addition to the documents ordinarily required for consular processing, you'll need to bring the child's final adoption decree or proof of custody from the foreign government.

After receiving an immigrant visa, the orphan child can then enter the United States as a permanent resident. If the child has not yet been adopted in the foreign country, the U.S. citizen or couple can proceed to adopt the child according to the laws of the state in which they live.

G. Automatic Citizenship for Adopted Orphans

Under the Child Citizenship Act of 2000, orphans who enter on IR-3 visas (meaning the adoption is legally complete before they enter the U.S.) become citizens as soon as they enter the United States, and should receive a citizenship certificate by mail from USCIS within about six weeks.

Orphans who enter the U.S. on IR-4 visas will become U.S. citizens as soon as their adoptions are complete. To obtain proof of their citizenship, the parents will need to apply to their local USCIS office, using Form N-643K.

Sample Form I-600A, Application for Advance Processing of Orphan Petition (page 1)

OMB No. 1615-0028; Expires 03/31/15

Department of Homeland Security
U.S. Citizenship and Immigration Services

Form I-600A, Application for Advance Processing of Orphan Petition

Do not write in this block   **For USCIS Use Only**

It has been determined that the:	Fee Stamp

☐ Married   ☐ Unmarried
prospective adoptive parent will furnish proper care to a beneficiary orphan if admitted to the United States.

There:

☐ are   ☐ are not
preadoptive requirements in the State of the child's proposed residence.

The following is a description of the preadoption requirements, if any, of the State of the child's proposed residence:

_____

_____

The preadoption requirements, if any:
☐ have been met.   ☐ have not been met.

DATE OF FAVORABLE
DETERMINATION

DD

DISTRICT

File number of applicant, if applicable: _____

Type or print legibly in black ink.
This application is made by the named prospective adoptive parent for advance processing of an orphan petition.

BLOCK I - Information About the Prospective Adoptive Parent

1. My name is: *(Last)*   *(First)*   *(Middle)*

LERNER   Cora   Lynn

2. Other names used *(including maiden name if appropriate)*:

ADAMS, Cora Lynn

3. I reside in the U.S. at: *(C/O if appropriate)*

444 5th Street
(Number and Street)   *(Apt. No.)*

Fremont   CA   94536
(Town or City)   *(State)*   *(Zip Code)*

4. Address abroad *(if any)*:

_____
(Number and Street)   *(Apt. No.)*

_____
(Town or City)   *(State or Province)*

_____
(Country)

5. I was born on: *(mm/dd/yyyy)*   09/16/1980

In:

Fort Bragg   CA
(Town or City)   *(State or Province)*

USA
(Country)

6. My telephone number is: *(include area code)*

510-555-1212

7. I am a citizen of the United States through:

☒ Birth   ☐ Parents   ☐ Naturalization

If acquired through naturalization, provide the following:

a. Name under which you naturalized:

_____

b. Naturalization certificate number:

_____

c. Date of naturalization *(mm/dd/yyyy)*:

_____

d. Place of naturalization:

_____

If acquired through parentage, have you obtained a certificate in your own name based on that acquisition?

☐ No   ☐ Yes

If not, submit evidence of citizenship. See **Page 2** of the instructions.

Have you or any person through whom you claimed citizenship ever lost U.S. citizenship?

☒ No   ☐ Yes *(If "Yes," attach detailed explanation)*

Received	Trans. In	Ret'd Trans. Out	Completed

Sample Form I-600A, Application for Advance Processing of Orphan Petition (page 2)

BLOCK I - Information About the Prospective Adoptive Parent *(Continued)*

8. My marital status is:

    a. [X] Married   [ ] Widowed   [ ] Divorced   [ ] Single

    b. If you are now or if you have been married, how may time have you been married (include current marriage if married): _____

9. If you are now married, provide the following information:

    Date of present marriage *(mm/dd/yyyy)*:   Place of present marriage:

    10/04/2009   Fremont, CA

    Name of present spouse:

LERNER	Kenneth	Jon	
(Last)	*(First)*	*(Middle)*	*(Maiden, if any)*

    Date of birth of present spouse *(mm/dd/yyyy)*:   Place of birth of present spouse:

    07/08/1979   Buffalo, NY

    My spouse has been married ___1___ time(s) (include current marriage)

    My spouse resides: [X] With me   [ ] Apart from me *(provide address below)*

Number and Street	Apt. No.	City	State	Country

BLOCK II - General Information

10. Name and address of organization or individual assisting you in locating or identifying an orphan.

    Name of organization or individual: Address of organization or individual:

    Adopt International   3705 Haven Avenue, Menlo Park, CA

11. Do you plan to travel abroad to locate or adopt a child?   [ ] No   [X] Yes

12. Does your spouse, if any, plan to travel abroad to locate or adopt a child?   [ ] No   [X] Yes

13. If the answer to **Question 11** or **12** is "Yes," provide the following information, if known:

    a. Your date of intended departure *(mm/dd/yyyy)*:   **b.** Your spouse's date of intended departure *(mm/dd/yyyy)*:

    02/10/2015   02/10/2015

    c. Names of city, province, country you are traveling to:

    Datong, Shanxi, China

14. Will the child be adopted abroad after having been personally seen and observed by you and your spouse (if married)?   [ ] No   [X] Yes

15. Will the preadoption requirements, if any, of the child's proposed State of residence be met prior to or after the child enters the United States?   [ ] No   [X] Yes

16. From what country do you plan to adopt, if known?

    China

17. Where do you wish to file your orphan petition? *(Complete **one** of the options below)*

    The USCIS office located at: The U.S. Embassy or consulate at:

    _____ **OR** Beijing, China

Form I-600A (Rev. 03/05/13) N Page 2

Sample Form I-600A, Application for Advance Processing of Orphan Petition (page 3)

BLOCK II - General Information *(Continued)*

18. Do you plan to adopt more than one child?   [X] No   [ ] Yes

    If "Yes," how many children do you plan to adopt? _____

BLOCK III - Accommodations for Individuals With Disabilities and Impairments *(Read the information in the instructions before completing this section.)*

19. **I am requesting an accommodation:**

    1. Because of my disability(ies) and/or impairment(s).   [X] No   [ ] Yes

    2. For my spouse because of his or her disability(ies) and/or impairment(s).   [X] No   [ ] Yes

    3. For my household member because of his or her disability(ies) and/or impairment(s).   [X] No   [ ] Yes

    If you answered "Yes," check any applicable box. Provide information on the disability(ies) and/or impairment(s) for each person:

    [ ] Deaf or hard of hearing and request the following accommodation(s) (if requesting a sign-language interpreter, indicate which language (e.g., American Sign Language)):

    _____

    [ ] Blind or sight-impaired and request the following accommodation(s):

    _____

    [ ] Other type of disability(ies) and/or impairment(s) (describe the nature of the disability(ies) and/or impairment(s) and accommodation(s) being requested):

    _____

Certification of Prospective Adoptive Parent

I certify, under penalty of perjury under the laws of the United States of America, that the foregoing is true and correct and that I will care for an orphan/orphans properly if admitted to the United States.

Cora Lynn Lerner
(Signature of Prospective Adoptive Parent)

July 15, 2014
Executed on (Date)

Certification of Married Prospective Adoptive Parent Spouse

I certify, under penalty of perjury under the laws of the United States of America, that the foregoing is true and correct and that my spouse and I will care for an orphan/orphans properly if admitted to the United States.

Kenneth John Lerner
(Signature of Prospective Adoptive Parent Spouse)

July 15, 2014
Executed on (Date)

Signature of Person Preparing Form, If Other Than Petitioner

I declare that this document was prepared by me at the request of the petitioner and is based entirely on information of which I have knowledge.

_____   _____
(Signature)   *Executed on (Date)*

Street Address and Room or Suite No./City/State/Zip Code

Form I-600A (Rev. 03/05/13) N Page 3

The Diversity Visa Lottery

In 1990, Congress created a new green card category to help balance out the numbers of immigrants coming from different countries, by opening up green card opportunities for people from countries that don't send many immigrants to the United States. Although the official name for this category is the "diversity visa," most people know it as the "visa lottery," because winners—50,000 in total—are selected through a random drawing. (The drawing is done by a computer.)

The visa lottery is held once a year. Every year the U.S. government looks to see which countries have sent the fewest immigrants to the United States in the last five years, and accordingly adds to or subtracts from the list of countries whose natives are allowed to put their names into the drawing. Diversity visas are divided among six geographic regions. No one country can receive more than 7% of the available diversity visas in any year.

You can enter the lottery if you are a native of one of the listed countries and meet certain other requirements. One of the latest requirements is purely technological—all applicants must now submit their applications through the Internet and attach a digital photo.

If you win the lottery, you've won the right to apply for green cards for yourself, your spouse, and your unmarried children under age 21—but no more than the right to apply. You can still be refused a green card for many reasons, including because of delays by the U.S. government causing you to miss the deadline, or because you've failed to meet the educational, health, or financial criteria for the diversity visa and green card.

Certain risks come with applying for the lottery. For example, if you win the lottery but are ultimately refused a green card, you've announced to the U.S. government that you're hoping to get a green card. That can make it more difficult to obtain or extend short-term visas to the United States—such as student or visitor visas. (Most short-term visas require you to assure the U.S. government that you have every intention of returning home afterward.) Even entering the lottery and losing is something you must declare on any later applications for U.S. visas, and it may be taken into account in considering whether you'll really return home on time.

! CAUTION

The lottery changes every year and could disappear entirely. It is an annual event, with a slightly different set of rules, including qualifying countries, every year. Recently the U.S. Congress discussed eliminating the diversity lottery, as part of its proposed comprehensive immigration reform. (The idea was to instead favor visas for highly educated workers in the science and engineering fields.) You'll need to keep your eyes on the Legal Updates on Nolo's website, and double check with the U.S. State Department during the year in which you'll be applying. The rules are usually announced around September, and posted on the State Department website at www.travel.state.gov.

Details of the Lottery That Began in 2013

At the time this book went to print, the most recent lottery had begun in 2013 (which the government calls "DV-2015"). Applications were accepted between noon on October 1, 2013 and noon on November 2, 2013. Entrants could check the status of their entries beginning May 1, 2014, at www.dvlottery.state.gov/ESC. Natives of the following countries were not eligible (meaning that people who were natives of any other country in the world were allowed to enter):

Bangladesh	Jamaica
Brazil	Mexico
Canada	Nigeria
China (mainland, not including Macau, Taiwan, or Hong Kong)	Pakistan
	Peru
Colombia	Philippines
Dominican Republic	South Korea
Ecuador	United Kingdom (except Northern Ireland) and its dependent territories
El Salvador	
Haiti	
India	Vietnam

CAUTION

Beware of lottery scams. Every year, fraudulent emails and letters are sent to DV applicants. The scammers pose as the U.S. government—with increasingly sophisticated methods, such as including official-looking images of the U.S. flag, Capitol building, or White House—then attempt to get money from DV applicants. Don't be fooled! Starting with DV-2012, the government does *not* personally contact winners. Information about your DV entry will be available only through the official government website. To double check that it's really a government website look for the ".gov" suffix on the Internet address. The same goes for any visa-related emails you receive. If they're not from an address ending with ".gov," be suspicious.

A. Who Qualifies for the Lottery

Whether or not you're allowed to enter the lottery depends on whether:

- you are a native of one of the countries that is eligible that year, and
- you meet the educational requirements.

It doesn't matter if you've already got an application for a green card underway in another category, for example through a family member or employer—you can still enter the diversity visa lottery.

1. What Country—or Countries— You're a Native Of

Lottery applicants should make sure that they can actually claim what the law describes as "nativity" in an eligible country. Nativity is usually based on having been born in the country. Living in a country is not enough, even if you have residence rights there.

You may, however, be a native of more than one country. This can be helpful for lottery purposes if you were born in one of the ineligible countries, or if your native country has a lot of people applying

for the lottery from it. There are two ways to gain nativity in a country other than having been born there:

- If your spouse was born in an eligible country, you can claim your spouse's country of birth for lottery purposes.
- If neither of your parents was born in your birth country or made a home there at the time of your birth, you may be able to claim nativity in one of your parents' countries of birth.

And remember, the list of eligible countries changes slightly every year, so check the State Department's instructions before you apply.

CAUTION

You must choose on which country to base your application. Even if you're a native of more than one eligible country, you can't apply for the lottery more than once within a single year.

Immigrant Story: Applying Based on Spouse's Country

Azu was born and lives in Nigeria. Although in past years he's been able to enter the visa lottery, he has never won—and this year, Nigeria was dropped off the list of eligible countries.

However, Azu's wife Marie is a native of Cameroon. So he submits a lottery application based on her country—and wins!

Assuming the U.S. consulate in Nigeria can process his case quickly enough, Azu, his wife, and their two unmarried children can become U.S. permanent residents.

2. The Educational Requirements

Applicants from qualifying countries must have either:

- a high school diploma or its equivalent, meaning a successfully completed twelve-year course of elementary plus secondary education that would qualify you to enter a U.S. college or university, or
- a minimum of two years' work experience (within the last five years) in a job that normally requires at least two years' training or experience. American job offers are not necessary. However, you won't be allowed to argue about how much experience your job requires—this judgment will be made based on a list of job titles and descriptions kept by the U.S. government in an online database called O*NET, at www.onetonline.org. (To check this out yourself, go to the website and click "Find Occupations.")

You won't be asked to prove your educational qualifications on the lottery application—but that doesn't mean you can puff up the truth. If you win the lottery, you will have to come up with proof of your education as part of the green card application.

B. How to Apply for the Lottery

A new application period starts every year, usually in early October. You can submit one application—and only one. People who try to apply more than once will have all their lottery visa applications tossed out of the running. Husbands, wives, and children in the same family can, however, submit separate applications if each one who applies separately meets the educational and other eligibility criteria.

No fee is charged for applying, so watch out for websites and consultants who claim that there is, or who charge you a lot of money for supposed "special" handling. The application is fairly simple and can be done by yourself, or with minimal help from another person.

> **CAUTION**
> **Registrations submitted one year are not held over to the next.** So if you are not selected one year, you need to reapply the next year to be considered.

1. The Application

We can't give you a sample application form, because there isn't one—the one and only way to apply is online, using a computer. (In previous years, paper applications were allowed, but no longer.)

The Web address at which to apply is www.dvlottery.state.gov. It doesn't matter what country you're in when you submit the online application. You can start the application and then stop without submitting it, for example if you realize you're missing a piece of information—but you cannot save or download your work. And if you try to submit an application and the system rejects it, you can try again until you succeed.

Once you start your application, the system will give you only an hour in which to submit it before it erases all the information you've entered. So, you'll need to assemble all the needed information ahead of time, and plan for a time when you can complete the entire application within that hour.

Here's what you'll probably be asked when you go to the State Department website to apply:

1. Full name—last name (family or surname), first name, middle name
2. Date of birth—day, month, year
3. Gender—male or female
4. City where you were born
5. Country where you were born (use your country's current name, even if it had a different name when you were born there—for example, Myanmar instead of Burma)
6. Country of eligibility or chargeability—normally, the same as your country of birth. However, if you were born in a country that is not eligible for the DV lottery, you may be able to claim your spouse's country of birth, or your parents' country of birth, if different

from your own. See "What Country—or Countries—You're a Native Of," above.

7. Entry photograph(s)—you'll need to submit digital photographs of you, your spouse, and all your children (unmarried, under age 21), if you have any. See the technical information on the State Department website, www.travel.state.gov.

CAUTION

Make sure to get the digital photographs right. Your entry will be disqualified—or your visa later refused—if you don't submit all the required photographs or the photographs are not recent, have been manipulated, or fail to meet the specifications detailed on the Department of State website.

8. Mailing address—in care of, address, city/town, district/country/province/state, postal code/zip code, country

9. Country where you live today

10. Phone number (optional)

11. Email address (optional)

12. What is the highest level of education you have achieved, as of today? (You don't need to list all your schooling, just the last type of school you completed, for example high school, vocational school, university, or graduate school.)

13. Marital status—unmarried, married, divorced, widowed, or legally separated.

14. Number of children that are unmarried and under 21 years of age (no need to mention children who are ineligible either because they are U.S. legal permanent residents or U.S. citizens or are over 21 years old or married).

15. Spouse information—name, date of birth, gender, city/town of birth, country of birth, photograph.

16. Children information—name, date of birth, gender, city/town of birth, country of birth, photograph.

CAUTION

If you are legally married and/or have children, be sure to include this information. This is important even if your spouse or children do not plan to become permanent residents. If you fail to include them on your original DV lottery entry, and they later try to apply for permanent residence based on your DV winning, your entire case will be disqualified. This applies only to people who were family members at the time the original application was submitted, not those acquired at a later date.

After you've successfully completed and submitted your online application, you'll get a confirmation screen, showing your name, other personal information, and a date/time stamp. It may take several minutes before you receive this screen. The confirmation doesn't mean you've won, it simply means your application went through okay. This is the only time you will be sent your confirmation number, so be sure to print out the confirmation screen for your records.

Be extra careful not to make typing errors. If your application contains a typing error, particularly in the spelling of your name, the State Department may throw it out. This is because it believes that people try to cheat the system by submitting more than one application with their name spelled slightly differently.

CAUTION

Don't sign off without writing down your confirmation number. You'll need this number in order to find out whether or not you are selected as a winner. But the one and only time you'll be given this number is right after you submit your online application. Write it down carefully and keep it in a safe place.

2. Notification of Winners

As of the DV-2012 lottery, winners are no longer notified by mail. The only way to find out whether or not you have been picked is to check the State Department website at www.dvlottery.state.gov. All entrants, including those not selected, will be able to check the status of their entries through this website. In order to access this information, you must have the confirmation number that was given you when you made your online entry.

C. After You Win—The Green Card Application

Unfortunately, winning the lottery doesn't guarantee you a green card. The government always declares more than 50,000 winners—but gives out only 50,000 green cards. This means if you don't follow up quickly or receive your interview on time, the supply of green cards could run out. You'll have to complete the process and have received your visa or green card by September 30th of the year following your selection. (For example, applicants in 2012, who will be notified in 2013, will lose their chance if they can't complete the process by September 30, 2014.)

This is a serious problem. The State Department and U.S. Citizenship and Immigration Services (USCIS, formerly called the INS) are so backed up that months can go by with no action, causing you to miss your opportunity altogether. One thing you can do to move your application forward is to make sure that the people handling it know about your September 30 deadline. Make a note, in big, bold letters, in the margins of your application, saying: **PLEASE EXPEDITE! DIVERSITY VISA APPLICANT. MUST PROCESS BY SEPTEMBER 30.** You can also write this on the front and back of the envelope that contains your application, and on your cover letter, if you have one. Despite these precautions, there may be delays over which you have little

control. Some people's applications get stalled while their security checks are being completed by the FBI (Federal Bureau of Investigation) and CIA (Central Intelligence Agency). Even if you've never done anything wrong, just having a common name can lead to delays, as the FBI and CIA check and double check your name and fingerprints against various databases.

Another problem is that, as with all green card applications, if you win the lottery, you still must prove that you are not "inadmissible" to the United States. For example, if you have been arrested for committing certain crimes, are considered a security risk, have spent too much time in the United States illegally, or are afflicted with certain physical or mental illnesses, you may be prevented from receiving a green card. (For more on inadmissibility, see Chapter 4.)

Proving that you'll be able to support yourself financially in the U.S. can be a challenge for lottery winners. If you can't show this, you'll be considered inadmissible as a potential "public charge"—that is, someone who may need government financial assistance. You will need to show that you are either self-supporting, have sufficient skills and/or education to find employment, or have friends or family who will support you once you're living in the United States. In 2014, for example, the U.S. government said that a family of four who were getting their green cards through the visa lottery would be presumed to need government assistance unless their income was $23,850 per year or more.

> **TIP**
> **You'll face less onerous financial requirements than most other green card applicants.** Most people applying for green cards must have a sponsor submit an Affidavit of Support for them on Form I-864, which shows that their sponsor can support them at 125% of the U.S. poverty guidelines. People getting green cards through the visa lottery, however, submit a shorter

and simpler Affidavit of Support, on Form I-134. Instead of showing an income that is at least 125% of the poverty guidelines, your sponsor needs only show an income that reaches 100%. You also have the option of filling out this form yourself if your income is sufficient, avoiding the need for a sponsor.

> **SEE AN EXPERT**
>
> **Don't miss your chance—get professional help.** A good lawyer will know the latest ways to get your application through the system quickly, and when and who to ask for speeded up handling.

The exact procedures for applying for the green card depend on where you're living now, and whether you've spent any time illegally in the United States. If you're currently overseas, see Chapter 17 regarding consular processing. If you're in the United States, see Chapter 16 regarding adjustment of status. Also, if you're in the United States, realize that it's very unlikely you'll be allowed to apply for the green card unless you are currently in status on a valid, unexpired visa or other status—if not, you should definitely see a lawyer for assistance.

An important note if you are able to use your DV winning to apply for adjustment of status: On Form I-485, Part 2, where the form asks what is the basis for your application, check box "h: other" and fill in the answer: Diversity Visa Lottery Winner.

> **CAUTION**
>
> **Don't forget to pay the extra fees.** Lottery winners must pay a "diversity visa surcharge" in addition to the regular fees for applying for a green card. At the time this book was published, the fee was $330.

D. How to Bring Your Spouse and Children

For the lottery application itself, it's very simple to include your spouse and children—in fact, you're required to name them on your application, unless you and your spouse are legally separated (by court order) or divorced, or your children are U.S. citizens or permanent residents. Simply include your spouse and children's names, and remember to attach a digital photograph of each one to your lottery submission. (And remember that your spouse may, if eligible, submit a separate lottery application for him- or herself, which includes your name and those of your children.)

It doesn't matter whether your spouse and children plan to come with you to the U.S. or not—you must still list their names and provide their photos with your lottery application. If you don't list them, not only will they lose their chance to immigrate with you if you win, but your entire application will be disqualified! In fact, even if you and your spouse are no longer living together, you must provide your spouse's photo unless you're either legally separated (by court order) or divorced—a requirement that causes problems for some applicants.

What if you give birth to a child or get married after submitting the lottery application? That's okay—your new child and spouse will be allowed to immigrate with you if you win. However, you may be asked to provide extra proof that this relationship wasn't created fraudulently, to get the newly added person a green card.

If you win the lottery, the rules and paperwork for your family get more complicated. First, you need to figure out which family members are allowed to immigrate with you. Your spouse will be allowed, so long as you're legally married. Your children will also be allowed, so long as they're under 21 years of age and remain unmarried up to the date you're approved for green cards. Warn your children that they must remain unmarried until they've entered the U.S., or they'll lose their eligibility!

Next, each family member must submit a separate green card application, as described in either Chapter 17 (discussing consular processing for people coming from overseas) or Chapter 16 (discussing adjustment of status for people already in the United States and lucky enough to have a right to apply for a green card without leaving). No matter where you apply, the application will consist of several forms, expensive fees, medical examination results, and more.

Fortunately, only the lead person—the one who won the lottery—is required to meet the educational and work requirements of the lottery. However, each of your family members must separately prove that he or she doesn't have any of the health, criminal, or other problems that make people inadmissible to the United States. And you'll have to show that the family as a whole isn't likely to need government assistance.

You'll also need to pay for your entire family's airfare to the United States, and for housing once you get here. You won't receive any U.S. government assistance with your transition.

CAUTION

Be careful if you have a child about to turn 21. Getting older is, of course, something your children have no control over. But a child who turns 21 before being approved for a green card is, technically, no longer eligible. Fortunately, the law contains some protections for children in this situation. When and if you are approved for green cards, your child will be allowed to subtract from his or her age the amount of time between the date you could have first applied for the lottery and the date the winners were announced.

EXAMPLE: Jorge applies for the DV-2014 lottery program. The first date for applying was October 2, 2012 (although Jorge didn't get around to applying until November 10th). The results of the DV-2014 lottery are posted on the State Department website on July 15, 2013. A total of 280 days passed between October 2, 2012 and July 15, 2013. Jorge, as well as his wife and daughter, submit immigrant visa (green card) applications through their local U.S. consulate. They attend their interview on September 5, 2014. The consular officer notices that Jorge's daughter already turned 21, on June 29, 2014. However, the daughter can subtract 280 days from her age, which brings her back to age 20. (An easy way to look at this is that the daughter has been 21 for fewer than 280 days.) The consular officer grants the entire family their immigrant visas.

Your Brothers and Sisters as Immigrants

If you are a U.S. citizen, whether by birth, naturalization, or some other means, you can petition for your brothers and sisters to immigrate—but you must be at least 21 years old when you file the petition.

What's more, your brothers and sisters will be put in the family fourth preference visa category, which is so overloaded with applicants that they'll face a wait of at least ten years, and up to 24 years for applicants from some countries. (See Chapter 5 for more information on waiting periods in visa preference categories.) Nevertheless, the years can pass surprisingly quickly, so it may be worthwhile to get the petition in and reserve your brother or sister a place on the waiting list.

Once a visa number becomes available, your brother or sister will also be able to bring in his or her spouse and any unmarried children under age 21.

CAUTION

Congress may eliminate the F4 immigrant preference category for siblings. One of the proposals for comprehensive immigration reform would stop allowing U.S. citizens to petition for green cards for their siblings. While that proposed law—and immigration reform as a whole—had been tabled as of this book's print date (mid-2014), the chance remains that a similar provision could be included in future reform efforts. The good news is that all visa petitions for brothers and sisters accepted by USCIS before the law changes would likely be allowed to go forward.

A. Who Counts As Your Brother or Sister

The immigration laws contain specific definitions setting out who qualifies as a brother and sister in every family.

When it comes time to submit the paperwork for your brothers or sisters (the "visa petition"), you'll need to prove that they fit into one of these relationship categories. The sections below will explain the different possibilities and list the documentation that you'll need to provide as proof.

1. Legitimate Brother and Sister

If your mother and father were married and had other children, all of them are your legitimate brothers and sisters.

Be sure to add the following to your visa petition:
- ☐ your birth certificate, and
- ☐ your brothers' and sisters' birth certificates (to show that you have the same mother and father).

EXAMPLE: Your parents raised your cook's baby as their own child. But to file a petition for that baby, you would have to present proof that your birth certificate and the other child's birth certificate show the same father and mother. Of course, you cannot do this. There is no way you can petition for this person as your brother or sister.

The only way around this strict rule is for someone in the family to legally adopt the child before the child turns 16. If that is not possible, you will have to look for another way for the child to immigrate to the United States, such as an employment visa.

2. Half-Brother and Half-Sister

If you and another person have the same mother or father, but not both parents in common, that other person is your half-brother or half-sister.

It does not matter when the relationship of half-brother or half-sister occurred. As far as the immigration law is concerned, you can petition for them just as if they were your full-blooded brothers or sisters.

Be sure to add the following to your visa petition:
- ☐ your birth certificate, and
- ☐ your half-brothers' or sisters' birth certificates (showing that you have one parent in common).

3. Stepbrother and Stepsister

If your mother or father has married somebody who had children from a previous marriage or relationship, the children of your stepfather or stepmother would be your stepbrothers and stepsisters.

However, for purposes of immigration into the United States, you can file a petition for them only on one condition: Your mother or father must have married your stepparent before your 18th birthday.

Be sure to include the following documents with your visa petition:

- ☐ your birth certificate
- ☐ the birth certificates of your stepbrothers or stepsisters, and
- ☐ the marriage certificate of your mother or father and your stepparent, as well as documents showing that any and all of their marriages ended by death, divorce, or annulment.

4. Adopted Brother and Adopted Sister

If your mother and father have adopted a child according to the laws of the state or country they are in, that child is your adopted brother or adopted sister. Or, you may have been adopted by parents who may have other legitimate children of their own. Their children became your brothers and sisters when you were adopted into their family.

However, you can petition for your adopted sibling only if the adoption decree occurs before the 16th birthday of your adopted brother or sister if they are the petitioners, or before your own 16th birthday if you were the adopted child.

Be sure to include the following with your visa petition:

- ☐ the adoption decree, and
- ☐ your and your siblings' birth certificates to show you had the same parents.

B. Quick View of the Application Process

To get a green card as a brother or sister, the U.S. citizen must begin the process by submitting what's called a "visa petition" (using USCIS Form I-130). We're going to assume that the person reading this is the U.S. citizen.

Form I-130 serves to prove to the immigration authorities that your siblings are truly and legally yours. After that petition is approved, your siblings must complete their half of the process (with your help, of course) by submitting green card applications and attending interviews, possibly with you accompanying them. Their applications serve to prove that not only do they qualify as the brothers or sisters of a U.S. citizen, but that they're otherwise eligible for U.S. permanent residence.

However, the details of when and how your brothers or sisters complete their half of the process depend on whether they are living overseas or in the United States, as described in Section D, below.

 TIP
Other people can petition for your brother and sister at the same time. There's no limit on the number of visa petitions that can be filed for a person—and it can be good to have more than one pending, in case one petitioner dies, for example. Let's say your parents are or become permanent U.S. residents—in that case, they could file visa petitions for your siblings (if your siblings are unmarried) in the second preference visa category, which moves much faster than the fourth preference. But you could file for your siblings as well, as a backup.

C. Detailed Instructions for the Application Process

Now we'll break the application process down into individual procedures, some of which will be covered in this chapter, and others in later chapters—we'll tell you exactly where to turn for your situation. We'll start by discussing the visa petition, which the U.S. citizen must always prepare to begin the process.

1. Preparing the Form I-130 Visa Petition

To prepare the visa petition, the U.S. citizen will need to assemble and prepare the following:

- ☐ Form I-130, Petition for Alien Relative (available at www.uscis.gov/i-130; see the sample at the end of this chapter).
- ☐ Copy of a document proving your U.S. citizenship, such as a birth certificate, naturalization certificate, or passport.
- ☐ Copy of your birth certificate.
- ☐ Copy of your immigrating brother or sister's birth certificate.
- ☐ Any other required proof of your relationship as detailed in Section A, above.
- ☐ If you or any of your brothers and sisters have changed your name from the name that appears on the birth certificate, a copy of a marriage certificate or court document that explains the change.
- ☐ Filing fee (currently $420, but double check the USCIS website at www.uscis.gov). Pay this by check or money order—don't send cash. Make it out to the U.S. Department of Homeland Security.
- ☐ Form G-1145. This is optional, but filing it is a good idea, so that you'll receive an email and/or text notification from USCIS when your application has been accepted. Once USCIS sends you a receipt number, you can use that number to sign up to receive automatic email updates letting you know whenever mail is sent regarding your application.

 TIP

Here's how to sign up for automatic email updates: Go to www.uscis.gov and click "Check your Case Status" on the home page. Then, click "Sign-up for Case Updates." Enter your email address or mobile phone number in order to receive updates from USCIS on your case.

2. Submitting the Form I-130 Visa Petition

When the U.S. citizen has prepared and assembled all the items on the above list, he or she should make a complete copy of everything (even the check or money order—this copy will be helpful if USCIS loses the application, which happens more often than it should). Then send it to USCIS's Chicago or Phoenix lockbox (depending on where the U.S. citizen lives). The lockbox facility will forward it to the appropriate USCIS office— mailing information is on the USCIS website, www.uscis.gov/i-130.

After USCIS receives the I-130 and determines that nothing was left out, it will send the U.S. citizen a receipt notice. In the upper left-hand corner of this notice will be a receipt number, which you can use to track the status of the petition on USCIS's website, www.uscis.gov. There, you can also sign up to have USCIS send you automatic email updates about the petition.

Don't expect a final decision on the visa petition for many years, however. USCIS often decides to wait until a visa will soon be available to the immigrants before making a decision on the application—which, in the case of brothers and sisters, could be ten or more years away.

If you move during that wait, be sure to send your change of address to the USCIS office that has the visa petition.

**Immigrant Story:
Reuniting Brother and Sister**

Karl, from Sweden, became a U.S. permanent resident after winning the visa lottery. Although most of his family is uninterested in joining him in the United States, his twin sister, Karla, is extremely close to Karl and swears she'll never live more than 20 miles away from him.

Unfortunately, Karl must wait until he is a U.S. citizen to file a visa petition for Karla. As soon as his required five years of permanent residence have passed, he files a petition for naturalization. Within a year, Karl is a U.S. citizen. Now he petitions for Karla in the fourth preference category: But unfortunately, the wait in this category is over ten years long. During that time, Karla marries and has two children.

At last, Karla's Priority Date becomes current. After talking to her husband, they agreed to give life in the U.S. a try. Based on Karl's original application, Karla and her husband and children all apply for and receive U.S. green cards.

D. What Happens After Filing Form I-130

And now, your brothers or sisters must sit back and wait. There is no way to hurry up the process—see Chapter 5 for details on the visa preference system, and for information on how to track your brothers' or sisters' progress on the waiting list (using their priority dates).

Having a visa petition on file does not give your brothers or sisters any right to stay in the United States. In fact, it could cause them problems when they apply for tourist or other temporary visas, because the State Department will know that they also have plans to stay in the U.S. permanently.

If your brothers or sisters are already in the United States, they cannot become permanent residents unless they remain in legal status during all the time they are in the country. They will probably have to return to their home country and proceed with consular processing (see Chapter 17), unless they're lucky enough to qualify for adjustment of status in the U.S. (see Chapter 16).

If your brothers or sisters are in the U.S. illegally, or have spent six or more months here illegally since 1997, they should talk to a lawyer about whether they'll be found inadmissible and barred from returning.

Once the immigrant visa is available to your brothers or sisters, they can extend the immigration privilege to their spouses and all unmarried children under 21 years of age at the same time, as "accompanying relatives."

CAUTION

A brother or sister who wants to come to the United States to visit during the waiting period must tell the U.S. consul when applying for a tourist or business visa that he or she has an approved visa petition. To be silent about this important fact will be looked upon as fraud in an immigrant visa file—and may mean a lost chance for a green card in the future. On the other hand, to be approved for the visa, the sibling will need plenty of evidence of intent to return on time.

Sample Form I-130, Petition for Alien Relative (as used for immigrating siblings of U.S. citizens) (page 1)

Department of Homeland Security
U.S. Citizenship and Immigration Services

OMB No. 1615-0012; Expires 12/31/2015

I-130, Petition for Alien Relative

DO NOT WRITE IN THIS BLOCK - FOR USCIS OFFICE ONLY

A#	Action Stamp	Fee Stamp

Section of Law/Visa Category
- [ ] 201(b) Spouse - IR-1/CR-1
- [ ] 201(b) Child - IR-2/CR-2
- [ ] 201(b) Parent - IR-5
- [ ] 203(a)(1) Unm. S or D - F1-1
- [ ] 203(a)(2)(A)Spouse - F2-1
- [ ] 203(a)(2)(A) Child - F2-2
- [ ] 203(a)(2)(B) Unm. S or D - F2-4
- [ ] 203(a)(3) Married S or D - F3-1
- [ ] 203(a)(4) Brother/Sister - F4-1

Petition was filed on: _____ (priority date)
- [ ] Personal Interview
- [ ] Pet. [ ] Ben. " A" File Reviewed
- [ ] Field Investigation
- [ ] 203(a)(2)(A) Resolved
- [ ] Previously Forwarded
- [ ] I-485 Filed Simultaneously
- [ ] 204(g) Resolved
- [ ] 203(g) Resolved

Remarks:

A. Relationship   You are the petitioner.   Your relative is the beneficiary.

1. I am filing this petition for my:
[ ] Spouse [ ] Parent [X] Brother/Sister [ ] Child

2. Are you related by adoption?
[ ] Yes [X] No

3. Did you gain permanent residence through adoption?
[ ] Yes [X] No

B. Information about you

1. Name (Family name in CAPS) / (First) / (Middle)
GRAY / Alexandria / Elaine

2. Address (Number and Street) / (Apt. No.)
555 Glasgow Road

(Town or City) / (State/Country) / (Zip/Postal Code)
Mission Hills / Kansas/USA / 66208

3. Place of Birth (Town or City) / (State/Country)
Brussels / Belgium

4. Date of Birth
03/22/1988

5. Gender
[ ] Male [X] Female

6. Marital Status
[ ] Married [ ] Single [ ] Widowed [ ] Divorced

7. Other Names Used (including maiden name)
BOFFIN, Alexandria Elaine

8. Date and Place of Present Marriage (if married)
06/15/2006, Bird City, Kansas

9. U.S. Social Security Number (If any)
123-12-1234

10. Alien Registration Number
N/A

11. Name(s) of Prior Spouse(s)
N/A

12. Date(s) Marriage(s) Ended

13. If you are a U.S. citizen, complete the following:
My citizenship was acquired through (check one):
- [ ] Birth in the U.S.
- [X] Naturalization. Give certificate number and date and place of issuance.
  14532, 12/13/2012, Kansas City, MO
- [ ] Parents. Have you obtained a certificate of citizenship in your own name?
  [ ] Yes. Give certificate number, date and place of issuance. [ ] No

14. If you are a lawful permanent resident alien, complete the following:
Date and place of admission for or adjustment to lawful permanent residence and class of admission.

14b. Did you gain permanent resident status through marriage to a U.S. citizen or lawful permanent resident?
[X] Yes [ ] No

C. Information about your relative

1. Name (Family name in CAPS) / (First) / (Middle)
BOFFIN / Ignace / Anton

2. Address (Number and Street) / (Apt. No.)
Van Cuppenstraat 85

(Town or City) / (State/Country) / (Zip/Postal Code)
Antwerp / Belgium / B-222

3. Place of Birth (Town or City) / (State/Country)
Brussels / Belgium

4. Date of Birth
07/29/1983

5. Gender
[X] Male [ ] Female

6. Marital Status
[ ] Married [ ] Single [ ] Widowed [ ] Divorced

7. Other Names Used (including maiden name)
none

8. Date and Place of Present Marriage (if married)
07/19/2003, Antwerp, Belgium

9. U.S. Social Security Number (If any)
None

10. Alien Registration Number
None

11. Name(s) of Prior Spouse(s)
N/A

12. Date(s) Marriage(s) Ended

13. Has your relative ever been in the U.S.? [X] Yes [ ] No

14. If your relative is currently in the U.S., complete the following:
He or she arrived as a:
(visitor, student, stowaway, without inspection, etc.)

Arrival/Departure Record (I-94)   Date arrived

Date authorized stay expired, or will expire, as shown on Form I-94 or I-95

15. Name and address of present employer (if any)
The Belgian Observer

Date this employment began
04/20/2003

16. Has your relative ever been under immigration proceedings?
[X] No [ ] Yes Where _____ When _____
[ ] Removal [ ] Exclusion/Deportation [ ] Rescission [ ] Judicial Proceedings

INITIAL RECEIPT _____ RESUBMITTED _____ RELOCATED: Rec'd _____ Sent _____ COMPLETED: Appv'd _____ Denied _____ Ret'd _____

Form I-130 (12/18/12) Y

Sample Form I-130, Petition for Alien Relative (as used for immigrating siblings of U.S. citizens) (page 2)

C. Information about your relative (continued)

17. List spouse and all children of your relative.

(Name)	(Relationship)	(Date of Birth)	(Country of Birth)
Eline Margaux BOFFIN	Wife	08/01/1984	Belgium
Justine Chloe BOFFIN	Daughter	09/04/2009	Belgium

18. Address in the United States where your relative intends to live.

(Street Address)	(Town or City)	(State)
555 Glasgow Road	Mission Hills	Kansas

19. Your relative's address abroad. (Include street, city, province and country)   Phone Number (if any)

Van Cuppenstraat 85, B-222 Antwerp, Belgium   02-123 45 67

20. If your relative's native alphabet is other than Roman letters, write his or her name and foreign address in the native alphabet.

(Name)   Address (Include street, city, province and country):

21. If filing for your spouse, give last address at which you lived together. (Include street, city, province, if any, and country):

From: To:

22. Complete the information below if your relative is in the United States and will apply for adjustment of status.

Your relative is in the United States and will apply for adjustment of status to that of a lawful permanent resident at the USCIS office in:

If your relative is not eligible for adjustment of status, he or she will apply for a visa abroad at the American consular post in:

(City)	(State)	(City)	(Country)

NOTE: Designation of a U.S. embassy or consulate outside the country of your relative's last residence does not guarantee acceptance for processing by that post. Acceptance is at the discretion of the designated embassy or consulate.

D. Other information

1. If separate petitions are also being submitted for other relatives, give names of each and relationship.

2. Have you ever before filed a petition for this or any other alien? ☐ Yes ☒ No

If "Yes," give name, place and date of filing and result.

WARNING: USCIS investigates claimed relationships and verifies the validity of documents. USCIS seeks criminal prosecutions when family relationships are falsified to obtain visas.

PENALTIES: By law, you may be imprisoned for not more than five years or fined $250,000, or both, for entering into a marriage contract for the purpose of evading any provision of the immigration laws. In addition, you may be fined up to $10,000 and imprisoned for up to five years, or both, for knowingly and willfully falsifying or concealing a material fact or using any false document in submitting this petition.

YOUR CERTIFICATION: I certify, under penalty of perjury under the laws of the United States of America, that the foregoing is true and correct. Furthermore, I authorize the release of any information from my records that U.S. Citizenship and Immigration Services needs to determine eligiblity for the benefit that I am seeking.

E. Signature of petitioner

Alexandria E. Gray   Date 08/05/2014   Phone Number (310) 555-1515

F. Signature of person preparing this form, if other than the petitioner

I declare that I prepared this document at the request of the person above and that it is based on all information of which I have any knowledge.

Print Name _____   Signature _____   Date _____

Address _____   G-28 ID or VOLAG Number, if any. _____

Form I-130 (12/18/12) Y Page 2

Refugees and Political Asylees

Since the Refugee Act of 1980 was passed by the U.S. Congress, many people fleeing persecution from their own countries have found a permanent haven in the United States. Those who made it to the U.S. on their own applied for what's called "asylum." (An unlimited number of people can apply for asylum every year.) Others were granted refugee status and a right to come to the U.S. while they were overseas. The U.S. president limits the number of refugees who'll be accepted every year—in recent years, the maximum has been set at between 70,000 and 90,000. Those fleeing natural disasters or war do not receive this permanent protection, but may receive what is called Temporary Protected Status. (See Section I, below.)

SEE AN EXPERT

You will need more help than what's in this book. This chapter explains the basic procedures and describes the immigration forms required for those claiming status as refugees and asylees. However, the full legal process requires much more than filling out forms. You must present the facts of your case, in detail, in a convincing and compelling manner. If, after reading the chapter, you decide that you may qualify as a refugee or asylee, it is best to consult an experienced immigration lawyer or other immigration professional. Many nonprofit organizations offer free or low-cost services to people fleeing persecution. (See Chapter 24.)

A. Who Qualifies

To qualify as either a refugee or asylee you must be unable or unwilling to return to your country because of actual persecution or a well-founded fear of persecution on account of your:

- race
- religion
- nationality
- membership in a particular social group, or
- political opinion.

Persecution can include such things as threats, violence, torture, inappropriate and abusive imprisonment, or a failure by the government to protect you from such things.

You do not have to provide evidence that you would be singled out individually for persecution if you can establish that:

- there is a pattern or practice in your country of persecuting groups of people similarly situated to you, and
- you belong to or identify with the groups of people being persecuted so that your fear is reasonable.

The persecution may have been by your government, or you can claim asylum by showing that you were persecuted by a group that your government is unable or unwilling to control, or that you fear such persecution.

For example, these might include guerrilla groups, warring tribes, or organized vigilantes. Again, however, the persecution must have some political or social basis—a member of a criminal network who comes after you just because you haven't paid him off is not persecution according to refugee law.

Although the law does not list types of persecution, it does, in one section, specify that refugees and asylees can include people who have undergone or fear a "coercive population control program" (such as forced abortion or sterilization). This provision was directed mainly at mainland China.

The most well-known kind of asylum is "political asylum," where an applicant is given safe haven in the U.S. because of persecution (past or future) based on political opinion. As mentioned earlier, however, asylum is also available if the persecution is based on race, religion, nationality, or membership in a particular social group. The definition of "membership in a particular social group" is still evolving. In recent years, this has allowed some applicants to gain protection based on having undergone or fearing cultural practices such as female genital cutting or forced marriage. Another social group recognized only in the last two decades is one based on sexual orientation. In some circumstances, gays, lesbians, and transgendered individuals who were persecuted in their home country, or fear such persecution in the future, have been granted asylum.

1. The Difference Between Asylees and Refugees

The difference between someone who can claim "asylee" status and someone who can claim "refugee" status has nothing to do with basic eligibility (both must meet the same standards). It simply refers to where you are when you file the application. To apply to be a refugee, you must be outside your country of nationality or country of residence but not within the borders of the United States. In addition, the president of the United States is empowered to recognize as a refugee any person who is still residing in his or her own country.

To apply to be an asylee, you must be either at the border or already inside the United States.

Although the standards are the same, there are major differences in the way that refugee and asylee applications are processed. One difference is that each year the U.S. President designates certain countries and areas of the world as places from which the U.S. will fill the annual refugee quota. No such designation exists for asylees. What that means is that if a person seeks refugee status from a country that is not designated under that year's quota, a U.S. consular officer can't accept the application, but will instead refer the person to the United Nations High Commissioner for Refugees.

Also, the U.S. government prioritizes the processing of refugee applications based on several factors, including familial relationships in the U.S. and country of origin. No such prioritizing occurs with asylum applications, which are generally handled on a first come, first served basis.

2. Challenges in Proving Your Case

The biggest challenge in applying, especially for asylees, is proving that you were, in fact, persecuted or you reasonably fear that you might be persecuted in the future. You can't just say "I was persecuted" or "I'm afraid" and expect to get a green card. But you probably didn't come to the U.S. with a lot of documents to prove what happened, if indeed any such documents exist. Nevertheless, you are required to at least attempt to obtain corroborating evidence of your persecution. (That's a fairly new development in U.S. asylum law, based on the 2005 REAL ID Act.)

Succeeding with your application will depend a great deal on your own ability to tell a detailed, compelling story of what occurred, including names, dates, places, and more. You'll probably need to write down the dates when everything you're talking about happened, and then read them several times to refresh your memory (unless you already have a better memory than most people, who probably couldn't tell you where they were on a particular date last week, much less last year).

Also realize that the person deciding your case is allowed to take into account your demeanor when testifying, as well as any previous statements you made while not under oath. This can create problems for people who, for example, have been culturally trained not to look anyone in the eye. Looking someone straight in the eye is, in the U.S., considered a sign of honesty, and the judge or asylum officer may interpret looking at your hands or at the floor as a sign that you're lying.

If you underwent torture or suffered other medical or psychological stress, it may help to get a written evaluation by a doctor who is trained in this area and can verify that you suffer from the effects of these things.

You'll also need to show that your own story matches up with accounts by independent sources of what goes on in your country. A good asylum application is accompanied by a thick stack of newspaper clippings, human rights reports, and more, all containing information about the kind of human rights violation you're describing. If, for example, you fled because local government officials were threatening to imprison you because you sent a letter to the editor protesting a political matter, you'd need to provide evidence that others who expressed similar political opinions have been imprisoned or threatened with prison. (And you'd definitely want to produce a copy of the newspaper's printing of your letter.)

B. Who Is Barred From Qualifying

A number of people are prohibited from becoming refugees or asylees in the United States.

1. Those Who Have Assisted in Persecution

The opportunity for refugee or asylum status is not open to anyone who has ordered, incited, assisted, or participated in the persecution of any other person owing to that person's race, religion, nationality, membership in a particular social group, or political opinion.

For example, this rule is often used to deny refugee status to military or police officials who assisted in persecuting minority or guerrilla groups (even though they may, indeed, fear for their life because members of those groups are seeking revenge against them).

2. Those Who Threaten U.S. Safety or Security

No one who has been convicted of a "particularly serious crime" and is therefore a danger to the community of the United States will be granted refugee or asylee status. There is no list of particularly serious crimes—the decision is made case by case, depending on the facts surrounding the crime. However, all "aggravated felonies" are considered particularly serious crimes—and, because of the immigration laws' strict definitions of aggravated felonies, some crimes that may have been called

misdemeanors when committed will be looked upon as aggravated felonies.

In addition, no person who has been convicted of a serious nonpolitical crime in a country outside the United States will be granted refugee or asylee status. However, people whose crimes were nonserious or political in nature may still qualify.

Furthermore, no person who has been involved in terrorist activity or who can reasonably be regarded as a threat to U.S. security will be granted refugee or asylee status.

As discussed in Chapter 4, the definition of who is a "terrorist" is broader than you might expect. It could, for example, be interpreted to cover people who have provided food or other "material support" to guerrillas or others trying to overthrow the government, or people who have given money to organizations whose aims the U.S. government believes are, at least in part, terrorist in nature. Asylum applicants who provided material support under duress (for example, at gunpoint) can in some cases overcome this barrier.

3. Those Who Have Resettled

Refugee status is also denied to refugees or asylees who have become "firmly resettled" in another country. A person is regarded as firmly resettled if he or she has been granted permanent residency, citizenship, or some other type of permanent resettlement in a nation other than the one from which he or she is seeking asylum. Other things taken into account are whether that person enjoyed the same kind of rights and privileges as citizens of the nation in which they lived, in areas like housing, employment, permission to hold property, and rights to travel.

C. How to Apply for Refugee Status

If you are outside the U.S. and believe you qualify as a refugee, there are a number of documents you are required to file—and a number of steps you must follow.

1. Filing the Application

You must prepare and submit the following forms:

- Form I-590, Registration for Classification as Refugee
- documentation of persecution or a detailed affidavit supporting your request for classification as a refugee
- Form G-325A, Biographic Information—for applicants 14 years old or over
- an assurance from a sponsor, which can be a responsible person or an organization, that employment and housing on entry will be arranged for you, and that you will be provided transportation to your final destination (usually accomplished through an umbrella organization called the American Council for Voluntary Agencies), and
- a medical examination report to ascertain that you are mentally sound and do not have a serious communicable disease.

2. Refugee Interview

After submitting your application, you will be interviewed by an overseas immigration officer who will decide whether you have been persecuted or have a well-founded fear of persecution because of your race, religion, nationality, political opinion, or membership in a particular social group.

3. Action on Your Refugee Application

If the overseas immigration officer decides that you meet the requirements and may be designated as a refugee, the application will be granted. You will have four months in which to enter the United States.

If the application is denied, there is no appeal. You have no further recourse because you are outside the United States and its legal mechanism of judicial review.

Once you have been granted status as a refugee, you will be granted work authorization for one year as soon as you enter the United States.

4. When Refugees Can Apply for a Green Card

After one year of physical presence as a refugee in the United States, during which you must not have violated certain laws or regulations, you, your spouse, and your children may apply for permanent residence (a green card).

If you are found to be eligible, you and your family will be given lawful permanent resident status. The date of your permanent residence will be the date that you first arrived in the United States as a refugee. You will be eligible to apply for citizenship five years from that date.

5. If Your Green Card Is Denied

If you are found ineligible for permanent residency, removal proceedings may be started against you and your family, and you will have to present your cases before an immigration judge. If this happens, consult with an experienced immigration lawyer who specializes in removal cases. (See Chapter 24.)

D. How to Apply for Asylum

If you are interested in applying for asylum, you must fill out various forms and explain your case to a USCIS officer or judge.

1. Where to Request Asylum

You can request asylum:

- upon arrival at the border or port of entry, if you are an alien stowaway, a crewman, or a passenger seeking admission into the United States
- at a removal hearing before the immigration judge, or
- by sending an application to USCIS, after which you'll be interviewed at one of the

Applying for a Work Permit

Some years ago, applicants for asylum were eligible for a work permit as soon as they submitted an I-589—but no more. Now, in order to apply for a work permit, you have to either win your case—which can take anywhere between a few months and several years—or be lucky enough to be left waiting for an unusually long time (150 days or more) with no initial decision by the U.S. government on your application.

This obviously creates hardships for asylum applicants, who have to find money to live on and potentially pay their lawyers with, until the case is won. You may want to find help from lawyers at a nonprofit organization who, if you're financially needy, will charge low or no fees.

Many asylum applicants do get a decision within 150 days, either an approval or a referral to an Immigration Judge, with an opportunity for the judge to decide your case within that time. If you do not, that is, the 150 days pass with no decision, or if your application for asylum is approved, you'll need to take steps to apply for a work permit (formally known as an Employment Authorization Document, or EAD).

Do so by filling out Form I-765 (available on the USCIS website). Most of this form is self-explanatory. On Question 16, if you've been waiting for 150 days or more with no decision, enter "(c)(8)." If your asylum application has already been approved, enter "(a)(5)." Follow the instructions on the form for what to include and where to send it.

Any steps on your part that delay processing of your application may lead USCIS or the Immigration Court to "stop the clock" on your case. That means that if you request a rescheduled asylum interview or do not accept the next available hearing date with the Immigration Judge, you may hurt your chances of getting a work permit before your asylum case is decided. For more information about this tricky rule, consult an experienced immigration attorney.

USCIS Asylum Offices. You can apply for asylum even if you're in the U.S. illegally— but understand that your application will be acted on within a matter of weeks, and if it is not approved, it will be forwarded to an Immigration Judge. If you cannot persuade the judge that you should be granted asylum, you may find yourself with an order of deportation and removal against you.

! CAUTION
Don't delay in preparing your application (if you're already in the U.S. and not in removal proceedings). The law says that applications for asylum must be submitted within one year of your entry into the United States. If you entered on a visa (that is, not illegally), USCIS policy is to allow you to proceed with your application period of "a reasonable time" after your visa-permitted stay expires. But this is up to the discretion of the USCIS officer deciding on your case. Similarly, time during which you had Temporary Protected Status (discussed in Section I, below) does not count toward your one year. If you've already spent more than a year here, talk to an immigration attorney. Exceptions are possible in rare cases, based on changed country conditions, changes in your circumstances that affect your eligibility for asylum, or other compelling reasons, such as your having been under the age of 18 when you first arrived in the United States.

2. Asylum Applications at the Border or Port of Entry

If you arrive at a U.S. border or port of entry and the officer says your visa isn't valid or you can't be admitted to the U.S., you can request asylum. The officer is supposed to refer you to another officer who is trained to understand, based on very little information, whether you have a believable and valid claim. Unfortunately, these officers do not act consistently, and there are many tragic reports of people being turned around and sent back to places where they were physically harmed.

If the officer denies your entry despite your request for asylum, you won't be allowed to reapply for U.S. entry for five years. You can, however, get around this by withdrawing your request for entry—in other words, by saying you changed your mind and don't want to enter the U.S. after all. But the border official has the option of deciding whether to allow you to get around the system in this way.

If the officer with whom you meet thinks you have a possible asylum case, you'll be placed in removal proceedings, where an immigration judge will consider your asylum claim (and any other relevant claims for immigration benefits you want to make). At this point, you'll have to prepare the application described in Section 3, below—and you should, if at all possible, get an attorney's help.

Immigrant Story: Filing Beyond the One-Year Deadline

Roberto came to the United States alone, without a visa or documents, when he was 14 years old. Three years later, he came out as a homosexual, and became publicly and actively involved in gay rights causes. Then, during a demonstration, Roberto was arrested by immigration agents.

Because Roberto had already been in the U.S. for three years, his lawyer had to make a special request to the judge to extend the one-year deadline for filing for political asylum.

Fortunately, the judge agreed to hear the asylum application based on two grounds: 1) that Roberto had entered the U.S. as an unaccompanied minor, and therefore could not have been expected to know about the one-year asylum filing deadline, and 2) that Roberto's circumstances had changed since he publicly came out as a homosexual, which could make him subject to persecution in El Salvador.

---

3. Preparing and Filing Your Asylum Application

The following documents should be mailed to a USCIS Regional Service Center, if you are not in removal proceedings, or submitted in person to the Immigration Judge, if you are already in proceedings:

☐ Form I-589, Application for Asylum and for Withholding of Removal—one original and two copies. (Available at www.uscis.gov/i-589; see the sample at the end of this chapter.) Also make two copies of all supplementary documents. There is no filing fee for this form. Your spouse and children may be included in the application, as long as you supply an additional copy of your filled-out Form I-589 and attached documents for each. If you include your family members, they will also be granted asylum if you win or be placed in removal proceedings with you if you lose. (Regardless of whether you take the required steps to officially include them, you must provide their names and other requested information on your Form I-589.)

☐ One color passport-style photo of you and each family member applying with you. Write the person's name in pencil on the back.

☐ Copies (three) of your passports (if you have them) and any other travel documents (including from USCIS or the border authorities, such as an I-94 card).

☐ Copies (three) of documents to prove your identity, such as a birth certificate, driver's license, or national identity document ("cedula").

☐ Copies (three) of documents to prove the relationships between the family members applying, such as birth and marriage certificates.

☐ Documentation (three copies) of your experience and the human rights situation in your country, showing why you fear to return, supported by your own detailed written statement.

☐ If possible, also include statements (three copies) by any witnesses, doctors, friends, relatives, or respected leaders of your community, relevant news reports, or letters from people in your country.

> ⚠ **CAUTION**
>
> **Documents not in English must be translated.** You'll have to provide a word-for-word English translation of any document in another language. Any capable person can do this, but should, on their translation, add the following text at the bottom: "I certify that I am competent in both English and [*your language*], and that the foregoing is a full and accurate translation into English, to the best of my knowledge and ability." The person should sign his or her name and add the date under this statement.

Not long after receiving your application, USCIS will call you in to have your fingerprints taken (if you're over age 14). This is to make sure that you don't have a record of criminal or terrorist acts and that you haven't applied for asylum before.

4. USCIS Asylum Offices—Where to File

There are four regional service centers that handle all asylum applications. Where you file depends on where you live. To find out which Service Center to use, go to www.uscis.gov, click "Forms," then search for "I-589," then see "Where to File."

5. USCIS Interview

After your papers have been processed at the USCIS Service Center, you will be called in to have your fingerprints taken. Within a few weeks, you are likely to get an appointment at one of the USCIS Asylum Offices. However, if you are one of the few people who live in an outlying area that asylum officers rarely visit, you're likely to wait much

longer. The purpose of your interview will be to determine whether you are eligible for asylum. Interviews can last anywhere from 30 minutes to two hours.

If you aren't comfortable in English, you'll need to bring your own interpreter. This doesn't have to be a hired professional—a family member or friend will do. But if your friends and family aren't truly fluent in both English and your own language, it's worth spending the money on a professional. Many asylum interviews have gone badly because the interpreter wasn't fully competent and the asylum officer, not knowing of the problem, assumed that the applicant couldn't get his or her story straight. For example, we know of a case in which the interpreter repeatedly translated the Spanish word "padres" (which means parents) as "father." The applicant was testifying about the death of both his parents in Guatemala, and the interviewer became very suspicious when he suddenly appeared to be talking about only his father.

The asylum officer will also call a translating service (on contract with the U.S. government), to have a monitor listen in on the interview by telephone. The monitor's job is to interrupt if he or she believes that your interpreter is not being accurate. The asylum officer will preserve your confidentiality by "muting" the telephone when asking you for identifying information.

Expect the interviewer to begin by reviewing some of the basic items in your application, such as your name, address, and date of entry into the U.S., then to move quickly into open-ended questions such as "Why are you afraid to return to your country?" The interviewer may interrupt you at any point. He or she may also ask questions you never expected, sometimes to test whether you are who you claim to be. For example, if you claim to be a member of a persecuted Christian minority in a Middle Eastern country, you might be asked questions about Christian doctrine. These interviewers are highly trained in the human rights situations of countries around the globe, and many of them have law degrees, so expect some intelligent, probing questions.

Whether the interviewer will behave courteously is another matter. Many of them are sympathetic people who took this job because they're interested in human rights issues—others are government bureaucrats whose first concern is to ferret out cases of fraud. You won't be able to choose your interviewer. Women who have been raped or experienced similar trauma can, however, request a female interviewer.

Protection Under the U.N. Convention Against Torture

Even if you don't qualify for asylum, you may be protected from deportation by the United Nations Convention Against Torture. This prohibits deporting anyone who can show that he or she is more likely than not to suffer torture at the hands of his or her home country's government. The asylum application has a place to mention whether you feel you qualify for this protection. However, it won't get you a green card—it will just stop USCIS from deporting you. Whether USCIS will also allow you a work permit is up to its discretion.

---

6. Comments of the Department of State

When USCIS receives your application, the officer may send a copy to the Bureau of Human Rights and Humanitarian Affairs (BHRHA) of the U.S. Department of State for comments on:

- the accuracy of the assertions on the conditions in the foreign country and the experiences described
- how an applicant who returned to the foreign country would be likely to be treated
- whether people who are similarly situated as the applicant are persecuted in the foreign country and the frequency of such persecution, and

- whether one of the grounds for denial may apply to the applicant.

However, the process usually goes faster than the BHRHA's ability to provide comments. Almost no one receives these comments anymore.

7. Decision by the Asylum Officer

After interviewing you, the asylum officer has full discretion to approve or deny your application for asylum. However, you won't be told the decision that day. Most likely, you'll have to return to the USCIS Asylum Office at an appointed time to pick up your decision from the front desk. Accommodations can be made if you live especially far from an Asylum Office.

CAUTION

You may have friends who applied for asylum years ago and are still waiting for an interview. Because of a huge backlog of applications, USCIS has started acting quickly on the cases of people who are just now applying, while it tries to deal with the older, backlogged cases a few at a time. Your case will probably be decided in six months or less—even though you may know people who've waited six years or more.

If you're approved, you'll be given a document stating this. Take good care of this document, and make copies to keep in safe places. You'll need it to apply for your Social Security card, work permit, and green card (permanent resident status) in a year.

CAUTION

Need to travel after you've gained asylum? Don't leave the U.S. without first obtaining a refugee travel document allowing you to return. The application is made on Form I-131; see the USCIS website at www.uscis.gov/i-131 for the form and instructions. Allow several weeks for your fingerprinting appointment and then possibly several additional months for the document to be approved. Also check the website to see the projected processing time, and take into account whether you will need any visas for your trip, to give yourself enough time to apply in advance of your trip. Also, if at all possible, do not return to the country that persecuted you—this will be taken as a sign that you aren't really in danger there after all, and you may not be allowed to return to the United States. If you feel you have no choice but to return to your home country, talk to an experienced immigration attorney before you leave.

E. If Your Asylum Application Is Denied

If the asylum officer denies your application for asylum, he or she will also serve you with papers to start your removal proceedings before the Immigration Court. Get an attorney to help you.

> ⚠ **CAUTION**
>
> **Missing the court hearing: an expensive mistake.** If, after you have been notified orally and in writing of the time, place, and date of the hearing, you fail to attend an asylum hearing before an Immigration Judge, you will be ordered deported and will never be able to adjust your status, obtain voluntary departure, or be granted suspension of deportation.
>
> The Immigration Judge may go ahead and hold the hearing without you being present—and issue an order of deportation if the evidence presented by USCIS supports it. You will be unable to request any green card until five years from the date of the asylum hearing that you failed to attend.
>
> Only "exceptional circumstances beyond your control," such as your own serious illness or the death of an immediate relative, are considered to be valid excuses for failing to appear before the Immigration Judge. Your lawyer will need to file a motion to reopen the order of your deportation.

If the Immigration Judge denies your case, you are free to pursue the case to the Board of Immigration Appeals (BIA) and from there to the federal circuit court of appeals. In the meantime,

while your case or your appeal is pending, you are able to remain in the United States. If you have already received work authorization, it will continue to be granted for one year at a time. If you haven't, you'll have to continue living with no income.

Some people turn around after they've been denied asylum and try to apply for it again. This won't work. First of all, it's not allowed, and second, USCIS has your fingerprints on file and will check them, so even if you change your name, you'll get caught.

F. Asylees Can Bring Overseas Spouses and Children to the United States

If you're granted political asylum and you have a husband, wife, or unmarried minor (under age 21) child still living in the country that persecuted you, you have the right to request asylum for them, too. But you must act within two years of when you're granted asylum, or they'll miss their chance (at least, until you're a permanent resident or U.S. citizen and can petition for them, but this takes years). No other relatives are eligible—you cannot, for example, bring your parents or grandchildren.

> ⚠ **CAUTION**
>
> **Getting married after you've won asylum won't do it.** As an asylee, you can bring in your spouse only if the two of you were already married when you were granted asylum. If, however, your wife gave birth to a child after you won asylum, you can bring the child in so long as it was in the womb when you were granted asylum.

The procedure for bringing your spouse and children to join you is to prepare and assemble the following (use separate forms and documents for each person):

☐ Form I-730, Refugee/Asylee Relative Petition, available from USCIS or on its website at www.uscis.gov/i-730 (see the sample at the end of this chapter; don't be confused by the second question on the sample, which says the asylee is filing for three relatives; that just means he and his wife have two children, who will be named in separate Forms I-730).

☐ a copy of the document granting you asylum

☐ a clear photograph of your family member

☐ a copy of proof of the relationship between you and the person you're applying for— a marriage certificate for your spouse, or a birth certificate for your child (if an adoption certificate, the adoption must have occurred before the child was 16), plus a marriage certificate in your child's petition if you're the child's father or stepparent, and

☐ if your child is adopted, evidence that he or she has been living in your legal custody for the last two years.

There is no filing fee. For more detailed information, see the instructions that come with Form I-730. After you've finished preparing the applications, make a complete copy for your records and send it the USCIS Service Center indicated on the form.

Despite your status as an asylee, be aware that your family members can be denied entry to the U.S. if they've committed serious nonpolitical crimes, been affiliated with terrorism, or otherwise violated the provisions of the immigration law in I.N.A. § 208(b)(2), 8 U.S.C. § 1158.

! CAUTION

Your children must remain unmarried and under age 21 until they enter the United States. Warn them not to get married, or they'll ruin their chance to claim asylum and join you. Of course, turning 21 is something your children have no control over. Fortunately, a law called the Child Status Protection Act (CSPA) offers them some protection. The law says that if your child was under age 21 when you filed your Form I-589 with USCIS, he or she will still be considered 21 years of age when you file the Form I-730 and the child comes to claim U.S. asylee status.

G. Getting a Green Card After Asylum Approval

One year after your asylum application has been approved, you and your family may apply to become permanent residents. (You can also wait more than a year, but it's safest to apply as soon as you can.) You are eligible for a green card if you:

• have been physically in the United States for 365 days after being granted asylum— although the 365 days do not have to be consecutive

• continue to be a refugee or asylee or the spouse or child of a refugee or asylee (as defined in Section A, above; if conditions in your country have improved a lot, see an attorney), and

• have not violated certain U.S. criminal laws.

If you meet these criteria, it's time to prepare and submit an application for adjustment of status, as described in Chapter 16. You can skip the sections of that chapter that discuss whether or not you're truly eligible to use the adjustment of status procedure—as an asylee, you are. You also don't need to worry about proving that you entered the U.S. legally, like some applicants do. And unlike most other adjustment of status applicants, you need not submit an Affidavit of Support (Form I-864).

There is no deadline to submit an application for adjustment of status. There is not even a requirement to ever do so. Asylee status is indefinite. However, the government has the authority to review your asylee status from time to time, to see if you are still eligible, and to see if conditions in your home country have improved to such an extent that it is no longer dangerous for you to return. Although the government does not often conduct such reviews, your safest course of action is to apply for permanent resident status as soon as you can.

H. Revocation of Asylee Status

Beware that if your country's political situation has improved or changed so that you are no longer in danger of being persecuted, USCIS may revoke your asylee status. However, it must first notify you and then convince either an asylum officer or an Immigration Judge that you either:

- no longer have a well-founded fear of persecution upon your return, due to a change of conditions in your country
- were guilty of fraud in your application so that you were not eligible for asylum when it was granted, or
- have committed any of the acts that would have caused your asylum application to be denied—such as a serious felony.

I. Temporary Protected Status (TPS)

Temporary Protected Status (TPS) is a legal category that was fashioned by the U.S. Congress to respond to situations when natural disasters, such as earthquakes, volcanic eruptions, or tidal waves occur, or when war is being waged in a foreign country. It is a form of temporary asylum or safe haven for aliens whose country is in turmoil. Congress responded with this humanitarian gesture to avoid the deportation of aliens to countries where their personal safety is threatened or in which normal living conditions are substantially disrupted. It does not, however, lead to permanent residence or a green card.

1. TPS Benefits

Temporary Protected Status offers several short-term benefits.

- **Stay of deportation.** You will not be placed in removal proceedings. If a removal case is already underway, you can claim TPS, and the proceedings will be adjourned until the end of the disruption period.
- **Work authorization.** You will receive work authorization as long as the TPS is in effect.
- **Temporary Treatment (TT).** When you file for TPS, so long as it is complete with such documentary proof as a birth certificate showing that you are a national of the designated country, you'll be granted a stay of deportation and work authorization immediately, and they won't be taken away until either the TPS designation is ended or your application is denied.

2. Who Designates the TPS Aliens

The U.S. attorney general, working through USCIS, will designate the countries whose nationals deserve Temporary Protected Status. The following situations may give rise to this designation:

- ongoing armed conflict and civil war that pose a serious threat to the lives and personal safety of deported aliens who are nationals of that country
- earthquakes, floods, droughts, epidemics, or other environmental disasters, resulting in a substantial disruption of living conditions and an inability to handle the return of its nationals, in a foreign country that has requested a TPS designation, or
- extraordinary and temporary conditions in the foreign country preventing its nationals in the United States from returning safely to their country.

3. Period of Protected Status

The attorney general will designate the initial period of protection as not less than six months or more than 18 months. Sixty days before the end of the period, the attorney general will review the conditions of the foreign country to determine whether to end the TPS, or to extend it for a period of six, 12, or 18 months.

The termination or the extension will be published in the *Federal Register.* Termination will be effective 60 days after publication.

4. Who Qualifies for TPS

Nationals or native-born citizens of the designated foreign countries may apply for Temporary Protected Status if they:

- have been physically present in the United States continuously since the date of the designation
- have continuously resided in the United States since a certain date
- register for TPS during a registration period of not less than 180 days, and
- pay the filing fee.

TPS-Designated Countries

At the time this book went to print, citizens from the countries on the list below could apply for TPS. However, this list changes rapidly, so keep your eyes on the news and USCIS website at www.uscis.gov.

El Salvador (through March 9, 2015)

Haiti (through January 22, 2016)

Honduras (through January 5, 2015)

Nicaragua (through January 5, 2015)

Somalia (through March 17, 2014)

Sudan (through November 2, 2014)

South Sudan (through November 2, 2014)

Syria (through March 31, 2015)

---

5. Who Is Not Eligible for TPS

TPS is not available to nationals or native-born citizens of a designated foreign country who are outside the United States. In addition, even if you are already in the United States, your application for TPS will be denied if you:

- have been convicted of any felony, or at least two misdemeanors, in the United States

- have ordered, incited, assisted, or participated in persecuting any person
- have committed a serious nonpolitical crime outside the United States, or
- are regarded as a terrorist or danger to the security of the United States.

6. No Departure From the U.S. Allowed

If a person who has been granted TPS leaves the United States without getting advance permission from USCIS, the agency may treat the TPS status as having been abandoned.

Brief, casual, and innocent absences from the United States—a few hours or days—shall not be considered as failure to be physically present in the United States. For humanitarian reasons, USCIS recognizes emergency and extenuating circumstances, and may give advance parole or permission to depart for a brief and temporary trip without affecting the TPS.

7. How to Apply for TPS

The following forms should be sent to the USCIS address indicated for your specific country on the Form I-821 instructions. You can also check the USCIS website at www.uscis.gov and under the heading "Humanitarian" click "Temporary Protected Status & Deferred Enforced Departure" for contact details.

- Form I-821, Application for Temporary Protected Status. It's available at www.uscis. gov/i-821. (Re-registrants may be able to file for TPS online, as long as the application is not their first and their country has not been "redesignated" for TPS.) The filing fee is $50 for your initial registration, plus an additional $85 for fingerprinting if you are age 14 or older. There is no filing fee to renew the I-821, but if you want to renew the work permit you must pay the I-765 fee again, which is currently $380.

- Form I-765, Employment Authorization Application. (It's available at www.uscis. gov/i-765.) If you do not plan to work, you must submit this form for biographic purposes, but you do not need to pay a separate filing fee. If you do plan to work, submit this form with the fee, which is currently $380. Work authorization, effective until TPS is ended, is granted for the TPS period or one year, whichever is shorter. The fee must be paid each time.
- Copies of documents showing your physical presence during the period designated: passport used in entering the United States, for example, Form I-94 (Arrival-Departure Record), rent receipts, school records, hospital records, pay stubs, banking records, employment records, and affidavits of responsible members of your community (such as a religious officer, school director, or employer).
- Two kinds of documents showing personal identity and nationality: birth certificate, a passport, driver's license, employment ID, or school ID.
- Two photographs, passport style.

8. Termination of TPS

After the U.S. government decides that the situation in the foreign country has improved and there is no longer any reason to retain the Temporary Protective Status for nationals of that country, it will announce that the TPS designation will be lifted. Your work authorization will continue until the TPS expiration date.

If you do not have any other legal right to be in the United States, you are expected to leave at that time. However, immigration authorities will usually not make special efforts to deport people at the end of the TPS period—though there are no guarantees.

J. Deferred Enforced Departure (DED)

Another benefit that may be available for people from countries that have political or civil conflicts is known as Deferred Enforced Departure (DED). This is a temporary form of relief that allows designated individuals to work and stay in the United States for a certain period of time, during which the authorities will not try to deport them.

At the time this book went to print, only Liberia was designated under the DED program, and DED status for Liberians was extended through September 30, 2014.

Certain people are ineligible for DED, including those who have committed certain crimes, persecuted others, or have been previously deported, excluded, or removed from the United States.

If you are already in removal proceedings, you may ask the Immigration Judge to defer action on your case based on DED. If your case is already up on appeal after a decision by an Immigration Judge at the Board of Immigration Appeals, you should receive notice automatically about the administrative or temporary closure of your proceeding.

To qualify for DED as a Liberian, you must have had TPS on September 30, 2007, and must have been covered by DED on September 30, 2011. To get a work permit valid through September 30, 2014, submit Form I-765 to the Vermont Service Center. Attach a copy of your latest I-797, Notice of Action, showing that you were previously approved for TPS as of September 30, 2007. State on your Form I-765 that you were previously a beneficiary of Liberian TPS and that you are covered by DED for Liberians through September 30, 2014.

Sample Form I-589, Application for Asylum and for Withholding of Removal (page 1)

Department of Homeland Security
U.S. Citizenship and Immigration Services

U.S. Department of Justice
Executive Office for Immigration Review

OMB No. 1615-0067; Expires 11/30/2014

**I-589, Application for Asylum
and for Withholding of Removal**

START HERE - Type or print in black ink. See the instructions for information about eligibilty and how to complete and file this application. There is NO filing fee for this application.

NOTE: Check this box if you also want to apply for withholding of removal under the Convention Against Torture. ☒

Part A.I. Information About You	
1. Alien Registration Number(s) (A-Number) (*if any*) A54750557	**2.** U.S. Social Security Number (*if any*)

3. Complete Last Name Romero	**4.** First Name Luiz	**5.** Middle Name Manuel

6. What other names have you used (*include maiden name and aliases*)?

None

7. Residence in the U.S. (*where you physically reside*)

Street Number and Name 156 Arbol Lane	Apt. Number

City Richmond	State CA	Zip Code 94666	Telephone Number (510) 555-2222

8. Mailing Address in the U.S. (*if different than the address in Item Number 7*) (same as above)

In Care Of (*if applicable*):	Telephone Number ( )

Street Number and Name	Apt. Number

City	State	Zip Code

9. Gender: ☒ Male ☐ Female   **10.** Marital Status: ☐ Single ☒ Married ☐ Divorced ☐ Widowed

11. Date of Birth (*mm/dd/yyyy*) 04/07/1973	**12.** City and Country of Birth Quetzaltenango, Guatemala

13. Present Nationality (Citizenship) Guatemalan	**14.** Nationality at Birth Guatemalan	**15.** Race, Ethnic, or Tribal Group Hispanic	**16.** Religion Catholic

17. *Check the box, a through c, that applies:* **a.** ☒ I have never been in Immigration Court proceedings.

b. ☐ I am now in Immigration Court proceedings.   **c.** ☐ I am **not** now in Immigration Court proceedings, but I have been in the past.

18. *Complete 18 a through c.*

a. When did you last leave your country? (*mmm/dd/yyyy*) 10/04/2011   **b.** What is your current I-94 Number, if any? 02654000102

c. List each entry into the U.S. beginning with your most recent entry. *List date (mm/dd/yyyy), place, and your status for each entry.* (*Attach additional sheets as needed.*)

Date 10/04/2011	Place San Francisco, CA	Status B-2	Date Status Expires 04/04/2013
Date 05/07/2007	Place Los Angeles, CA	Status B-2	
Date	Place	Status	

19. What country issued your last passport or travel document? Guatemala	**20.** Passport Number Travel Document Number 775824	**21.** Expiration Date (*mm/dd/yyyy*) 01/01/2015

22. What is your native language (*include dialect, if applicable*)? Spanish	**23.** Are you fluent in English? ☒ Yes ☐ No	**24.** What other languages do you speak fluently? None

For EOIR use only.	For USCIS use only.	Action: Interview Date: _____ Asylum Officer ID#: _____	Decision: Approval Date: _____ Denial Date: _____ Referral Date: _____

Form I-589 (Rev. 11/01/12) Y

Sample Form I-589, Application for Asylum and for Withholding of Removal (page 2)

Part A.II. Information About Your Spouse and Children

Your spouse   ☐ I am not married. *(Skip to **Your Children** below.)*

1. Alien Registration Number (A-Number) *(if any)*	2. Passport/ID Card Number *(if any)*	3. Date of Birth *(mm/dd/yyyy)*	4. U.S. Social Security Number *(if any)*
A54571570	775825	05/09/1976	

5. Complete Last Name	6. First Name	7. Middle Name	8. Maiden Name
Romero	Maria	Beatriz	Carcamo

9. Date of Marriage *(mm/dd/yyyy)*	10. Place of Marriage	11. City and Country of Birth
11/07/1997	Antigua, Guatemala	Panajachel, Guatemala

12. Nationality *(Citizenship)*	13. Race, Ethnic, or Tribal Group	14. Gender
Guatemalan	Hispanic	☐ Male ☒ Female

15. Is this person in the U.S.?

☒ Yes *(Complete Blocks 16 to 24.)*   ☐ No *(Specify location)*:

16. Place of last entry into the U.S.	17. Date of last entry into the U.S. *(mm/dd/yyyy)*	18. I-94 Number *(if any)*	19. Status when last admitted *(Visa type, if any)*
San Francisco, CA	10/04/2011	02654000103	B-2 visitor

20. What is your spouse's current status?	21. What is the expiration date of his/her authorized stay, if any? *(mm/dd/yyyy)*	22. Is your spouse in Immigration Court proceedings?	23. If previously in the U.S., date of previous arrival *(mm/dd/yyyy)*
B-2	04/04/2013	☐ Yes ☒ No	None

24. If in the U.S., is your spouse to be included in this application? *(Check the appropriate box.)*

☒ Yes *(Attach one photograph of your spouse in the upper right corner of Page 9 on the extra copy of the application submitted for this person.)*

☐ No

Your Children. List **all** of your children, regardless of age, location, or marital status.

☒ I do not have any children. *(Skip to Part A.III., **Information about your background.**)*

☐ I have children.   Total number of children: _____.

(NOTE: *Use Form I-589 Supplement A or attach additional sheets of paper and documentation if you have more than four children.)*

1. Alien Registration Number (A-Number) *(if any)*	2. Passport/ID Card Number *(if any)*	3. Marital Status *(Married, Single, Divorced, Widowed)*	4. U.S. Social Security Number *(if any)*

5. Complete Last Name	6. First Name	7. Middle Name	8. Date of Birth *(mm/dd/yyyy)*

9. City and Country of Birth	10. Nationality *(Citizenship)*	11. Race, Ethnic, or Tribal Group	12. Gender
			☐ Male ☐ Female

13. Is this child in the U.S. ?   ☐ Yes *(Complete Blocks 14 to 21.)*   ☐ No *(Specify location)*:

14. Place of last entry into the U.S.	15. Date of last entry into the U.S. *(mm/dd/yyyy)*	16. I-94 Number *(If any)*	17. Status when last admitted *(Visa type, if any)*

18. What is your child's current status?	19. What is the expiration date of his/her authorized stay, if any? *(mm/dd/yyyy)*	20. Is your child in Immigration Court proceedings?
		☐ Yes ☐ No

21. If in the U.S., is this child to be included in this application? *(Check the appropriate box.)*

☐ Yes *(Attach one photograph of your spouse in the upper right corner of Page 9 on the extra copy of the application submitted for this person.)*

☐ No

Sample Form I-589, Application for Asylum and for Withholding of Removal (page 3)

Part A.II. Information About Your Spouse and Children (Continued)

1. Alien Registration Number (A-Number) *(if any)*	2. Passport/ID Card Number *(if any)*	3. Marital Status *(Married, Single, Divorced, Widowed)*	4. U.S. Social Security Number *(if any)*
5. Complete Last Name	6. First Name	7. Middle Name	8. Date of Birth *(mm/dd/yyyy)*
9. City and Country of Birth	10. Nationality *(Citizenship)*	11. Race, Ethnic, or Tribal Group	12. Gender ☐ Male ☐ Female

13. Is this child in the U.S. ? ☐ Yes *(Complete Blocks 14 to 21.)* ☐ No *(Specify location):* _____

14. Place of last entry into the U.S.	15. Date of last entry into the U.S. *(mm/dd/yyyy)*	16. I-94 Number *(If any)*	17. Status when last admitted *(Visa type, if any)*
18. What is your child's current status?	19. What is the expiration date of his/her authorized stay, if any? *(mm/dd/yyyy)*	20. Is your child in Immigration Court proceedings? ☐ Yes ☐ No	

21. If in the U.S., is this child to be included in this application? *(Check the appropriate box.)*

☐ Yes *(Attach one photograph of your spouse in the upper right corner of Page 9 on the extra copy of the application submitted for this person.)*

☐ No

1. Alien Registration Number (A-Number) *(if any)*	2. Passport/ID Card Number *(if any)*	3. Marital Status *(Married, Single, Divorced, Widowed)*	4. U.S. Social Security Number *(if any)*
5. Complete Last Name	6. First Name	7. Middle Name	8. Date of Birth *(mm/dd/yyyy)*
9. City and Country of Birth	10. Nationality *(Citizenship)*	11. Race, Ethnic, or Tribal Group	12. Gender ☐ Male ☐ Female

13. Is this child in the U.S. ? ☐ Yes *(Complete Blocks 14 to 21.)* ☐ No *(Specify location):* _____

14. Place of last entry into the U.S.	15. Date of last entry into the U.S. *(mm/dd/yyyy)*	16. I-94 Number *(If any)*	17. Status when last admitted *(Visa type, if any)*
18. What is your child's current status?	19. What is the expiration date of his/her authorized stay, if any? *(mm/dd/yyyy)*	20. Is your child in Immigration Court proceedings? ☐ Yes ☐ No	

21. If in the U.S., is this child to be included in this application? *(Check the appropriate box.)*

☐ Yes *(Attach one photograph of your spouse in the upper right corner of Page 9 on the extra copy of the application submitted for this person.)*

☐ No

1. Alien Registration Number (A-Number) *(if any)*	2. Passport/ID Card Number *(if any)*	3. Marital Status *(Married, Single, Divorced, Widowed)*	4. U.S. Social Security Number *(if any)*
5. Complete Last Name	6. First Name	7. Middle Name	8. Date of Birth *(mm/dd/yyyy)*
9. City and Country of Birth	10. Nationality *(Citizenship)*	11. Race, Ethnic, or Tribal Group	12. Gender ☐ Male ☐ Female

13. Is this child in the U.S. ? ☐ Yes *(Complete Blocks 14 to 21.)* ☐ No *(Specify location):* _____

14. Place of last entry into the U.S.	15. Date of last entry into the U.S. *(mm/dd/yyyy)*	16. I-94 Number *(If any)*	17. Status when last admitted *(Visa type, if any)*
18. What is your child's current status?	19. What is the expiration date of his/her authorized stay, if any? *(mm/dd/yyyy)*	20. Is your child in Immigration Court proceedings? ☐ Yes ☐ No	

21. If in the U.S., is this child to be included in this application? *(Check the appropriate box.)*

☐ Yes *(Attach one photograph of your spouse in the upper right corner of Page 9 on the extra copy of the application submitted for this person.)*

☐ No

Sample Form I-589, Application for Asylum and for Withholding of Removal (page 4)

Part A.III. Information About Your Background

1. List your last address where you lived before coming to the United States. If this is not the country where you fear persecution, also list the last address in the country where you fear persecution. *(List Address, City/Town, Department, Province, or State and Country.)*
   (NOTE: *Use Form I-589 Supplement B, or additional sheets of paper, if necessary.)*

Number and Street *(Provide if available)*	City/Town	Department, Province, or State	Country	Dates From *(Mo/Yr)*	To *(Mo/Yr)*
123 Avenida 7	Guatemala City	Guatemala City	Guatemala	11/1993	10/2011

2. Provide the following information about your residences during the past 5 years. List your present address first.
   (NOTE: *Use Form I-589 Supplement B, or additional sheets of paper, if necessary.)*

Number and Street	City/Town	Department, Province, or State	Country	Dates From *(Mo/Yr)*	To *(Mo/Yr)*
156 Arbol Lane	Richmond	California	USA	10/2011	present
123 Avenida 7	Guatemala City	Guatemala City	Guatemala	11/1993	10/2011
321 Calle de la Paz	Quetzaltenango		Guatemala	birth	11/1993

3. Provide the following information about your education, beginning with the most recent.
   (NOTE: *Use Form I-589 Supplement B, or additional sheets of paper, if necessary.)*

Name of School	Type of School	Location *(Address)*	Attended From *(Mo/Yr)*	To *(Mo/Yr)*
San Carlos University	College	Guatemala City	09/1990	06/1994
Quetzal High School	High School	Quetzaltenango	09/1986	06/1990
Sta. Maria Academy	Elementary/Middle	Quetzaltenango	09/1978	06/1986

4. Provide the following information about your employment during the past 5 years. List your present employment first.
   (NOTE: *Use Form I-589 Supplement B, or additional sheets of paper, if necessary.)*

Name and Address of Employer	Your Occupation	Dates From *(Mo/Yr)*	To *(Mo/Yr)*
Jose Torres Ramirez, Attorney	Legal Assistant	08/2003	10/2011

5. Provide the following information about your parents and siblings (brothers and sisters). Check the box if the person is deceased.
   (NOTE: *Use Form I-589 Supplement B, or additional sheets of paper, if necessary.)*

Full Name	City/Town and Country of Birth	Current Location
Mother Gloria Alcala de Romero	Quetzaltenango, Guatemala	☐ Deceased Quetzaltenango, Guatemala
Father Jorge Romero	Quetzaltenango, Guatemala	☒ Deceased
Sibling Felipe Romero	Quetzaltenango, Guatemala	☒ Deceased
Sibling Laura Romero	Quetzaltenango, Guatemala	☐ Deceased Antigua, Guatemala
Sibling		☐ Deceased
Sibling		☐ Deceased

Sample Form I-589, Application for Asylum and for Withholding of Removal (page 5)

Part B. Information About Your Application

(NOTE: *Use Form I-589 Supplement B, or attach additional sheets of paper as needed to complete your responses to the questions contained in Part B.)*

When answering the following questions about your asylum or other protection claim (withholding of removal under 241(b)(3) of the INA or withholding of removal under the Convention Against Torture), you must provide a detailed and specific account of the basis of your claim to asylum or other protection. To the best of your ability, provide specific dates, places, and descriptions about each event or action described. You must attach documents evidencing the general conditions in the country from which you are seeking asylum or other protection and the specific facts on which you are relying to support your claim. If this documentation is unavailable or you are not providing this documentation with your application, explain why in your responses to the following questions.

Refer to Instructions, Part 1: Filing Instructions, Section II, "Basis of Eligibility," Parts A - D, Section V, "Completing the Form," Part B, and Section VII, "Additional Evidence That You Should Submit," for more information on completing this section of the form.

1. Why are you applying for asylum or withholding of removal under section 241(b)(3) of the INA, or for withholding of removal under the Convention Against Torture? Check the appropriate box(es) below and then provide detailed answers to questions A and B below.

    I am seeking asylum or withholding of removal based on:

    ☐ Race   ☒ Political opinion

    ☐ Religion   ☒ Membership in a particular social group

    ☐ Nationality   ☒ Torture Convention

A. Have you, your family, or close friends or colleagues ever experienced harm or mistreatment or threats in the past by anyone?

   ☐ No   ☒ Yes

If "Yes," explain in detail:
1. What happened;
2. When the harm or mistreatment or threats occurred;
3. Who caused the harm or mistreatment or threats; and
4. Why you believe the harm or mistreatment or threats occurred.

> During the months of July through September 2011, jeeps with darkened windows have been circling our office and followed me home on at least two occasions. The neighbors told me that a military officer has been asking questions about me. I received a phone call on September 4, in which an anonymous voice said "drop the Diaz case or your wife will be a widow."

B. Do you fear harm or mistreatment if you return to your home country?

   ☐ No   ☒ Yes

If "Yes," explain in detail:
1. What harm or mistreatment you fear;
2. Who you believe would harm or mistreat you; and
3. Why you believe you would or could be harmed or mistreated.

> I believe that members of the Guatemalan military would torture, imprison, or kill me because of my work assisting victims of human rights abuses to gain judicial relief.

Sample Form I-589, Application for Asylum and for Withholding of Removal (page 6)

Part B. Information About Your Application (Continued)

2. Have you or your family members ever been accused, charged, arrested, detained, interrogated, convicted and sentenced, or imprisoned in any country other than the United States?

[X] No ☐ Yes

If "Yes," explain the circumstances and reasons for the action.

3.A. Have you or your family members ever belonged to or been associated with any organizations or groups in your home country, such as, but not limited to, a political party, student group, labor union, religious organization, military or paramilitary group, civil patrol, guerrilla organization, ethnic group, human rights group, or the press or media?

☐ No [X] Yes

If "Yes," describe for each person the level of participation, any leadership or other positions held, and the length of time you or your family members were involved in each organization or activity.

> I was a member of Students United for Free Speech from 1986 to 1990. I was a member of the Legal Committee for Redress from 2003 until I left Guatemala in 2011.

3.B. Do you or your family members continue to participate in any way in these organizations or groups?

[X] No ☐ Yes

If "Yes," describe for each person your or your family members' current level of participation, any leadership or other positions currently held, and the length of time you or your family members have been involved in each organization or group.

4. Are you afraid of being subjected to torture in your home country or any other country to which you may be returned?

☐ No [X] Yes

If "Yes," explain why you are afraid and describe the nature of torture you fear, by whom, and why it would be inflicted.

> Other human rights activists, including a former clerk at the office where I worked, have been questioned and tortured by members of the Guatemalan police and military, or by members of clandestine groups believed to be linked with the government. Reported methods of torture and interrogation include putting a hood filled with insecticides over the victim's head, and administering electric shock, particularly to the genital area.

Sample Form I-589, Application for Asylum and for Withholding of Removal (page 7)

Part C. Additional Information About Your Application

(NOTE: *Use Form I-589 Supplement B, or attach additional sheets of paper as needed to complete your responses to the questions contained in Part C.)*

1. Have you, your spouse, your child(ren), your parents or your siblings ever applied to the U.S. Government for refugee status, asylum, or withholding of removal?

[X] No   [ ] Yes

If "Yes," explain the decision and what happened to any status you, your spouse, your child(ren), your parents, or your siblings received as a result of that decision. Indicate whether or not you were included in a parent or spouse's application. If so, include your parent or spouse's A-number in your response. If you have been denied asylum by an immigration judge or the Board of Immigration Appeals, describe any change(s) in conditions in your country or your own personal circumstances since the date of the denial that may affect your eligibility for asylum.

2.A. After leaving the country from which you are claiming asylum, did you or your spouse or child(ren) who are now in the United States travel through or reside in any other country before entering the United States?

[X] No   [ ] Yes

2.B. Have you, your spouse, your child(ren), or other family members, such as your parents or siblings, ever applied for or received any lawful status in any country other than the one from which you are now claiming asylum?

[X] No   [ ] Yes

If "Yes" to either or both questions (2A and/or 2B), provide for each person the following: the name of each country and the length of stay, the person's status while there, the reasons for leaving, whether or not the person is entitled to return for lawful residence purposes, and whether the person applied for refugee status or for asylum while there, and if not, why he or she did not do so.

3. Have you, your spouse or your child(ren) ever ordered, incited, assisted or otherwise participated in causing harm or suffering to any person because of his or her race, religion, nationality, membership in a particular social group or belief in a particular political opinion?

[X] No   [ ] Yes

If "Yes," describe in detail each such incident and your own, your spouse's, or your child(ren)'s involvement.

Sample Form I-589, Application for Asylum and for Withholding of Removal (page 8)

Part C. Additional Information About Your Application (Continued)

4. After you left the country where you were harmed or fear harm, did you return to that country?

[X] No   [ ] Yes

If "Yes," describe in detail the circumstances of your visit(s) (for example, the date(s) of the trip(s), the purpose(s) of the trip(s), and the length of time you remained in that country for the visit(s).)

5. Are you filing this application more than 1 year after your last arrival in the United States?

[X] No   [ ] Yes

If "Yes," explain why you did not file within the first year after you arrived. You must be prepared to explain at your interview or hearing why you did not file your asylum application within the first year after you arrived. For guidance in answering this question, see Instructions, Part 1: Filing Instructions, Section V. "Completing the Form," Part C.

6. Have you or any member of your family included in the application ever committed any crime and/or been arrested, charged, convicted, or sentenced for any crimes in the United States?

[X] No   [ ] Yes

If "Yes," for each instance, specify in your response: what occurred and the circumstances, dates, length of sentence received, location, the duration of the detention or imprisonment, reason(s) for the detention or conviction, any formal charges that were lodged against you or your relatives included in your application, and the reason(s) for release. Attach documents referring to these incidents, if they are available, or an explanation of why documents are not available.

Sample Form I-589, Application for Asylum and for Withholding of Removal (page 9)

Part D. Your Signature

I certify, under penalty of perjury under the laws of the United States of America, that this application and the evidence submitted with it are all true and correct. Title 18, United States Code, Section 1546(a), provides in part: Whoever knowingly makes under oath, or as permitted under penalty of perjury under Section 1746 of Title 28, United States Code, knowingly subscribes as true, any false statement with respect to a material fact in any application, affidavit, or other document required by the immigration laws or regulations prescribed thereunder, or knowingly presents any such application, affidavit, or other document containing any such false statement or which fails to contain any reasonable basis in law or fact - shall be fined in accordance with this title or imprisoned for up to 25 years. I authorize the release of any information from my immigration record that U.S. Citizenship and Immigration Services (USCIS) needs to determine eligibility for the benefit I am seeking.

| Staple your photograph here or the photograph of the family member to be included on the extra copy of the application submitted for that person. |

WARNING: Applicants who are in the United States illegally are subject to removal if their asylum or withholding claims are not granted by an asylum officer or an immigration judge. Any information provided in completing this application may be used as a basis for the institution of, or as evidence in, removal proceedings even if the application is later withdrawn. Applicants determined to have knowingly made a frivolous application for asylum will be permanently ineligible for any benefits under the Immigration and Nationality Act. You may not avoid a frivolous finding simply because someone advised you to provide false information in your asylum application. If filing with USCIS, unexcused failure to appear for an appointment to provide biometrics (such as fingerprints) and your biographical information within the time allowed may result in an asylum officer dismissing your asylum application or referring it to an immigration judge. Failure without good cause to provide DHS with biometrics or other biographical information while in removal proceedings may result in your application being found abandoned by the immigration judge. See sections 208(d)(5)(A) and 208(d)(6) of the INA and 8 CFR sections 208.10, 1208.10, 208.20, 1003.47(d) and 1208.20.

Print your complete name.	Write your name in your native alphabet.
Luiz Manuel Romero	n/a

Did your spouse, parent, or child(ren) assist you in completing this application? [X] No [ ] Yes *(If "Yes," list the name and relationship.)*

_____	_____	_____	_____
(Name)	*(Relationship)*	*(Name)*	*(Relationship)*

Did someone other than your spouse, parent, or child(ren) prepare this application? [X] No [ ] Yes *(If "Yes," complete Part E.)*

Asylum applicants may be represented by counsel. Have you been provided with a list of persons who may be available to assist you, at little or no cost, with your asylum claim? [ ] No [X] Yes

Signature of Applicant *(The person in Part A.I.)*

[*Luiz Manuel Romero*]   10/03/2013
Sign your name so it all appears within the brackets   Date *(mm/dd/yyyy)*

Part E. Declaration of Person Preparing Form, if Other Than Applicant, Spouse, Parent, or Child

I declare that I have prepared this application at the request of the person named in Part D, that the responses provided are based on all information of which I have knowledge, or which was provided to me by the applicant, and that the completed application was read to the applicant in his or her native language or a language he or she understands for verification before he or she signed the application in my presence. I am aware that the knowing placement of false information on the Form I-589 may also subject me to civil penalties under 8 U.S.C. 1324c and/or criminal penalties under 18 U.S.C. 1546(a).

Signature of Preparer	Print Complete Name of Preparer		
Daytime Telephone Number ( )	Address of Preparer: Street Number and Name		
Apt. Number	City	State	Zip Code

Sample Form I-589, Application for Asylum and for Withholding of Removal (page 10)

Part F. To Be Completed at Asylum Interview, if Applicable

NOTE: *You will be asked to complete this part when you appear for examination before an asylum officer of the Department of Homeland Security, U.S. Citizenship and Immigration Services (USCIS).*

I swear (affirm) that I know the contents of this application that I am signing, including the attached documents and supplements, that they are ☐ all true or ☐ not all true to the best of my knowledge and that correction(s) numbered _____ to _____ were made by me or at my request. Furthermore, I am aware that if I am determined to have knowingly made a frivolous application for asylum I will be permanently ineligible for any benefits under the Immigration and Nationality Act, and that I may not avoid a frivolous finding simply because someone advised me to provide false information in my asylum application.

Signed and sworn to before me by the above named applicant on:

_____
Signature of Applicant

_____
Date *(mm/dd/yyyy)*

_____
Write Your Name in Your Native Alphabet

_____
Signature of Asylum Officer

Part G. To Be Completed at Removal Hearing, if Applicable

NOTE: *You will be asked to complete this Part when you appear before an immigration judge of the U.S. Department of Justice, Executive Office for Immigration Review (EOIR), for a hearing.*

I swear (affirm) that I know the contents of this application that I am signing, including the attached documents and supplements, that they are ☐ all true or ☐ not all true to the best of my knowledge and that correction(s) numbered _____ to _____ were made by me or at my request. Furthermore, I am aware that if I am determined to have knowingly made a frivolous application for asylum I will be permanently ineligible for any benefits under the Immigration and Nationality Act, and that I may not avoid a frivolous finding simply because someone advised me to provide false information in my asylum application.

Signed and sworn to before me by the above named applicant on:

_____
Signature of Applicant

_____
Date *(mm/dd/yyyy)*

_____
Write Your Name in Your Native Alphabet

_____
Signature of Immigration Judge

Sample Form I-589, Application for Asylum and for Withholding of Removal (page 11)

Supplement A, Form I-589

A-Number *(If available)*	Date
Applicant's Name	Applicant's Signature

List All of Your Children, Regardless of Age or Marital Status
(NOTE. Use this form and attach additional pages and documentation as needed, if you have more than four children)

1. Alien Registration Number (A-Number) *(if any)*	2. Passport/ID Card Number *(if any)*	3. Marital Status *(Married, Single, Divorced, Widowed)*	4. U.S. Social Security Number *(if any)*
5. Complete Last Name	6. First Name	7. Middle Name	8. Date of Birth *(mm/dd/yyyy)*
9. City and Country of Birth	10. Nationality *(Citizenship)*	11. Race, Ethnic, or Tribal Group	12. Gender ☐ Male ☐ Female

13. Is this child in the U.S. ? ☐ Yes *(Complete Blocks 14 to 21.)* ☐ No *(Specify location):*

14. Place of last entry into the U.S.	15. Date of last entry into the U.S. *(mm/dd/yyyy)*	16. I-94 Number *(If any)*	17. Status when last admitted *(Visa type, if any)*
18. What is your child's current status?	19. What is the expiration date of his/her authorized stay, if any? *(mm/dd/yyyy)*	20. Is your child in Immigration Court proceedings? ☐ Yes ☐ No	

21. If in the U.S., is this child to be included in this application? *(Check the appropriate box.)*
☐ Yes *(Attach one photograph of your spouse in the upper right corner of Page 9 on the extra copy of the application submitted for this person.)*
☐ No

1. Alien Registration Number (A-Number) *(if any)*	2. Passport/ID Card Number *(if any)*	3. Marital Status *(Married, Single, Divorced, Widowed)*	4. U.S. Social Security Number *(if any)*
5. Complete Last Name	6. First Name	7. Middle Name	8. Date of Birth *(mm/dd/yyyy)*
9. City and Country of Birth	10. Nationality *(Citizenship)*	11. Race, Ethnic, or Tribal Group	12. Gender ☐ Male ☐ Female

13. Is this child in the U.S. ? ☐ Yes *(Complete Blocks 14 to 21.)* ☐ No *(Specify location):*

14. Place of last entry into the U.S.	15. Date of last entry into the U.S. *(mm/dd/yyyy)*	16. I-94 Number *(If any)*	17. Status when last admitted *(Visa type, if any)*
18. What is your child's current status?	19. What is the expiration date of his/her authorized stay, if any? *(mm/dd/yyyy)*	20. Is your child in Immigration Court proceedings? ☐ Yes ☐ No	

21. If in the U.S., is this child to be included in this application? *(Check the appropriate box.)*
☐ Yes *(Attach one photograph of your spouse in the upper right corner of Page 9 on the extra copy of the application submitted for this person.)*
☐ No

Sample Form I-589, Application for Asylum and for Withholding of Removal (page 12)

Additional Information About Your Claim to Asylum	
A-Number *(if available)*	Date
Applicant's Name	Applicant's Signature

NOTE: *Use this as a continuation page for any additional information requested. Copy and complete as needed.*

Part _____

Question _____

Sample Form I-730, Refugee/Asylee Relative Petition (page 1)

Department of Homeland Security
U.S. Citizenship and Immigration Services

OMB No. 1615-0037; Expires 01/31/2015

I-730, Refugee/Asylee Relative Petition

DO NOT WRITE IN THIS BLOCK - FOR USCIS OFFICE ONLY

Section of Law	Action Stamp	Receipt
☐ 207 (c)(2) Spouse		
☐ 207 (c)(2) Child		
☐ 208 (b)(3) Spouse		
☐ 208 (b)(3) Child		

Reserved		Remarks

☐ Beneficiary Not Previously Claimed
☐ Beneficiary Previously Claimed On: _____ (e.g., Form I-590, Form I-589, etc.)   CSPA Eligible: ☐ Yes ☐ No ☐ N/A

START HERE - Type or print legibly in black ink.

My Status: ☐ Refugee ☐ Lawful Permanent Resident based on previous Refugee status
☒ Asylee ☐ Lawful Permanent Resident based on previous Asylee status

The beneficiary is my: ☒ Spouse
☐ Unmarried child who is a (n):   ☐ Biological Child ☐ Stepchild ☐ Adopted Child

Number of relatives for whom I am filing separate Form I-730s.   __3__ (__1__ of __3__)

Part 1. Information About You, the Petitioner	Part 2. Information About Your Alien Relative, the Beneficiary
Family Name (Last name), Given Name (First name), Middle Name: BERA, John Paul	Family Name (Last name), Given Name (First name), Middle Name: BERA, Gladys Mary

Part 1:

Address of Residence (*Where you physically reside*)

Street Number and Name: 876 5th Street	Apt. Number 14
City: Providence	State or Province: RI
Country: USA	Zip/Postal Code: 02901

Mailing Address (*If different from residence*) - C/O.
same as above

Street Number and Name:	Apt. Number:
City:	State or Province:
Country:	Zip/Postal Code:

Telephone Number including Country and City/Area Code:
401-555-2121

Your E-Mail Address, if available:
n/a

Gender: a. ☒ Male b. ☐ Female	Date of Birth (*mm/dd/yyyy*): 12/15/74
Country of Birth: Nigeria	Country of Citizenship/Nationality: Nigeria
U.S. Alien Registration Number: A-012345678	U.S. Social Security Number (*If applicable*): 123-45-6789

Part 2:

Address of Residence (*Where the beneficiary physically resides*)

Street Number and Name: 17 Ozumba Mbadicue Avenue	Apt. Number 2
City: Lagos	State or Province:
Country: Nigeria	Zip/Postal Code:

Mailing Address (*If different from residence*) - C/O:
same as above

Street Number and Name:	Apt. Number
City:	State or Province:
Country:	Zip/Postal Code:

Telephone Number including Country and City/Area Code:
none

The Beneficiary's E-Mail Address, if available:
none

Gender: a. ☐ Male b. ☒ Female	Date of Birth (*mm/dd/yyyy*): 07/24/1976
Country of Birth: Nigeria	Country of Citizenship/Nationality: Nigeria
U.S. Alien Registration Number: A- none	U.S. Social Security Number (*If applicable*): none

Sample Form I-730, Refugee/Asylee Relative Petition (page 2)

Part 1. Information About You, the Petitioner (Continued)	Part 2. Information About Your Alien Relative, the Beneficiary (Continued)
Other Name(s) Used (Including maiden name): none	Other Name(s) Used (Including maiden name): Gladys Mary Amah
If married, Name of Spouse, Date (*mm/dd/yyyy*), and Place of Present Marriage:	If married, Name of Spouse, Date (*mm/dd/yyyy*), and Place of Present Marriage: John, Paul Bera 07/18/1996 Lagos, Nigeria
If previously married, name(s) of prior spouse(s): Gladys Bera 07/18/1996 Lagos, Nigeria	If previously married, name(s) of Prior Spouse(s):
Date(s) (*mm/dd/yyyy*) and Place(s) Previous Marriage(s) Ended: Please provide documentation indicating how marriage(s) ended (e.g., death certificate, divorce certificate, etc.):	Date(s) (*mm/dd/yyyy*) and Place(s) Previous Marriage(s) Ended: Please provide documentation indicating how marriage(s) ended (e.g., death certificate, divorce certificate, etc.):

Date (*mm/dd/yyyy*) and Place Asylee Status was granted in the United States

08/15/2013   Immigration Court, Boston, MA

OR

Date (*mm/dd/yyyy*) and Place you received your approval for Refugee Status while living abroad

If You Were Approved for Refugee Status, Date (*mm/dd/yyyy*) and Place Admitted to the United States as a Refugee:

☐ Beneficiary is currently in the United States.
☒ Beneficiary is outside the United States and will apply for travel authorization at a USCIS Office or a U.S. Embassy or consulate in:

   Lagos Nigeria
   City and Country

To Be Completed By Attorney or Representative, if any.

☐ Fill in box if G-28 is attached to represent the petitioner.

Volag Number: [ ]

Attorney State License Number: [ ]

Part 2. Information About Your Alien Relative, the Beneficiary (Continued)

Name and **mailing** address of the beneficiary written in the language of the country where he or she now **resides**:

Family Name:	Given Name:	Middle Name:
Bera	Gladys	Mary

Address - C/O:

Street Number and Name:		Apt. Number:
17 Ozumba Mbadicue Ave.		2
City/State or Province:	Country:	Zip/Postal Code:
Lagos	Nigeria	

Check the box, a through d, that applies:

a. ☒ The beneficiary has never been in the United States

b. ☐ The beneficiary is now in immigration court proceedings in the United States Where? _____

c. ☐ The beneficiary has never been in immigration court proceedings in the United States

d. ☐ The beneficiary is not now in immigration court proceedings in the United States, but has been in the past. Where? _____

What is the beneficiary's native language?	Is the beneficiary fluent in English?	What other language(s) does the beneficiary speak fluently:
Igbo	☐ No ☒ Yes	none

Sample Form I-730, Refugee/Asylee Relative Petition (page 3)

Part 2. Information About Your Alien Relative, the Beneficiary (Continued)

List each of the beneficiary's entries into the United States; if any, beginning with the most recent entry. Submit a copy of each I-94 and/or copy of the beneficiary's passport showing all the entry and exit stamps for each entry. Attach an additional sheet if the beneficiary has more than two entries into the United States:

Date of Arrival *(mm/dd/yyyy)*: none	Place *(City and State)*:		Status:
I-94 Number:	Date Status Expires *(mm/dd/yyyy)*:	Passport Number:	
Travel Document Number:	Expiration Date for Passport or Travel Document:	Country of Issuance for Passport or Travel Document:	

Date of Arrival *(mm/dd/yyyy)*:	Place *(City and State)*:		Status:
I-94 Number:	Date Status Expires *(mm/dd/yyyy)*:	Passport Number:	
Travel Document Number:	Expiration Date for Passport or Travel Document:	Country of Issuance for Passport or Travel Document:	

Part 3. 2-Year Filing Deadline

Are you filing this application more than 2 years after the date you were admitted to the United States as a refugee or granted asylee status? ☒ No ☐ Yes

If you answered "Yes" to the previous question, explain the delay in filing and submit evidence to support your explanation (Attach additional sheets of paper if necessary):

Part 4. Warning

WARNING: Any beneficiary who is in the United States illegally is subject to removal if Form I-730 is not granted by USCIS. Any information provided in completing this petition may be used as a basis for the institution of, or as evidence in, removal proceedings, even if the petition is later withdrawn. Unexcused failure by the beneficiary to appear for an appointment to provide biometrics (such as fingerprints and photographs) and biographical information within the time allowed may result in denial of Form I-730. Information provided on this form and biometrics and biographical information provided by the beneficiary may also be used in producing an Employment Authorization Document if the beneficiary is granted derivative refugee or asylee status.

Sample Form I-730, Refugee/Asylee Relative Petition (page 4)

| **Part 5. Signature of Petitioner** | *Read the information on penalties in the instructions and the warning in **Part 4** before completing this section and sign below. If someone other than the beneficiary helped you to prepare this petition, that person must complete **Part 7**.* |

I certify or, if outside the United States, I swear or affirm, under penalty of perjury under the laws of the United States of America, that this petition and the evidence submitted with it is all true and correct. I authorize the release of any information from my record that U.S. Citizenship and Immigration Services needs to determine eligibility for the benefit I am seeking.

Signature	Print Full Name	Date *(mm/dd/yyyy)*	Daytime Telephone Number
John P. Bera	John Paul Bera	08/30/13	401-555-2121

NOTE: If you do not completely fill out this form or if you fail to submit the required documents listed in the instructions, your relative may not be found eligible for the requested benefit and this petition may be denied.

| **Part 6. Signature of Beneficiary, if in the United States** | *Read the information on penalties in the instructions and the warning in **Part 4** before completing this section and sign below. If someone other than the petitioner helped you to prepare this petition, that person must complete **Part 7**.* |

NOTE: If the beneficiary is not currently in the United States, this section should be left blank.

I certify under penalty of perjury under the laws of the United States of America, that this petition and the evidence submitted with it is all true and correct. I authorize the release of any information from my record that U.S. Citizenship and Immigration Services needs to determine eligibilty for the benefit I am seeking.

Signature	Print Full Name	Date *(mm/dd/yyyy)*	Daytime Telephone Number

NOTE: If you do not completely fill out this form or if you fail to submit the required documents and biometrics listed in the instructions, you may not be found eligible for the requested benefit and this petition may be denied.

Part 7. Signature of Person Preparing Form, If Other Than Petitioner or Beneficiary Above

I declare that I prepared this petition at the request of _____ (name of person(s) above), and it is based on all of the information of which I have knowledge.

Signature	Print Full Name	Date *(mm/dd/yyyy)*	Daytime Telephone Number

Firm Name and Address	E-Mail Address (If any)

Part 8. To Be Completed at Interview of Beneficiary, If Applicable (14 years of age or older)

Beneficiaries in the United States will be interviewed by USCIS officers. Their petitioners may also be interviewed. Beneficiaries living overseas will be interviewed by a USCIS officer or a DOS consular officer.

I swear (affirm) that I know the contents of this petition that I am signing, including the attached documents and supplements, and that they are ☐ all true or ☐ not all true to the best of my knowledge and that correction(s) numbered _____ to _____ were made by me or at my request. With these corrections, the information on this form is now true.

Signed and sworn before me by the beneficiary named herein on:

_____
Signature of Beneficiary

_____
Date *(mm/dd/yyyy)*

_____
Write your Name in your Native Alphabet

_____
Signature of USCIS Officer or DOS Consular Officer

☐ Beneficiary Approved for Travel, Admission Code: _____

☐ Petition Returned to Service Center via NVC

CBP Action Block

Military Veterans and Enlistees

The immigration laws recognize the patriotism and valor of aliens who have defended the U.S. Constitution by serving in the military. Some veterans can jump directly to becoming U.S. citizens. Others have a path to a U.S. green card.

A. Who Qualifies to Apply for Citizenship Without a Green Card

If you have honorably and actively served the U.S. military in a time of war or conflict, you are exempt from all green card requirements and qualify for immediate citizenship. (See J.N.A. § 329, 8 U.S.C. § 1440.) This special benefit depends, however, on the war or conflict in which you fought under the U.S. Armed Forces. It includes:

- World War I
- World War II, specifically between September 1, 1939 and December 31, 1946; a special provision allowed Filipino war veterans to file applications for citizenship until February 3, 2001
- the Korean War, specifically between June 25, 1950, and July 1, 1955
- the Vietnam War, specifically between February 28, 1961 and October 15, 1978
- the Persian Gulf Conflict, specifically between August 2, 1990 and April 11, 1991, and
- the "War on Terror" (also called "Operation Enduring Freedom"), which began on September 11, 2001 and will end on a date to be determined by the U.S. president.

It also depends on where you were when you enlisted. Your enlistment, reenlistment, extension of enlistment, or induction must have been in the United States, the Canal Zone, American Samoa, or Swains Island, or on board a public vessel owned or operated by the U.S. for noncommercial service.

You'll need to submit an application for naturalization in order to become a citizen. Your application will consist of Form N-400, Application for Naturalization; Form N-426, Request for Certification of Military or Naval Service (certified by the military); and Form G-325B, Biographic Information. However, you'll be able to take advantage of streamlined application procedures, and will not have to pay a fee. Your military installation should have a designated point of contact to help you with your application.

You'll ultimately need to attend an interview and pass a test of your knowledge of the English language and U.S. civics and government. But you won't have to worry about many of the other citizenship requirements, including your age and your period of residence within the United States.

If you're eventually separated from the Armed Forces under other-than-honorable conditions before you've served honorably for a total of five years, your citizenship can be revoked (taken away).

**Immigrant Story:
Major Diaz Becomes a U.S. Citizen**

Reynaldo Diaz came to the U.S. from Mexico as a four-year-old, with his family. A cousin helped smuggle them across the border near San Diego. After completing high school in the U.S., Reynaldo decided to join the U.S. Army. He was sent to serve in Iraq, where he received many awards and commendations.

As soon as Reynaldo learns of the law permitting him to apply for citizenship, he talks to a superior officer, who helps him fill out the paperwork. Reynaldo attends his naturalization interview while at home in Kansas on leave, and passes the test easily.

As a U.S. citizen, he can now petition for residency for his parents, brothers, and sisters.

B. Who Qualifies for Permanent Residence

If you were outside the U.S. when you enlisted in the military, or for other reasons don't qualify for immediate U.S. citizenship, you may still be able to apply for a U.S. green card, under the employment-based classification of "special immigrant."

The spouse and minor children under 21 years of age who are joining or accompanying the veteran or enlistee are also entitled to immigrant visas.

In order to have enlisted outside the U.S., you must be in a country that has a treaty with the United States allowing this.

RESOURCE

You can call or email for advice. Members of the U.S. military and their families stationed around the world can call USCIS for help with immigration services and benefits by using a dedicated, toll-free telephone help line, at 877-CIS-4MIL (877-247-4645). Alternatively, you can email a customer service representative at militaryinfo.nsc@dhs.gov.

1. Veterans

An alien veteran of the U.S. Armed Forces can apply for permanent residence if he or she:

- has served honorably
- has served on active duty
- has served after October 15, 1978
- is recommended for a special immigrant visa by the U.S. Armed Forces or Navy officer under whom he or she serves
- originally enlisted outside the United States
- has served for an aggregate of 12 years, and
- was honorably discharged when separated from the service.

2. Enlistees

An alien enlistee in the U.S. Armed Forces can apply for permanent residence if he or she:

- originally enlisted outside the United States for six years
- is on active duty when applying for adjustment of status under this law
- has reenlisted for another six years, giving a total of 12 years active duty service, and

- is recommended for a special immigrant visa by the U.S. Armed Forces or Navy officer under whom he or she serves.

A Break for Illegal Workers

Because of this special law for alien members of the U.S. Armed Forces, the Immigration and Nationality Act allows the applicant—and his or her spouse and children—to get permanent residence even if they may have worked illegally in the United States.

3. Iraqi or Afghan Translators for U.S. Armed Forces

You may also apply for a U.S. green card if you are a national of Iraq or Afghanistan and you:

- worked directly with the U.S. Armed Forces as a translator for at least 12 months
- received a letter of recommendation from a general or flag officer in your unit, and
- have passed background checks and screening.

Your application process will be similar to the one described below, except that you'll need to provide documents proving the above three things (instead of the certifications required of other members of the military). Also, you must submit Form I-360 to the USCIS Nebraska Service Center to start the process; you can't combine it with an adjustment of status application even if you're in the United States. You can either mail your I-360 or email it (preferably in pdf format) to NSCI360SIVAPP@uscis.dhs.gov.

4. How to File for Permanent Residence

The following forms must be completed and filed, along with a filing fee of $405 in a money order or certified check made payable to U.S. Department of Homeland Security:

☐ Form I-360, Petition for Amerasian, Widow(er), or Special Immigrant (available at www.uscis.gov/i-360; see sample at the end of this chapter; note that it includes only the pages relevant to veterans and enlistees; but you'll still need to submit all the pages, even the ones you don't fill in)

☐ Form N-426, Request for Certification for Military or Naval Service

☐ Form G-325A/G-325B, Biographic Information

☐ certification of past active duty status of 12 years for the veteran, or certified proof of reenlistment after six years of active duty service for the enlistee, issued by an authorized Armed Forces official, and

☐ your birth certificate to show that you are a national of the country that has an agreement with the United States allowing the enlistment of its nationals in the U.S. Armed Forces.

These papers have to be filed with either:

- the USCIS office having jurisdiction over the veteran or enlistee's current residence or intended place of residence in the United States, or
- the overseas USCIS office having jurisdiction over the residence abroad.

If you are in the U.S., you may (unless you're an Afghan or Iraqi translator, as described in Section B3, above) apply directly for adjustment of status (see Chapter 16), and so may your spouse and your children under 21 years of age. Form I-360 and accompanying materials should be included with the rest of the adjustment of status application.

If your spouse and children are outside the United States, you may file Form I-824, Application for Action on an Approved Application or Petition, to be sent to the U.S. consulate where they will apply for immigrant visas as derivative relatives of a special immigrant.

! CAUTION

USCIS will automatically revoke the petition and bar the enlistee from getting a green card if he or she:

- fails to complete the period of reenlistment, or
- receives other than an honorable discharge.

The enlistee's spouse and children will also be barred from getting green cards. If any of them already have green cards, USCIS will begin proceedings to have them taken away.

5. Applying for Citizenship After Getting a Green Card

If you got your green card as a veteran or enlistee, you're only a few short steps away from being eligible for U.S. citizenship. Although most people must wait five years after getting their green card, you are immediately able to apply for citizenship.

Servicepeople who got their green cards in other ways than through their military service can apply for citizenship as soon as they've served honorably for one year; it doesn't matter how long they've had the green card for—one day is enough. However, if they've been discharged, the discharge must have been honorable, and they must apply for citizenship within six months of the discharge date.

To file for naturalization, you must file the following forms and documents with USCIS:

☐ Form N-400, Application for Naturalization

☐ Form N-426, Request for Certification for Military or Naval Service

☐ a copy of your green card

☐ Form G-325A/G-325B, Biographic Information, and

☐ two photographs.

There is no fee for filing a naturalization application for servicemembers filing for citizenship on the basis of their military service.

📖 RESOURCE

Want complete information on the application process for U.S. citizenship, including special exceptions applying to members of the military? See *Becoming a U.S. Citizen: A Guide to the Law, Exam & Interview,* by Ilona Bray (Nolo).

Sample Form I-360, Petition for Amerasian, Widow(er), or Special Immigrant (page 1)

OMB No. 1615-0020; Expires 03/31/2015

Department of Homeland Security
U.S. Citizenship and Immigration Services

I-360, Petition for Amerasian, Widow(er), or Special Immigrant

START HERE - Type or print in black ink

For USCIS Use Only

Part 1. Information About Person or Organization Filing This Petition (Individuals use the top name line; organizations use the second line.) If you are a self-petitioning spouse or child and do not want USCIS to send notices about this petition to your home, you may show an alternate mailing address here. If you are filing for yourself and do not want to use an alternate mailing address, skip to Part 2.

1a. Family Name	**1b.** Given Name	**1c.** Middle Name
ZAPATO	Dante	Diego

2. Company or Organization Name

3. Address - C/O

4. Street Number and Name	**5.** Apt. Number
122 Jupiter St.	3

6. City	**7.** State or Province
Makati	Metro Manila

8. Country	**9.** Zip/Postal Code
Philippines	

10. U.S. Social Security Number	**11.** A-Number	**12.** IRS Tax No. (if any)
123-45-6767	None	None

For USCIS Use Only:

Returned
_____
_____

Receipt

Resubmitted
_____
_____

Reloc Sent
_____
_____

Reloc Rec'd
_____
_____

☐ Petitioner/Applicant Interviewed
☐ Beneficiary Interviewed

☐ I-485 Filed Concurrently
☐ Bene "A" File Reviewed

Classification

Consulate

Priority Date

Remarks:

Part 2. Classification Requested (Check one):

☐ **a.** Amerasian

☐ **b.** Widow(er) of a U.S. citizen

☐ **c.** Special Immigrant Juvenile

☐ **d.** Special Immigrant Religious Worker

　　Will the alien be working as a minister? ☐ Yes ☐ No

☒ **e.** Special Immigrant based on employment with the Panama Canal Company, Canal Zone Government, or U.S. Government in the Canal Zone

☐ **f.** Special Immigrant Physician

☐ **g.** Special Immigrant International Organization Employee or family member

☐ **h.** Special Immigrant Armed Forces Member

☐ **i.** Self-Petitioning Spouse of Abusive U.S. Citizen or Lawful Permanent Resident

☐ **j.** Self-Petitioning Child of Abusive U.S. Citizen or Lawful Permanent Resident

☐ **k.** Special Immigrant Afghanistan or Iraq National who worked with the U.S. Armed Forces as a translator

☐ **l.** Special Immigrant Iraq National who was employed by or on behalf of the U.S. Government

☐ **m.** Other, explain: _____

Action Block

To Be Completed By
☐ *Attorney or Representative,* **if any**
Fill in box if Form G-28 is attached to represent the applicant

VOLAG Number

ATTY State License Number

Form I-360 (03/05/13) N

Sample Form I-360, Petition for Amerasian, Widow(er), or Special Immigrant (page 2)

Part 3. Information About the Person for Whom This Petition Is Being Filed

1a. Family Name *(Last Name)* ZAPATO	**1b.** Given Name *(First Name)* Dante	**1c.** Middle Name Diego

2. Address - C/O

3a. Street Number and Name 122 Jupiter St.	**3b.** Apt. Number 3

4. City Makati	**5.** State or Province Metro Manila

6. Country Philippines	**7.** Zip/Postal Code

8. Date of Birth *(mm/dd/yyyy)* 04/06/1966	**9.** Country of Birth Philippines	**10.** U.S. Social Security Number 123-45-6767	**11.** A-Number *(if any)* none

12. Marital Status: ☐ Single ☒ Married ☐ Divorced ☐ Widowed

13. Complete the items below if this person is in the United States. If an item is not applicable or the answer is "none," leave the space blank. Provide data below for the passport or other document used at the time of last arrival to the United States.

a. Date of Arrival *(mm/dd/yyyy)*	**b.** I-94 Number
c. Passport Number	**d.** Travel Document Number
e. Country of Issuance for Passport or Travel Document	**f.** Expiration Date for Passport or Travel Document
g. Current Nonimmigrant Status	**h.** Current Status Expires on *(mm/dd/yyyy)*

Part 4. Processing Information

1. Provide information on which U.S. consulate you want notified if this petition is approved, and if any requested adjustment of status cannot be granted.

a. U.S. Consulate: City Manila	**b.** Country Philippines

2. If you gave a U.S. address in **Part 3**, print the person's foreign address below. If his or her native alphabet does not use Roman letters, print his or her name and foreign address in the native alphabet.

a. Name	**b.** Address

c. Gender of the person for whom this petition is being filed: ☒ Male ☐ Female

d. Are you filing any other petitions or applications with this one? ☒ No ☐ Yes (How many? _____)

e. Is the person this petition is for in deportation or removal proceedings? ☒ No ☐ Yes (Explain on a separate sheet of paper)

f. Has the person for whom this petition is being filed ever worked in the U.S. without permission? ☒ No ☐ Yes (Explain on a separate sheet of paper)

g. Is an application for adjustment of status attached to this petition? ☒ No ☐ Yes (Attach a full explanation)

Sample Form I-360, Petition for Amerasian, Widow(er), or Special Immigrant (page 10)

Part 9. Information About the Spouse and Children of the Person for Whom This Petition Is Being Filed

A widow/widower or a self-petitioning spouse of an abusive citizen or lawful permanent resident should also list the children of the deceased spouse or of the abuser. This includes biological and adopted children and stepchildren.

1a. Family Name	1b. Given Name	1c. Middle Name
ZAPATO	Isabella	Aday

1d. Date of Birth (mm/dd/yyyy)	1e. Country of Birth	1f. Relationship	1g. A Number
07/12/1969	Philippines	☒ Spouse ☐ Child	None

2a. Family Name	2b. Given Name	2c. Middle Name
ZAPATO	Ricardo	Jesus

2d. Date of Birth (mm/dd/yyyy)	2e. Country of Birth	2f. Relationship	2g. A-Number
06/12/1994	Philippines	☒ Child	None

3a. Family Name	3b. Given Name	3c. Middle Name

3d. Date of Birth (mm/dd/yyyy)	3e. Country of Birth	3f. Relationship	3g. A-Number
		☐ Child	

4a. Family Name	4b. Given Name	4c. Middle Name

4d. Date of Birth (mm/dd/yyyy)	4e. Country of Birth	4f. Relationship	4g. A-Number
		☐ Child	

5a. Family Name	5b. Given Name	5c. Middle Name

5d. Date of Birth (mm/dd/yyyy)	5e. Country of Birth	5f. Relationship	5g. A-Number
		☐ Child	

6a. Family Name	6b. Given Name	6c. Middle Name

6d. Date of Birth (mm/dd/yyyy)	6e. Country of Birth	6f. Relationship	6g. A-Number
		☐ Child	

Cancellation of Removal:

Do Ten Illegal Years Equal One Green Card?

Immigration law does provide a green card as a form of relief from removal (deportation) to a person who has been in the United States for more than ten years. However, the process is long and arduous, and can normally be started only if you're already in immigration court proceedings, facing removal from the United States. This relief is called "cancellation of removal," formerly known as "suspension of deportation." When granted, an alien immediately becomes a lawful permanent resident—and receives a green card soon after the court hearing.

This area of immigration law has changed drastically in recent years. The rules controlling who qualifies have become much tougher since Congress passed changes in 1996. Some people can still qualify under the former, more flexible rules; others will qualify only if they meet the more restrictive rules passed more recently.

A. Applying in Court Proceedings

You cannot file an application to begin cancellation of removal directly with USCIS, as you can with other immigration applications. This process is available only when you are already in Immigration Court (EOIR) proceedings, where the government is trying to deport and remove you from the United States. It is a defense against deportation and removal. (The only exception to this rule is for people who qualify for benefits under the Nicaraguan Adjustment and Central American Relief Act.)

Unlike the other kinds of applications discussed in this book, with cancellation of removal, USCIS is not involved in the decision making. The decision on your case will be made by the Immigration Judge. The other branch of the government that gets involved is a part of the Department of Homeland Security (DHS) called Immigration and Customs Enforcement (ICE). DHS/ICE is the "opposing counsel" in your case.

Being in removal proceedings means that DHS has learned of your illegal status and has served you with a summons called a Notice to Appear (which was once called an Order to Show Cause). The notice is a formal order giving you the time, date, and place to appear for a hearing on whether or not you should be deported.

If DHS has not started removal proceedings against you, and you want to apply for cancellation of removal, your sole possibility is to turn yourself in to DHS—and it may then start removal proceedings against you. But you should not do this before consulting an experienced immigration attorney. The attorney can help evaluate whether you qualify for relief and assess the chances of DHS cooperating with you. More often, DHS just lets your application sit in their files for years and years, perhaps waiting for the laws to turn against you.

B. Who Qualifies for Cancellation

If you have been in the United States for ten years or more and you are of good moral character, and your deportation would cause hardship to certain close family members who are either U.S. citizens or permanent residents, there is a chance that your application for cancellation of removal will be granted.

> **SEE AN EXPERT**
>
> **It is very risky to ask to be placed in removal proceedings solely to request cancellation.** If you are contemplating turning yourself in to DHS, discuss your situation first with an immigration attorney who specializes in cancellation issues or with an immigration law clinic or a group that specializes in counseling on immigration matters.

C. Who Is Not Eligible for Cancellation

A number of people cannot apply for cancellation of removal. They include:

- aliens who entered the United States as crewmen after June 30, 1964
- J-1 visa holders who have not fulfilled a two-year home country residency requirement if they are required to do so, and those who came to the U.S. to receive graduate medical education or training
- those who belong to certain categories of inadmissible aliens, including those who the U.S. government believes are coming to the U.S. to engage in espionage, unlawful activities to overturn the U.S. government, or terrorist activities, and those who have been members of totalitarian or some communist parties
- people who are deportable for offenses involving national security, espionage, or terrorism
- people who have participated in persecuting others
- certain people previously given relief from removal or deportation
- people who have been convicted of certain crimes involving morally bad conduct or illegal drugs
- people convicted of a crime involving morally bad conduct in the five years after being admitted to the U.S. if the crime is punishable by a sentence of one year or more
- people who have been convicted of certain offenses involving failure to comply with alien registration or change of address requirements, or certain offenses involving document fraud, and
- people convicted of an aggravated felony. This includes murder, rape, sexual abuse of a minor, illegal trafficking in drugs or firearms, money laundering, crimes of violence, some theft crimes, burglary, or other offenses, including some misdemeanors. If you have

been convicted of a crime, get advice from an experienced attorney.

D. Preparing a Convincing Case

If you decide that your best approach is to file for cancellation of removal, know that you will have some difficult times ahead. Nationwide, Immigration Judges are not allowed to grant more than 4,000 cancellation of removal cases per year, so applicants are effectively competing against each other to show who is most worthy of this relief—usually by showing whose family will be most devastated by their removal from the United States.

Your first task will be to find a lawyer. (See Chapter 24 for advice on finding a good one.) Together, you and your lawyer will figure out what kinds of evidence you can submit to show that you should be granted cancellation of removal. The following three sections will get you started thinking about what evidence is most relevant to you.

1. Proof of Good Moral Character

You must show that you've been a person of good moral character for at least the last ten years. You may be able to secure a certificate of good conduct from your local police station. This certificate will attest that, according to computer records, you have never been in trouble with the police. Although DHS will also send your fingerprints to the Federal Bureau of Investigation in Washington, DC, submitting your own record from the local police will help prove to the court that you are a person of good moral character.

You can also submit declarations from relatives, friends, and community members verifying that you have participated in religious institutions, volunteered at schools or other civic places, or in any other way demonstrated that you are a good person.

If you have committed any serious crime during the ten years you were in the United States, the Immigration Judge may find that you lack good moral character. Ten years must pass from the time you committed the crime until the time you can apply for a suspension of deportation. However, committing certain serious crimes will make you ineligible forever.

2. Proof That You Stayed in the U.S. Ten Years

You must show also that you have lived in the United States continuously for at least ten years. A copy of your passport and I-94 (Arrival-Departure Record) from when you first arrived in the United States are the best proof of this.

In addition, copies of your apartment lease, bank statements, and income tax returns are good evidence that you have been in the United States for ten years. School and medical records, subscriptions and memberships, and statements from friends, landlords, or coworkers are also useful.

What Does "Continuous Physical Presence" Mean?

The court will consider that you have been continuously present in the U.S. even if you departed from the country, as long as your absences did not exceed more than 90 days per trip or 180 days total. There are exceptions for individuals who served honorably in the Armed Forces for at least two years. Also, the time that can be used toward the ten-year presence period will be cut short if you commit an act that makes you deportable or inadmissible, or when DHS issues you a Notice to Appear.

---

3. Proof of Hardship

You must convince the court that if you are deported from the United States, it would cause "exceptional and extremely unusual hardship" to your spouse, child, or parent who is a U.S. citizen or a permanent resident. (The law in effect before 1996 allowed an individual to qualify by showing extreme hardship to himself or herself as well as to one of those family members, but this no longer works.)

Of course, if your spouse, parent, or adult child (21 or over) is a U.S. citizen, you qualify as a candidate for an immigrant visa as an immediate relative or as a family preference beneficiary (see Chapter 4). Cancellation of removal is considered a remedy of last resort, so if you are able to adjust your status based on a visa petition filed by any of those family members, you are expected to do so. If for some reason you are not able to adjust your status, however, cancellation of removal might be your only available avenue.

Because cancellation of removal depends almost completely on the discretion of the judge, you can only hope for a judge who is compassionate and humane. You and your lawyer must convince the judge that leaving the United States and returning to your own country would cause exceptional and extremely unusual hardship for your family members due to any combination of personal, economic, sociocultural, and psychological reasons.

Personal reasons. The Immigration Court will need the birth certificate of your child, your marriage certificate, and your own birth certificate (if your parents are the U.S. citizens or permanent residents who will suffer hardship should you leave the United States).

For starters, your relatives should be prepared to testify in court about how much you mean to them, how much they depend on you, and how disastrous it would be for them if you were not allowed to remain in the United States. Since nearly every family would face some similar pain, the judge wants to see that the hardship your family would face is "exceptional and extremely unusual."

If your American-born children are under 14, the judge will normally not ask to hear their testimony. However, the testimony of such young children, detailing their affection for you and the hardships they would endure if they accompanied you to your native country—problems with language, problems being uprooted from friends and schools—could strengthen your case.

Although testimony by your young children that, as Americans, they would rather stay in the United States with their grandparents or with a foster family than leave for a country they don't know could be hurtful for you to hear, such testimony would be further evidence that your deportation would cause them hardship.

Proof that any illness for which you or a family member is being treated in the United States, and evidence that the same treatment or medicine is either lacking or too expensive in your own country should also be given to the judge, supported by letters from doctors and pharmacists in the United States and the foreign country.

Provided they are either U.S. citizens or permanent residents, more distant relatives—including the grandparents or the biological parents of your child, their aunts, uncles, or cousins, or your own brothers and sisters—may all testify that your departure would also be an extreme hardship to them and to the family in general.

Whether or not these people testify, they should all submit letters of support for you. Letters that are sworn under penalty of perjury are usually given more weight than other letters.

If you have a boyfriend or girlfriend who is married to somebody else, it is not recommended that he or she testify either on your behalf, or on behalf of the child he or she had with you. Although adultery has been repealed from immigration law as proof of the lack of good moral character, many judges will not look with favor upon such situations.

Economic reasons. Although you are probably earning much more in the United States than you would earn in your own country, economic reasons are the least persuasive arguments against deportation. Economic hardship by itself has never been considered by the Immigration Court as sufficient reason to cancel deportation. If you would be completely unable to support yourself and your family in your home country, however, the Judge may consider that a hardship factor.

If you are receiving welfare, government subsidies, or any form of public assistance, you may have a more difficult time receiving mercy from the judge. A judge is unlikely to grant you permission to stay in the United States permanently if you may be seen as a burden to the government.

Proof of regular and continuous employment is very important. Letters from your employers, past and present, detailing your employment history and your value as an employee, your most current pay stubs, and evidence of your work product, in the form of photos or newspaper articles, are all useful in demonstrating your contribution to the economic life of the nation. Try to contrast this to how different your employment opportunities would be in your home country.

You should have filed income tax returns for the past ten years, so submit copies as proof. These will show that, except for your illegal immigration status, you have been law-abiding. If you have not filed any tax returns because you do not have a Social Security number or because you have always been paid in cash, you should consult a tax expert at once. You may have to pay back taxes.

If you are in business for yourself, submit copies of documents demonstrating this. These could include your business license, your business checking account showing activity, a financial statement from an accountant to the court, and incorporation papers showing you as the major or only stockholder. Also consider providing photos of your business in operation, payroll records for any employees, and a letter from your bank giving your account history and the average balance of your business account. Letters from your business partners and testimony in court explaining how the business would be affected if you were forced to leave it should also be presented during the hearing.

If you have invested in real estate, present proof of ownership, mortgage papers, and a letter from a real estate broker concerning how much your property would be worth if sold in the present market and especially how much financial loss this would cause you.

Sociocultural reasons. Convince the court that you are in good standing in your community. Present letters from your church, temple, or mosque about your active membership, from your block or village association, from the Parent-Teacher Association, from volunteer organizations, and from people you have cared for or helped. All are important to show that your life has been intimately entwined with U.S. society and that you have been a useful member of your community.

Letters from the union supervisor or from your coworkers explaining the kind of person you are and how valuable you are to them personally and in terms of work are also persuasive documents to present to the judge.

The judge will want to know whether you have any other possible forms of relief from deportation, whether you have any pending petitions submitted on your behalf by a relative or an employer, and why it is advantageous for the U.S. government to grant you permanent residence through an immediate cancellation of removal instead of waiting for the Priority Date of any other immigration petition that may be pending.

Psychological reasons. You will have to acquaint the judge with the social, cultural, and political situation in your country and how your family may be subjected to prejudice, bigotry, or ostracism.

If you have a child born outside of marriage, or who is of a different race or is physically handicapped, provide evidence of how such children are treated in your country. Explain how going back to your country would affect your emotional and psychological health, thereby affecting your U.S. citizen and permanent resident family members. Also explain how going back would directly affect the emotional or psychological health of any relative who is a U.S. citizen or permanent resident. Testimony from an expert witness, such as a psychiatrist or a psychologist, would bolster your case.

If you have a child who is a U.S. citizen, explain how the child's inability to speak the language of your native country would be harmful to the child's education, and how removal from relatives, friends, and classmates could cause the child great psychological trauma.

E. How to File

You and your lawyer must submit the following documents to the immigration judge, along with a filing fee of $100:

- Form EOIR-42B, Application for Cancellation of Removal and Adjustment of Status for Certain Nonpermanent Residents
- Form G-325A, Biographic Information
- documentary evidence as described in Section D, above
- two color photographs taken within 30 days of submitting the application, and
- $80 fingerprinting fee.

Notice that we don't provide sample, filled-in forms in this chapter. That's because you'd be foolish to go into Immigration Court without the help of an attorney; and the attorney will help you fill out the forms.

You can apply for a work permit once you have filed Form EOIR-42B, by filing Form I-765 at the Chicago lockbox address indicated on the form's instructions, along with the filing fee of $380. Your answer to question #16 (eligibility category) is (c)(10).

The Immigration Judge will set a hearing date for your case—giving enough time for you and your lawyer to prepare and for USCIS to investigate your case. In the meantime, USCIS should issue you a work permit.

The hearing may not finish the first day. In fact, it may be postponed one or more times because the Immigration Court devotes only a few hours at a time to each case on its calendar. Unless you are being detained at the immigration jail, your case may take one or two years before it is fully heard and a decision is reached.

F. Approving Your Application

If the Immigration Judge approves your application for cancellation of removal, you will be granted permanent residence that day (if there are still visa numbers available for the current year).

Because you have shown that you have lived a productive and useful life in the United States all those years that you were living illegally, and that your deportation would be extremely hard for your American or lawful permanent resident spouse, child, or parents, the U.S. government wants you to remain in the United States legally.

Winning Is Not Enough

Even if an Immigration Judge decides to cancel your removal order, you could face a delay. Only 4,000 people each year are granted formal cancellation of removal. Immigration judges have the power to grant conditional or temporary cancellation of removal orders until the person becomes eligible. The removal proceedings will not be formally ended, and permanent residence will not be formally granted, until your waiting number is reached.

G. Additional Forms of Cancellation of Removal

There are two additional forms of cancellation of removal. One is for permanent residents (green card holders) who have become deportable or removable. The other is for people who have been subjected to extreme cruelty or battery by a spouse or parent who is a U.S. citizen or permanent resident while in the United States.

1. Permanent Residents

An immigration judge may cancel the removal of, and re-grant a green card to, a permanent resident if the person:

- has five years as a permanent resident
- has lived continuously in the U.S. for at least seven years after having been admitted in any status, and
- has not been convicted of an aggravated felony.

This relief will serve as a waiver of removal for many permanent residents who commit acts that make them deportable. See a lawyer for help with this (and Chapter 24).

2. Abused Spouse or Child

An abused spouse or child of a U.S. citizen or permanent resident may apply for cancellation of removal under different rules. In this case, the applicant must show that he or she:

- suffered physical abuse or extreme mental cruelty in the U.S. at the hands of a permanent resident or U.S. citizen who is or was the applicant's parent or spouse—or the applicant is the parent of such an abused child
- has been physically present in the U.S. for a continuous period of at least three years at the time of the application
- has had good moral character for at least the three-year period, and
- is not inadmissible due to a conviction for a crime involving moral turpitude or drugs, or on national security or terrorism grounds or other specified grounds, and has not been convicted of an aggravated felony.

The applicant must also show that the removal would result in extreme hardship to the applicant, or to his or her child or parent (if the applicant is a child).

Congress added this provision as part of the Violence Against Women Act, or VAWA, so that spouses and children who are victims of abuse by their petitioning relative would have a way to obtain status if they left the household of the abuser.

Again, seek a lawyer's help with this type of application. Many nonprofits offer free or low-cost help.

Adjustment of Status

Are you ready for the final step toward getting a green card while you're living in the United States? By now, you should have already completed some preliminary steps, such as winning the visa lottery, receiving approval of a visa petition (Form I-130) filed by a member of your family, or having spent one year in the U.S. as an asylee or refugee. Or you should have figured out that, because of special circumstances (most likely that you're the immediate relative of a U.S. citizen and entered the U.S. legally), you don't need to get advance approval of a Form I-130 before continuing with your application. In any case, it's now your turn, as the immigrant, to file your application for a green card.

The procedure for obtaining a green card while you're in the United States is called adjustment of status. It involves submitting forms to USCIS and attending an interview at a local USCIS office. It literally means you're changing your status from that of an undocumented person or a nonimmigrant visa holder to that of permanent resident. The alternate way to obtain a green card is through what's called "consular processing" (discussed in Chapter 17), in which you correspond with and attend interviews at an overseas U.S. embassy or consulate.

If you're living or staying in the United States right now, you might prefer the convenience of applying for your green card without leaving, using the adjustment of status process. Unfortunately, it's not always that easy. Many people who are eligible for green cards—because they're family members of U.S. citizens or permanent residents, or fall into other immigration categories—are nevertheless not allowed to stay in the United States to get their green card. Read on to find out the possibilities and potential problems that surround adjustment of status.

This chapter will discuss:

- who is allowed to use the adjustment of status procedure (Section A)
- who doesn't qualify, and what effect this has on the person's efforts to immigrate (Section B), and
- if you qualify, what forms and application procedures you'll need to use (Section C).

How Do You Decide?

If you are eligible for both adjustment of status in the United States or consular processing abroad, it is often best to choose adjustment of status because:

- you will save the expense of traveling back to your home country
- if your application to adjust your status is denied, you can remain and work in the U.S. while you appeal that decision
- if you go for consular processing and your application is denied, there is no right to appeal, and
- when adjusting status, there is no risk of being kept out for three or ten years due to past illegal stays in the United States.

Nevertheless, adjustment of status is not the best choice for everyone. For example, if you don't face any problems with the time bars, and the U.S. consulate in your home country is processing cases a lot faster than your local USCIS office—as was the case several years ago—you might want to choose consular processing for the sake of a speedier and less expensive green card. For example, people who are eager to start the clock ticking on their eligibility for U.S. citizenship, perhaps in order to help parents or other relatives immigrate, may want to choose the speedier way.

A. Who Is Allowed to Use the Adjustment of Status Procedure

You are allowed to choose adjustment of status as your green card application method only if you fall into one of the following three categories:

- You are the immediate relative of a U.S. citizen and your last entry into the U.S. was done legally (see Section 1, below).

- Your last entry into the U.S. was done legally and you have remained in legal status ever since (see Section 2, below).
- You are "grandfathered in" under certain old laws because you had a visa petition on file before the laws changed (unlikely; see Section 3, below).

In addition, you must not be inadmissible based on the "permanent bar." This bar applies to people who lived in the United States illegally for more than a year and then left or were deported, but who returned to the United States illegally (or were caught trying to). Such people may never be allowed to get a green card. See a lawyer if you believe this bar might apply to you.

1. Immediate Relatives Who Entered Legally

If you meet the following two criteria, you are one of the lucky few allowed to use the adjustment of status procedure:

- You are the immediate relative (spouse, parent, or minor, unmarried child) of a U.S. citizen.
- Your most recent entry to the United States was done legally, most likely using a visa (such as a tourist or a student visa), a visa waiver (in which you simply showed your passport and were admitted for a 90-day tourist stay), or some other entry document like a border crossing card. There are exceptions, however: You cannot adjust under this category if you entered as a crewman on a boat or plane, regardless of what visa you had, or you were in transit to another country without a visa (for example, changing planes in a U.S. airport).

> CAUTION
> **Remember, this chapter discusses only procedures, not your underlying eligibility for a green card.** Unless you've already completed the steps explained in another chapter—most likely one describing family- or lottery-based visas—you shouldn't be in this chapter. It's only for people with approved visa petitions—or immediate relatives who are filing a visa petition with their application for adjustment of status—or for people with winning lottery letters who are now completing their green card application process.

> **EXAMPLE:** Katerina is a foreign student from Germany who has used her student visa to enter the United States many times, most recently on her return trip after summer vacation. She is engaged to marry a fellow student named Mark, a U.S. citizen. Once they're married, Katerina will be an immediate relative, whose last entry to the U.S. was done legally. (In fact, it wouldn't matter if she let her student visa expire before applying to adjust status, though we don't recommend this method, since it means spending time in the U.S. illegally.) Katerina will be able to apply for her green card without leaving the U.S., using the adjustment of status procedure.

However, there's one major, and common, difficulty for some immediate relatives: Your use of the visa or visa waiver to enter the U.S. has to have been an innocent one, merely to study, travel, or whatever it was your visa was meant for. If instead you used the visa specifically for the purpose of getting yourself to the U.S. so you could adjust status, that's visa fraud, and will make you ineligible for a green card. Visas are meant to be used only for the limited purpose of coming to the U.S. for a temporary stay—any secret plans to stay permanently can be seen as a big problem.

> **EXAMPLE:** While Sally was a foreign student in the Netherlands, she met Joost, and they became engaged. After Sally's studies ended, she returned to the United States. Joost stayed behind for a few months, to finish an architecture project. Because citizens of the Netherlands are not required to obtain visas to visit the U.S., Joost simply picked up his passport when he was ready, and flew to New York. He told the border official he was there

to visit friends for a few months, and was let in. They got married at city hall the next week, and Joost immediately began preparing his green card application. Joost's actions could easily be considered visa fraud. Although, technically, Joost would be able to use the adjustment of status procedure—in fact, he would probably have no problem submitting his full green card application—when the time comes for Joost's interview, the USCIS officer may question him closely about whether he purposely lied when he entered the U.S. and told the border official that he would stay here for only a few months. If Joost can't come up with a good answer, his application will be denied. (There is a waiver Joost can apply for, with the help of an attorney, but it's hard to get.)

An unbelievable number of married couples make the same mistake that Sally and Joost did. A few get lucky and the immigration official who interviews them simply overlooks the problem. If you wait long enough after your entry to either get married or submit the green card application—hopefully two months, at least—you'll face fewer questions, because USCIS may presume you were thinking your plans over in between. And some people are able to convincingly explain that their intentions when entering the U.S. were truly just to visit (or do whatever their visa was intended for), but while here, they talked it over with their relative (or soon-to-be spouse) and decided that the immigrant should stay and apply for a green card.

Additional difficulties can occur if you entered the U.S. on the visa waiver program. In this situation, you should submit a complete adjustment application to USCIS and, ideally, submit it before the expiration of the 90-day period of your visa-waiver–authorized stay. USCIS may approve your I-485 application even if you overstayed, but in most jurisdictions, if your application is denied, you won't get a "second bite at the apple" by asking an Immigration Judge to consider your application.

2. People Who Entered Legally and Remain Legal

Even if you're not the immediate relative of a U.S. citizen, you're allowed to get a green card using the adjustment of status procedure if you meet all the following criteria:

- You entered the U.S. legally, most likely using a visa (such as a tourist or a student visa) or some other entry document like a border crossing card. There are exceptions, however: You cannot adjust under this rule if you entered using a visa waiver, you entered as a crewman on a boat or plane (regardless of what visa you had), or you were in transit to another country without a visa (for example, changing planes in a U.S. airport).
- You have never been out of legal status (your right to stay, as most likely shown on your I-94, hasn't expired).
- You have never worked without INS or USCIS authorization.

Whether or not your permitted stay has expired is an important issue. If you were granted a tourist visa (B-2), for example, the visa itself may be valid for many years and allow multiple entries. However, the important issue is how long the border officials said you could stay on this particular trip. You'll find this information on your I-94, which you must obtain online, and will show the expiration date of your authorized stay. You might also find this date stamped on your passport. If you've overstayed that date, and didn't get any extension or change of status, your status is now illegal, no matter how long your visa is good for.

Note to students: Your I-94 may not have an expiration date, but may simply say "D/S," which means "duration of status." In other words, you're allowed to stay in the U.S. as long as you continue your studies (and don't violate the other terms of your student visa).

Working without authorization is also a troublesome issue for many immigrants. Tourist and student visa holders, for example, are frequent violators of the work permit rules (tourists aren't allowed to work at all, and students can work only under limited circumstances).

EXAMPLE: Ahmed and Ali, two brothers age 24 and 26, come to visit their mother in the United States, where she lives as a permanent resident. A month into their six-month stay, their mother's U.S. citizenship finally comes through. Because the mother petitioned for the brothers some years ago, they can use their old Priority Date, and they find that they're immediately eligible for green cards in the family first preference category (see Chapter 9). But can they apply for adjustment of status? They entered legally, and their stay is still legal. However, Ali has picked up a part-time job in a local restaurant. Only Ahmed will be able to adjust status. Ali will have to return home and try to get his green card through consular processing (where he may face questions about his illegal work).

Another problem that comes up for some applicants is the use of visa fraud to enter the United States. After waiting outside the United States for many years for their Priority Date to become current, many applicants figure they can simply get a visa to the U.S. and submit an adjustment of status application once they're here. Many of them are disappointed to find out they've just committed visa fraud. Again, visas are meant to be used only for the limited purpose of coming to the U.S. for a temporary stay, and your activities on that visa must remain within its purposes—visitor visa holders must act like tourists, student visa holders must act like students, and so on. Although immigration officials will sometimes look the other way, it's best to avoid the problem, stay in your home country, and finish your application through the local consulate.

EXAMPLE: Meijin is a U.S. permanent resident who filed visa petitions for her two children, aged 26 and 28, in the second preference category, many years ago. Their Priority Date finally becomes current, and they receive forms and information from the U.S. consulate in Beijing, China, near where they live. The older child, Guofeng, can't wait—he uses a tourist visa he already happens to have to enter the United States. He tells the border officials in San Francisco he's just coming to sightsee (otherwise they would have turned Guofeng around and sent him home). Guofeng submits a green card application. The application is denied, because Guofeng inappropriately used a tourist visa when his real intention was to stay permanently. His sister, Jinqing, stays home and files her paperwork with the U.S. consulate, and she succeeds in getting an immigrant visa and a green card.

SEE AN EXPERT

Not sure whether you can adjust status under these rules? If you have any doubts at all about whether you qualify to adjust status, consult a qualified immigration attorney. See Chapter 24 for advice on finding a good one.

3. People Who Qualify Under Old Laws

As you've seen, a number of people are barred from adjusting status, including those who entered the U.S. illegally; overstayed their visa or other permitted time; worked without authorization; entered while in transit without a visa; or entered as crew on planes or boats. However, there are two exceptions, based on changes in the laws over the years.

At one time, a law called "245(i)" allowed all people who were otherwise unable to adjust status to do so by paying a penalty fee. That law is now gone, but a few people who were around when the law was still in effect are allowed to make use of it. You can apply to adjust status under § 245(i) if:

- you had an approvable visa petition or labor certification filed on your behalf before January 14, 1998 (it doesn't matter whether it was filed by the same person or employer as the one through whom you're now immigrating)
- you had an approvable visa petition or labor certification filed on your behalf before April 30, 2001, as long as you were physically in the U.S. on December 21, 2000 (again, it doesn't matter whether it was filed by the same person or employer as the one through whom you're now immigrating), or
- in certain circumstances, if you are the spouse or child of someone described above.

EXAMPLE: Amina's father, a U.S. citizen, filed a visa petition for her in 1996, when she was already married. She was in the U.S. on a student visa (F-1) with her husband, on an F-2 visa as the spouse of a student. Amina and her husband overstayed their visas after graduation, and went out of status. They planned to file for adjustment of status when her Priority Date became current. Unfortunately, although the visa petition was approved, the father died before Amina could complete the green card application process. Amina's brother, a U.S. citizen, then files a visa petition for her. When her Priority Date on her brother's petition becomes current (and assuming USCIS hasn't caught and deported her), Amina and her husband can use the approval notice from her father's 1996 petition to make them eligible to adjust status in the United States.

There is a financial catch to using these old laws to adjust status, however: You'll have to pay a penalty fee, currently $1,000.

B. People Who Can't Adjust Status at All

If you don't fall into any of the categories described above, you do not qualify to use adjustment of status as your green card application method. This means that many people who only recently became eligible to immigrate—for example, by marrying a U.S. citizen—but who entered the U.S. without being inspected and admitted by a border official, and had no visa petitions filed for them by any of the important 1998 or 2001 dates, will be ineligible to adjust status.

Unfortunately, this is a difficult trap, because if a person has spent more than 180 days in the U.S. illegally, leaving the U.S. to try to apply through an overseas U.S. consulate could result in being barred from returning for three or ten years. Some, but not all people facing this trap may be able to get around it by applying for a provisional waiver of unlawful presence, allowing them to receive an answer before leaving the United States. (Review Chapter 4 for details.) See a lawyer if you're in this or a similar situation.

C. How to File

If you are one of the lucky people who can adjust status in the U.S., a number of picky rules control how and when you can submit your various application forms. Follow them exactly, to be sure that your paperwork can be processed quickly and properly.

1. Whether You Need to Wait for Approval of Form I-130

Most people who are eligible to adjust status can do so only after receiving some official government statement about their basic eligibility for a green card—for example, USCIS approval of their Form I-130 visa petition, a State Department letter indicating they won the lottery, or a grant of political asylum (which can be used as the basis for a green card after one year). However, one exception allows certain applicants applying through family to turn this two-step application process into one step.

If you are the spouse, parent, or minor child of a U.S. citizen (an immediate relative), then you can file the I-130 and adjustment of status paperwork at the same time. If you've already filed the I-130, file your adjustment application with either the approval or with a request for USCIS to request that the pending file be transferred.

If you are applying through a family member but do not match the description in the paragraph above, then your family member must file Form I-130 and accompanying documents at a USCIS Service Center first. (The procedures for I-130 submissions are explained in the various chapters of this book that apply to different types of eligibility for family members.) Only after the I-130 is approved and your Priority Date is current can you continue with your application.

2. Adjustment of Status Forms and Documents

To apply for adjustment of status, you must submit the following forms to USCIS:

- ☐ **Copy of government document proving your basic green card eligibility.** This might be an approved I-130 visa petition (unless you're a family member who can submit this petition together with the adjustment of status application as described in Section 1, above), a State Department letter notifying you that you've won the lottery, a grant of political asylum or refugee status, or, if you entered on a K-1 or K-2 fiancé visa, copies of the fiancé visa petition approval notice, your marriage certificate, and your Form I-94 (which is either a card tucked into your passport or a page you've printed from the U.S. Customs and Border Protection (CBP) website).

 TIP

Getting a copy of your I-94. Until 2013, all nonimmigrants (such as students and tourists) entering the U.S. needed to complete Form I-94, Arrival/Departure Record, a small white piece of paper. The border agent would then indicate the date by which the entrant would need to depart the U.S., and staple the form to the person's passport. Now, paper I-94s have been phased out. You will, however, still need your I-94 number for your adjustment of status application. To find and print it, go to https://i94.cbp.dhs.gov/I94/request.html. If you can't locate your information on the first try, try different variations of your name. For example, include your middle name along with your first name, or both last names, if applicable. Still out of luck? Call a Customs and Border Patrol Deferred Inspection Site for more information, or simply submit an explanation that you were unable to locate your I-94 number online.

- ☐ **Proof that you're eligible to use the adjustment of status procedure.** What you use as proof depends on the reason you're able to adjust status. For example, if you're an immediate relative who entered the U.S. legally, a copy of your Form I-94 would be sufficient. If you're an asylee or refugee and have been present in the U.S. for one year or more, submit proof of the day your status started. This could be your I-94, the Asylum Office Approval letter, or the Order of the Immigration Judge. If you entered the U.S. on a fiancé visa (K-1, K-2, K-3, or K-4) and got married or met your other visa requirements, submit a copy of your visa and I-94. If you're claiming eligibility because you fall under the Section 245(i) law from 1998, you'll need to submit a copy of your I-130 visa petition or labor certification. Approval Notice, with proof that your application was received by the January 14, 1998 deadline. If you are claiming eligibility under the Section 245(i) law from 2001, you'll need to submit the Approval Notice with proof that the application was received by April 30, 2001, as well as proof that you were in the U.S. on December 21, 2000. Such proof might include medical or dental records from that date, a pay stub, or even a traffic ticket. If you don't have a document issued exactly on December 21, 2000—and most people don't—submit documents that are close in time to that date.

☐ **Form I-485, Application to Register Permanent Resident or Adjust Status.** This is the primary form used to adjust status, which collects information on who you are, where you live, how you're eligible for a green card, and whether any of the grounds of inadmissibility (disqualification) apply to you. (See the sample at the end of this chapter.)

☐ **Form I-485 Supplement A.** Use this form only if you're applying to adjust status based on old laws (245(i)). Also remember to pay the penalty fee.

☐ **If you want permission to work, Form I-765.** (See the sample at the end of this chapter.) Several months may pass before you're approved for a green card, during which time you can't work without getting permission. Use this form to ask permission (you don't have to pay any fee with it—it's included in your overall application fee—but if for some reason you submit your work permit application later, you'll have to submit a copy of your Form I-797C Notice of Action receipt showing you filed the I-485, in order to avoid paying a separate fee). You'll be given an Employment Authorization Document (EAD), which is an identification card with your photo. Even if you don't plan to work, this card is a handy way to prove who you are. The last question on the form, number 16, can be confusing (and the instructions list many ways that different types of applicants must answer it). As an adjustment applicant, you simply answer it (c)(9), regardless of how you became eligible for your green card.

☐ **Form G-325A, Biographic Information.** This form asks for information on where you have lived and worked for the last five years, for background investigation. (See the sample at the end of Chapter 7.)

☐ **Form I-131, Application for Travel Document.** This is optional, but very handy. Submitting it will result in your obtaining an "Advance Parole" (AP) document, which you'll need if you leave the U.S. before your green card application has been approved. Even if you don't have plans to leave the U.S. anytime soon, having this AP document will save a lot of time and worry if circumstances arise requiring you to leave before you receive your green card (such as an emergency in your home country or a required trip abroad for work). See the sample at the end of this chapter; and ignore the part of the form that says you have to supply a separate explanation as to why you deserve Advance Parole. Approval is fairly automatic for adjustment of status applicants who haven't already left the U.S., so you really don't need to explain anything.) Leaving the U.S. without Advance Parole will lead to your adjustment of status application being canceled. There is no additional fee to submit your I-131 along with Form I-485 or after if USCIS has already accepted the adjustment application. If you also apply for an EAD and are approved, you will receive an "EAD-AP" combo card, which both serves as your work permission and enables you to leave the USCIS while you await a decision on Form I-485.

TIP

Advance Parole does NOT guarantee readmission into the U.S. You can still be denied reentry at the discretion of Customs and Border Protection (CBP), including if you're inadmissible. This was, in the past, a particular problem for people who'd been unlawfully present in the U.S. for 180 days or more. Fortunately, the Board of Immigration Appeals (BIA) ruled in *Matter of Arrabally Yerrabelly*, 25 I&N Dec. 771 (BIA 2012) that people with a pending permanent residency application who leave the U.S. with Advance Parole do not trigger the three- and ten-year unlawful presence bars. However, to be cautious, you might want to consult an immigration attorney before leaving.

☐ **Form I-864, Affidavit of Support.** (See the sample in Chapter 17.) If you're applying through a family member (not through an employer or as an asylee or refugee, nor if you're a self-petitioning widow(er) or a battered spouse or child), you must submit this sworn statement from the petitioner (the U.S. citizen or lawful permanent resident who submitted the visa petition for you, who has sufficient income and who promises to support you and to reimburse the U.S. government if you must receive public assistance after receiving your permanent residence).

☐ **Form I-864W (if you fall within an exception to Form I-864 requirement).** Certain exceptions apply: The petitioner need not submit a Form I-864 if either the immigrant or the immigrant's spouse or parent has already worked in the U.S. for 40 quarters as defined by the Social Security system—about ten years. Nor do you need the Form I-864 if the beneficiary is a child (adopted or natural born) who will become a U.S. citizen automatically upon entering the U.S. If you're exempt from the affidavit of support requirement due to one of these exceptions, fill out Form I-864W instead of the regular Form I-864.

☐ **Documents to support Form I-864.** The latest year's tax returns (or IRS transcripts) of the citizen or permanent resident should be attached to the affidavit as proof of financial capacity (or up to three years' worth if it will strengthen your case). Proof of the sponsor's employment should also be attached.

☐ **Additional Form I-864 or I-864A (Contract Between Sponsor and Household Member) if getting help with sponsorship.** If your petitioner doesn't earn enough to meet the government requirements, you'll have to find an additional financial sponsor or another member of the sponsor's household who can add income and assets to the mix.

☐ **Form I-864EZ (for simple cases).** If you are the only person that your petitioner is sponsoring, and your petitioner can meet the sponsorship requirements based upon his or her income alone, it's okay to use a shorter version of the form called I-864EZ.

☐ **Job letter for immigrant.** If you are working (with USCIS authorization), you can submit a job letter from your employer in the United States stating your work history, when you started to work, whether your employment is permanent, and how much you earn, along with a payroll statement confirming your earnings.

If you are applying for a green card based on marriage, the job letter should include your marital status, name of spouse, and name and telephone number of person to be notified in case of an emergency.

Sample Sponsor's Job Letter

ABC Company
123 Main Street
Anytown, Anystate 12345

April 24, 20xx

U.S. Citizenship and Immigration Services
26 Federal Plaza
New York, NY 10278

Dear Sir or Madam:

This letter is to certify that Jon Fratellanza has been employed by this company since March 2005 as a widget inspector.

His salary is $850 per week and he is employed on a full-time, permanent basis. His prospects for continued employment with this company are excellent.

Our personnel records indicate that this employee is married. In case of emergency, his spouse, Danielle Fratellanza, must be notified at their home telephone: 111-222-3456.

Sincerely,

Milton Mutter

Milton Mutter
Personnel Director, ABC Company

☐ **Form I-693, Medical Examination of Aliens Seeking Adjustment of Status.** This must be filled out by a USCIS-approved doctor and submitted in an unopened envelope. To find a USCIS-approved doctor, go to the USCIS website at www.uscis.gov/i-693 and click "Immigration Medical Examinations" then "USCIS Civil Surgeons Locator" or call USCIS Customer Service (1-800-375-5283). **Refugees, I-730 derivative asylees, and fiancés take note:** If you had an exam overseas within the last year, submit a copy of the results of that medical rather than submitting a new medical. An exception to this is if medical grounds of inadmissibility were noted during your exam or when you entered the United States; then you'll need a new exam and may have to request a waiver of inadmissibility. If you had the medical but did not get all of the vaccines before entering the U.S., you will have to get them now and submit the "Vaccination Supplemental Form to I-693" with your application. This can be filled out only by a USCIS-approved doctor.

☐ **If applying as an asylee or refugee, proof that you've been physically present in the U.S. for at least a year.** This could be a letter verifying your employment, an apartment lease, or school records. You'll also need to include evidence of any trips you've made outside the U.S. since gaining asylum. (Remember, if you've made any trips to the country you fled from, you may have canceled your eligibility and should see a lawyer.)

☐ **A copy of your birth certificate.** Include a word-for-word translation, if it is not in English.

☐ **Two passport-style color photographs.**

☐ **Filing fee.** USCIS charges fees for handling applications, based on which forms you submit. They regularly raise the fees, so check with USCIS for the latest before you turn in your application. As of the date that this book went to print, the fee to file Form I-485 is $985. Refugees pay no fee. Applicants under age 14 who are filing with at least one parent owe a fee total of $635. Applicants under age 14 who are not filing with a parent have a fee total of $985. Neither needs to pay a separate fingerprinting fee. Pay by money order or personal check made payable to the U.S. Department of Homeland Security. In addition, if you file Form I-485 Supplement A, you'll have to pay the penalty fee of $1,000 (see Section A). Fingerprints ("biometrics") are an additional $85 (but are not required if you're age 79 or older). The filing fee and the fingerprinting fee can be paid in one check.

☐ **Form G-1145.** While not required, it is a good idea to also file Form G-1145, so as to receive an email and/or text notification from USCIS letting you know that your application has been accepted.

3. Submission Procedures

The procedures for submitting an adjustment of status application have changed a lot in recent years. In the past, you could ordinarily walk your application right into a local USCIS office. Now, however, you'll have to mail your application to a service center or an out-of-state processing office. See the chart below for the appropriate address.

D. After You Apply

After you've submitted your adjustment of status application, USCIS should send you a receipt notice (on Form I-797). This will confirm that your application contained everything it should have, and that you're now in line for an adjustment of status interview.

You can use the number on your receipt notice to sign up for automatic email and/or text updates letting you know when mail is sent regarding your application. To sign up for these, go to the USCIS website, www.uscis.gov, and click "Check Your Case Status." Enter your receipt number, then click "Check status." On this page, click "creating an account."

If your application was incomplete, you will receive a letter indicating what's missing, and you should reply as soon as possible. How long you'll have to wait for your adjustment of status interview depends on how backed up your local USCIS office is. (These interviews are held locally, at a different office than the one you submitted your application to.) Several months is typical.

Some weeks before your interview is scheduled, you'll be called in to have your fingerprints taken for your security checks.

During this wait, it's best not to take any long trips or move to a different address. USCIS won't give you much advance notice of your interview date, usually about a month or so.

**Travel Outside the U.S.
While Awaiting Your Interview**

As discussed earlier, you or your minor children should not leave the United States while waiting for your adjustment of status interview without first applying for and receiving "Advance Parole." If you didn't apply for Advance Parole when you filed your adjustment of status application, you can do so later, by submitting Form I-131 to the office handling your file. There is no additional fee for the Form I-131 application as long as your adjustment of status application is pending.

If you leave without this permission, USCIS will cancel your adjustment of status application. It will assume that your departure shows your lack of interest in receiving your green card in the United States and that you have abandoned your application.

E. Interview and Approval

Although USCIS makes some exceptions, it requires most applicants to attend an interview at a local USCIS office before approving them for permanent residence and a green card. You'll get a form letter (see the sample below) advising you of the interview date and location, and telling you what to bring along.

The required documents normally include a photo identification; recent financial records from whoever signed the affidavit of support, to show continuing employment and ownership of assets; documents updating other information in your application, for example if you've changed your name; and originals of your birth certificate, passport, visas, and other

Where to Send an Adjustment of Status Application	
If you're applying based on:	**Send your adjustment of status application to:**
A family relationship (for example, you're the spouse, widow, parent, or child of a U.S. citizen, or the spouse or child of a U.S. permanent resident); as a winner of the diversity visa lottery; as someone eligible for registry; as a special immigrant member of the Armed Forces; or as an Amerasian	U.S. Citizenship and Immigration Services, P.O. Box 805887, Chicago, IL 60680-4120 (if you're using the U.S. Postal Service) or U.S. Citizenship and Immigration Services, Attn: FBAS, 131 South Dearborn—3rd Floor, Chicago, IL 60603-5520 (if you're using a private courier)
Having held asylum or refugee status for at least one year and you live in one of the following states: AK, AZ, CA, CO, Commonwealth of Northern Mariana Islands, Guam, HI, IA ID, IL, IN, , KS, MI, MN, MO, MT, ND, NE, NV, OH, OR, SD, UT, WA, WI, or WY	USCIS, Phoenix Lockbox, P.O. Box 21281, Phoenix, AZ 85036 (if you're using the U.S. Postal Service) or USCIS, Attn: AOS, 1820 E. Skyharbor Circle S, Suite 100, Phoenix, AZ 85034 (if you're using a private courier)
Having held asylum or refugee status for at least one year and you live in one of the following states: AL, AR, CT, DE, FL, GA, KY, LA, MA, MD, ME, MS, NC, NH, NJ, NM, NY, OK, PA, Puerto Rico, RI, SC, TN, TX, VA, VT, U.S. Virgin Islands, WV, or Washington, DC	USCIS, Dallas Lockbox, P.O. Box 660867, Dallas, TX 75266 (if you're using the U.S. Postal Service) or USCIS, Attn: AOS, 2501 S State Hwy. 121 Business, Suite 400, Lewisville, TX 75067 (if you're using a private courier)
Having an approved petition as an Afghan or Iraqi translator	USCIS, Nebraska Service Center, P.O. Box 87485, Lincoln, NE 68501-7485 (if you're using the U.S. Postal Service) or USCIS, Nebraska Service Center, 850 S. Street, Lincoln, NE 68508-1225 (if you're using a private courier)
As a battered spouse or child	USCIS, Vermont Service Center, Attn: CRU, 75 Lower Welden Street, St. Albans, VT 05479-0001

documents you've submitted copies of in connection with your application (these are for the USCIS officer to view, not keep); and documents showing any changes in the information on your application, such as a new employer.

If you're applying based on marriage, you'll also need to bring documents proving that your marriage is the real thing, such as copies of your home mortgage or lease, joint credit card statements, children's birth certificates, and more.

Then there's the question of whom to bring along. Everyone who submitted a green card application and is mentioned in the interview notice should go along, including children. And if the green cards are based on marriage, the U.S. petitioner needs to be there as well. For other family relationships, however—for example if you're getting a green card as the brother, sister, parent, or child of a U.S. citizen—the rules are less strict. USCIS would prefer to see the petitioner there, first off to make sure that he or she is still alive, and in case questions arise about the affidavit of support. But if that's inconvenient, for example if the petitioner lives in another part of the U.S., you can go to your appointment without the petitioner. However, it's best to bring a recent, signed, sworn statement by the petitioner explaining the situation and providing a phone number in case USCIS wants to follow up.

When bringing new documents, be sure to make copies of any that you don't want to leave with USCIS—they're usually happy with copies, particularly if they can view the original when you bring it. They're unwilling, however, to make photocopies for you, so you must either bring a copy or lose your original to the USCIS file.

If you don't speak English, you'll need to bring your own interpreter. You don't need to spend money on a professional—a friend or family member over 18 who is a legal U.S. resident will do. But it's worth spending the money if you don't know anyone who's truly fluent in both English and your native language—your future is at stake here,

and a little confusion may delay or destroy your hopes of getting a green card.

CAUTION
Arrive on time—and follow the rules. Leave extra time for parking and passing through the security guard post at the USCIS office. Remember, this is a federal government building, so they'll X-ray your possessions and confiscate pocket knives or other illegal materials. They may also prohibit other items, such as cell phones and food. If you arrive late, you will probably lose your chance to be interviewed that day, and go through major hassles getting USCIS to reschedule you.

Interview Tips for Spouses

If you are requesting an adjustment of status as the spouse of a U.S. citizen or permanent resident, USCIS will require a personal interview with you both before granting your application.

Bring copies of all the forms relevant to your application, along with evidence of a bona fide marriage—such as wedding pictures, joint bank statements, rental agreements, children's birth certificates, health insurance contracts, and more. (See Chapter 7.)

If you've got solid documentary evidence of your real marriage, the officer is likely to ask only a few questions. If, on the other hand, the documents are weak, or you and your spouse don't seem able to answer the questions about your marriage, you may be sent for what's called a "fraud interview." This means that you and your spouse will each separately meet with the USCIS officer, who will ask each of you the same set of questions, and then check whether your answers match up. If you don't already have an attorney, this is a good time to ask that the interview be postponed, so that you can return with legal help.

At your interview, a USCIS officer will review your application, ask you some questions, and presumably approve you for a green card. Most of the questions will relate to what's already on your application, such as your current address, how you last entered the United States, and whether you have a criminal record or are otherwise ineligible for a green card.

If you're applying based on marriage, be prepared to answer additional questions to prove that your marriage is the real thing, such as how you met, details of your wedding, and details about your house and your life together.

Most interviews last about 20 minutes. Answer the questions courteously and honestly—but don't volunteer extra information. Saying too much wastes the officer's time and may bring to light information that would have been better left unsaid.

If everything is in order, your application for adjustment of status should be approved. Your passport may be stamped with a temporary approval, good for one year, authorizing you to stay in the United States. If you are not approved at your interview, you will later be notified of the approval and requested to bring your passport to the nearest USCIS office.

Your green card—which resembles a driver's license in size and format—will be sent by mail to your address in several weeks or months. Be sure to inform USCIS of any change of address, because your green card might not be forwarded to you by the post office. Even after you get your green card, you are obligated to send USCIS written word every time your address changes—see Chapter 23 for this and other important rules on keeping your right to a green card.

It's wonderful! You are now a lawful permanent resident who is authorized to work and stay in the United States legally.

SEE AN EXPERT

If your application is denied, consult an experienced immigration attorney. Unless you have some other visa or legal status in the United States, your file will be transferred to the Immigration Court for removal proceedings. See Chapter 24 for advice on finding a good attorney.

Immigrant Story: Proving a Real Marriage

Brian, a U.S. citizen, and Toshi, from Japan, met and fell in love while they were in college in Champaign, Illinois. Brian graduated two years ahead of Toshi, and got a great job in Atlanta. They corresponded long distance, and the next year got married and applied for Toshi's green card.

However, by the time Toshi got called for her adjustment of status interview, the couple was still not living together. They were worried that the immigration officer would not believe that their marriage was the real thing. After much thought, here are the documents they came up with to prove their relationship:

- college receipts showing that Brian was helping pay for Toshi's education
- sworn statements from Toshi's dormmates attesting to Brian's frequent visits
- documents showing that Toshi is the beneficiary of Brian's life insurance policy and 401(k)
- letter from a fertility specialist that Brian and Toshi had consulted about her difficulty in getting pregnant, and
- copies of emails and phone bills showing their frequent communication.

Brian and Toshi easily answered all the officer's questions at the interview, and Toshi was granted U.S. permanent residence.

Sample Interview Appointment Notice

Department of Homeland Security
U.S. Citizenship and Immigration Services

I-797C, Notice of Action

REQUEST FOR APPLICANT TO APPEAR FOR INITIAL INTERVIEW	NOTICE DATE January 31, 2011
CASE TYPE FORM I-485, APPLICATION TO REGISTER PERMANENT RESIDENCE OR ADJUST STATUS	A# A 099 909 909

APPLICATION NUMBER MSC0712345678	RECEIVED DATE January 12, 2011	PRIORITY DATE January 12, 2011	PAGE 1 of 1

HAI-ZI ZHANG
c/o ILONA BRAY
950 PARKER ST.
BERKELEY, CA 94710

You are hereby notified to appear for the interview appointment, as scheduled below, for the completion of your Application to Register Permanent Residence or Adjust Status (Form I-485) and any supporting applications or petitions. *Failure to appear for this interview and/or failure to bring the below listed items will result in the denial of your application.* (8 CFR 103.2(b)(13))

<u>Who should come with you?</u>

☐ **If your eligibility is based on your marriage, your husband or wife must come with you to the interview.**
☐ **If you do not speak English fluently, you should bring an interpreter.**
☐ Your attorney or authorized representative may come with you to the interview.
☐ If your eligibility is based on a parent/child relationship and the child is a minor, the petitioning parent and the child must appear for the interview.

NOTE: Every adult (over 18 years of age) who comes to the interview must bring Government-issued photo identification, such as a driver's license or ID card, in order to enter the building and to verify his/her identity at the time of the interview. You do not need to bring your children unless otherwise instructed. Please be on time, but do not arrive more than 45 minutes early. We may record or videotape your interview.

<u>YOU MUST BRING THE FOLLOWING ITEMS WITH YOU:</u> (Please use as a checklist to prepare for your interview)

☐ This Interview Notice and your Government issued photo identification.
☐ A completed medical examination (Form I-693) and vaccination supplement in a sealed envelope (unless already submitted).
☐ A completed Affidavit(s) of Support (Form I-864) with all required evidence, including the following, for <u>each</u> of your sponsors (unless already submitted):
    ☐ Federal Income Tax returns and W-2's, or certified IRS printouts, for the past 3 years;
    ☐ Letters from each current employer, verifying current rate of pay and average weekly hours, and pay stubs for the past 2 months;
    ☐ Evidence of your sponsor's and/or co-sponsor's United States Citizenship or Lawful Permanent Resident status.
☐ All documentation establishing your eligibility for Lawful Permanent Resident status.
☐ Any immigration-related documentation ever issued to you, including any Employment Authorization Document (EAD) and any Authorization for Advance Parole (Form I-512).
☐ All travel documents used to enter the United States, including Passports, Advance Parole documents (I-512) and I-94s (Arrival/Departure Document).
☐ Your Birth Certificate.
☐ Your petitioner's Birth Certificate and your petitioner's evidence of United States Citizenship or Lawful Permanent Resident Status.
☐ If you have children, bring a Birth Certificate for each of your children.
☐ If your eligibility is based on your marriage, in addition to your spouse coming to the interview with you, bring:
    ☐ A certified copy of your Marriage Document issued by the appropriate civil authority.
    ☐ Your spouse's Birth Certificate and your spouse's evidence of United States Citizenship or Lawful Permanent Resident status;
    ☐ If either you or your spouse were ever married before, all divorce decrees/death certificates for each prior marriage/former spouse;
    ☐ Birth Certificates for all children of this marriage, and custody papers for your children and for your spouse's children not living with you;
☐ Supporting evidence of your relationship, such as copies of any documentation regarding joint assets or liabilities you and your spouse may have together. This may include: tax returns, bank statements, insurance documents (car, life, health), property documents (car, house, etc.), rental agreements, utility bills, credit cards, contracts, leases, photos, correspondence and/or any other documents you feel may substantiate your relationship.
☐ Original and copy of each supporting document that you submitted with your application. Otherwise, we may keep your originals for our records.
☐ If you have ever been arrested, bring the related Police Report and the original or certified Final Court Disposition for each arrest, even if the charges have been dismissed or expunged. If no court record is available, bring a letter from the court with jurisdiction indicating this.
☐ A certified English translation for each foreign language document. The translator must certify that s/he is fluent in both languages, and that the translation in its entirety is complete and accurate.

<u>YOU MUST APPEAR FOR THIS INTERVIEW-</u> If an emergency, such as your own illness or a close relative's hospitalization, prevents you from appearing, call the U.S. Citizenship and Immigration Services (USCIS) National Customer Service Center at 1-800-375-5283 as soon as possible. Please be advised that rescheduling will delay processing of application/petition, and may require some steps to be repeated. It may also affect your eligibility for other immigration benefits while this application is pending.

If you have questions, please call the USCIS National Customer Service Center at 1-800-375-5283 (hearing impaired TDD service is 1-800-767-1833).

PLEASE COME TO: U.S. Citizenship and Immigration Services 630 SANSOME ST 2ND FLOOR - ADJUSTMENT OF STATUS SAN FRANCISCO CA 94111	ON: **Monday, March 28, 2011** AT: **02:15 PM**
3	REPRESENTATIVE COPY

Form I-797C (Rev. 01/31/05) N

Sample Form I-485, Application to Register Permanent Residence or Adjust Status (page 1)

OMB No. 1615-0023; Expires 06/30/15

Department of Homeland Security
U.S. Citizenship and Immigration Services

Form I-485, Application to Register
Permanent Residence or Adjust Status

START HERE - Type or Print (Use black ink)

	For USCIS Use Only

Part 1. Information About You

Family Name *(Last Name)*	Given Name *(First Name)*	Middle Name
Michelski	Anda	

Address - Street Number and Name	Apt. No.
68 Watertown Boulevard	12

C/O *(in care of)*

City	State	ZIP Code
Erie	Pennsylvania	19380

Date of Birth *(mm/dd/yyyy)*	Country of Birth
06/28/1984	Bulgaria

Country of Citizenship/Nationality	U.S. Social Security No. *(if any)*	A-Number *(if any)*
Bulgaria	128-46-9255	

Date of Last Arrival *(mm/dd/yyyy)*	I-94 Number
11/04/2011	000000000 00

Current USCIS Status	Expires on *(mm/dd/yyyy)*
B-2	05/3/2014

For USCIS Use Only

Returned

Receipt

Resubmitted

Reloc Sent

Reloc Rec'd

Applicant Interviewed

Part 2. Application Type *(Check one)*

I am applying for an adjustment to permanent resident status because:

a. ☒ An immigrant petition giving me an immediately available immigrant visa number that has been approved. (Attach a copy of the approval notice, or a relative, special immigrant juvenile, or special immigrant military visa petition filed with this application that will give you an immediately available visa number, if approved.)

b. ☐ My spouse or parent applied for adjustment of status or was granted lawful permanent residence in an immigrant visa category that allows derivative status for spouses and children.

c. ☐ I entered as a K-1 fiancé(e) of a U.S. citizen whom I married within 90 days of entry, or I am the K-2 child of such a fiancé(e). (Attach a copy of the fiancé(e) petition approval notice and the marriage certificate.)

d. ☐ I was granted asylum or derivative asylum status as the spouse or child of a person granted asylum and am eligible for adjustment.

e. ☐ I am a native or citizen of Cuba admitted or paroled into the United States after January 1, 1959, and thereafter have been physically present in the United States for at least 1 year.

f. ☐ I am the husband, wife, or minor unmarried child of a Cuban described above in **(e)**, and I am residing with that person, and was admitted or paroled into the United States after January 1, 1959, and thereafter have been physically present in the United States for at least 1 year.

g. ☐ I have continuously resided in the United States since before January 1, 1972.

h. ☐ Other basis of eligibility. Explain (for example, I was admitted as a refugee, my status has not been terminated, and I have been physically present in the United States for 1 year after admission). If additional space is needed, see **Page 3** of the instructions. _____

I am already a permanent resident and am applying to have the date I was granted permanent residence adjusted to the date I originally arrived in the United States as a nonimmigrant or parolee, or as of May 2, 1964, whichever date is later, and: *(Check one)*

i. ☐ I am a native or citizen of Cuba and meet the description in **(e)** above.

j. ☐ I am the husband, wife, or minor unmarried child of a Cuban and meet the description in **(f)** above.

Section of Law
☐ Sec. 209(a), INA
☐ Sec. 209(b), INA
☐ Sec. 13, Act of 9/11/57
☐ Sec. 245, INA
☐ Sec. 249, INA
☐ Sec. 1 Act of 11/2/66
☐ Sec. 2 Act of 11/2/66
☐ Other _____

Country Chargeable

Eligibility Under Sec. 245
☐ Approved Visa Petition
☐ Dependent of Principal Alien
☐ Special Immigrant
☐ Other

Preference

Action Block

To be Completed by
Attorney or Representative, **if any**
☐ Fill in box if Form G-28 is attached to represent the applicant.

VOLAG No

ATTY State License No.

Form I-485 (Rev. 06/20/13) Y

Sample Form I-485, Application to Register Permanent Residence or Adjust Status (page 2)

Part 3. Processing Information

A. City/Town/Village of Birth

Sofia

Current Occupation

Language teacher

Your Mother's First Name

Anastasia

Your Father's First Name

Liski

Give your name exactly as it appears on your Form I-94, Arrival-Departure Record

Anda Michelski

Place of Last Entry Into the United States
(City/State)

JFK Airport, New York

In what status did you last enter? (*Visitor, student, exchange visitor, crewman, temporary worker, without inspection, etc.*)

Visitor

Were you inspected by a U.S. Immigration Officer?   Yes [X]   No [ ]

Nonimmigrant Visa Number

1062745139652

Consulate Where Visa Was Issued

Sofia

Date Visa Issued (*mm/dd/yyyy*)

09/06/2013

Gender

[ ] Male   [X] Female

Marital Status

[ ] Married   [X] Single   [ ] Divorced   [ ] Widowed

Have you ever applied for permanent resident status in the U.S.?   [ ] Yes (*If "Yes" give date and place of filing and final disposition.*)   [X] No

B. List your present spouse and all of your children (include adult sons and daughters). (If you have none, write "None." If additional space is needed, see **Page 3** of the instructions.)

Family Name (*Last Name*)	Given Name (*First Name*)	Middle Initial	Date of Birth (*mm/dd/yyyy*)
Country of Birth	Relationship	A-Number (*if any*)	Applying with you? Yes [ ] No [ ]
Family Name (*Last Name*)	Given Name (*First Name*)	Middle Initial	Date of Birth (*mm/dd/yyyy*)
Country of Birth	Relationship	A-Number (*if any*)	Applying with you? Yes [ ] No [ ]
Family Name (*Last Name*)	Given Name (*First Name*)	Middle Initial	Date of Birth (*mm/dd/yyyy*)
Country of Birth	Relationship	A-Number (*if any*)	Applying with you? Yes [ ] No [ ]
Family Name (*Last Name*)	Given Name (*First Name*)	Middle Initial	Date of Birth (*mm/dd/yyyy*)
Country of Birth	Relationship	A-Number (*if any*)	Applying with you? Yes [ ] No [ ]
Family Name (*Last Name*)	Given Name (*First Name*)	Middle Initial	Date of Birth (*mm/dd/yyyy*)
Country of Birth	Relationship	A-Number (*if any*)	Applying with you? Yes [ ] No [ ]

Sample Form I-485, Application to Register Permanent Residence or Adjust Status (page 3)

Part 3.   Processing Information *(Continued)*

C. List your present and past membership in or affiliation with every organization, association, fund, foundation, party, club, society, or similar group in the United States or in other places since your 16th birthday. Include **any military service** in this part. If none, write "None." Include the name of each organization, location, nature, and dates of membership. If additional space is needed, attach a separate sheet of paper. Continuation pages must be submitted according to the guidelines provided on **Page 3** of the instructions under **General Instructions**.

Name of Organization	Location and Nature	Date of Membership From	Date of Membership To
None			

Answer the following questions. (If your answer is **"Yes"** to any question, explain on a separate piece of paper. Continuation pages must be submitted according to the guidelines provided on **Page 3** of the instructions under **General Instructions**. Information about documentation that must be include with your application is also provide in this section.) Answering **"Yes"** does not necessarily mean that you are not entitled to adjust status or register for permanent residence.

1. Have you **EVER**, in or outside the United States:

    a. Knowingly committed any crime of moral turpitude or a drug-related offense for which you have not been arrested?   Yes ☐ No ☒

    b. Been arrested, cited, charged, indicted, convicted, fined, or imprisoned for breaking or violating any law or ordinance, excluding traffic violations?   Yes ☐ No ☒

    c. Been the beneficiary of a pardon, amnesty, rehabilitation decree, other act of clemency, or similar action?   Yes ☐ No ☒

    d. Exercised diplomatic immunity to avoid prosecution for a criminal offense in the United States?   Yes ☐ No ☒

2. Have you received public assistance in the United States from any source, including the U.S. Government or any State, county, city, or municipality (other than emergency medical treatment), or are you likely to receive public assistance in the future?   Yes ☐ No ☒

3. Have you **EVER**:

    a. Within the past 10 years been a prostitute or procured anyone for prostitution, or intend to engage in such activities in the future?   Yes ☐ No ☒

    b. Engaged in any unlawful commercialized vice, including, but not limited to, illegal gambling?   Yes ☐ No ☒

    c. Knowingly encouraged, induced, assisted, abetted, or aided any alien to try to enter the United States illegally?   Yes ☐ No ☒

    d. Illicitly trafficked in any controlled substance, or knowingly assisted, abetted, or colluded in the illicit trafficking of any controlled substance?   Yes ☐ No ☒

4. Have you **EVER** engaged in, conspired to engage in, or do you intend to engage in, or have you ever solicited membership or funds for, or have you through any means ever assisted or provided any type of material support to any person or organization that has ever engaged or conspired to engage in sabotage, kidnapping, political assassination, hijacking, or any other form of terrorist activity?   Yes ☐ No ☒

Sample Form I-485, Application to Register Permanent Residence or Adjust Status (page 4)

Part 3. Processing Information *(Continued)*

5. Do you intend to engage in the United States in:

    a. Espionage?   Yes ☐   No ☒

    b. Any activity a purpose of which is opposition to, or the control or overthrow of, the Government of the United States, by force, violence, or other unlawful means?   Yes ☐   No ☒

    c. Any activity to violate or evade any law prohibiting the export from the United States of goods, technology, or sensitive information?   Yes ☐   No ☒

6. Have you **EVER** been a member of, or in any way affiliated with, the Communist Party or any other totalitarian party?   Yes ☐   No ☒

7. Did you, during the period from March 23, 1933 to May 8, 1945, in association with either the Nazi Government of Germany or any organization or government associated or allied with the Nazi Government of Germany, ever order, incite, assist, or otherwise participate in the persecution of any person because of race, religion, national origin, or political opinion?   Yes ☐   No ☒

8. Have you **EVER** been deported from the United States, or removed from the United States at government expense, excluded within the past year, or are you now in exclusion, deportation, removal, or rescission proceedings?   Yes ☐   No ☒

9. Are you under a final order of civil penalty for violating section 274C of the Immigration and Nationality Act (INA) for use of fraudulent documents or have you, by fraud or willful misrepresentation of a material fact, ever sought to procure, or procured, a visa, other documentation, entry into the United States, or any immigration benefit?   Yes ☐   No ☒

10. Have you **EVER** left the United States to avoid being drafted into the U.S. Armed Forces?   Yes ☐   No ☒

11. Have you **EVER** been a J nonimmigrant exchange visitor who was subject to the 2-year foreign residence requirement and have not yet complied with that requirement or obtained a waiver?   Yes ☐   No ☒

12. Are you now withholding custody of a U.S. citizen child outside the United States from a person granted custody of the child?   Yes ☐   No ☒

13. Do you plan to practice polygamy in the United States?   Yes ☐   No ☒

14. Have you **EVER** ordered, incited, called for, committed, assisted, helped with, or otherwise participated in any of the following:

    a. Acts involving torture or genocide?   Yes ☐   No ☒

    b. Killing any person?   Yes ☐   No ☒

    c. Intentionally and severely injuring any person?   Yes ☐   No ☒

    d. Engaging in any kind of sexual contact or relations with any person who was being forced or threatened?   Yes ☐   No ☒

    e. Limiting or denying any person's ability to exercise religious beliefs?   Yes ☐   No ☒

15. Have you **EVER**:

    a. Served in, been a member of, assisted in, or participated in any military unit, paramilitary unit, police unit, self-defense unit, vigilante unit, rebel group, guerrilla group, militia, or insurgent organization?   Yes ☐   No ☒

    b. Served in any prison, jail, prison camp, detention facility, labor camp, or any other situation that involved detaining persons?   Yes ☐   No ☒

16. Have you **EVER** been a member of, assisted in, or participated in any group, unit, or organization of any kind in which you or other persons used any type of weapon against any person or threatened to do so?   Yes ☐   No ☒

Sample Form I-485, Application to Register Permanent Residence or Adjust Status (page 5)

Part 3.   Processing Information *(Continued)*

17. Have you **EVER** assisted or participated in selling or providing weapons to any person who to your knowledge used them against another person, or in transporting weapons to any person who to your knowledge used them against another person?   Yes ☐   No ☒

18. Have you **EVER** received any type of military, paramilitary, or weapons training?   Yes ☐   No ☒

Part 4.   Accommodations for Individuals With Disabilities and/or Impairments *(See Page 7 of the instructions before completing this section.)*

Are you requesting an accommodation because of your disability(ies) and/or impairment(s)?   Yes ☐   No ☒

If you answered "Yes," check any applicable box:

☐   **a.** I am deaf or hard of hearing and request the following accommodation(s) (if requesting a sign-language interpreter, indicate which language (e.g., American Sign Language)):

☐   **b.** I am blind or sight-impaired and request the following accommodation(s):

☐   **c.** I have another type of disability and/or impairment (describe the nature of your disability(ies) and/or impairment(s) and accommodation(s) you are requesting):

Part 5.   Signature *(Read the information on penalties on Page 8 of the instructions before completing this section. You must file this application while in the United States.)*

Your Registration With U.S. Citizenship and Immigration Services

"I understand and acknowledge that, under section 262 of the Immigration and Nationality Act (INA), as an alien who has been or will be in the United States for more than 30 days, I am required to register with U.S. Citizenship and Immigration Services (USCIS). I understand and acknowledge that, under section 265 of the INA, I am required to provide USCIS with my current address and written notice of any change of address within **10** days of the change. I understand and acknowledge that USCIS will use the most recent address that I provide to USCIS, on any form containing these acknowledgements, for all purposes, including the service of a Notice to Appear should it be necessary for USCIS to initiate removal proceedings against me. I understand and acknowledge that if I change my address without providing written notice to USCIS, I will be held responsible for any communications sent to me at the most recent address that I provided to USCIS. I further understand and acknowledge that, if removal proceedings are initiated against me and I fail to attend any hearing, including an initial hearing based on service of the Notice to Appear at the most recent address that I provided to USCIS or as otherwise provided by law, I may be ordered removed in my absence, arrested, and removed from the United States."

Selective Service Registration

The following applies to you if you are a male at least 18 years of age, but not yet 26 years of age, who is required to register with the Selective Service System: "I understand that my filing Form I-485 with U.S. Citizenship and Immigration Services (USCIS) authorizes USCIS to provide certain registration information to the Selective Service System in accordance with the Military Selective Service Act. Upon USCIS acceptance of my application, I authorize USCIS to transmit to the Selective Service System my name, current address, Social Security Number, date of birth, and the date I filed the application for the purpose of recording my Selective Service registration as of the filing date. If, however, USCIS does not accept my application, I further understand that, if so required, I am responsible for registering with the Selective Service by other means, provided I have not yet reached 26 years of age."

Sample Form I-485, Application to Register Permanent Residence or Adjust Status (page 6)

Part 5. **Signature** *(Continued)*

Applicant's Statement *(Check one)*

[X] I can read and understand English, and I have read and understand each and every question and instruction on this form, as well as my answer to each question.

[ ] Each and every question and instruction on this form, as well as my answer to each question, has been read to me in the _____ language, a language in which I am fluent, by the person named in **Interpreter's Statement and Signature**. I understand each and every question and instruction on this form, as well as my answer to each question.

I certify, under penalty of perjury under the laws of the United States of America, that the information provided with this application is all true and correct. I certify also that I have not withheld any information that would affect the outcome of this application.

I authorize the release of any information from my records that U.S. Citizenship and Immigration Services (USCIS) needs to determine eligibility for the benefit I am seeking.

Signature *(Applicant)*	Print Your Full Name	Date *(mm/dd/yyyy)*	Daytime Phone Number *(include area code)*
Anda Michelski	Anda Michelski	04/15/2014	314-276-9440

NOTE: *If you do not completely fill out this form or fail to submit required documents listed in the instructions, you may not be found eligible for the requested benefit, and this application may be denied.*

Interpreter's Statement and Signature

I certify that I am fluent in English and the below-mentioned language.

Language Used *(language in which applicant is fluent)*

I further certify that I have read each and every question and instruction on this form, as well as the answer to each question, to this applicant in the above-mentioned language, and the applicant has understood each and every instruction and question on the form, as well as the answer to each question.

Signature *(Interpreter)*	Print Your Full Name	Date *(mm/dd/yyyy)*	Phone Number *(include area code)*

Part 6. **Signature of Person Preparing Form, If Other Than Above**

I declare that I prepared this application at the request of the above applicant, and it is based on all information of which I have knowledge.

Signature	Print Your Full Name	Date *(mm/dd/yyyy)*	Phone Number *(include area code)*

Firm Name and Address	E-Mail Address *(if any)*

Form I-485 (Rev. 06/20/13) Y Page 6

Sample Form I-765, Application for Employment Authorization

OMB No. 1615-0040; Expires 04/30/2016

Department of Homeland Security
U.S. Citizenship and Immigration Services

I-765, Application For Employment Authorization

Do not write in this block.

Remarks	Action Block	Fee Stamp
A#		

Applicant is filing under §274a.12 _____

☐ Application Approved. Employment Authorized / Extended *(Circle One)*   until _____ (Date).
_____ (Date).

Subject to the following conditions: _____
Application Denied.
☐ Failed to establish eligibility under 8 CFR 274a.12 (a) or (c).
☐ Failed to establish economic necessity under 8 CFR 274a.12(c)(14), (18) and 8 CFR 214.2(f)

I am applying for:
☒ Permission to accept employment.
☐ Replacement *(of lost employment authorization document).*
☐ Renewal of my permission to accept employment *(attach previous employment authorization document).*

1. Name (Family Name in CAPS)   (First)   (Middle)
MANZETTI   Juliet   Anna

2. Other Names Used (include Maiden Name)
Juliet Stefano

3. U.S. Mailing Address (Street Number and Name)   (Apt. Number)
280 Mosher Street

(Town or City)   (State/Country)   (ZIP Code)
Baltimore   Maryland   21216

4. Country of Citizenship/Nationality
Italy

5. Place of Birth (Town or City)   (State/Province)   (Country)
Verona   Italy

6. Date of Birth (mm/dd/yyyy)   **7. Gender**
12/23/1968   ☐ Male ☒ Female

8. Marital Status   ☒ Married   ☐ Single
☐ Widowed   ☐ Divorced

9. Social Security Number (Include all numbers you have ever used, if any)
none

10. Alien Registration Number (A-Number) or I-94 Number (if any)
A456789103

11. Have you ever before applied for employment authorization from USCIS?
☐ Yes (Complete the following questions.)   ☒ No (Proceed to Question 12.)

Which USCIS Office?   Date(s)

Results (Granted or Denied - attach all documentation)

12. Date of Last Entry into the U.S., on or about: (mm/dd/yyyy)
09/01/2013

13. Place of Last Entry into the U.S.
New York, New York

14. Status at Last Entry (B-2 Visitor, F-1 Student, No Lawful Status, etc.)
Parolee

15. Current Immigration Status (Visitor, Student, etc.)
Parolee

16. Go to the **"Who May File Form I-765?"** section of the instructions. In the space below, place the letter and number of the eligibility category you selected from the instructions. (For example, (a)(8), (c)(17)(iii), etc.).

(c) (9) ( )

17. If you entered the eligibility category, (c)(3)(C), in Question 16 above, list your degree, your employer's name as listed in E-Verify, and your employer's E-Verify Company Identification Number or a valid E-Verify Client Company Identification Number in the space below.

Degree: _____
Employer's Name as listed in E-Verify: _____
Employer's E-Verify Company Identification Number or a valid E-Verify Client Company Identification Number _____

Certification

Your Certification: I certify, under penalty of perjury under the laws of the United States of America, that the foregoing is true and correct. Furthermore, I authorize the release of any information that U.S. Citizenship and Immigration Services needs to determine eligibility for the benefit I am seeking. I have read the **"Who May File Form I-765?"** section of the instructions and have identified the appropriate eligibility category in **Question 16.**

Signature	Telephone Number	Date
Juliet Manzetti	301-123-4567	May 25, 2014

Signature of Person Preparing Form, If Other Than Above: I declare that this document was prepared by me at the request of the applicant and is based on all information of which I have any knowledge.

Print Name	Address	Signature	Date

Remarks	Initial Receipt	Resubmitted	Relocated		Completed		
			Received	Sent	Approved	Denied	Returned

Form I-765 04/01/13 Y

Sample Form I-131, Application for Travel Document (page 1)

Application for Travel Document
Department of Homeland Security
U.S. Citizenship and Immigration Services

USCIS
Form I-131
OMB No. 1615-0013
Expires 03/31/2016

For USCIS Use Only	Receipt	Action Block	To Be Completed by an *Attorney/Representative*, if any.

☐ **Document Hand Delivered**

By: _____ Date: ____ / ____ / ____

☐ Fill in box if G-28 is attached to represent the applicant.

Document Issued

☐ Re-entry Permit *(Update "Mail To" Section)*   ☐ Refugee Travel Document *(Update "Mail To" Section)*

☐ Single Advance Parole   ☐ Multiple Advance Parole *Valid Until:* ____ / ____ / ____

Mail To *(Re-entry & Refugee Only)*
☐ Address in *Part 1*
☐ US Consulate at: _____
☐ Intl DHS Ofc at: _____

Attorney State License Number:
_____

▶ **Start Here.** Type or Print in Black Ink

Part 1. Information About You

1.a. Family Name *(Last Name)* MANZETTI

1.b. Given Name *(First Name)* Juliet

1.c. Middle Name Anna

Physical Address

2.a. In Care of Name

2.b. Street Number and Name 280 Mosher Street

2.c. Apt. ☐ Ste. ☐ Flr. ☐

2.d. City or Town Baltimore

2.e. State MD   **2.f.** Zip Code 21216

2.g. Postal Code

2.h. Province

2.i. Country

Other Information

3. Alien Registration Number (A-Number)

▶ A- 4 5 6 7 8 9 1 0 3

4. Country of Birth Italy

5. Country of Citizenship Italy

6. Class of Admission Parolee

7. Gender ☐ Male ☒ Female

8. Date of Birth *(mm/dd/yyyy)* ▶ 12/13/1968

9. U.S. Social Security Number *(if any)*

▶

Sample Form I-131, Application for Travel Document (page 2)

Part 2. Application Type

1.a. ☐ I am a permanent resident or conditional resident of the United States, and I am applying for a reentry permit.

1.b. ☐ I now hold U.S. refugee or asylee status, and I am applying for a Refugee Travel Document.

1.c. ☐ I am a permanent resident as a direct result of refugee or asylee status, and I am applying for a Refugee Travel Document.

1.d. ☒ I am applying for an Advance Parole Document to allow me to return to the United States after temporary foreign travel.

1.e. ☐ I am outside the United States, and I am applying for an Advance Parole Document.

1.f. ☐ I am applying for an Advance Parole Document for a person who is outside the United States.

If you checked box "1.f." provide the following information about that person in 2.a. through 2.p.

2.a. Family Name *(Last Name)*

2.b. Given Name *(First Name)*

2.c. Middle Name

2.d. Date of Birth *(mm/dd/yyyy)* ▶

2.e. Country of Birth

2.f. Country of Citizenship

2.g. Daytime Phone Number (☐☐☐) ☐☐☐ - ☐☐☐☐

Physical Address (If you checked box 1.f.)

2.h. In Care of Name

2.i. Street Number and Name

2.j. Apt. ☐ Ste. ☐ Flr. ☐

2.k. City or Town

2.l. State ☐ **2.m.** Zip Code

2.n. Postal Code

2.o. Province

2.p. Country

Part 3. Processing Information

1. Date of Intended Departure
(mm/dd/yyyy) ▶ 07/12/2014

2. Expected Length of Trip *(in days)* 21

3.a. Are you, or any person included in this application, now in exclusion, deportation, removal, or rescission proceedings? ☐ Yes ☒ No

3.b. If "Yes", Name of DHS office:

4.a. Have you ever before been issued a reentry permit or Refugee Travel Document? *(If "Yes" give the following information for the last document issued to you):*
☐ Yes ☒ No

4.b. Date Issued *(mm/dd/yyyy)* ▶

4.c. Disposition *(attached, lost, etc.):*

If you are applying for a non-DACA related Advance Parole Document, skip to Part 7; *DACA recipients must complete Part 4 before skipping to Part 7.*

Sample Form I-131, Application for Travel Document (page 3)

Part 3. Processing Information (continued)

Where do you want this travel document sent? (Check one)

5. ☒ To the U.S. address shown in **Part 1 (2.a through 2.i.)** of this form.

6. ☐ To a U.S. Embassy or consulate at:

6.a. City or Town

6.b. Country

7. ☐ To a DHS office overseas at:

7.a. City or Town

7.b. Country

If you checked "6" or "7", where should the notice to pick up the travel document be sent?

8. ☐ To the address shown in **Part 2 (2.h. through 2.p.)** of this form.

9. ☐ To the address shown in **Part 3 (10.a. through 10.i.)** of this form.:

10.a. In Care of Name

10.b. Street Number and Name

10.c. Apt. ☐ Ste. ☐ Flr. ☐

10.d. City or Town

10.e. State

10.f. Zip Code

10.g. Postal Code

10.h. Province

10.i. Country

10.j. Daytime Phone Number ( ) -

Part 4. Information About Your Proposed Travel

1.a. Purpose of trip. (If you need more space, continue on a separate sheet of paper.)

Visit family

1.b. List the countries you intend to visit. (If you need more space, continue on a separate sheet of paper.)

Spain and Italy

Part 5. Complete Only If Applying for a Re-entry Permit

Since becoming a permanent resident of the United States (or during the past 5 years, whichever is less) how much total time have you spent outside the United States?

1.a. ☐ less than 6 months
1.b. ☐ 6 months to 1 year
1.c. ☐ 1 to 2 years

1.d. ☐ 2 to 3 years
1.e. ☐ 3 to 4 years
1.f. ☐ more than 4 years

2. Since you became a permanent resident of the United States, have you ever filed a Federal income tax return as a nonresident or failed to file a Federal income tax return because you considered yourself to be a nonresident? (If "Yes" give details on a separate sheet of paper.)

☐ Yes ☐ No

Sample Form I-131, Application for Travel Document (page 4)

Part 6. Complete Only If Applying for a Refugee Travel Document

1. Country from which you are a refugee or asylee:

[   ]

If you answer "Yes" to any of the following questions, you must explain on a separate sheet of paper. Include your Name and A-Number on the top of each sheet.

2. Do you plan to travel to the country named above? ☐ Yes ☐ No

Since you were accorded refugee/asylee status, have you ever:

3.a. Returned to the country named above? ☐ Yes ☐ No

3.b. Applied for and/or obtained a national passport, passport renewal, or entry permit of that country? ☐ Yes ☐ No

3.c. Applied for and/or received any benefit from such country (for example, health insurance benefits)? ☐ Yes ☐ No

Since you were accorded refugee/asylee status, have you, by any legal procedure or voluntary act:

4.a. Reacquired the nationality of the country named above? ☐ Yes ☐ No

4.b. Acquired a new nationality? ☐ Yes ☐ No

4.c. Been granted refugee or asylee status in any other country? ☐ Yes ☐ No

---

Part 7. Complete Only If Applying for Advance Parole

On a separate sheet of paper, explain how you qualify for an Advance Parole Document, and what circumstances warrant issuance of advance parole. Include copies of any documents you wish considered. *(See instructions.)*

1. How many trips do you intend to use this document?
☒ One Trip ☐ More than one trip

If the person intended to receive an Advance Parole Document is outside the United States, provide the location (City or Town and Country) of the U.S. Embassy or consulate or the DHS overseas office that you want us to notify.

2.a. City or Town

[   ]

2.b. Country

[   ]

If the travel document will be delivered to an overseas office, where should the notice to pick up the document be sent?:

3. ☐ To the address shown in **Part 2 (2.h. through 2.p.)** of this form.

4. ☐ To the address shown in **Part 7 (4.a. through 4.i.)** of this form.

4.a. In Care of Name

[   ]

4.b. Street Number and Name

[   ]

4.c. Apt. ☐ Ste. ☐ Flr. ☐ [   ]

4.d. City or Town [   ]

4.e. State [   ] **4.f.** Zip Code [   ]

4.g. Postal Code [   ]

4.h. Province [   ]

4.i. Country [   ]

4.j. Daytime Phone Number ([   ]) [   ] - [   ]

Sample Form I-131, Application for Travel Document (page 5)

Part 8. Signature of Applicant *(Read the information on penalties in the Form Instructions before completing this Part.)* If you are filing for a Re-entry Permit or Refugee Travel Document, you must be in the United States to file this application.

1.a. I certify, under penalty of perjury under the laws of the United States of America, that this application and the evidence submitted with it is all true and correct. I authorize the release of any information from my records that U.S. Citizenship and Immigration Services needs to determine eligibility for the benefit I am seeking.

Signature of Applicant

Juliet Manzetti

1.b. Date of Signature *(mm/dd/yyyy)* ▶ 05/25/2014

2. Daytime Phone Number (301) 123 - 4567

NOTE: If you do not completely fill out this form or fail to submit required documents listed in the instructions, your application may be denied.

Part 9. Information About Person Who Prepared This Application, If Other Than the Applicant

NOTE: If you are an attorney or representative, you must submit a completed Form G-28, Notice of Entry of Appearance as Attorney or Accredited Representative, along with this application.

Preparer's Full Name

Provide the following information concerning the preparer:

1.a. Preparer's Family Name *(Last Name)*

1.b. Preparer's Given Name *(First Name)*

2. Preparer's Business or Organization Name

Preparer's Mailing Address

3.a. Street Number and Name

3.b. Apt. ☐ Ste. ☐ Flr. ☐

3.c. City or Town

3.d. State

3.e. Zip Code

3.f. Postal Code

3.g. Province

3.h. Country

Preparer's Contact Information

4. Preparer's Daytime Phone Number   Extension

( ) -

5. Preparer's E-mail Address *(if any)*

Declaration

To be completed by all preparers, including attorneys and authorized representatives: I declare that I prepared this benefit request at the request of the applicant, that it is based on all the information of which I have knowledge, and that the information is true to the best of my knowledge.

6.a. Signature of Preparer

6.b. Date of Signature *(mm/dd/yyyy)* ▶

NOTE: If you require more space to provide any additional information, use a separate sheet of paper. You must include your Name and A-Number on the top of each sheet.

Consular Processing

The second type of government procedure for getting a green card (other than adjustment of status) is "consular processing." It means that the immigrant goes to a U.S. embassy or consulate to complete the green card application. Only after the consulate interviews and approves the immigrant for an immigrant visa can he or she enter the United States and claim permanent resident status.

Most immigrants will have no choice but to use consular processing as their application method. Immigrants who are overseas are almost all required to use consular processing, though many would love to enter the U.S. and finish their application there. However, with the exception of fiancés and people immigrating based on marriage (who can use a K-3 fiancé visa to enter the U.S. and then adjust status) most immigrants will only get themselves in trouble (for example, accused of visa fraud) if they try to enter the U.S. to finish their green card application.

Immigrants who are already in the United States may be required to use consular processing if they are not eligible to use the adjustment of status procedure described in Chapter 16. Unfortunately, this lack of choice creates a potential trap for immigrants who have lived illegally in the U.S. for 180 days or more. By leaving the U.S., they become subject to penalties for their illegal stay. Even if they otherwise qualify for a green card, the consulate must, under the law, bar them from reentering the U.S. for three years (if their illegal stay was between 180 days and one year) or ten years (for illegal stays over one year). See an attorney if you're in this situation—there are waivers you can apply for, including a "provisional waiver" that allows some applicants to receive an answer before they actually leave the U.S., but it's hard to get one approved.

This chapter will discuss the paperwork and other requirements involved in consular processing.

! CAUTION

Remember, this chapter discusses only procedures, not your underlying eligibility for a green card. Unless you've already completed the steps explained in another chapter—most likely one describing family- or lottery-based visas—you shouldn't be in this chapter. It's only for people with approved visa petitions or winning lottery letters who are now completing their green card application process.

If You Have a Choice of Procedure

While the requirements for adjustment of status (getting a green card at a USCIS office) are rather restrictive, if you qualify, there are a number of advantages to that procedure over consular processing. If you are currently in the U.S., read Chapter 16 carefully to see whether you qualify to get a green card through adjustment of status.

A. How Your Case Gets to the Consulate

When your relative filled out your visa petition, or when you filled out your lottery application, your address or other information will have indicated to the U.S. government which consulate would be most convenient for you. After your visa petition has been approved or you've won the lottery, a central office known as the National Visa Center (NVC) will take care of transferring your file to the appropriate consulate. (Remember that if you're not an immediate relative but a "preference relative," you may have to wait several years before your Priority Date becomes current and your case is transferred to a consulate—see Chapter 5 for details.)

A lot has to happen, however, before the NVC transfers your case. You will have to visit the Consular Electronic Application Center (CEAC) at http://ceac.state.gov/ceac and complete DS-261, Online Choice of Address and Agent. Log in using the invoice number that the NVC sent you either by mail or email. It's a fairly simple form, but keep in mind that by choosing an "agent," you are essentially deciding where and how all the important notices from the U.S. government will be sent—to your overseas address or to the petitioner or via email. If mail service from the U.S. has been at all unreliable where you live, or if you might be moving before your visa interview, it's safest to choose the petitioner (in the U.S.) as your agent or to indicate that you'd rather be contacted by email. Since the majority of the steps you need to take on your visa petition are online, it makes sense to enroll in email notifications.

After you submit the DS-261, you will receive some information about filing fees. If you are immigrating through a family member, the NVC will send the U.S. family member petitioner a bill for the Affidavit of Support review and send either you or your agent a bill for the immigrant visa processing fee (currently $230). If any family members who are included on your petition are immigrating with you, a separate filing fee of $230 will also be required. However, all family members can be included on the one $88 filing fee for the Affidavit of Support.

Diversity lottery winners also have to pay an additional fee of $330.

The NVC prefers that you pay these fees online, by entering your checking account number and bank routing number. That's also the best way to ensure that your fees get credited to your account, all your documents are kept together, and that the NVC doesn't lose your paper check.

However, if you don't have a checking account, you will need to pay by mail using a bank check or money order. Make sure to have your visa bill handy, because it contains a bar code that the NVC will need in order to credit your fee to your application.

After paying your fees, you will need to submit DS-260, the online immigrant visa application. This form will ask you a number of biographical questions, such as all names used, all addresses where you have lived, work and educational history, and family member information. You will also be asked questions to determine your admissibility to the United States.

The DS-260 application can be submitted only online. You will again need your NVC invoice number and receipt number in order to complete this form. You can save your DS-260 and come back to it later if you need to. Keep in mind that you do need to complete this form in English using English characters only, so have someone ready to help you if you aren't confident in your English ability.

This online form isn't much different from the paper one that preceded it (known as DS-230) except that it requires a lot more detail. You'll be asked for all your addresses since the age of 16 and the exact dates that you lived there. Make sure that all your answers correspond with the answers you gave on the Form G-325A submitted with the petitioner's Form I-130. If an answer does not apply to you (such as U.S. Social Security number), you will be given the option to choose "Does Not Apply." You can see more tips for filling out immigration forms in Chapter 21.

After you submit the DS-260, print the confirmation page and bring it to your interview. Although you are not required to do so, it doesn't hurt to print out a copy of the entire form as well, so that you can refer to it when needed.

TIP

Got questions? The Department of State website has a good step-by-step outline of the entire process. Go to http://immigrantvisas.state.gov for a wonderful diagram of the immigrant visa process. You can also contact the remarkably accessible NVC at NVCINQUIRY@state.gov or call 603-334-0070 on weekdays from 7:00 a.m. to midnight, Eastern Standard Time.

You will receive further instructions and a checklist on what else the NVC needs from you before your interview. See the next section for our own checklist of the forms and documents you'll need. For consulate-specific information, visit http://travel.state.gov and click "Immigrate," then "Learn About Immigrating to the United States" then, on the flowchart, click "Submit Documents to NVC." Here, you'll find information about how to obtain proper police certification, birth and marriage certificates, and divorce decrees in your home country.

All foreign-language documents must be translated as well. For more information on how to certify translations for foreign language documents, see Chapter 21.

After the NVC is satisfied that you have submitted the necessary documentation and have paid all your fees, it will schedule an interview date and transfer your visa file to the appropriate U.S. consulate or embassy.

Before your interview, you will need to attend a medical examination with an authorized physician. To find one in your country, go to the State Department flowchart link described just above and click "Prepare for the Interview."

Medical exam fees may vary among doctors, so it's best to call around to inquire. Bringing your vaccination records and any recent chest X-rays will help you to avoid additional costs for shots and X-rays (if necessary).

This exam is not like the ordinary one you'd have with your own doctor. Its sole purpose is to spot any grounds of inadmissibility that might prevent you from getting a green card. See Chapter 4 for a discussion of the grounds of inadmissibility. If you do have a medical ground of inadmissibility, you may be eligible for a waiver (also discussed in Chapter 4), and should consult an immigration lawyer. See Chapter 24 for tips on finding a good lawyer.

B. Forms and Documents You'll Need to Provide

Here's a summary of the forms and documents that you'll need to give to either the NVC or the consulate between now and the end of the process:

- ☐ Form DS-260, which you'll fill out online (as described above).
- ☐ Copies of current passports. You'll be asked to send in a copy of the key pages of your family members' passports—but not the originals. You'll bring the original passports to your interview at the U.S. consulate.
- ☐ Birth certificates for you and for your spouse or children, with English translations if they are not in the language of the country in which you are interviewed.
- ☐ A police clearance certificate for each person over 16 years of age from the country of nationality or current residence if he or she has lived there for more than six months, and from any other country where the applicant lived for more than one year.
- ☐ Marriage certificate, death certificate, divorce or annulment decree—whichever shows your current marital status and history.
- ☐ Military record of any service in your country, or any country, including certified proof of military service and of honorable or dishonorable discharge.
- ☐ Certified copy of court and prison records if you have been convicted of a crime.
- ☐ Form I-864 or I-864EZ, Affidavit of Support. (See the sample Form I-864 at the end of this chapter. Notice that in our sample, the sponsor didn't have enough income, and therefore had to add a Form I-864A in which his daughter, who lives with him, also promised to add her income to help the immigrant.) Which form you must submit depends on your situation. You must file Form I-864 if your petition is family-

based (except K-1 fiancé visas). But if you are the only person that your petitioner is sponsoring, and your petitioner can meet the sponsorship requirements based upon his or her income alone, he or she can use a shorter version of the form, called I-864EZ. On both Form I-134 and I-864, a U.S. citizen or permanent resident promises to repay the U.S. government if you become impoverished and go on public assistance after you arrive in the United States.

☐ **Documents to support form I-864.** Your sponsor who fills out the form must also include financial documents, including an employment verification letter or other proof of income such as a "year-to-date" pay stub, the sponsor's latest U.S. income tax transcript and W-2s (or the last three years', if it will strengthen the case). If the sponsor is relying on assets to meet the poverty guidelines, then proof of those assets—such as bank statements—must be submitted.

☐ **Form I-864W (in cases where an I-864 is not required).** In certain exceptional cases, a Form I-864 need not be filed. One of these is where the beneficiary is a child (adopted or natural born) who will become a U.S. citizen automatically upon entering the United States (see Chapter 20 for details). The other is where the beneficiary, or the beneficiary's spouse or parent, has worked 40 "quarters" (about ten years, as defined by the Social Security Administration) in the United States. If you're exempt from the affidavit of support requirement due to one of these exceptions, the sponsor should fill out Form I-864W instead of the regular Form I-864.

You will also be required to submit to fingerprinting, for a background check by the FBI and CIA. (See Chapter 21, Section F, for more about these security checks.)

The final set of documents you'll normally need to prepare for your interview include:

☐ Two color photographs, passport style.

☐ Current passports for you and for everyone in your family who is getting an immigrant visa (they must not expire earlier than six months after your interview date).

☐ Medical examination report. During the exam, your blood will be tested and you will be X-rayed. You may be barred from immigrating if these tests show that you have a contagious disease of public health concern such as tuberculosis, or if you have a severe mental disorder. If any of these bars apply to you, you may be eligible for a waiver (see Chapter 4), and should consult an immigration lawyer.

☐ U.S. income tax transcripts. If you have worked in the U.S. and intend to immigrate, you must present proof that you filed income tax returns for every year you worked.

☐ Visa fees, if not already paid. (The charge for a fiancé visa is $240; the charge for an immigrant visa is $230 in total.)

> **CAUTION**
>
> **Unmarried children beware.** If you are an unmarried son or daughter of a permanent resident or a U.S. citizen, and you marry before you have your immigration visa interview, be prepared for a shock: Your visa will be denied because you are no longer in the immediate relative or second preference category under which you were petitioned.
>
> If you married after your visa interview but before you entered the U.S. with your immigrant visa, you may also be in serious trouble. Although you may be admitted into the United States (because USCIS has no way of knowing that you are no longer eligible), the agency could discover this fact if you later apply to bring your spouse or try to become a U.S. citizen.

It will not matter that you have been admitted as a permanent resident. Removal proceedings will be started against you, you and your spouse will not be reunited in the United States, and you will eventually have to go back to your country and start all over again in the preference category of the married son or daughter of a U.S. citizen. You could completely lose your immigrant eligibility if your parent is only a green card holder.

If you fall into this category, see an experienced attorney (Chapter 24 offers tips on finding one).

C. Attending Your Visa Interview

The final step in obtaining your visa is to attend an interview with a U.S. consular official. Until the date of your interview, it's quite possible that neither you nor your petitioning spouse or family members (if any) will have had any personal contact with any immigration official. At last, you can deal with a real human being—for better and for worse.

With all the paperwork you've submitted by now, you might wonder why the interview is even necessary. However, the government views the interview as its opportunity to confirm the contents of your application after you've sworn to tell the truth. If you're applying based on marriage, it also allows them to ask personal questions designed to reveal whether your marriage is the real thing or a sham.

If you're being petitioned by a spouse or other family member, they're not expected to attend the interview—although it can only help to have them there. If yours is a marriage case, your spouse's willingness to travel and be with you at the interview is a good sign that your marriage is not a sham. Some, but not all, consulates also allow you to bring a lawyer, if you feel you need one.

To prepare for your interview, the most important thing is to review all your paperwork. Look at all the questions and answers on all the forms, including any that were submitted for you by your U.S. family member. Though boring, this information is all important to the consular officials. Be alert for any inconsistencies and mistakes, and bring along any documents that will help correct them.

If you're applying through a spouse or fiancé, spend some time together reviewing the details of how you met, how you've corresponded and visited each other or each other's families, and when and why you decided to get married. If already married, review the details of the wedding—number of guests, where it was held, what food and drink was served, and the like.

If you don't live in the same city as the consulate, it's a good idea to get there a few days in advance, particularly for purposes of getting your medical exam and photos done. Arrive early, in case there's a line. Consulates often schedule applicants in large groups, telling them all to arrive at the same time. And be careful of personal security outside the consulate—it's a common place for pickpockets and con artists to hang around. The interview itself will probably last 30 minutes.

Tips for the Interview

The most important thing to do is relax. Wear conservative but comfortable clothes. The interviewer will ask you mostly about information you have already given in response to questions on your immigration forms and other documents.

Answer all questions truthfully. If you cannot understand a question, be brave and ask for an interpreter. It is better to be embarrassed about not understanding English very well than to be denied your immigrant visa because you misunderstood the question.

D. Approval of Your Immigrant Visa

If the U.S. consulate or embassy needs more information, it will tell you that further administrative processing is necessary and what types of documents it needs. If it denies your case, it will give you a letter detailing the reasons. In any case, you are unlikely to receive the visa at the end of the interview.

The consulate will let you know the method by which you can check on your case status, submit any required documents, and after you're approved, receive your visa (either by mail or in-person pickup). It will give you back your passport with your immigrant visa, a sealed packet (DO NOT open this), and an envelope with your X-rays, all of which you will need to carry with you when you arrive at the U.S. border and are inspected by Customs and Border Protection.

Check the visa for any spelling or other factual errors. Immigrants will also have to pay one additional fee, the USCIS immigrant fee, in order to receive their actual green card after entering the United States. You can do so at http://www.uscis.gov/forms/uscis-immigrant-fee.

Your immigrant visa is valid for six months, and you must arrive in the United States within those six months. Keep in mind that your permanent resident status does not start until you actually enter the United States.

If you are unable to leave for the United States and your visa is about to expire, you may apply for an extension of your immigrant visa by means of an affidavit, or written statement signed before a notary public, explaining why you are unable to leave on time. But unless you have a very good reason, the U.S. consulate will be reluctant to approve an extension.

E. Arriving in the United States

When you arrive at your U.S. port of entry, the U.S. citizens who were on the plane with you will be admitted in one line, while all the noncitizens will be queuing in another line.

When it is your turn, the immigration officer will take your immigrant documents and keep them—all but your X-rays—and make them part of your permanent record in the USCIS office. Your passport will be stamped to show that you have entered as a lawful permanent resident.

Your green card will be mailed to you within several weeks to months. You must inform USCIS if you change addresses within ten days of your move (or you can be deported). Besides, if you don't tell them, you may not receive your green card until you have made several trips to the USCIS office and filled out countless forms. See Chapter 23 for more information on changing addresses and keeping your right to a green card.

At last! You are now a bona fide immigrant—able to live and work legally in the United States. Welcome.

Sample Form I-864, Affidavit of Support Under Section 213A of the Act (page 1)

Affidavit of Support Under Section 213A of the Act

Department of Homeland Security
U.S. Citizenship and Immigration Services

**USCIS
Form I-864**
OMB No. 1615-0075
Expires 03/31/2015

For USCIS Use Only	Affidavit of Support Submitter	Section 213A Review	Number of Support Affidavits in File
	☐ Petitioner ☐ 1st Joint Sponsor ☐ 2nd Joint Sponsor ☐ Substitute Sponsor ☐ 5% Owner	☐ MEETS requirements ☐ DOES NOT MEET requirements Reviewed By:_____ Office: _____ Date: MM / DD / YYYY	☐ 1 ☐ 2 **Remarks**

▶ **START HERE - Type or print in black ink.**

Part 1. Basis For Filing Affidavit of Support

1. Alberto Ilario Mancini

am the sponsor submitting this affidavit of support because *(Check only one box):*

1.a. ☒ I am the petitioner. I filed or am filing for the immigration of my relative.

1.b. ☐ I filed an alien worker petition on behalf of the intending immigrant, who is related to me as my

1.c. ☐ I have an ownership interest of at least 5 percent in

which filed an alien worker petition on behalf of the intending immigrant, who is related to me as my

1.d. ☐ I am the only joint sponsor.

1.e. ☐ I am the ☐ first ☐ second of two joint sponsors.

1.f. ☐ The original petitioner is deceased. I am the substitute sponsor. I am the intending immigrant's

NOTE: If you check box 1.b., 1.c., 1.d., 1.e., or 1.f., you must include proof of your citizen, national, or lawful permanent resident status.

Part 2. Information on the Principal Immigrant

1.a. Family Name *(Last Name)* Mancini

1.b. Given Name *(First Name)* Terese

1.c. Middle Name Maria

Mailing Address

2.a. Street Number and Name 108 Piazza D'Azaglio

2.b. Apt. ☐ Ste. ☐ Flr. ☐

2.c. City or Town Venice

2.d. State ___ **2.e.** Zip Code ___

2.f. Postal Code 99999

2.g. Province Venice

2.h. Country Italy

Other Information

3. Country of Citizenship

Italy

4. Date of Birth *(mm/dd/yyyy)* ▶ 02/02/1981

5. Alien Registration Number (A-Number)

▶ A- | N | O | N | E | | | | |

Sample Form I-864, Affidavit of Support Under Section 213A of the Act (page 2)

Part 3. Information on the Immigrant(s) You Are Sponsoring

1. I am sponsoring the principal immigrant named in **Part 2**.

   [X] Yes [ ] No (Applicable only in cases with two joint sponsors)

2. [X] I am sponsoring the following family members immigrating at the same time or within 6 months of the principal immigrant named in **Part 2**. Do not include any relative listed on a separate visa petition

Family Member 1

2.a. Family Name *(Last Name)* — Moreno

2.b. Given Name *(First Name)* — Glovana

2.c. Middle Name — Mara

2.d. Relationship to Sponsored Immigrant — Daughter

2.e. Date of Birth *(mm/dd/yyyy)* ▶ 06/01/2009

2.f. Alien Registration Number (A-Number)

   ▶ A- N O N E

Family Member 2

3.a. Family Name *(Last Name)*

3.b. Given Name *(First Name)*

3.c. Middle Name

3.d. Relationship to Sponsored Immigrant

3.e. Date of Birth *(mm/dd/yyyy)* ▶

3.f. Alien Registration Number (A-Number) ▶ A-

Family Member 3

4.a. Family Name *(Last Name)*

4.b. Given Name *(First Name)*

4.c. Middle Name

4.d. Relationship to Sponsored Immigrant

4.e. Date of Birth *(mm/dd/yyyy)* ▶

4.f. Alien Registration Number (A-Number)

   ▶ A-

Family Member 4

5.a. Family Name *(Last Name)*

5.b. Given Name *(First Name)*

5.c. Middle Name

5.d. Relationship to Sponsored Immigrant

5.e. Date of Birth *(mm/dd/yyyy)* ▶

5.f. Alien Registration Number (A-Number)

   ▶ A-

Family Member 5

6.a. Family Name *(Last Name)*

6.b. Given Name *(First Name)*

6.c. Middle Name

Sample Form I-864, Affidavit of Support Under Section 213A of the Act (page 3)

For USCIS Use Only	

Part 3. Information on the Immigrant(s) You Are Sponsoring *(continued)*

Family Member 5 *(Continued)*

6.d. Relationship to Sponsored Immigrant

6.e. Date of Birth *(mm/dd/yyyy)* ▶

6.f. Alien Registration Number (A-Number)

▶ A-

7. Enter the total number of immigrants you are sponsoring on this form from Items **1** through **6**.   `2`

Part 4. Information on the Sponsor

Sponsor's Full Name

1.a. Family Name *(Last Name)*   Mancini

1.b. Given Name *(First Name)*   Alberto

1.c. Middle Name   Ilario

Sponsor's Mailing Address

2.a. Street Number and Name   800 Broadway

2.b. Apt. ☐ Ste. ☐ Flr. ☐

2.c. City or Town   Lindenhurst

2.d. State   NY   **2.e.** Zip Code   11757

2.f. Postal Code

2.g. Province

2.h. Country   USA

Sponsor's Place of Residence

3.a. Street Number and Name   800 Broadway

3.b. Apt. ☐ Ste. ☐ Flr. ☐

3.c. City or Town   Lindenhurst

3.d. State   NY   **3.e.** Zip Code   11757

3.f. Postal Code

3.g. Province

3.h. Country

Other Information

4. Telephone Number   (2 1 2) 2 2 2 - 2 1 2 1

5. Country of Domicile   USA

6. Date of Birth *(mm/dd/yyyy)* ▶ 03/30/1968

Sample Form I-864, Affidavit of Support Under Section 213A of the Act (page 4)

For USCIS Use Only	

Part 4. Information on the Sponsor *(continued)*

7. City or Town of Birth

Los Angeles

8. State or Province of Birth

California

9. Country of Birth

USA

10. U.S. Social Security Number *(Required)*

► 2 2 2 3 3 2 2 2 2

Citizenship/Residency

11.a. ☒ I am a U.S. citizen.

11.b. ☐ I am a U.S. national (for joint sponsors only).

11.c. ☐ I am a lawful permanent resident.

My alien registration number is:

► A- ☐☐☐☐☐☐☐☐☐

Military Service *(To be completed by petitioner sponsors only.)*

12. I am currently on active duty in the U.S. armed services.

☐ Yes   ☒ No

Part 5. Sponsor's Household Size

Your Household Size - <u>DO NOT COUNT ANYONE TWICE</u>

Persons you are sponsoring in this affidavit:

1. Enter the number you entered on line 7 of Part 3. `2`

Persons NOT sponsored in this affidavit:

2. Yourself. `1`

3. If you are currently married, enter "1" for your spouse.

4. If you have dependent children, enter the number here.

5. If you have any other dependents, enter the number here.

6. If you have sponsored any other persons on an I-864 or I-864 EZ who are now lawful permanent residents, enter the number here.

7. **OPTIONAL:** If you have <u>siblings, parents, or adult children</u> with the same principal residence who are combining their income with yours by submitting Form I-864A, enter the number here. `1`

8. Add together lines 1-7 and enter the number here. **Household Size:** `4`

Part 6. Sponsor's Income and Employment

I am currently:

1. ☒ Employed as a/an

Cook

1.a. Name of Employer #1 *(if applicable)*

Bob's Diner

1.b. Name of Employer #2 *(if applicable)*

2. ☐ Self-employed as a/an

3. ☐ Retired from:

3.a. Company Name

3.b. Date of Retirement

(mm/dd/yyyy) ►

Sample Form I-864, Affidavit of Support Under Section 213A of the Act (page 5)

For USCIS Use Only	Household Size	Poverty Guideline	Remarks
	☐ 1 ☐ 2 ☐ 3 ☐ 4 ☐ 5 ☐ 6 ☐ 7 ☐ 8 ☐ 9 ☐ Other_____	Year: 20YY Poverty Line: $_____	

Part 6. Sponsor's Income and Employment *(continued)*

4. ☐ Unemployed since

(mm/dd/yyyy) ▶ [_____]

5. My current individual annual income is:

(See Instructions) $ 21,000

Income you are using from any other person who was counted in your household size, including, in certain conditions, the intending immigrant. (See Instructions.) Please indicate name, relationship and income.

Person 1

6.a. Name

Beatrice Mancini

6.b. Relationship

Daughter

6.c. Current Income $ 46,000

Person 2

7.a. Name

[_____]

7.b. Relationship

[_____]

7.c. Current Income $ [_____]

Person 3

8.a. Name

[_____]

8.b. Relationship

[_____]

8.c. Current Income $ [_____]

Person 4

9.a. Name

[_____]

9.b. Relationship

[_____]

9.c. Current Income $ [_____]

10. **My current Annual Household Income** *(Total all lines from 5, 6.c., 7.c., 8.c., and 9.c. Will be Compared to Poverty Guidelines -- See Form I-864P.)*

$ 67,000

11. ☒ The person(s) listed in 6.a., 7.a., 8.a., and 9.a. have completed Form I-864A. I am filing along with this form all necessary Forms I-864A completed by these persons.

12. ☐ The person(s) listed in 6.a., 7.a., 8.a., or 9.a. does not need to complete Form I-864A because he/she is the intending immigrant and has no accompanying dependents.

Name(s)

[_____]

Federal income tax return information

13. ☒ I have filed a Federal tax return for each of the three most recent tax years. I have attached the required photocopy or transcript of my Federal tax return for **only the most recent tax year.**

Sample Form I-864, Affidavit of Support Under Section 213A of the Act (page 6)

For USCIS Use Only	Household Size	Poverty Guideline	Sponsor's Household Income *(Page 5, Line 10)*	Remarks
	☐ 1 ☐ 2 ☐ 3 ☐ 4 ☐ 5 ☐ 6 ☐ 7 ☐ 8 ☐ 9 ☐ Other_____	Year: 2 0 Y Y Poverty Line: $_____	$_____	The total value of all assets, line 10, must equal 5 times (3 times for spouses and children of USC's, or 1 time for orphans to be formally adopted in the U.S.) the difference between the poverty guidelines and the sponsor's household income, line 10.

Part 6. Sponsor's Income and Employment *(continued)*

My total income (adjusted gross income on IRS Form 1040EZ) as reported on my Federal tax returns for the most recent 3 years was:

	Tax Year			Total Income
13.a.	2013	*(most recent)*	**13.a.1.** $	21,000
13.b.	2012	*(2nd most recent)*	**13.b.1.** $	20,000
13.c.	2011	*(3rd most recent)*	**13.c.1.** $	18,000

14. ☐ *(Optional)* I have attached photocopies or transcripts of my Federal tax returns for my second and third most recent tax years.

Part 7. Use of Assets to Supplement Income *(optional)*

If your income, or the total income for you and your household, from Part 6, line 10 exceeds the Federal Poverty Guidelines for your household size, YOU ARE NOT REQUIRED to complete this Part. Skip to Part 8.

Your assets *(Optional)*

1. Enter the balance of all savings and checking accounts.

$ _____

2. Enter the net cash value of real-estate holdings. (Net means current assessed value minus mortgage debt.)

$ _____

3. Enter the net cash value of all stocks, bonds, certificates of deposit, and any other assets not already included in lines 1 or 2.

$ _____

4. Add together lines 1-3 and enter the number here.

TOTAL: $ _____

Part 7. Use of Assets to Supplement Income *(optional) (continued)*

Assets from Form I-864A, line 12d for:

5.a. Name of Relative

_____

5.b. **Your household member's assets from Form I-864A.** *(Optional)*

$ _____

Assets of the principal sponsored immigrant *(Optional)*. The principal sponsored immigrant is the person listed in lines 1.a. - 1.c. in Part 2.

6. Enter the balance of the sponsored immigrant's savings and checking accounts.

$ _____

7. Enter the net cash value of all the sponsored immigrant's real estate holdings. (Net means investment value minus mortgage debt.)

$ _____

8. Enter the current cash value of the sponsored immigrant's stocks, bonds, certificates of deposit, and other assets not included on line 6 or 7.

$ _____

9. **Add together lines 6-8 of Part 7 and enter the number here.**

$ _____

Total value of assets.

10. **Add together lines 4, 5.b., and 9 of Part 7 and enter the number here.**

TOTAL: $ _____

Sample Form I-864, Affidavit of Support Under Section 213A of the Act (page 7)

Part 8. Sponsor's Contract

Please note that, by signing this Form I-864, you agree to assume certain specific obligations under the Immigration and Nationality Act and other Federal laws. The following paragraphs describe those obligations. Please read the following information carefully before you sign the Form I-864. If you do not understand the obligations, you may wish to consult an attorney or accredited representative.

What is the Legal Effect of My Signing a Form I-864?

If you sign a Form I-864 on behalf of any person (called the "intending immigrant") who is applying for an immigrant visa or for adjustment of status to a permanent resident, and that intending immigrant submits the Form I-864 to the U.S. Government with his or her application for an immigrant visa or adjustment of status, under section 213A of the Immigration and Nationality Act these actions create a contract between you and the U. S. Government. The intending immigrant's becoming a permanent resident is the "consideration" for the contract.

Under this contract, you agree that, in deciding whether the intending immigrant can establish that he or she is not inadmissible to the United States as an alien likely to become a public charge, the U.S. Government can consider your income and assets to be available for the support of the intending immigrant.

What If I choose Not to Sign a Form I-864?

You cannot be made to sign a Form I-864 if you do not want to do so. But if you do not sign the Form I-864, the intending immigrant may not be able to become a permanent resident in the United States.

What Does Signing the Form I-864 Require Me to do?

If an intending immigrant becomes a permanent resident in the United States based on a Form I-864 that you have signed, then, until your obligations under the Form I-864 terminate, you must:

-- Provide the intending immigrant any support necessary to maintain him or her at an income that is at least 125 percent of the Federal Poverty Guidelines for his or her household size (100 percent if you are the petitioning sponsor and are on active duty in the U.S. Armed Forces and the person is your husband, wife, unmarried child under 21 years old.)

-- Notify USCIS of any change in your address, within 30 days of the change, by filing Form I-865.

What Other Consequences Are There?

If an intending immigrant becomes a permanent resident in the United States based on a Form I-864 that you have signed, then until your obligations under the Form I-864 terminate, your income and assets may be considered ("deemed") to be available to that person, in determining whether he or she is eligible for certain Federal means-tested public benefits and also for State or local means-tested public benefits, if the State or local government's rules provide for consideration ("deeming") of your income and assets as available to the person.

This provision does **not** apply to public benefits specified in section 403(c) of the Welfare Reform Act such as, but not limited to, emergency Medicaid, short-term, non-cash emergency relief; services provided under the National School Lunch and Child Nutrition Acts; immunizations and testing and treatment for communicable diseases; and means-tested programs under the Elementary and Secondary Education Act.

What If I Do Not Fulfill My Obligations?

If you do not provide sufficient support to the person who becomes a permanent resident based on the Form I-864 that you signed, that person may sue you for this support.

Sample Form I-864, Affidavit of Support Under Section 213A of the Act (page 8)

Part 8. Sponsor's Contract *(continued)*

If a Federal, State or local agency, or a private agency provides any covered means-tested public benefit to the person who becomes a permanent resident based on the Form I-864 that you signed, the agency may ask you to reimburse them for the amount of the benefits they provided. If you do not make the reimbursement, the agency may sue you for the amount that the agency believes you owe.

If you are sued, and the court enters a judgment against you, the person or agency that sued you may use any legally permitted procedures for enforcing or collecting the judgment. You may also be required to pay the costs of collection, including attorney fees.

If you do not file a properly completed Form I-865 within 30 days of any change of address, USCIS may impose a civil fine for your failing to do so.

When Will These Obligations End?

Your obligations under a Form I-864 will end if the person who becomes a permanent resident based on a Form I-864 that you signed:

1. Becomes a U.S. citizen;

2. Has worked, or can be credited with, 40 quarters of coverage under the Social Security Act;

3. No longer has lawful permanent resident status, and has departed the United States;

4. Becomes subject to removal, but applies for and obtains in removal proceedings a new grant of adjustment of status, based on a new affidavit of support, if one is required; or

5. Dies.

Note that divorce **does not** terminate your obligations under this Form I-864.

Your obligations under a Form I-864 also end if you die. Therefore, if you die, your Estate will not be required to take responsibility for the person's support after your death. Your Estate may, however, be responsible for any support that you owed before you died.

I, | Alberto Ilario Mancini |
(Print Sponsor's Name)

certify under penalty of perjury under the laws of the United States that:

a. I know the contents of this affidavit of support that I signed.

b. **All the factual statements in this affidavit of support are true and correct.**

c. I have read and I understand each of the obligations described in Part 8, and I agree, freely and without any mental reservation or purpose of evasion, to accept each of those obligations in order to make it possible for the immigrants indicated in Part 3 to become permanent residents of the United States;

d. I agree to submit to the personal jurisdiction of any Federal or State court that has subject matter jurisdiction of a lawsuit against me to enforce my obligations under this Form I-864;

e. Each of the Federal income tax returns submitted in support of this affidavit are true copies, or are unaltered tax transcripts, of the tax returns I filed with the U.S. Internal Revenue Service; and

f. I authorize the Social Security Administration to release information about me in its records to the Department of State and U.S. Citizenship and Immigration Services.

g. Any and all other evidence submitted is true and correct.

1.a. Signature of Sponsor

Alberto Ilario Mancini

1.b. Date of Signature *(mm/dd/yyyy)* ► 03/06/2014

Sample Form I-864, Affidavit of Support Under Section 213A of the Act (page 9)

Part 9. Information on Preparer, If Prepared By Someone Other Than the Sponsor

Preparer's Full Name

Provide the following information concerning the preparer:

1.a. Preparer's Family Name *(Last Name)*

1.b. Preparer's Given Name *(First Name)*

2. Preparer's Business or Organization Name

Preparer's Mailing Address

3.a. Street Number and Name

3.b. Apt. ☐ Ste. ☐ Flr. ☐

3.c. City or Town

3.d. State

3.e. Zip Code

3.f. Postal Code

3.g. Province

3.h. Country

Preparer's Contact Information

4. Preparer's Daytime Phone Number

(___) ___ - ____

5. Preparer's Email Address

6. Business State ID # *(if any)*

Declaration

I certify under penalty of perjury under the laws of the United States that I prepared this affidavit of support at the sponsor's request and that this affidavit of support is based on all information of which I have knowledge.

7.a. Signature of Preparer

7.b. Date of Signature *(mm/dd/yyyy)* ▶

Poverty Guidelines Chart for Immigrants

2014 HHS Poverty Guidelines for Affidavit of Support

Department of Homeland Security
U.S. Citizenship and Immigration Services

**USCIS
Form I-864P**
Supplement

2014 HHS Poverty Guidelines*
Minimum Income Requirements for Use in Completing Form I-864

For the 48 Contiguous States, the District of Columbia, Puerto Rico, the U.S. Virgin Islands, Guam, and the Commonwealth of the Northern Mariana Islands:

Sponsor's Household Size	100% of HHS Poverty Guidelines* For sponsors on active duty in the U.S. Armed Forces who are petitioning for their spouse or child	125% of HHS Poverty Guidelines* For all other sponsors
2	$15,730	$19,662
3	$19,790	$24,737
4	$23,850	$29,812
5	$27,910	$34,887
6	$31,970	$39,962
7	$36,030	$45,037
8	$40,090	$50,112
	Add $4,060 for each additional person.	Add $5,075 for each additional person.

For Alaska:

Sponsor's Household Size	100% of HHS Poverty Guidelines* For sponsors on active duty in the U.S. Armed Forces who are petitioning for their spouse or child	125% of HHS Poverty Guidelines* For all other sponsors
2	$19,660	$24,575
3	$24,740	$30,925
4	$29,820	$37,275
5	$34,900	$43,625
6	$39,980	$49,975
7	$45,060	$56,325
8	$50,140	$62,675
	Add $5,080 for each additional person.	Add $6,350 for each additional person.

For Hawaii:

Sponsor's Household Size	100% of HHS Poverty Guidelines* For sponsors on active duty in the U.S. Armed Forces who are petitioning for their spouse or child	125% of HHS Poverty Guidelines* For all other sponsors
2	$18,090	$22,612
3	$22,760	$28,450
4	$27,430	$34,287
5	$32,100	$40,125
6	$36,770	$45,962
7	$41,440	$51,800
8	$46,110	$57,637
	Add $4,670 for each additional person.	Add $5,837 for each additional person.

Means - Tested Public Benefits

Federal Means-Tested Public Benefits. To date, Federal agencies administering benefit programs have determined that Federal means-tested public benefits include Food Stamps, Medicaid, Supplemental Security Income (SSI), Temporary Assistance for Needy Families (TANF), and the State Child Health Insurance Program (SCHIP).

State Means-Tested Public Benefits. Each State will determine which, if any, of its public benefits are means-tested. If a State determines that it has programs which meet this definition, it is encouraged to provide notice to the public on which programs are included. Check with the State public assistance office to determine which, if any, State assistance programs have been determined to be State means-tested public benefits.

Programs Not Included: The following Federal and State programs are **not** included as means-tested benefits: emergency Medicaid; short-term, non-cash emergency relief; services provided under the National School Lunch and Child Nutrition Acts; immunizations and testing and treatment for communicable diseases; student assistance under the Higher Education Act and the Public Health Service Act; certain forms of foster-care or adoption assistance under the Social Security Act; Head Start Programs; means-tested programs under the Elementary and Secondary Education Act; and Job Training Partnership Act programs.

* These poverty guidelines remain in effect for use with Form I-864, Affidavit of Support, from March 1, 2014 until new guidelines go into effect in 2015.

Sample Form I-864A, Contract Between Sponsor and Household Member (page 1)

OMB No. 1615-0075; Expires 03/31/2015

Department of Homeland Security
U.S. Citizenship and Immigration Services

**I-864A, Contract Between
Sponsor and Household Member**

Part 1. Information on the Household Member. (You.)			For Government Use Only
1. Name	Last Name Mancini		This I-864A relates to a household member who:
	First Name Beatrice	Middle Name Stella	
2. Mailing Address	Street Number and Name *(include apartment number)* 800 Broadway		☐ is the intending immigrant.
	City Lindenhurst	State or Province New York	
	Country U.S.	Zip/Postal Code 11757	☐ is not the intending immigrant.
3. Place of Residence *(if different from mailing address)*	Street Number and Name *(include apartment number)*		
	City	State or Province	Reviewer
	Country	Zip/Postal Code	
4. Telephone Number	*(Include area code or country and city codes)* 212-222-2121		Location
5. Date of Birth	*(mm/dd/yyyy)* 03/06/1986		Date *(mm/dd/yyyy)*
6. Place of Birth	City State/Province Country Horseheads NY U.S.		
7. U.S. Social Security Number *(if any)*	206-45-9872		

8. Relationship to Sponsor (Check either a, b or c.)

a. ☐ I am the intending immigrant and also the sponsor's spouse.

b. ☐ I am the intending immigrant and also a member of the sponsor's household.

c. ☒ I am not the intending immigrant. I am the sponsor's household member. I am related to the sponsor as his/her.

    ☐ Spouse

    ☒ Son or daughter *(at least 18 years old)*

    ☐ Parent

    ☐ Brother or sister

    ☐ Other dependent (specify)

Form I-864A (03/22/13) Y

Sample Form I-864A, Contract Between Sponsor and Household Member (page 2)

9. I am currently:

For Government Use Only

a. [X] Employed as a/an _____ Legal secretary _____ .

Name of Employer No. 1 *(if applicable)* __Wynken, Blynken & Nodd__ .

Name of Employer No. 2 *(if applicable)* _____ .

b. [ ] Self-employed as a/an _____ .

c. [ ] Retired from_____ since _____ .
          (Company Name)   *(mm/dd/yyyy)*

d. [ ] Unemployed since _____
                        (mm/dd/yyyy)

10. My current individual annual income is: $ __46,000__ .

11. Federal income tax information.

[X] I have filed a Federal tax return for each of the three most recent tax years. I have attached the required photocopy or transcript of my Federal tax return for only the most recent tax year.

My total income (adjusted gross income on IRS Form 1040EZ) as reported on my Federal tax returns for the most recent three years was:

Tax Year		Total Income
__2013__	*(most recent)*	$ __46,000__
__2012__	*(2nd most recent)*	$ __43,000__
__2011__	*(3rd most recent)*	$ __27,000__

[ ] *(Optional)* I have attached photocopies or transcripts of my Federal tax returns for my second and third most recent tax years.

12. My assets (complete only if necessary).

a. Enter the balance of all cash, savings, and checking accounts. $_____ .

b. Enter the net cash value of real-estate holdings. (Net means assessed value minus mortgage debt.) $_____ .

c. Enter the cash value of all stocks, bonds, certificates of deposit, and other assets not listed on line a or b. $_____ .

d. **Add together Lines a, b, and c and enter the number here.** $_____ .

Sample Form I-864A, Contract Between Sponsor and Household Member (page 3)

			For Government Use Only
Part 2. Sponsor's Promise.			

13. **I, THE SPONSOR,** _____Alberto Ilario Mancini_____
(Print Name)

in consideration of the household member's promise to support the following intending immigrant(s)

and to be jointly and severally liable for any obligations I incur under the affidavit of support, promise

to complete and file an affidavit of support on behalf of the following ____2____ named intending
(Indicate Number)

immigrant(s) (see Step-by-Step instructions).

	Name	Date of Birth *(mm/dd/yyyy)*	A-number *(if any)*	U.S. Social Security Number *(if any)*
a.	Terese M. Mancini	02/15/1981	none	none
b.	Giovana Moreno	06/01/2009	none	none
c.				
d.				
e.				

14. _____Alberto I. Mancini_____   03/06/2014
       (Sponsor's Signature)   *(Date--mm/dd/yyyy)*

Part 3. Household Member's Promise.

15. **I, THE HOUSEHOLD MEMBER,** _____Beatrice Stella Mancini_____
(Print Name)

in consideration of the sponsor's promise to complete and file an affidavit of support on behalf of the

above _____2_____ named intending immigrant(s):
(Number from line 13)

  a. Promise to provide any and all financial support necessary to assist the sponsor in maintaining the sponsored immigrant(s) at or above the minimum income provided for in section 213A(a)(1)(A) of the Act (not less than 125 percent of the Federal Poverty Guidelines) during the period in which the affidavit of support is enforceable;

  b. Agree to be jointly and severally liable for payment of any and all obligations owed by the sponsor under the affidavit of support to the sponsored immigrant(s), to any agency of the Federal Government, to any agency of a State or local government, or to any other private entity that provides means-tested public benefit;

  c. Certify under penalty under the laws of the United States that all the information provided on this form is true and correct to the best of my knowledge and belief and that the Federal income tax returns submitted in support of the contract are true copies or unaltered tax transcripts filed with the Internal Revenue Service.

  d. **Consideration where the household member is also the sponsored immigrant:** I understand that if I am the sponsored immigrant and a member of the sponsor's household that this promise relates only to my promise to be jointly and severally liable for any obligation owed by the sponsor under the affidavit of support to any of my dependents, to any agency of the Federal Government, to any agency of a State or local government, and to provide any and all financial support necessary to assist the sponsor in maintaining any of my dependents at or above the minimum income provided for in section 213A(s)(1)(A) of the Act (not less than 125 percent of the Federal poverty line) during the period which the affidavit of support is enforceable.

  e. I authorize the Social Security Administration to release information about me in its records to the Department of State and U.S. Citizenship and Immigration Services.

16. _____Beatrice Stella Mancini_____   03/06/2014
      (Household Member's Signature)   *(Date--mm/dd/yyyy)*

Deferred Action for Childhood Arrivals

In June of 2012, the Obama administration created a new remedy for young immigrants in the U.S. with no legal status. Called "Deferred Action for Childhood Arrivals" or "DACA," it allows noncitizens who were brought to the U.S. as children and who meet other requirements (described below) to apply for two years' protection from deportation (removal), as well a work permit. Another benefit is that DACA approval stops accrual of "unlawful presence" (which is a problem if you ever apply for a visa or green card, as described in Chapter 4).

Since DACA does not confer actual or long-term legal immigration status, you might wonder why this remedy is included in a book about green cards. One good reason is that Congress has considered legislation on a similar theme, known as the "DREAM Act," which would grant conditional residency and later, permanent residency, to successful applicants. But it's impossible to say when or whether Congress will ever take action on the DREAM Act and whether DACA applicants (sometimes known as "DREAMers") will ever receive recognized immigration status. In the meantime, however, DACA can fill the gap and improve your ability to ultimately qualify for a green card.

It's important to note what the DACA remedy is not. It does not confer amnesty, a green card, or U.S. citizenship. It simply means that U.S. immigration authorities are expected to exercise their discretion and decline to deport an otherwise removable person who meets the legal criteria. Furthermore, family members of the applicant cannot claim any derivative rights to deferred action status.

As with any new government policy, the road to implementation has been bumpy. Although DACA can be renewed after its two-year expiration (and renewal applications were already being accepted when this book went to print), it provides no protection against the possibility that a later administration or Congress will change or override the policy. Such a change could leave former applicants—especially those whose applications were denied—with a clear record of unlawful U.S. presence, which would present a problem for their future green card eligibility.

A. Who Is Eligible for DREAM-Act Deferred Action

You may apply for deferred action status if you:

☐ had not yet turned age 31 as of June 15, 2012

☐ had not yet turned age 16 when you came to the U.S. to live

☐ have continuously lived ("resided") in the U.S. since June 15, 2007 up to when you apply (excluding any brief, casual, and innocent departures from the U.S.)

☐ were physically present in the U.S. on June 15, 2012, and also at the time you apply for deferred action

☐ either entered the U.S. without inspection before June 15, 2012, or if you entered with inspection, your lawful immigration status (such as a visa or Temporary Protected Status (TPS)) had expired as of June 15, 2012

☐ are either in school now (unless absent for emergency reasons), have graduated or earned a certificate of completion from an accredited high school, have obtained a general education development (GED) certificate, or are an honorably discharged veteran of the Coast Guard or Armed Forces of the U.S., and

☐ have not been convicted of a felony, significant misdemeanor, or three or more other misdemeanors; and do not otherwise present a threat to U.S. national security or public safety (such as by being a member of a gang).

You will, when it comes time to apply, need to supply proof of each item on this list.

TIP
No, you probably haven't missed the deadline.
As of the time this book went to print, there was no set deadline to apply for DACA, nor any known end date to the program. Applications will be accepted on a rolling basis for as long as the program remains in existence (which it's likely to do at least through the conclusion of the Obama administration, or until Congress passes comprehensive immigration reform and hopefully replaces DACA with an actual long-term legal program).

B. Who Is Ineligible for Deferred Action Status

Eligibility depends on meeting each and every criterion listed above. If, for example, you fit nearly all the criteria but were already 17 when you came to the U.S. to live, you will not qualify. The same goes if you haven't lived in the U.S. "continuously" for the required period but spent a few years in your home country. USCIS will also look closely at whether the schools from which you claim to have graduated are in fact recognized, accredited (in most cases, public) schools.

What "Currently in School" Means

If you are currently in school, or have graduated, you will need to make sure your school or program qualifies for DACA. USCIS has set forth narrow guidelines for those schools or programs that qualify.

You are "currently in school" if you are enrolled in one of the following.

1. **Elementary, junior high, or high school.** Applicants enrolled in a public or private elementary school, junior high school, or high school meet the "currently in school" requirement.

2. **ESL program.** An English as a second language program (ESL) can qualify you for DACA, but only if the program is a prerequisite for postsecondary education, job training, or employment and you are working toward one of these after completing the ESL program.

3. **Educational program; preparation for diploma or GED.** Other educational programs qualify if they are designed to help obtain a high school diploma or GED. The program must be funded by state or federal grants or, if privately operated, be of demonstrated effectiveness. Demonstrated effectiveness is measured by the success and quality of the program, including its length of operation and track record of success in placing participants in the workplace or in higher education. In other words, if you choose a privately run GED program, you will need to be selective and steer clear of ones that are recently opened or do not have a solid reputation. Programs run by local universities, adult schools, or community colleges are probably the best options.

4. **Education, literacy, vocational, or career training program.** One of these will meet the "currently in school" requirement if:
   - the program is funded by state or federal grants or the applicant can prove that the program is of demonstrated effectiveness (as described above)
   - the program is intended to place the applicant into postsecondary education, job training, or employment, and
   - the applicant is preparing for post-program placement.

If you are not now in school, you may still become DACA-eligible if you enroll in one of the programs described above. USCIS will look at whether you are enrolled in school at the time you submit your DACA application.

The criminal grounds of ineligibility are especially challenging for some applicants; especially because the term "significant misdemeanor" is not one that previously appeared in the immigration law, and thus has not yet been applied to many individual fact patterns by USCIS or the courts.

According to USCIS statements, significant misdemeanors include any, regardless of the prison or other sentence imposed, that involved violence, threats, assault, burglary, domestic violence, sexual abuse or exploitation, larceny, fraud, unlawful possession or use of a firearm, driving under the influence of drugs or alcohol (DUI or DWI), obstruction of justice or bribery, drug possession, drug distribution or trafficking, fleeing from a lawful arrest or prosecution, or leaving the scene of an accident.

Significant misdemeanors may also include any other misdemeanor for which the applicant was sentenced to more than 90 days in prison, not including suspended sentences, pretrial detention, or time held on an immigration detainer. (Again, three or more misdemeanors of any sort are a disqualifier for DACA deferred action status.)

USCIS has also explained a "non-significant misdemeanor" as including one punishable by imprisonment of more than five days and less than a year that is not on the USCIS list of significant misdemeanors.

C. Risks and Downsides to Applying for DACA

If you are considering applying for DACA but haven't yet done so, first consider your own personal, immigration, and criminal history and the risks of providing these details to the U.S. government, as described in this section.

1. DACA Offers No Long-Term Benefits

DACA is a discretionary, stopgap remedy that provides a stay of deportation from the U.S. for two years at a time and a work permit. It is not an amnesty, does not forgive past grounds of inadmissibility, and does not provide a pathway to U.S. legal residency or citizenship. And the longer you wait to apply, the less time you may have in which to enjoy DACA's benefits.

2. DACA Requires Sharing Personal Information That Could Later Lead to Deportation

USCIS has stated that DACA applicants' information will not be shared with Immigration and Customs Enforcement (ICE) unless applicants present national security, fraud, or public safety concerns. Nevertheless, the risk remains that a future event (such as a terrorist attack or a change in administration) could cause USCIS to interpret those categories more broadly.

Immigrants who have criminal records (including certain "significant misdemeanors," juvenile offenses, and expunged convictions), links to organizations flagged by the FBI, or past instances of committing immigration fraud are not only not eligible for DACA, but also risk being placed into removal proceedings if they submit a DACA application.

Similarly, USCIS may share the personal information of family members who are undocumented and listed on a DACA application with certain branches of the U.S. government if those family members are deemed a national security or public safety threat.

3. DACA's Travel Possibilities Create Risks of Being Stopped Upon Return to the U.S.

If you are granted relief under DACA, you may not freely travel in and out of the U.S.—but you do gain the ability to apply for and obtain what's called "Advance Parole" (a travel document) for "humanitarian, work or school purposes."

Even so, your travel will trigger the scrutiny of border agents upon your return. DACA is relatively new territory in immigration law, and many questions remain as to how other agencies will treat its beneficiaries. Because U.S. Customs and Border Protection (CBP) is separate from USCIS and restricts U.S. entry to foreign travelers with valid visas, DACA recipients have no guarantee that they will not be detained when attempting to reenter the U.S., based on their past immigration offenses or criminal history.

4. DACA Benefits Vary State by State

Immigrants who are approved for DACA in certain states may see more benefits than those living in others. While some states, such as California and Texas, allow DACA beneficiaries with an EAD to apply for a driver's license, others, such as Arizona and Nebraska, have forbidden this. In-state tuition regulations also differ from state to state.

D. Who Shouldn't Apply for DACA

If you face a significant risk that your case may be referred to Immigration and Customs Enforcement (ICE), which may lead to removal proceedings being instituted against you in the future, DACA may not be an appropriate remedy for you.

1. Don't Apply If You Have an Incident of Fraud in Your Past

If you entered the U.S. by means of fraud, you should not apply for DACA relief. Doing so would risk having your case referred to ICE. Common ways in which entrants commit fraud include using a counterfeit identity document such as a fake passport or a falsified birth certificate to obtain a visa or another immigration benefit.

Even if you entered the U.S. as a minor child or your parent or guardian used a false document on your behalf without your knowledge, until a law is passed that forgives fraud that was committed unknowingly, USCIS will still consider it to be part of your immigration history.

2. Don't Apply If You Have Committed Serious Immigration Offenses

USCIS may disqualify applicants who have serious immigration violations in their history or have committed several offenses, such as multiple unlawful reentries, as well as immigrants who have been deported in the past.

If and when the DACA program ends, immigrants who have submitted such information may undergo scrutiny from immigration enforcement authorities.

3. Don't Apply If You Have a Criminal Record

You are ineligible for DACA if you have been convicted of a felony, one "significant" misdemeanor, or three or more misdemeanor offenses that do not arise from a single event. Minor traffic offenses will not count as a misdemeanor for purposes of DACA even if they were classified as a misdemeanor under state law.

Fortunately for DACA applicants, USCIS does not immediately disqualify those who have just one or two misdemeanors or juvenile convictions or expunged offenses. USCIS will look at applicants' juvenile or expunged records and decide on a case-by-case basis whether or not to grant DACA relief. But even after that, immigration officials might still deny your application.

If you have any doubt as to whether a criminal conviction could disqualify you from DACA relief and possibly lead to an ICE referral, consult an immigration attorney. The attorney can help you obtain a copy of your state criminal record or a FBI background check and advise you whether or not to apply.

4. Don't Apply If You May Be Viewed as a Public Safety or National Security Threat

You may also be disqualified from receiving benefits under DACA and may be placed into removal proceedings if you are considered a threat to public safety or national security. USCIS may take into consideration any criminal activity that did not result in a conviction—even arrests and dismissed charges.

USCIS has stated that membership in a gang or an organization whose criminal activities threaten the U.S. public welfare would qualify as a public safety or national security threat. Again, since DACA is considered discretionary relief, any membership in a group that is flagged as having terrorist ties or anti-American views might lead to denial of your application and possible investigation by ICE in the future.

E. How to Apply for DACA

The application process for DACA involves submitting two government forms, supporting evidence showing that you qualify for this status, and a fee.

> ! **CAUTION**
> **The procedures described here apply only to people who are not in removal (deportation) proceedings.** You can submit a DACA application if you are in proceedings, but the procedures will be somewhat different—definitely get an attorney's help.

1. DACA Application Forms

The forms to submit to apply for DACA include:
- ☐ Form I-821-D, Consideration of Deferred Action for Childhood Arrivals, and
- ☐ Form I-765, Application for Employment Authorization, accompanied by a worksheet called Form I-765WS.

These are available as free downloads on the USCIS website, www.uscis.gov/forms. See the samples at the end of this chapter.

2. Preparing Documents in Support of DACA Application

In addition to filling out the forms, you will need to submit documents showing that you meet all the criteria mentioned above, including proof of your identity, age, entry date in the U.S., academic record, presence in the U.S. on June 15, 2012, and continuous physical presence in the United States. Such evidence might include:
- ☐ birth certificate
- ☐ copy of passport or other photo identity document
- ☐ copy of visa and Form I-94 (if you overstayed)
- ☐ past documents from immigration authorities, even if they showed you were stopped or ordered into removal proceedings
- ☐ travel receipts, for example showing plane tickets to the U.S.
- ☐ school records and correspondence, including acceptance letters, report cards, transcripts, progress reports, diplomas, and GED certificates, showing the name of the school and a description of the program, your dates of attendance, and degrees received
- ☐ copy of U.S. driver's license

- ☐ personal affidavits or statements by friends, teachers, employers, religious leaders, and others in authority
- ☐ tax records
- ☐ bank, credit card, and other financial records showing activity in the U.S.
- ☐ store, restaurant, and online shopping receipts in your name and/or indicating items sent to your address
- ☐ Facebook check-ins or Tweets indicating presence in the U.S.
- ☐ medical and dental records of your presence at U.S. doctors' offices or hospitals
- ☐ records of working for U.S. employers, and
- ☐ U.S. military records.

These are simply examples. Also think about what other documents might show that you meet the criteria. If, for example, you won a swimming contest at a U.S. summer camp, a copy of your certificate would be a good form of evidence of your physical presence here. Some people have even submitted traffic or speeding tickets as evidence (though any more serious run-in with police might be problematic for your DACA eligibility—talk to a lawyer).

The fee for this application is $465, which includes the standard $85 biometrics (fingerprinting) fee for a background check and the $380 fee for an EAD (work permit). In limited circumstances, USCIS may grant a fee exemption for applicants who fall below the U.S. poverty line.

Sample Form I-821D, Consideration of Deferred Action for Childhood Arrivals (page 1)

Consideration of Deferred Action
for Childhood Arrivals
Department of Homeland Security
U.S. Citizenship and Immigration Services

USCIS
Form I-821D
OMB No. 1615-0124
Expires 06/30/2015

		Receipt	Action Block
For USCIS Use Only	A- ☐☐☐☐☐☐☐		
	Case ID:		
	☐ Requestor interviewed on _____		

Returned: ___/___/___		Received: ___/___/___	Remarks
Resubmitted: ___/___/___	Relocated	Sent: ___/___/___	

To Be Completed by an *Attorney or* *Accredited Representative*, **if any.**	☐ Fill in box if G-28 is attached to represent the requestor.	Attorney State License Number: _____

▶ **START HERE - Type or print in black ink. Read the instructions for information on how to complete this form.**

Part 1. Information About You

I am not in immigration detention *and* I am requesting consideration of deferred action for childhood arrivals *and* I have included Form I-765, Application for Employment Authorization, and Form I-765WS, Form I-765 Worksheet.

Full Name

1.a. Family Name *(Last Name)* — Henriquez-Santos

1.b. Given Name *(First Name)* — Jorge

1.c. Middle Name — Adam

U.S. Mailing Address (Enter the same address on Form I-765)

2.a. In Care Of Name *(if applicable)* — [blank]

2.b. Street Number and Name — 14 W. Harbor Drive

2.c. Apt. ☒ Ste. ☐ Flr. ☐ 3

2.d. City or Town — San Diego

2.e. State — CA **2.f.** Zip Code — 92101

Removal Proceedings Information

3.a. Are you **now or have you ever been** in removal proceedings (which includes exclusion or deportation proceedings initiated before April 1, 1997, an INA section 240 removal proceeding, expedited removal, reinstatement of removal, an INA section 217 removal after admission under the Visa Waiver Program, or removal as a criminal alien under INA section 238), or do you have a removal order issued in any other context (for example, at the border or within the United States by an immigration agent)?   ☐ Yes ☒ No

If you answered "Yes" to the above question, you must check a box below indicating your current status or outcome of your removal proceedings.

3.b. Status or outcome:

1. ☐ Currently in Proceedings (Active)
2. ☐ Currently in Proceedings (Administratively Closed)
3. ☐ Terminated
4. ☐ Subject to a Final Order

3.c. Most Recent Date of Proceedings

(mm/dd/yyyy) ▶ [blank]

3.d. Location of Proceedings

[blank]

For USCIS
Use Only

Sample Form I-821D, Consideration of Deferred Action for Childhood Arrivals (page 2)

Part 1. Information About You *(continued)*

Other Information

4. Alien Registration Number (A-Number)*(if any)*
   ▶ A- ☐☐☐☐☐☐☐☐☐

5. U.S. Social Security Number *(if any)*
   ▶ ☐☐☐☐☐☐☐☐☐

6. Date of Birth *(mm/dd/yyyy)* ▶ 05/12/1985

7. Gender ☒ Male ☐ Female

8.a. City/Town/Village of Birth

   Zacatecas

8.b. Country of Birth

   Mexico

9. Current Country of Residence

   U.S.A.

10. Country of Citizenship/Nationality

   Mexico

11. Marital Status
   ☐ Married ☐ Widowed ☒ Single ☐ Divorced

Other Names Used (including maiden name)

If you require additional space, use **Part 7., Additional Information**.

12.a. Family Name *(Last Name)*

12.b. Given Name *(First Name)*

12.c. Middle Name

U.S. Entry and Status Information

13. Date of *Initial* Entry into the United States, on or about
   (mm/dd/yyyy) ▶ 08/15/1996

14. Place of Entry into the United States

   El Paso, TX

15. Status on June 15, 2012 *(e.g., No Lawful Status, Status Expired, Parole Expired)*

   No lawful status

16.a. Do you have an Arrival/Departure Record (I-94)?
   ☐ Yes ☒ No

16.b. If you answered "Yes", provide your I-94 number *(if applicable)* ▶ ☐☐☐☐☐☐☐☐☐☐☐

17. Date authorized stay expired, as shown on Form I-94, I-95, or I-94W *(if applicable)*
   (mm/dd/yyyy) ▶

Education Information

18. Education Status *(e.g., High School Graduate, Recipient of GED, or Currently in School)*

   Currently in school

19. Name, City, and State of School Currently Attending or Where Education Received

   San Diego State University

20. Date of Graduation (e.g., Receipt of a Certificate of Completion, GED Certificate, or other equivalent State-authorized exam) or, if Currently in School, Date of Last Attendance *(mm/dd/yyyy)* ▶ 06/20/2014

Military Service Information

21.a. Were you a member of the U.S. Armed Forces or Coast Guard?
   ☐ Yes ☒ No

If you answered "Yes" to the above question, you must provide responses to Item Numbers 21.b. through 21.e.

21.b. Military Branch

21.c. Service Start Date *(mm/dd/yyyy)* ▶

21.d. Discharge Date
   (mm/dd/yyyy) ▶

21.e. Type of Discharge

For USCIS Use Only

Sample Form I-821D, Consideration of Deferred Action for Childhood Arrivals (page 3)

Part 2. Arrival/Residence Information

1.a. I initially arrived and established residence in the U.S. prior to the age of 16. [X] Yes [ ] No

1.b. I have been continuously residing in the U.S. since at least June 15, 2007 up to the present time. [X] Yes [ ] No

Note: If you departed the United States for some period of time before your 16th birthday and returned to the United States on or after your 16th birthday to begin your current period of continuous residence, submit evidence that you established residence in the United States prior to age 16 as set forth in the instructions to this form.

List your current address and, to the best of your knowledge, the addresses where you resided since your initial entry into the United States. If you require additional space, use **Part 7., Additional Information**.

Present Address

2.a. Dates at this residence *(mm/dd/yyyy)*
From: ▶ 08/31/2013   To: ▶ Present

2.b. Street Number and Name   14 W. Harbor Dr.

2.c. Apt. [X] Ste. [ ] Flr. [ ]   3

2.d. City or Town   San Diego

2.e. State CA   **2.f.** Zip Code 92101

Address 1

3.a. Dates at this residence *(mm/dd/yyyy)*
From: ▶ 07/15/2009   To: ▶ 08/31/2013

3.b. Street Number and Name   960 47th St.

3.c. Apt. [X] Ste. [ ] Flr. [ ]   12E

3.d. City or Town   San Diego

3.e. State CA   **3.f.** Zip Code 92105

Address 2

4.a. Dates at this residence *(mm/dd/yyyy)*
From: ▶ 08/27/1996   To: ▶ 07/15/2009

4.b. Street Number and Name   4327 Crockett St.

4.c. Apt. [ ] Ste. [ ] Flr. [ ]

4.d. City or Town   Amarillo

4.e. State TX   **4.f.** Zip Code 79110

Address 3

5.a. Dates at this residence *(mm/dd/yyyy)*
From: ▶   To: ▶

5.b. Street Number and Name

5.c. Apt. [ ] Ste. [ ] Flr. [ ]

5.d. City or Town

5.e. State   **5.f.** Zip Code

List all your absences from the United States since June 15, 2007. If you require additional space, use **Part 7., Additional Information**.

6.a. Departure Date 1 *(mm/dd/yyyy)* ▶ 08/07/2000

6.b. Return Date 1 *(mm/dd/yyyy)* ▶ 09/01/2000

6.c. Reason for Departure
Visit grandparents

7.a. Departure Date 2 *(mm/dd/yyyy)* ▶

7.b. Return Date 2 *(mm/dd/yyyy)* ▶

7.c. Reason for Departure

**For USCIS
Use Only**

Sample Form I-821D, Consideration of Deferred Action for Childhood Arrivals (page 4)

Part 3. Criminal, National Security and Public Safety Information

If any of the following questions apply to you, use **Part 7., Additional Information**, to describe the circumstances and include a full explanation.

1. Have you ever been arrested for, charged with, or convicted of a felony or misdemeanor in the United States? *Do not include minor traffic violations unless they were alcohol- or drugs-related. Do include incidents handled in juvenile court.* ☐ Yes ☒ No

   If you answered "Yes" you must include a certified court disposition, arrest record, charging document, sentencing record, etc., for each arrest, unless disclosure is prohibited under state law.

2. Have you ever been arrested for, charged with, or convicted of a crime in any country other than the United States? ☐ Yes ☒ No

   If you answered "Yes" you must include a certified court disposition, arrest record, charging document, sentencing record, etc., for each arrest.

3. Have you ever engaged in or do you continue to engage in or plan to engage in terrorist activities? ☐ Yes ☒ No

4. Are you now or have you ever been a member of a gang? ☐ Yes ☒ No

Have you ever engaged in, ordered, incited, assisted or otherwise participated in any of the following:

5.a. Acts involving torture, genocide, or human trafficking? ☐ Yes ☒ No

5.b. Killing any person? ☐ Yes ☒ No

5.c. Severely injuring any person? ☐ Yes ☒ No

5.d. Any kind of sexual contact or relations with any person who was being forced or threatened? ☐ Yes ☒ No

Part 4. Signature of Requestor

Requestor's Statement *(check one)*

1.a. ☒ I can read and understand English, and have read and understand each and every question and instruction on this form, as well as my answer to each question.

1.b. ☐ Each and every question and instruction on this form, as well as my answer to each question, has been read to me by the person named below

   in a language in which I am fluent. I understand each and every question and instruction on this form, as well as my answer to each question.

Requestor's Certification

I certify, under penalty of perjury under the laws of of the United States of America, that the foregoing is true and correct. Copies of documents submitted are exact photocopies of unaltered original documents, and I understand that I may be required to submit original documents to USCIS at a later date. Furthermore, I authorize the release of any information from my records that USCIS needs to reach a determination on deferred action.

2.a. Signature of Requestor

   Jorge Henriquez-Santos

2.b. Date of Signature *(mm/dd/yyyy)* ▶ 09/10/2014

3. Daytime Phone Number (858) 555 - 1212

NOTE: Deferred action is unlikely to be considered for anyone who fails to completely fill out this form or to submit required documents listed in the instructions. Deferred action does not confer lawful status upon an individual. Furthermore, a decision on deferred action is wholly within the discretion of DHS.

4. Did someone help you prepare this form or a portion of it? (You must answer Yes or No.) ☐ Yes ☒ No

If yes, complete **Part 5., Signature of Person Preparing This Request, If Other Than the Requestor.**

For USCIS Use Only

Sample Form I-821D, Consideration of Deferred Action for Childhood Arrivals (page 5)

Part 5. Signature and Contact Information of Person Preparing This Form, If Other Than the Requestor

Preparer's Full Name

Provide the following information concerning the preparer:

1.a. Preparer's Family Name *(Last Name)*

1.b. Preparer's Given Name *(First Name)*

2. Preparer's Business or Organization Name

Preparer's Mailing Address

3.a. Street Number and Name

3.b. Apt. ☐ Ste. ☐ Flr. ☐

3.c. City or Town

3.d. State

3.e. Zip Code

Preparer's Contact Information

4. Daytime Phone Number ( ) -

5. Email Address

Preparer's Declaration

To be completed by all preparers, including attorneys and authorized representatives.

I declare that I prepared this Form I-821D at the requestor's behest, and it is based on all the information of which I have knowledge.

6.a. Signature of Preparer

6.b. Date of Signature *(mm/dd/yyyy)* ▶

Part 6. Signature of Interpreter

1. Language Used

I certify that I am fluent in English and the language above. I further certify that I have read each and every question and instruction on this form, as well as the answer to each question, to this requestor in the above-mentioned language, and that the requestor has informed me that he or she has understood each and every instruction and question of the form, as well as the answer to each question.

2.a. Signature of Interpreter

2.b. Date of Signature *(mm/dd/yyyy)* ▶

Interpreter's Information

3.a. Interpreter's Family Name *(Last Name)*

3.b. Interpreter's Given Name *(First Name)*

**For USCIS
Use Only**

Sample Form I-821D, Consideration of Deferred Action for Childhood Arrivals (page 6)

Part 7. Additional Information

If you require more space to provide any additional information within this request, please use the space below. If you require more space than what is provided to complete this request, you may use a separate sheet(s) of paper. You must include your full name on each sheet of paper along with the page number, Part Number, and Item Number related to your explanation.

Your Full Name

1.a. Family Name *(Last Name)*

1.b. Given Name *(First Name)*

1.c. Middle Name

2.a. Page Number   **2.b.** Part Number   **2.c.** Item Number

2.d.

3.a. Page Number   **3.b.** Part Number   **3.c.** Item Number

3.d.

4.a. Page Number   **4.b.** Part Number   **4.c.** Item Number

4.d.

**For USCIS
Use Only**

Sample Form I-765, Application for Employment Authorization

OMB No. 1615-0040; Expires 04/30/2016

I-765, Application For
Employment Authorization

Department of Homeland Security
U.S. Citizenship and Immigration Services

Do not write in this block.

Remarks	Action Block	Fee Stamp
A#		

Applicant is filing under §274a.12 _____

☐ Application Approved. Employment Authorized / Extended *(Circle One)*   until _____ (Date).

_____ (Date).

Subject to the following conditions: _____

Application Denied.
☐ Failed to establish eligibility under 8 CFR 274a.12 (a) or (c).
☐ Failed to establish economic necessity under 8 CFR 274a.12(c)(14), (18) and 8 CFR 214.2(f)

I am applying for:
☐ Permission to accept employment.
☐ Replacement *(of lost employment authorization document).*
☐ Renewal of my permission to accept employment *(attach previous employment authorization document).*

1. Name (Family Name in CAPS) (First)   (Middle)

HENRIQUEZ-SANTOS   Jorge   Adam

2. Other Names Used (include Maiden Name)

3. U.S. Mailing Address (Street Number and Name)   (Apt. Number)

14 W. Harbor Dr.   3

(Town or City)   (State/Country)   (ZIP Code)

San Diego   CA   92101

4. Country of Citizenship/Nationality

Mexico

5. Place of Birth (Town or City) (State/Province) (Country)

Atolinga   Zacatecas   Mexico

6. Date of Birth (mm/dd/yyyy)   **7.** Gender

05/12/1995   [X] Male ☐ Female

8. Marital Status   ☐ Married   [X] Single   ☐ Widowed   ☐ Divorced

9. Social Security Number (Include all numbers you have ever used, if any)

10. Alien Registration Number (A-Number) or I-94 Number (if any)

11. Have you ever before applied for employment authorization from USCIS?

☐ Yes (Complete the following questions.)   [X] No (Proceed to Question 12.)

Which USCIS Office?   Date(s)

Results (Granted or Denied - attach all documentation)

12. Date of Last Entry into the U.S., on or about: (mm/dd/yyyy)

08/15/1996

13. Place of Last Entry into the U.S.

El Paso, TX

14. Status at Last Entry (B-2 Visitor, F-1 Student, No Lawful Status, etc.)

No lawful status

15. Current Immigration Status (Visitor, Student, etc.)

DACA applicant

16. Go to the "Who May File Form I-765?" section of the instructions. In the space below, place the letter and number of the eligibility category you selected from the instructions. (For example, (a)(8), (c)(17)(iii), etc.).

(c) (33) ( )

17. If you entered the eligibility category, (c)(3)(C), in Question 16 above, list your degree, your employer's name as listed in E-Verify, and your employer's E-Verify Company Identification Number or a valid E-Verify Client Company Identification Number in the space below.

Degree: _____

Employer's Name as listed in E-Verify: _____

Employer's E-Verify Company Identification Number or a valid E-Verify Client Company Identification Number _____

Certification

Your Certification: I certify, under penalty of perjury under the laws of the United States of America, that the foregoing is true and correct. Furthermore, I authorize the release of any information that U.S. Citizenship and Immigration Services needs to determine eligibility for the benefit I am seeking. I have read the **"Who May File Form I-765?"** section of the instructions and have identified the appropriate eligibility category in **Question 16.**

Signature	Telephone Number	Date
Jorge Henriquez-Santos	858-555-1212	09-10-2014

Signature of Person Preparing Form, If Other Than Above: I declare that this document was prepared by me at the request of the applicant and is based on all information of which I have any knowledge.

Print Name	Address	Signature	Date

Remarks	Initial Receipt	Resubmitted	Relocated		Completed		
			Received	Sent	Approved	Denied	Returned

Form I-765 04/01/13 Y

Sample Form I-765 Worksheet

Form I-765 Worksheet
Department of Homeland Security
U.S. Citizenship and Immigration Services

USCIS
Form I-765WS
OMB No. 1615-0040
Expires 04/30/2016

If you are applying for employment authorization under the (c)(14), Deferred Action, or (c)(33), Consideration of Deferred Action for Childhood Arrivals, categories, you must complete this worksheet so that USCIS can determine whether you have an economic need to work. In the spaces provided, please indicate your current annual income, your current annual expenses, and the total current value of your assets. It is not necessary to submit supporting documentation, though it will be accepted and reviewed if you choose to submit it. You do not need to include other household members' financial information to establish your own economic necessity.

Part 1. Full Name

1.a. Family Name
(Last Name)   HENRIQUEZ-SANTOS

1.b. Given Name
(First Name)   Jorge

1.c. Middle Name   Adam

Part 2. Financial Information

2. My current annual income is: $ 10,000

3. My current annual expenses are: $ 35,000

4. The total current value of my assets is: $ 750

Part 3. Explanation

If you would like to provide an explanation regarding your current financial information or your economic need for employment authorization, please use the space below.

While I earn some money doing odd jobs, I am mostly supported by my parents and a scholarship, which covers one half of my school tuition. I need to work in order to be self-supporting, especially after graduation.

Form I-765WS 04/01/13 N

Page 1 of 1

U Visas for Crime Victims Assisting Law Enforcement

The Victims of Trafficking and Violence Protection Act of 2000 authorized a new visa for immigrant victims of serious crimes, called the "U" visa. The legislation was enacted in response to rising public safety concerns, with the idea that foreign victims of crimes in the U.S. should be allowed to remain here so as to provide law enforcement officials with information helpful in apprehending and prosecuting criminal offenders.

Although the U visa is temporary in nature, it can lead to a U.S. green card. It has, in fact, become an important option for many noncitizens in the United States. (The same legislation also created a "T" visa for victims of severe human trafficking, but because this is used less commonly, we will not cover it within this book.)

If you are approved for a U visa, you will be granted legal status in the U.S. for up to four years (which may be extended in "exceptional circumstances"). After you have held your U status for three years, you may be eligible to apply for a green card.

As with all U.S. visas, you will need to take several steps to prove that you qualify for it. In other words, it is not enough to simply claim that you have been a victim of a serious crime. You will need to provide a "certificate of helpfulness" from a qualifying government agency and also prove that you suffered mental or physical abuse by the U.S. criminal perpetrator.

Additionally, if you are "inadmissible" to the U.S. due to past immigration violations or for other reasons, you will need to apply for a waiver of these grounds.

This chapter will discuss the eligibility criteria for a U visa and how to apply. A final note: Although we use the word "U visa" throughout this chapter, only the applicants who come from outside the U.S. will, in literal terms, receive a visa in their passport. (A visa is an entry document.) Applicants from within the U.S. will receive "U status," and will, if they leave the U.S., need to go to a U.S. consulate to get an actual visa stamp in their passport before returning.

A. Who Is Eligible for a U Visa

In order to qualify for a U visa or U status in the U.S., you must meet the following criteria:

- ☐ You must have been a victim of a "qualifying criminal activity," and this crime must have occurred in the U.S. or violated U.S. law. Indirect and bystander victims are also eligible to apply in certain circumstances. For example, a murder victim obviously cannot benefit from a U visa, but a person who witnessed the murder, or a close family member who was impacted by it, may have information that can help law enforcement.
- ☐ In the course of or as a result of this criminal activity, you must have suffered substantial physical or mental abuse.
- ☐ You can provide useful information about the criminal activity (or if under age 16, your parent, guardian, or "next friend" such as a counselor or social worker can provide this information for you).
- ☐ You (or your parent, guardian, or next friend) are cooperating with U.S. law enforcement in order to bring the perpetrator of the crime to justice.
- ☐ You are admissible to the U.S. or you are applying for a waiver using Form I-192, Application for Advance Permission to Enter as a Non-Immigrant.

You can apply for a U visa either from within the U.S. or abroad (at a U.S. consulate).

1. What Crimes Qualify Their Victims for a U Visa

In a typical U visa case, you will have been the victim of a serious crime that took place in the United States. In some cases, however, the crime might have violated U.S. laws overseas (such as a human trafficking or kidnapping crime). Examples of qualifying crimes are:

- **Violent crimes:** murder, manslaughter, vehicular homicide, robbery, felonious assault (which usually involves the use of a deadly weapon, and can include statutory rape and other offenses), domestic violence, or stalking.
- **Enslavement crimes:** criminal restraint, kidnapping, abduction, being held hostage, forced labor, slavery, human trafficking, indentured or debt servitude, or false imprisonment.
- **Sex crimes:** rape, incest, sexual trafficking, sexual assault and abusive sexual contact, prostitution, sexual exploitation, or female genital mutilation.
- **Obstruction of justice crimes:** perjury, witness tampering, or withholding evidence.

The crime need not have been "completed" in order for it to qualify. An attempt, solicitation, or conspiracy to commit one of the above-mentioned crimes is enough. For example, obviously a murder victim wouldn't be applying for a U visa. But if you are the victim of attempted murder, you may qualify for a U visa.

2. When Indirect Victims May Be Eligible for U Status

USCIS may grant U status to noncitizen bystanders to crimes who suffered unusually severe harm as a result of having witnessed the criminal activity. The example most often used is that of a pregnant woman who suffers a miscarriage as a result of witnessing a criminal activity.

Also, certain family members can apply for U visas as indirect victims if the primary victim died due to murder or manslaughter or was rendered incompetent or incapacitated and therefore cannot help authorities with the criminal investigation. For crime victims who are age 21 or older, their spouse, as well as their children under 21 years of age, may be considered indirect victims. For victims under age 21, their parents and unmarried siblings under 18 can be considered indirect victims.

Indirect victims still need to establish that they meet the other eligibility requirements for U status, meaning that they:

- ☐ have been helpful, are being helpful, or will be helpful in the investigation of the crime
- ☐ suffered substantial harm as a result of the crime, and
- ☐ are either admissible to the U.S. or qualify for a waiver of inadmissibility.

EXAMPLE: Leticia's son Rodrigo was murdered when he was 20 years old. The mother, from Mexico, had a nervous breakdown soon after hearing the news. She helped the police investigation by providing information about her son and the events that happened on the day of the murder. Leticia would qualify as an indirect victim because she is the parent of a deceased victim under 21, she suffered harm as a result of the crime, and she helped in the investigation. She may still qualify even if several years have passed since the murder, because USCIS looks at the age of the victim when the murder took place to determine whether parents were indirect victims, and Rodrigo was 20.

USCIS generally considers minors to be "incapacitated," and therefore their family members often qualify as indirect victims.

EXAMPLE: Minjun, who overstayed a visa from Korea, has a four-year-old daughter, born in the United States. The daughter became the victim of child molestation by a nanny. As soon as Minjun realized his daughter was being abused, he reported the incident to the police, and assisted with the investigation. He suffered serious emotional harm because of what the daughter went through, especially because he was also the victim of abuse as a child. Because the daughter was born in the U.S., she does not need to apply for immigration relief. Minjun therefore could not be a derivative on her U status application. However, he may qualify for U status as an indirect victim, because his daughter was incapacitated (by definition, due to her young age), he helped the investigation, and he suffered harm as a result of the crime.

In both the above examples of indirect victims, the noncitizen would also have to meet the other requirements for eligibility for U status or a U visa, by showing admissibility to the U.S. or qualifying for a waiver of inadmissibility.

3. Satisfying the Requirement That You Suffered Substantial Physical or Mental Abuse

It is not enough to merely be the victim of a qualifying crime. You must have also suffered "substantial" physical injury or mental anguish as a result of this criminal activity and must provide USCIS with supporting evidence of this, such as medical records and affidavits.

In determining whether the injury was "substantial," USCIS will consider how severe the injury was, for how long the abuse occurred, and how likely it is to cause you lasting or permanent harm.

You will need to provide a personal statement detailing the physical or mental harm you suffered, as well as medical records or statements from treating physicians and psychologists, photographs of physical injuries, and affidavits from social workers.

4. Satisfying the Requirement That You Are Helping Law Enforcement

One of the reasons that Congress authorized U visas was out of concern that many U.S. immigrants refuse to provide information to U.S. police and other law enforcement authorities, due to cultural differences, language barriers, and fear of deportation. The unfortunate result is that many perpetrators of serious crimes view immigrants as easy targets.

In order to further the public safety objectives of the U visa, your visa petition must be certified by a police officer or other law enforcement official. The official must attest that you were a victim of a qualifying crime and that you are likely to be helpful to an investigation or prosecution of the crime.

The chances of your getting a law enforcement official to cooperate with your U visa application are greatly improved if you are forthcoming with information that could lead to the identification, arrest, and conviction of a serious criminal. This could include (but is not limited to) your providing:

- ☐ an identification of the criminals involved, such as their names and addresses, or by your choosing the correct person in a lineup identification
- ☐ information that helps apprehend the perpetrators, such as your tips as to where they may be "hiding out," names of their friends and family who might give information about their whereabouts, or identifying details about their vehicle (make, color, license plate number)
- ☐ descriptive details that help the prosecution convince a jury that the accused is guilty of the crime, rebut the criminal's alibi, support a motive for committing the crime, or determine what penalty (or sentencing) it should request
- ☐ evidence that could help law enforcement classify the crime as more serious or charge the criminals with additional crimes. (This might be the situation if, for example, the officer is investigating a felony assault but you have evidence that could lead to an attempted murder charge, or you have information that might lead to an additional charge of sexual assault.)
- ☐ agreement to testify as a witness if the case goes to trial

5. Available Waiver If You Are Inadmissible

To be eligible for a U visa, you must not be "inadmissible" to the United States. This means that you are not barred from U.S. entry due to factors such as multiple criminal convictions, immigration violations, certain medical conditions, or any of several other reasons.

In order to apply for a waiver of inadmissibility, you must submit to USCIS Form I-192, Application for Advance Permission to Enter as a Nonimmigrant. Unlike many other immigration waivers, this one does not require a showing of "extreme hardship." U visa waiver applications are reviewed on a case-by-case basis. You'll definitely want to get a lawyer's help, however, in order to identify and prove the reasons you deserve the waiver.

6. Qualifying Family Members May Receive Derivative U Visas

Certain family members may be eligible to become derivative U visa recipients if the principal petitioner's application is approved. These include your:

- unmarried children under age 21
- spouse
- parents (if principal petitioner is under age 21), and
- unmarried siblings under 18 years old (if principal petitioner is under age 21).

To obtain derivative status for family members, you (as the primary petitioner) would submit Form I-918, Supplement A, Petition for Qualifying Family Member of U Visa Recipient, along with your own petition or after your U visa is approved. Any derivative relatives that you include must also be "admissible" to the U.S. (or apply for a waiver) and have good moral character.

B. How to Apply for a U Visa

Applying for a U visa involves the following steps:

- Prepare USCIS Form I-918, Petition for U Nonimmigrant Status (see sample at end of this chapter).
- Have a qualifying agency provide certification of your helpfulness, to accompany this I-918 petition.
- Gather evidence to substantiate your eligibility and claim of substantial injury.
- If you have derivative family members who wish to work in the U.S., prepare Form I-765 for a work permit.
- Submit your petition and supporting documents to USCIS, and
- Attend an interview at a USCIS office or your local U.S. consulate, if required.

We'll explain each of these steps below. And here is a summary of the items you will need to assemble:

- ☐ Form I-918 (No fee is required with this form.)
- ☐ Form I-918, Supplement A (if you want derivative status for a qualifying family member)
- ☐ Form I-918, Supplement B (completed and certified by a qualifying law enforcement agency)
- ☐ supporting documents, as described above
- ☐ Evidence that you have helpful information about the crime. Form I-918, Supplement B should be sufficient, but if you have any further information about how you are being helpful to authorities in providing information about the crime, you should submit it.
- ☐ Evidence that the crime violated U.S. laws. Again, Form I-918, Supplement B should cover this, but if you have any additional information about the crime, especially if it occurred outside of the U.S. (but violated federal law), you should provide this.

☐ Waiver of Grounds of Inadmissibility, if applicable. Submit Form I-192, Application for Advance Permission to Enter as a Nonimmigrant, with check or money order ($585 as of this book's print date), made payable to "U.S. Department of Homeland Security." If you cannot afford this amount, you may apply for a fee waiver.

☐ Information to prove relationship of derivative family members. Provide documentation to prove that your family member qualifies for derivative U status (for example, birth or marriage certificates). Make sure that any foreign language documents are accompanied by a full English translation that is certified as complete and accurate by a translator competent to translate from the foreign language into English.

☐ Form I-765, Application for Employment Authorization Document (EAD), with appropriate filing fees, for any derivative family members who wish to work and are currently in the United States.

1. Line-by-Line Instructions for Preparing I-918 Petition for U Visa

Here are instructions for filling out the required visa petition, on USCIS Form I-918. The application form, its supplements, and further instructions are available on the I-918 page of the USCIS website (www.uscis.gov/i-918).

Part 1, "Information about you." You will need to provide your name (including maiden name and nicknames), address, and phone number, as well as your alien number (A#) and Social Security number (if any). Also provide your birth date, passport information, marital status, I-94# and other arrival/departure information, and current immigration status.

Part 2, "Additional information." Your answers to these questions will determine whether or not you are eligible for a U visa or whether USCIS will require more information from you. If you answer "no" to any of questions 1-5, your application will be denied. Definitely see an attorney if the true answer is "no;" lying on an application can get you into serious trouble.

Question 1. (Qualifying crime.) Answer "yes" if you are the victim of any crime listed at Section 101(a)(15)(u) of the I.N.A.

Question 2. (Substantial physical or mental abuse.) Answer "yes" to certify that you have been substantially injured as the result of the criminal activity.

Question 3. (Information about the crime.) Answer "yes" if you have information concerning the crime that you were a victim of.

Question 4. (Certification of helpfulness.) You'll definitely need to answer "yes," to show that a qualifying official will be providing a Certification of Helpfulness on Form I-918, Supplement B.

Question 5. (Place of the crime.) Answer "yes" if the qualifying crime took place in the U.S. or violated U.S. laws.

Question 6. If you are under age 16, answer "yes." Your parent, guardian, or "next friend" will need to cooperate with the agency and provide information on your behalf.

Question 7. (Employment Authorization Document.) If you want to apply for a work permit, answer "yes."

Question 8. (Immigration proceedings.) If you have ever been in U.S. removal (deportation) or exclusion proceedings, answer "yes" and provide dates.

Question 9. (Admissions to U.S.) List your date and place of entry to the U.S. and the status you held at the time. Write the visa you entered with or "EWI" (entered without inspection) if you did not have legal status.

Question 10. (Application outside the U.S.) If you are applying for a U visa from abroad, complete this section. Otherwise, write "N/A."

Part 3, "Processing information." The questions that follow will determine whether you are "admissible" to the United States. If you answer "yes" to any of these, your application may be denied or you may have to file Form I-192, Application for Advance Permission to Enter as a Nonimmigrant, along with your petition. Consult an immigration attorney if you need to answer "yes" to any of these questions.

Question 1. (Criminal history.) The form asks about any arrests, convictions, sentences, imprisonment, probation, parole, alternative sentencing, or rehabilitation. You will need to answer truthfully and list the charge, date, place, and outcome for each event.

Question 2. (Likeliness to become a public charge.) If you have received food stamps, free medical care (other than emergency medical treatment) or any other form of welfare or public assistance, or are likely to need this type of help in the future, answer "yes."

Question 3. (Moral character.) These questions about prostitution, gambling, helping others to evade immigration laws, and drug trafficking are meant to determine whether you are "inadmissible" because of poor moral character.

Questions 4–13, 20. (Public safety, persecution of others, totalitarian and Nazi Party membership, polygamy.) Your answers to these questions will indicate whether you pose a threat to public safety, present a terrorist threat, have persecuted others, or are voluntarily involved with an unaccepted political party. If you need to answer "yes" to any of these, you will need to explain your involvement on a separate sheet of paper. Absent very good reason (you were forced to participate in these activities, for example) your U visa application will likely be denied.

Question 14. (Removal proceedings.) If you are currently in removal (deportation) proceedings, you can still apply for a U visa. If you were ever ordered removed (or deported) or requested voluntary departure in the past, answer "yes."

Questions 15–16. (False documentation, fraud.) If you have used false documents to obtain a U.S. visa or otherwise enter the U.S. or lied to obtain an immigration benefit, you must answer "yes" here. Your visa application will be denied and you will be placed into removal proceedings.

Question 17. (Military draft.) If you left the U.S. to avoid being drafted into the military, answer "yes."

Question 18. (J exchange visitor visa.) If you hold a J visa that came with a two-year foreign residency requirement (requiring you to leave at the end of your J status and spend two years outside the U.S. before qualifying for another visa or green card), answer "yes." You may have to submit a waiver application, and receive an approval of that, before your U visa petition can be approved.

Question 19. (Withholding child custody.) Self-explanatory.

Question 21. (Stowaways.) Self-explanatory.

Question 22. (Communicable disease and drug abuse.) Self-explanatory.

Part 4, "Information about your spouse or children." You will need to fill out personal information for your spouse and children (if applicable).

Part 5, "Filing on behalf of family members." If you are applying for U derivative status for a qualifying family member, check "Yes." Qualifying family members include your spouse, unmarried children under age 21, parents (if you are under age 21), and unmarried siblings (if you are under age 18).

Part 6, "Attestation, release, and signature." You must sign and date your application.

2. Obtaining a Certification of Helpfulness

As part of your application for a U visa, you will need to show USCIS that a law enforcement official has "vouched" for your petition. A judge, police officer, prosecutor, or other law enforcement official must complete a "certification of helpfulness" (I-918 Supplement B, U Nonimmigrant Status Certification) on your behalf. This document is a vital part of your application. It shows that you have been a victim of qualifying criminal activity, have information that will be useful to law enforcement, and are cooperating in order to bring the perpetrator to justice.

The agencies that will most commonly certify a U visa petition are local, state, and federal police departments and prosecutors. Even a judge may sign a U visa certification, although many will refuse to do so in order to avoid a showing of bias for the prosecution. However, any state or federal agency that has "responsibility for the investigation or prosecution of a qualifying crime or criminal activity" may complete the certification of helpfulness. For example, if you are the victim of a crime that requires the involvement of Child Protective Services (CPS), you could bypass the police and justice departments and instead have CPS help you with your application.

USCIS states that people who are in a supervisory role and have responsibility for issuing certificates of helpfulness must sign the petition, but it allows the agency to designate another certifying official if it chooses to do so.

Ultimately, it's up to the law enforcement authorities acting in your case to decide whether or not you are "helpful" to them and whether they should fill out the certification of helpfulness for you.

> **TIP**
> **Get to work on obtaining the certification of helpfulness as soon as possible.** Not only is it a vital part of your application, but by showing interest and providing helpful evidence to authorities, you will help show that you are eager to participate in the investigation. Also, if the criminals involved are arrested and plead guilty to the criminal charges before you contact police or answer a request for cooperation from law enforcement, your evidence and testimony may not be as useful, since the case will not go to trial.

3. Preparing Documents to Support Your U Visa Petition

Filling out the required forms will not be enough, by itself, to qualify you for a U visa. You will also need to prepare or gather various documents to support your claim, such as:

- ☐ Personal narrative statement, describing how you are a victim of criminal activity and the circumstances surrounding the crime. You can use this statement to show that you were not at fault in the criminal activity and that you were helpful (if you called the authorities to report the crime, for example). Also describe the extent of your injuries.

- ☐ Evidence that you are the victim of a qualifying criminal activity. This could include trial transcripts, newspaper articles, police reports, affidavits, or orders of protection (restraining orders).

- ☐ Evidence that you suffered substantial physical or mental abuse. This could include affidavits from case or social workers, medical personnel, and police; photographs of injuries; and affidavits from people who have personal knowledge of the criminal activity.

An attorney can help you gather these documents, but you will still need to play a role in considering what the best sources might be, and in talking to friends, doctors, and others who might help.

4. Filling Out Form I-765

The principal petitioner does not need to worry about applying for a work permit (EAD). If the I-918 is approved, he or she will be sent an EAD automatically. Any derivative family members who want to work must, however, separately submit Form I-765 to request an EAD. They can do so either by including their form with the I-918 petition or by sending in a separate Form I-765 after USCIS has approved the I-918 petition.

Form I-765 is fairly short and self-explanatory. For Question 16, the applicant's eligibility category, you would fill in "(a)(19)" for the principal applicant and "(a)(20)" for any derivative family members.

Your family members will also need to pay the Form I-765 fee ($380 as of this book's print date) or request a fee waiver.

5. Submitting Your U Visa Petition to USCIS

After you have completed the application, make a copy for your files. Then send the packet of forms and documents to the following USCIS address:

Vermont Service Center
75 Lower Welden Street
St. Albans, VT 05479

6. Attending a U Visa Interview

If you are applying from within the U.S., chances are you will not be required to attend an interview at a local USCIS office, which is why it is important to provide a strong statement with your I-918 applications. However, it's always possible that you may be required to attend an in-person interview at a local USCIS office. If you (or your family members) are applying from overseas, this interview would be held at the U.S. embassy or consulate in your home country.

The purpose of the interview will be for U.S. officials to review your file and talk with you personally about your eligibility for a U visa or your relationship with the principal applicant (if you are a family member applying for derivative status) and to make sure you are not inadmissible to the United States.

How Long Does It Take to Get a U Visa?

It typically takes about a year for USCIS to fully process a U visa application, which includes taking biometrics (photographs and fingerprints), processing all forms and supporting information (such as the certification of helpfulness by a qualifying agency), and finally, issuing an approval notice and your work permit.

Use that estimate only as a guideline, however. The amount of time USCIS takes to process your Form I-918 can vary, depending on the particulars of your case.

For example, if the USCIS officer assigned to your case needs more information, he or she will send you a Request for Evidence (RFE). That will put a hold on your file until you send in the requested documents

---

C. Green Card Possibilities After U Visa Approval

If you have received a U visa or U status as a victim of a serious crime assisting law enforcement, you may be able to adjust your status (receive your green card) after three years of continuous presence in the United States. If interested, you should apply for a green card as soon you can, because you must continue to be eligible as a U visa crime victim at the time you apply.

1. Which U Nonimmigrants Are Eligible for a Green Card

Here's a breakdown of the requirements you must meet in order to apply for a U.S. green card:

- ☐ You must continue to be eligible for U nonimmigrant status. This means that you must continue to assist law enforcement by providing helpful information used to investigate and prosecute the criminals who victimized you.
- ☐ You must not have abandoned this status (for example, by refusing to cooperate with government agencies or by living outside the U.S. for an extended period of time).
- ☐ You have been physically present in the U.S. continuously for at least three years.
- ☐ You have not unreasonably refused to cooperate with the law enforcement officials investigating and prosecuting the crime against you, and
- ☐ Your continued presence in the U.S. is justified either on humanitarian grounds, to ensure family unity, or because it is in the public interest.

You will have a difficult time showing USCIS that you are eligible for a green card if your help is no longer necessary to investigate and prosecute the crime against you (for example, the criminal case is now closed and a government official will not vouch for your "helpfulness").

2. You Have Continuous U.S. Physical Presence of at Least Three Years

In order to successfully apply for permanent residence, you must show that you have lived in the U.S. continuously for three years. "Continuous" presence for immigration purposes means that you have not taken a trip outside the U.S. for 90 days or more or spent more than 180 days abroad during your time in U status.

You can demonstrate your continuous presence by documenting each trip outside the U.S. (to show that you were abroad only briefly) and providing proof that you now make your life in the United States. This can include pay stubs, tax transcripts, school records, and affidavits from people who know you and can attest to your U.S. presence.

If you can't show continuous presence, you will need to provide a written explanation by a government official who is working on your case, stating that your presence outside the U.S. was necessary in order to assist the investigation or prosecution of the crime or that it was otherwise justified.

3. You Must Continue to Cooperate With Law Enforcement

In order to be eligible for a green card, you must continue to provide helpful information to law enforcement officials, and you cannot have "unreasonably refused" to provide requested assistance.

Ideally, you will submit another certification of helpfulness (Form I-918 Supplement B, U Nonimmigrant Status Certification) with your green card application. This will prove that you are a willing participant in the investigation and prosecution of the crime (or crimes) against you.

If you are unable to obtain another certification of helpfulness, contact an experienced immigration attorney to help, because you will need to instead submit an affidavit and other supporting evidence showing all of your contacts and meetings with law enforcement officials. You will also need to explain that you attempted to obtain a certification from a qualifying agency, but were unable to for good reason.

Additionally, if you ever refused a request for cooperation, you must explain your reasons. USCIS will determine whether the request was "unreasonable" given a variety of factors. Its decision will depend on the nature of the crime, your circumstances, and the extent of the assistance required.

For example, if you are a rape victim and a police investigator asked you to meet with your attacker, USCIS would likely consider this to be an unreasonable request, and would excuse you for refusing it. However, if a police officer asked you to identify your attacker in a lineup where he would not see you and you refused, your denial might cost you a green card.

4. Your Residence Is Justified on Humanitarian, Family Unity, or Public Interest Grounds

Unlike many other green card applicants, U visa holders do not have to apply for a waiver of any applicable inadmissibility grounds. The only ground of inadmissibility that applies to U adjustment applicants concerns participants in Nazi persecution, genocide, or extrajudicial killings. There is no waiver available for these grounds.

However, adjustment of status to permanent residence from a U visa is a discretionary benefit, which means it is completely up to the USCIS officer handling your case whether or not to grant it. Therefore, you should submit evidence with your application to show USCIS that you "deserve" a green card. For example, your family ties in the U.S., achievements and accomplishments, and any reasons why you would be subjected to hardship if you were to return to your home country will be relevant. This is especially true if there are any negative factors in your record (such as arrests or criminal convictions).

5. Your Immediate Relatives May Also Apply for Green Cards

If you have qualifying family members in the U.S. in derivative U status, the procedures to apply for adjustment of status are the same as for the principal U applicant.

However, if you have an immediate family member—spouse, child, or parents (if you are under age 21)—who has never received U derivative status, that person can also apply for adjustment of status or an immigrant visa at the same time you apply or after your approval. To bring this about, file Form I-929, Petition for Qualifying Family Member of U-1 Nonimmigrant, with USCIS.

You must show that you or your family member would be subjected to "extreme hardship" if he or she was not permitted to reside with you in the United States. This is not an easy task, so you would do best to consult an immigration attorney to help you.

Keep in mind that these relatives (unlike you) WILL be subject to the inadmissibility grounds that prevent many noncitizens from entering the United States.

6. How to File for a U.S. Green Card

If you meet all the requirements, the next step is to file for adjustment of status. You (and each of your derivative family members) will need to assemble:

- ☐ Form I-485, Application to Register Permanent Residence or to Adjust Status
- ☐ filing fee or, or if you cannot afford it, a waiver request filed on Form I-912, Request for Fee Waiver
- ☐ Form I-693, Report of Medical Examination and Vaccination Record
- ☐ Form G-325A, Biographic Information Sheet (if you are between 14 and 79 years old)
- ☐ Form I-765, Application for Employment Authorization and supporting documentation
- ☐ Form I-131, Application for Travel Document and supporting documentation
- ☐ a copy of Form I-797, Notice of Action, showing that USCIS approved you for U nonimmigrant status
- ☐ a copy of your I-94, Arrival/Departure Record. All arriving foreign visitors had this white card stapled into their passports until this form was automated in April 2013; subsequent visitors can obtain a copy of their I-94 from the U.S. Customs and Border Protection (CBP) website at www.cbp.gov (click "Travel" then "Arrival/Departure Forms: I-94 and I-94W")
- ☐ if any of your family members has not yet obtained derivative status, Form I-929, Petition for Qualifying Family Member of U-1 Nonimmigrant, as described in Section C5, above

☐ a copy of all pages of your passport, including the U nonimmigrant visa page. If you do not have a U visa, because you have not departed the U.S. since you were granted U status, make copies of all of your passport pages regardless. If you don't have a passport, provide an explanation as to why you do not have one, such as loss or theft

☐ a copy of your birth certificate (along with an English translation)

☐ two passport-style photos

☐ evidence that you have three years of continuous physical presence in the U.S.: this can include tax transcripts, pay stubs, leases, receipts, and utility bills for a U.S. residence, a letter from your school or employer, and affidavits from people who can vouch for your U.S. presence

☐ Evidence that you complied with requests for assistance from law enforcement officials. The best evidence of this is a new Form I-918 Supplement B. Second-best would be your affidavit, describing your attempts to contact law enforcement officials during your time in U status and reasons for any failure to comply with a request for cooperation.

☐ Evidence that you "deserve" permanent residence. U visa holders are not subject to a majority of the inadmissibility grounds that others face when applying for a green card. However, because adjustment of status for U visa holders depends on whether USCIS believes it is justified, be prepared to submit evidence that you should be granted a green card on humanitarian, public interest, or family unity grounds.

> **CAUTION**
>
> **What if your U status will expire before you can apply for a green card?** Your U status, as the principal applicant, will likely last four years. However, due to consular processing delays, many derivative U visa holders are authorized to stay in the U.S. for only three years or less. If your U status will expire before you are able to accrue the continuous presence needed, you may able to extend the time to a period not exceeding four years. Do so by filling out and submitting USCIS Form I-539. Provide the documents described on the USCIS instructions to the form (available at www.uscis.gov/i-539), and be prepared to describe how USCIS or consular processing delays slowed your entry into the U.S. or that you would be unable to adjust to permanent residence if your U visa was not extended, through no fault of your own.

After you compile all of the above items, make a copy for your files and send it to:

Vermont Service Center
75 Lower Welden Street
St. Alban's, VT 05479

7. What Happens After Submitting Adjustment of Status Application

After you file Form I-485, you should first receive a receipt notice. Later, you will be sent a biometrics appointment notice, requiring you to appear to have your photograph, fingerprints, and signature taken.

If USCIS has questions about your application, it may schedule you for interview at a local USCIS field office. Bring a copy of everything you sent to USCIS and an interpreter if you are not fluent in English.

Sample Form I-918, Petition for U Nonimmigrant Status (page 1)

OMB No. 1615-0104; Expires 01/31/2016

Department of Homeland Security
U.S. Citizenship and Immigration Services

Form I-918, Petition for U Nonimmigrant Status

START HERE - Please type or print in black ink.

Part 1. Information about you. *(Person filing this petition as a victim)*

Family Name	Given Name	Middle Name
Chen	Xing	Mei

Other Names Use (Include maiden name/nickname)

Sally

Home Address - Street Number and Name	Apt. No.
812 142nd St	

City	State/Province	Zip/Postal Code
Puyallup	WA	98371

Safe Mailing Address (if other than above) - Street Number and Name | Apt. No.

C/O (*in care of*):

City	State/Province	Zip/Postal Code

Home Telephone No. *(with area code)*	Safe Daytime Phone No. *(with area code)*	E-Mail Address *(optional)*
253-555-1313		xmchen@email.com

A-No. *(if any)*	U.S. Social Security No. *(if any)*	Gender
		☐ Male ☒ Female

Marital Status
☐ Single ☐ Married ☒ Divorced ☐ Widowed

Date of Birth *(mm/dd/yyyy)*	Country of Birth
09/18/1990	China

Country of Citizenship	Passport No.
China	131234667

Place of Issuance	Date of Issue *(mm/dd/yyyy)*
Beijing, China	01/03/2009

Place of Last Entry	Date of Last Entry *(mm/dd/yyyy)*
Seattle, WA	10/12/2012

I-94 No. *(Arrival/Departure Document)*	Current Immigration Status
12123456799	Visa overstay

For USCIS Use Only

Returned	Receipt
Date	
Date	
Resubmitted	
Date	
Date	
Reloc Sent	
Date	
Date	
Reloc Rec'd	
Date	
Date	

U.S. Embassy/Consulate:

Validity Dates
From: _____
To: _____

Remarks

Conditional Approval
Stamp No.: _____ Date

Action Block

To Be Completed by *Attorney or Representative,* if any.

☐ Fill in box if G-28 is attached to represent the applicant.

ATTY State License Number

Sample Form I-918, Petition for U Nonimmigrant Status (page 2)

Part 2. Additional information.

Answers to the questions below require explanations and supporting documentation. Attach relevant documents in support of your claims that you are a victim of criminal activity listed in the Immigration and Nationality Act (INA), section 101(a)(15)(U). You must also attach a personal narrative statement describing the criminal activity of which you were the victim. If you are only petitioning for U derivative status for a qualifying family member(s) subsequent to your (the principal petitioner) initial filing, evidence supporting the original petition is not required to be submitted with the new Form I-918.

Attach additional sheets of paper as needed. Write your name and Alien Registration Number (A #), if any, at the top of each sheet and indicate the number of the item that refers to your answer. Include the Part and letter or number relating to the additional information you provided (example: Part 2, Z).

Check either "Yes" or "No" as appropriate to each of the following questions.

1. I am a victim of criminal activity listed in the INA at section 101(a)(15)(U). [X] Yes ☐ No

2. I have suffered substantial physical or mental abuse as a result of having been a victim of this criminal activity. [X] Yes ☐ No

3. I possess information concerning the criminal activity of which I was a victim. [X] Yes ☐ No

4. I am submitting a certification from a certifying official on Form I-918 Supplement B, U Nonimmigrant Status Certification. [X] Yes ☐ No

5. The crime of which I am a victim occurred in the United States including Indian country and military installations) or violated the laws of the United States. [X] Yes ☐ No

6. I am under the age of 16 years. ☐ Yes [X] No

7. I want an Employment Authorization Document. [X] Yes ☐ No

8. Have you ever been in immigration proceedings? ☐ Yes [X] No

   If "Yes," what type of proceedings? *(Check all that apply.)*

   ☐ Removal Date *(mm/dd/yyyy)*   ☐ Exclusion Date *(mm/dd/yyyy)*   ☐ Deportation Date *(mm/dd/yyyy)*   ☐ Recission Date *(mm/dd/yyyy)*   ☐ Judicial Date *(mm/dd/yyyy)*

9. List each date, place of entry and status under which you entered the United States during the five years preceding the filing of this petition.

Date of Entry *(mm/dd/yyyy)*	Place of Entry	Status at Entry
10/12/2012	Seattle, WA	B-2 Visitor

Sample Form I-918, Petition for U Nonimmigrant Status (page 3)

Part 2. Additional information.	(Continued.)

10. If you are outside the United States, give the U.S. Consulate or inspection facility you want notified if this petition is approved.

Type of Office *(Check one)*:   ☐ Consulate   ☐ Pre-flight inspection   ☐ Port of Entry

Office Address *(City)*

U.S. State or Foreign Country

Safe Foreign Address Where You Want Notification Sent - Street Number and Name   Apt. No.

City	State/Province	Country	Zip/Postal Code

Part 3. Processing information.

Please answer the following questions about yourself. For the purposes of this petition, you must answer "Yes" to the following questions, if applicable, even if your records were sealed or otherwise cleared or if anyone, including a judge, law enforcement officer or attorney, told you that you no longer have a record. *(Answering "Yes" does not necessarily mean that you will be denied U nonimmigrant status.)*

1. Have you **EVER**:

a. Committed a crime or offense for which you have not been arrested?   ☐ Yes   ☒ No

b. Been arrested, cited or detained by any law enforcement officer (including DHS, former INS and military officers) for any reason?   ☐ Yes   ☒ No

c. Been charged with committing any crime or offense?   ☐ Yes   ☒ No

d. Been convicted of a crime or offense (even if violation was subsequently expunged or pardoned)?   ☐ Yes   ☒ No

e. Been placed in an alternative sentencing or a rehabilitative program (for example: diversion, deferred prosecution, withheld adjudication, deferred adjudication)?   ☐ Yes   ☒ No

f. Received a suspended sentence, been placed on probation or been paroled?   ☐ Yes   ☒ No

g. Been in jail or prison?   ☐ Yes   ☒ No

h. Been the beneficiary of a pardon, amnesty, rehabilitation, or other act of clemency or similar action?   ☐ Yes   ☒ No

i. Exercised diplomatic immunity to avoid prosecution for a criminal offense in the United States?   ☐ Yes   ☒ No

If you answered "Yes" to any of the above questions, complete the following table. If you need more space, use a separate sheet of paper to give the same information.

Why were you arrested, cited, detained or charged?	Date of arrest, citation, detention, charge. *(mm/dd/yyyy)*	Where were you arrested, cited, detained or charged? *(City, State, Country)*	Outcome or disposition. *(e.g., no charges filed, charges dismissed, jail, probation, etc.)*

Sample Form I-918, Petition for U Nonimmigrant Status (page 4)

Part 3. Processing information. *(Continued.)*

2. Have you ever received public assistance in the United States from any source, including the U.S. government or any State, county, city or other municipality (other than emergency medical treatment), or are you likely to receive public assistance in the future? ☐ Yes ☒ No

3. Have you:

   a. Engaged in prostitution or procurement of prostitution or do you intend to engage in prostitution or procurement of prostitution? ☐ Yes ☒ No

   b. Ever engaged in any unlawful commercialized vice, including, but not limited to illegal gambling? ☐ Yes ☒ No

   c. Ever knowingly encouraged, induced, assisted, abetted or aided any alien to try to enter the United States illegally? ☐ Yes ☒ No

   d. Ever illicitly trafficked in any controlled substance, or knowingly assisted, abetted or colluded in the illicit trafficking of any controlled substance? ☐ Yes ☒ No

4. Have you ever committed, planned or prepared, participated in, threatened to, attempted to, or conspired to commit, gathered information for, solicited funds for any of the following:

   a. Highjacking or sabotage of any conveyance (including an aircraft, vessel, or vehicle? ☐ Yes ☒ No

   b. Seizing or detaining, and threatening to kill, injure, or continue to detain, another individual in order to compel a third person (including a governmental organization) to do or abstain from doing any act as an explicit or implicit condition for the release of the individual seized or detained? ☐ Yes ☒ No

   c. Assassination? ☐ Yes ☒ No

   d. The use of any firearm with intent to endanger, directly or indirectly, the safety of one or more individual or to cause substantial damage to property? ☐ Yes ☒ No

   e. The use of any biological agent, chemical agent, or nuclear weapon or device, or explosive, or other weapon or dangerous device, with intent to endanger, directly or indirectly, the safety of one or more individuals or to cause substantial damage to property? ☐ Yes ☒ No

5. Have you ever been a member of, solicited money or members for, provided support for, attended military training (as defined in section 2339D(c)(1) of title 18, United States Code) by or on behalf of, or been associated with an organization that is:

   a. Designated as a terrorist organization under section 219 of the Immigration and Nationality Act? ☐ Yes ☒ No

   b. Any other group of two or more individuals, whether organized or not, which has engaged in or has a subgroup which has engaged in: ☐ Yes ☒ No

   c. Highjacking or sabotage of any conveyance (including an aircraft, vessel, or vehicle? ☐ Yes ☒ No

   d. Seizing or detaining, and threatening to kill, injure, or continue to detain, another individual in order to compel a third person (including a governmental organization) to do or abstain from doing any act as an explicit or implicit condition for the release of the individual seized or detained? ☐ Yes ☒ No

   e. Assassination? ☐ Yes ☒ No

   f. The use of any firearm with intent to endanger, directly or indirectly, the safety of one or more individual or to cause substantial damage to property? ☐ Yes ☒ No

Sample Form I-918, Petition for U Nonimmigrant Status (page 5)

Part 3. Processing information. *(Continued.)*

g. The use of any biological agent, chemical agent, or nuclear weapon or device, or explosive, or other weapon or dangerous device, with intent to endanger, directly or indirectly, the safety of one or more individuals or to cause substantial damage to property? ☐ Yes ☒ No

h. Soliciting money or members or otherwise providing material support to a terrorist organization? ☐ Yes ☒ No

6. Do you intend to engage in the United States in:

   a. Espionage? ☐ Yes ☒ No

   b. Any unlawful activity, or any activity the purpose of which is in opposition to, or the control or overthrow of the government of the United States? ☐ Yes ☒ No

   c. Solely, principally, or incidentally in any activity related to espionage or sabotage or to violate any law involving the export of goods, technology, or sensitive information? ☐ Yes ☒ No

7. Have you ever been or do you continue to be a member of the Communist or other totalitarian party, except when membership was involuntary? ☐ Yes ☒ No

8. Have you, during the period of March 23, 1933 to May 8, 1945, in association with either the Nazi Government of Germany or any organization or government associated or allied with the Nazi Government of Germany, ever ordered, incited, assisted or otherwise participated in the persecution of any person because of race, religion, nationality, membership in a particular social group or political opinion? ☐ Yes ☒ No

9. Have you EVER ordered, committed, assisted, helped with, or otherwise participated in any act that involved:

   a. Torture or genocide? ☐ Yes ☒ No

   b. Killing, beating, or injuring any person? ☐ Yes ☒ No

   c. Displacing or moving any persons from their residence by force, threat of force, compulsion, or duress? ☐ Yes ☒ No

   d. Engaging in any kind of sexual contact or relations with any person who was being subjected to force, threat of force, compulsion, or duress? ☐ Yes ☒ No

   e. Limiting or denying any person's ability to exercise religious beliefs? ☐ Yes ☒ No

   f. The persecution of any person because of race, religion, national origin, membership in a particular social group, or political opinion? ☐ Yes ☒ No

   If you answer "Yes," please describe the circumstances on a separate sheet(s) of paper.

10. Have you EVER advocated that another person commit any of the acts described in the preceding question, urged, or encouraged another person, to commit such acts? (If you answer "Yes," describe the circumstances on a separate sheet(s) of paper.) ☐ Yes ☒ No

Sample Form I-918, Petition for U Nonimmigrant Status (page 6)

Part 3. Processing information.	*(Continued.)*

11. Have you EVER been present or nearby when any person was:

    a. Intentionally killed, tortured, beaten, or injured?   ☐ Yes   ☒ No

    b. Displaced or moved from his or her residence by force, compulsion or duress?   ☐ Yes   ☒ No

    c. In any way compelled or forced to engage in any kind of sexual contact or relations?   ☐ Yes   ☒ No

    If you answer "Yes," please describe the circumstances on a separate sheet(s) of paper.

---

12. Have you (or has any member of your family) EVER served in, been a member of, or been involved in any way with:

    a. Any military unit, paramilitary unit, police unit, self-defense unit, vigilante unit, rebel group, guerrilla group, or insurgent organization?   ☐ Yes   ☒ No

    b. Any prison, jail, prison camp, detention camp, labor camp, or any other situation that involved guarding prisoners?   ☐ Yes   ☒ No

    c. Any group, unit, or organization of any kind in which you or other persons possessed, transported, or used any type of weapon?   ☐ Yes   ☒ No

    If you answer "Yes," please describe the circumstances on a separate sheet(s) of paper.

---

13. Have your EVER received any type of military, paramilitary or weapons training? (If you answer "Yes," please describe the circumstances on a separate sheet(s) of paper.)   ☐ Yes   ☒ No

---

14. **a.** Are removal, exclusion, rescission or deportation proceedings pending against you?   ☐ Yes   ☒ No

    b. Have removal, exclusion, rescission or deportation proceedings EVER been initiated against you?   ☐ Yes   ☒ No

    c. Have you EVER been removed, excluded or deported from the United States?   ☐ Yes   ☒ No

    d. Have you EVER been ordered to be removed, excluded or deported from the United States?   ☐ Yes   ☒ No

    e. Have you EVER been denied a visa or denied admission to the United States? *(If a visa was denied, explain why on a separate sheet of paper.)*   ☐ Yes   ☒ No

    f. Have you EVER been granted voluntary departure by an immigration officer or an immigration judge and failed to depart within the allotted time?   ☐ Yes   ☒ No

---

15. Are you under a final order or civil penalty for violating section 274C (producing and/or using false documentation to unlawfully satisfy a requirement of the Immigration and Nationality Act)?   ☐ Yes   ☒ No

---

16. Have you ever, by fraud or willful misrepresentation of a material fact, sought to procure, or procured, a visa or other documentation, for entry into the United States or any immigration benefit?   ☐ Yes   ☒ No

---

17. Have you ever left the United States to avoid being drafted into the U.S. Armed Forces?   ☐ Yes   ☒ No

---

Sample Form I-918, Petition for U Nonimmigrant Status (page 7)

Part 3. Processing information. *(Continued.)*		

18. Have you ever been a J nonimmigrant exchange visitor who was subject to the two-year foreign residence requirement and not yet complied with that requirement or obtained a waiver of such? ☐ Yes ☒ No

19. Have you ever detained, retained, or withheld the custody of a child, having a lawful claim to United States citizenship, outside the United States from a United States citizen granted custody? ☐ Yes ☒ No

20. Do you plan to practice polygamy in the United States? ☐ Yes ☒ No

21. Have you entered the United States as a stowaway? ☐ Yes ☒ No

22. a. Do you have a communicable disease of public health significance? ☐ Yes ☒ No

b. Do you have or have you had a physical or mental disorder and behavior (or a history of behavior that is likely to recur) associated with the disorder which has posed or may pose a threat to the property, safety, or welfare of yourself or others? ☐ Yes ☒ No

c. Are you now or have you been a drug abuser or drug addict? ☐ Yes ☒ No

Part 4. Information about spouse and/or children.		

1. ☐ Spouse

Family Name	Given Name	Middle Name

Date of Birth *(mm/dd/yyyy)*	Country of Birth	Relationship	Current Location

2. ☒ Children

Family Name	Given Name	Middle Name
Chen	Anna	Lee

Date of Birth *(mm/dd/yyyy)*	Country of Birth	Relationship	Current Location
9/12/2013	U.S.A.	Daughter	With me

Family Name	Given Name	Middle Name

Date of Birth *(mm/dd/yyyy)*	Country of Birth	Relationship	Current Location

(If more space is needed, attach additional sheet(s) of paper.)

Sample Form I-918, Petition for U Nonimmigrant Status (page 8)

Part 5.	Filing on behalf of family members.

I am now petitioning for one or more qualifying family member(s). *(If "Yes," complete and include Form I-918, Supplement A and Supplement B, for each family member for whom you are petitioning.)*   ☐ Yes   ☒ No

Part 6. Attestation, release and signature.	*(Read information on penalties in the instructions before completing this part.)*

I certify, under penalty of perjury under the laws of the United States of America, that the information provided with this petition is all true and correct. I certify also that I have not withheld any information that would affect the outcome of this petition.

Signature

Xing Mei Chen

Date *(mm/dd/yyyy)*

05/22/2014

NOTE: *If you do not completely fill out this form or fail to submit required documents listed in the instructions, you may not be found eligible for the benefit sought and this petition will be denied.*

Part 7. Signature of person preparing form, if other than above.	*(Sign below.)*

I declare that I prepared this petition at the request of the above person, and it is based on all information of which I have knowledge. I have not knowingly withheld any material information that would affect the outcome of this petition.

Attorney or Representative: In the event of a Request for Evidence, may USCIS contact you by Fax or E-Mail?   ☐ Yes   ☐ No

Preparer's Signature

Date *(mm/dd/yyyy)*

Preparer's Printed Name

Preparer's Firm Name *(if applicable)*

Preparer's Address

Daytime Phone Number *(with area code)*	Fax Number *(if any)*	E-Mail Address *(if any)*
( )	( )	

Acquiring Citizenship Through U.S. Citizen Parents

Okay, we know it's unlikely, but every so often someone struggling to qualify for a U.S. green card discovers that he or she was a U.S. citizen all along. How? Because the person's parents or even grandparents held U.S. citizenship at the time of the person's birth in another country. This is called "acquisition" of citizenship. This chapter will describe who qualifies for acquisition of citizenship, how to prove you're a U.S. citizen, and how to figure out whether you qualify for dual citizenship (simultaneous citizenship in the United States and your home country).

RESOURCE

This book does not describe how people who have already gotten their green card can apply to become naturalized citizens. For complete information on your eligibility and the application process, see *Becoming a U.S. Citizen: A Guide to the Law, Exam & Interview*, by Ilona Bray (Nolo).

What If You Were Born "Out of Wedlock" to a U.S. Citizen Father?

In many cases, your right to U.S. citizenship may depend on your relationship to a U.S. citizen father. However, if your parents weren't married at the time you were born, the laws of the time may refer to you as "illegitimate," meaning in legal terms that you have no recognized father. As you'll see in the sections below, your right to claim citizenship may depend on you providing evidence that your father took the actions necessary to satisfy the legitimation law of your birth country. Legitimation laws require fathers to legally acknowledge their children.

A. Who Qualifies for Acquisition of Citizenship

In many circumstances, even though a child is born outside the U.S., if at least one parent was a U.S. citizen at the time of the child's birth, the child automatically "acquires" U.S. citizenship. When this child marries and has children, those children may also acquire U.S. citizenship at birth.

The laws governing whether or not a child born outside U.S. boundaries acquires U.S. citizenship from his or her parents have changed several times. The law that was in effect on the date of the child's birth determines whether the child acquired U.S. citizenship from a parent or grandparent. If there is anyone in your direct line of ancestry whom you believe may be a U.S. citizen, it is worth your time to read what the U.S. laws were on the date of your birth and that of your ancestor.

Most laws controlling the passing of U.S. citizenship from parent to child require that the parent, the child, or both have had a period of living in the United States ("residence"). Sometimes the residence is required to be for a specified length of time (for example, five years) and sometimes it is not. When the law doesn't say exactly how long the residence period must be, you can assume that even a brief time, such as a month, might be enough. The key element is often not the amount of time but whether or not USCIS or the State Department believes it was a residence and not a visit. If the period of stay has the character of a residence, the length of time doesn't matter.

1. Birth Prior to May 24, 1934

If you were born before May 24, 1934, the law originally provided that only your U.S. citizen father (not mother) could pass citizenship on to you. The rules were very simple. In order to pass on U.S. citizenship, the father must have resided in the U.S. at some time before the child's birth. The law didn't require any particular length of time or dates when the residence took place. Technically, a day or a week would be enough if it could be regarded as a residence and not just a visit. Once a child obtained U.S. citizenship at birth through a U.S. citizen father, there were no conditions to retaining it. These rules also applied to so-called illegitimate children (children born to unmarried parents), provided the U.S. citizen father had at some time legally legitimated the child (acknowledged his paternal responsibility). U.S. citizenship was then acquired at the time of legitimation, without regard to the child's age.

This law has been challenged several times as discriminatory, with some courts holding that citizenship could also be passed by the mother to the children. Congress finally addressed this issue in 1994 and amended the law, retroactively, to provide that either parent could pass his or her U.S. citizenship to children.

Consider that if you were born before May 24, 1934, and either of your parents was a U.S. citizen, that citizenship might have been passed on to you. Consider also that if either of your parents was born before May 24, 1934, they may have acquired U.S. citizenship from either of their parents, which they then passed on to you under laws in existence at a later date. A check of the family tree may well be worth your while.

2. Birth Between May 25, 1934, and January 12, 1941

If you were born between May 25, 1934, and January 12, 1941, you acquired U.S. citizenship at birth on the conditions that both your parents were U.S. citizens and at least one had resided in the U.S. prior to your birth. The law at this time placed no additional conditions on retaining U.S. citizenship acquired in this way.

You could also get U.S. citizenship if only one of your parents was a U.S. citizen, as long as that parent had a prior U.S. residence. If your U.S. citizenship came from only one parent, you too would have been required to reside in the U.S. for at least two years between the ages of 14 and 28 in order to retain the citizenship you got at birth. Alternately,

you could retain citizenship if your noncitizen parent naturalized before you turned 18 and you began living in the U.S. permanently before age 18. Otherwise, your citizenship would be lost. If the one U.S. citizen parent was your father and your birth was illegitimate (took place while your parents weren't married), the same rules applied provided your father legally legitimated you (acknowledged paternal responsibility). Citizenship was passed at the time of legitimation without regard to your age, as long as you had met the retention requirements.

3. Birth Between January 13, 1941, and December 23, 1952

If you were born between January 13, 1941, and December 23, 1952, both your parents were U.S. citizens, and at least one had a prior residence in the U.S., you automatically acquired U.S. citizenship at birth, with no conditions to retaining it.

If only one parent was a U.S. citizen, that parent must have resided in the U.S. for at least ten years prior to your birth, and at least five of those years must have been after your parent reached the age of 16. With a parent thus qualified, you then acquired U.S. citizenship at birth, but with conditions for retaining it. To keep your citizenship, you must have resided in the U.S. for at least two years between the ages of 14 and 28. Alternately, you could retain citizenship if your noncitizen parent naturalized before you turned 18 and you began living in the U.S. permanently before age 18. As a result of a U.S. Supreme Court decision, if you were born after October 9, 1952, your parent still had to fulfill the residence requirement in order to confer citizenship on you, but your own residence requirements for retaining U.S. citizenship were abolished—you need not have lived in the U.S. at all.

If your one U.S. citizen parent was your father and your birth was illegitimate (took place while your parents weren't married), the same rules apply provided you were legally legitimated (your father acknowledged paternal responsibility) prior to your 21st birthday and you were unmarried at the time of legitimation.

4. Birth Between December 24, 1952, and November 13, 1986

If at the time of your birth both your parents were U.S. citizens and at least one had a prior residence in the U.S., you automatically acquired U.S. citizenship, with no other conditions for retaining it.

If only one parent was a U.S. citizen at the time of your birth, that parent must have resided in the U.S. for at least ten years, and at least five of those years must have been after your parent reached the age of 14. If your one U.S. citizen parent is your father and your birth was illegitimate (took place while your parents weren't married), the same rules apply provided you were legally legitimated (your father acknowledged paternal responsibility) prior to your 21st birthday and you were unmarried at the time of legitimation.

5. Birth Between November 14, 1986, and the Present

If at the time of your birth both your parents were U.S. citizens and at least one had a prior residence in the U.S., you automatically acquired U.S. citizenship, with no conditions for retaining it.

If only one parent was a U.S. citizen at the time of your birth, that parent must have resided in the U.S. for at least five years and at least two of those years must have been after your parent reached the age of 14. Even with only one U.S. citizen parent, there are still no conditions to retaining your citizenship. If your one U.S. citizen parent is your father and your birth was illegitimate (took place while your parents weren't married), the same rules apply provided you were legally legitimated (your father acknowledged paternal responsibility) prior to your 18th birthday. Additionally, your father must have established paternity prior to your 18th birthday either by acknowledgment or by court order, and must have stated, in writing, that he would support you financially until your 18th birthday.

> **CAUTION**
>
> **The situation is more complicated for children born through in vitro fertilization.** Before such children can be recognized as U.S. citizens, the U.S. citizen parents must show a biological link with the child. In the past, this was held to mean solely a genetic link, thus excluding children whose U.S. mother carried the child after donation of both sperm and egg. In 2014, however, the U.S. State Department changed its policy so as to acknowledge a biological connection based on gestation as well.

6. Exception to Requirements for Retaining Citizenship

It is not unusual for a child born and raised outside the U.S. to have acquired U.S. citizenship at birth from parents or grandparents without knowing it. The child, ignorant of the laws and circumstances affecting his or her birthright, then proceeds to lose U.S. citizenship by failing to fulfill U.S. residency requirements.

Congress sought to address this by adding a law for people who once held U.S. citizenship but lost it by failing to fulfill the residency requirements that were in effect before 1978. Such persons can regain their citizenship by simply taking the oath of allegiance to the United States. It is not necessary that the person apply for naturalization. Contact a U.S. consulate or USCIS office for more information. The relevant statute is 8 U.S.C. § 1435(d)(1), I.N.A. § 324(d)(1).

B. Obtaining Proof of U.S. Citizenship

If you have a legitimate claim to U.S. citizenship, in order to establish that claim you must apply for some kind of citizenship document; either a:

- U.S. passport
- certificate of citizenship, or
- certificate of consular registration of birth.

1. U.S. Passport

If you were born abroad to U.S. citizen parents, you can apply for a U.S. passport in the same way as someone born in the United States. However, you will have the added requirement of establishing your citizenship claim. Passports are available from passport offices in the U.S. (run by the U.S. Department of State) and at U.S. consulates outside the U.S., but experience shows that you have a better chance at a U.S. consulate. Wherever you apply, you will be required to present proof of your parents' U.S. citizenship and evidence that they—and you—complied with any applicable U.S. residency requirements. Review the sections on birth to a U.S. citizen for what you must prove under these circumstances. You will need to present documents such as birth or citizenship records of your parent or grandparent and work or tax records establishing U.S. residency for your parent or grandparent.

2. Certificate of Citizenship

Certificates of citizenship are issued only inside the U.S. by USCIS offices. Anyone with a claim to U.S. citizenship can apply for a certificate of citizenship. In most cases it is more difficult and takes much longer to get a certificate of citizenship than a U.S. passport.

Certificates of citizenship must be applied for on Form N-600. The current fee is $600. Copies of the form and detailed instructions are available on the USCIS website, www.uscis.gov.

We recommend that you also prepare a cover letter explaining the basis of your claim to U.S. citizenship and describing the documents you are offering as proof. These should include your parents' birth certificates, marriage certificate, and citizenship or naturalization certificates.

You should also present your own birth certificate, as well as marriage certificates and any divorce decrees to show legal changes in your name since birth. Your letter should also list whatever evidence you will be presenting to show that you have met any residency requirements as described in this chapter.

Form N-600, the documents, and the cover letter should be submitted to the USCIS local office having jurisdiction over your place of residence. You will most likely be called in for an interview on your application. In the busier USCIS offices, it can take up to a year to get a decision on an application for certificate of citizenship.

3. Certificate of Consular Report of Birth

Your parents may have registered your birth with a U.S. consulate to establish your right to U.S. citizenship and create an official birth record. If so, the consulate would have created a Consular Report of Birth, which would provide conclusive proof that you are a U.S. citizen. A Consular Report of Birth (FS-240) can be prepared only at a U.S. consular office overseas, and only while the child is under the age of 18. Replacement copies of it can be obtained at any time, either overseas or in the United States. If an application for a replacement is made in the U.S., a Certification of Report of Birth (DS-1350) is issued, rather than a replacement Consular Report of Birth.

C. Dual Citizenship

Whenever a child is born to U.S. citizen parents but the birth takes place outside U.S. territory, the child may acquire dual citizenship. In this situation, the child will, depending on the laws of the country where the birth took place, usually have the nationality of the country in which he or she was actually born, in addition to U.S. citizenship through the nationality of the parents. U.S. law recognizes dual citizenship under these circumstances, and if you have acquired dual citizenship in this manner, under U.S. law you will be entitled to maintain dual status for your lifetime.

Filling Out and Submitting Immigration Applications

The most important part of obtaining a green card is the paperwork. The key to getting one is to pay very close attention to the immigration forms and other documents you submit as evidence to the U.S. government.

A. Don't Give False Answers

There is one primary rule to keep in mind while answering the questions on the immigration forms: Honesty Is the Best Policy.

For example, if you have been previously married, admit this and provide the documents to prove that your previous marriage ended by divorce, annulment, or the death of your spouse.

If you have children by a previous marriage, or you have had any children while you were unmarried, list all of them on the immigration form, together with their correct names and dates of birth as shown on their birth certificates.

If the immigration form requests such information, be sure to list all your brothers and sisters, whether they are full-blood siblings, half-siblings, or stepbrothers or stepsisters.

Once you submit the immigration forms, it is very difficult to change your answers. If you attempt later changes, you run the risk of having your petition denied.

> **EXAMPLE:** Suppose you never told your American husband that you had an illegitimate child. For this reason, you do not mention this child in your immigration papers. Later on, you decide to reveal the truth to your husband. If you want to petition for an immigrant visa for the child you left behind in your country, you will have a hard time convincing USCIS that you had a child prior to your marriage.

1. Criminal Penalties

Lying or failing to mention things on your immigration paperwork can have consequences beyond your immigration case. You also run the risk of being prosecuted criminally for obtaining entry by a "willfully false or misleading representation or willful concealment of a material fact." This can also affect U.S. citizens or permanent residents who file petitions for an immigrant.

If you are found guilty of committing these offenses, you may be imprisoned for as long as five years or fined as much as $10,000, or receive both forms of punishment. If you received your green card by a fraudulent marriage, the punishment is more severe.

2. Civil Penalties

There are also civil (noncriminal) penalties for those who "forge, counterfeit, alter, or falsely make any document" to satisfy a requirement of immigration law.

If you are found guilty, you can be fined $250 to $5,000 for each fraudulent document that you have in your possession or have already submitted to USCIS. In addition, if you are an alien, you may be excluded from entering the United States or, if you are already there, you may be removed or deported.

B. Get the Latest Forms and Fee Amounts

The law and the rules on immigration procedures change frequently. Using old, outdated forms may cause your immigration petition to be delayed or, worse, denied. And if your immigration papers are filed with the wrong fee, they will be returned; this will further delay your legal entry as an immigrant.

Therefore, before mailing any immigration applications, take the time to request the most recent forms and to double check the filing fees with the local USCIS office, at www.uscis.gov/forms, or on the State Department website at www.travel.state.gov, or with an American consulate in your country of residence, whichever is most convenient.

You must pay the fees by personal check or money order, made out to the Department of Homeland Security. Don't send cash!

C. Tips for Filling Out Forms

A number of immigration forms ask for the same kinds of identifying information—your name, address, identification numbers. While the answers may often seem obvious, USCIS requires that they be phrased in specific ways.

Try to Answer Every Question

Answer all questions and do not leave a line on the form blank unless clearly directed to do otherwise. If the question being posed does not apply to you, it is best to write "not applicable" ("N/A") or, if you do not have a number or document, write "none." If you do not know the answer, write "not known."

What's the difference between "not applicable" and "none"? There is one, and it's important that you get it right. If, for example, a form asks for "other names used," and you've never used another name, you'd write "none." That's because the question applies to you, just like it does to everyone. Entering "not applicable" or "N/A" is appropriate only if there's a question like "Have you ever been married?" and you answer "no," followed by another question asking the "date of marriage." You can answer "N/A" to "date of marriage" because that question is truly irrelevant and doesn't apply to your situation.

If you fail to answer all questions, processing of your forms may be delayed while USCIS sends them back and asks for more complete information. There's one important exception to the advice above, however. Some newer USCIS forms, particularly the online forms, will not permit you to write "none" in fields where numbers are usually input, such as for a Social Security number or an alien registration number. If that's the case, skip that field.

1. Your Family Name

When an immigration form asks you to fill in your name, write the complete name that you were given on your birth certificate or the name written in your passport, to match whichever document is required. Add your full middle name (if you have one), even if the form asks only for your middle initial. USCIS asks all applicants to add this for security check purposes, and it may delay your application if you don't.

If the name on your birth certificate is not your name at present, explain the difference in a letter and submit the corresponding court papers or other documents that show the change.

> **EXAMPLE:** If you are a woman named Jane and you're using the surname of your husband, John Smith, as your family name, write your husband's surname—that is, Jane Smith.
>
> On the space that says "other names used," write your maiden name and any other names you have used—that is, Jane Doe.
>
> If you were married previously, write your previous married name on that space. Attach your marriage certificate or divorce decree.

2. Your Address

Your address, as far as USCIS is concerned, is the place where you receive mail. The post office is very important in your immigration relationship because everything from USCIS will come by mail—notice of approval of petition, notice of incomplete submission, notice of interview, notice of proceedings, and your green card.

If the mail carrier does not deliver mail in your locality, rent a post office box. However, some USCIS forms ask not only for your mailing address but also for your actual address. In that case, write the exact address or location of your home or indicate c/o—meaning "in care of"—if another person at that address wil be receiving your mail.

3. Your Social Security and Alien Registration Numbers

The Social Security number requested on immigration forms is issued by the U.S. government, not by your country's own Social Security administration. You should have one only if you've lived in the U.S. and had a legal right to work there.

An alien registration number, also called your "A#," is issued by USCIS (or, formerly, the INS). If you have not been assigned one or both of these numbers, write "none" in the space provided on the immigration forms—unless you can't, because the e-form does not allow you to use letters instead of numbers.

4. Technical Difficulties Filling Out USCIS Forms Online

The latest version of many USCIS forms allows you to save them as a PDF document and fill them out on your computer before printing and mailing them. However, a lot of kinks have yet to be worked out. In fact, you may find that some of your answers will be changed or erased after you save and print the form.

Ironically, this was all part of a USCIS effort to ensure the accurate transfer of information into its databases, by creating new versions of certain forms with a bar code at the bottom that can be scanned. Unfortunately, USCIS released many of these forms without working out all the technical glitches first.

You may find that some answer boxes are impossible to place a check mark in, or that checking one box will erase the answer in another. What's more, some of the blanks are too short to include accurate information in (such as long names and foreign addresses). And because the forms cannot tell the difference between numbers and letters, writing "N/A" or "none" in the blanks for things like Social Security number (which was once the best practice) is often not allowed.

Our advice? Do your best until the kinks are eventually worked out, but double (and triple) check everything before you send it to USCIS, to make sure it is accurate and unchanged from what you entered.

You may, for example, need to manually write an "X" in your boxes using black ink, after printing the form. Although it may be USCIS's fault that your answer was changed or deleted, that excuse won't do you much good if USCIS rejects or delays your application as a result.

D. When Additional Proof Is Required

USCIS requires specific proof to be submitted along with the answers on many of its forms. This is because you are entitled to a green card only when you can prove by convincing documentation that you meet specific qualifications. You can go a long way toward eliminating delays and confusion if you take the time to make sure your additional proof is accurate and complete.

1. Proving a Family Relationship

As requested on the immigration forms, you must provide copies of documents to prove that a relationship permits you to apply as a family-based immigrant. If you do not submit the right documents, your materials will be returned and the whole process will be delayed.

You must have the official documents. To prove a family relationship, you must have the original birth certificate, marriage certificate, or death certificate issued by the civil registry of your country with the official government seal, stamp, or ribbon attached, depending on how official documents are marked in your country. Nongovernmental documents, such as church or hospital certificates, are usually not sufficient. Although you won't mail the originals in—unless you are processing through the National Visa Center and are instructed to send the NVC the originals—you'll probably be asked to show them to USCIS at your interview.

Use your fingers to verify the indentation of the government seal that is embossed or pressed into the paper. USCIS will often assume that a document without such a seal is fraudulent.

If you have lost the documents, you can request certified copies from your government for an additional charge. Be sure these copies also have the official government seal. Because some unscrupulous people create counterfeit documents, USCIS has to carefully examine the documents presented.

You should write or type the following statement on the back of each photocopy:

> Copies of documents submitted are exact photocopies of unaltered original documents, and I understand that I may be required to submit original documents to an immigration or consular official at a later date.

Include your signature and the date. There is no need to have your signature verified by a notary public.

Do Not Send Your Originals to USCIS

Whenever possible, make a copy of your original document—and send the copy to USCIS. Things often get lost in the mail. And added to that, the USCIS offices are busy places crowded with many people and even more documents, so things can get lost there, too. USCIS often makes no effort to return originals to you, and takes no responsibility if they are lost. Keep the originals of your documents in a safe place—one that's fireproof if possible. Then show them to the USCIS officer at your interview.

If you are consular processing, however, you may be required to send your original documents to the National Visa Center. Whenever you send original documents, use a form of delivery that comes with a receipt, so you can track your documents through the system and have proof of delivery.

Using the Department of State Documents Finder

Ever wonder how to get a birth certificate in Belarus or a divorce certificate in Djibouti? Go to http://travel.state.gov to find out. (Click "Immigrate" then "A-Z Index" then go to the "R" section and click "Reciprocity.")

This tremendously helpful Web page tells you how to get documents you need for immigration cases (like proof of military service or lack of a police record) or replace documents you thought you had but can't lay your hands on. If you really can't get a certain document (such as a birth certificate), the website will give you suggestions on alternatives.

If you don't have the official document. Sometimes, you cannot get your original documents because of war, destruction of the civil registry, your government's prohibition on emigration, or simple oversight or ignorance.

In such cases, family relationships such as parent-child, brother-sister, or husband-wife can be proved by what is called secondary evidence—a combination of documents that may not come from the civil registry, but which nevertheless prove a relationship.

- Church records, for example, can sometimes be submitted. A baptismal certificate will show the parents' names and the date and place of birth of the child.
- Annotations in a family Bible, old letters, school records, or data from a relevant government census are other types of secondary evidence.
- USCIS may also accept the sworn statements, or affidavits, of two people who have witnessed your birth, your marriage, the death of a spouse, or whatever event you need to prove. The statement should include the witnesses' names and addresses, their relationship to you or your family, and why and how they know about the alleged event. The strongest evidence is from witnesses who were present at the event you need to prove.

For example, if you've never had a birth certificate or you could not obtain a copy, a sworn statement written by your sister could read as the sample below.

Sample Sworn Statement

My name is Jane Doe, and I am the older sister of John Doe.

I live at 123 Middle Abbey Street, Dublin, Ireland.

I was seven years old when my brother, John Doe, was born to our mother, Carolyn Doe, on July 4, 1952, at our home in Cork, Ireland. I remember the midwife coming to our house and I was sent outside to play. After it got dark, my brother was born and they called me inside to see him.

This affidavit is submitted because the civil registry in Cork was burned in 1954 and my brother's birth certificate was lost when the family moved to Dublin in the same year.

Signature: _____

Signed and sworn to before me on March 1, 20xx

[Notary Stamp]

The witnesses have to swear to the truth of their statements before a notary public—a person who is authorized by the state to verify signatures. You can find a notary by looking in the telephone book, although most banks have one on staff. Most notaries will charge for their services, so it may be worthwhile to shop around for the one with the most reasonable fee. If required by the U.S. embassy in your country, the affidavits may have to be sworn to before the U.S. consular official, who will also charge a fee for the service.

You may need to submit your own affidavit stating why you cannot obtain the original documents and what efforts you have made to try to do so.

USCIS may further investigate your family relationship, or request that you and your relative undergo blood tests or give additional testimony. An investigation may even be conducted in the neighborhood in which you lived in your native country.

Before it confers an immigration benefit, the U.S. government must be certain that the person immigrating is truly the child, brother, sister, husband, or wife—and not the niece, nephew, aunt, uncle, cousin, or friend—of the U.S. citizen or permanent resident petitioner.

Documents in Languages Other Than English

If the documents you are submitting are not in English, have them translated accurately. The only exception to this is if you are consular processing, and the document is in the language of the country where the consulate is located. In that situation the document does not need to be translated. Any translations should be word for word. An English summary of the main points in the document is usually not enough. However, you do not have to hire a professional translator to do the job. Somebody who has competent knowledge of both English and the language in which the documents are written should be able to do the translation.

The translator must attach the following statement to the translated document and sign and date it:

I hereby certify that I am competent to translate this document from [the foreign language] to English and that this translation is accurate and complete to the best of my knowledge and ability.

2. Proving an INS or USCIS Approval

In some situations, you may have an application or petition that has been approved by the USCIS (or the formerly named INS) but need further action because:

- you lost the approval notice or you need a duplicate

- the U.S. embassy or consulate that originally received the approval notice closed down or you simply could not go to your home country, and another U.S. consulate is willing to process your immigration visa and needs to be officially notified, or
- you need USCIS to notify the U.S. consulate in your country that you became a green card holder in the United States so that your spouse and children can receive visas to join you.

In any of these circumstances, you must file Form I-824, Application for Action on an Approved Application or Petition, with the USCIS office that approved the original application or petition. The filing fee was $405 at the time this book went to print.

If you have a copy of the approval, make a copy of that and attach it to your Form I-824.

3. Proving U.S. Citizenship

A U.S. citizen has the right to petition for their spouse, parent, child, brother, sister, fiancée or fiancé, so that their relative can apply for permanent resident status. The widow or widower of a U.S. citizen can sometimes derive status from their deceased spouse. But in all of these situations, USCIS must first see documents proving the petitioning person's U.S. citizenship.

The following are accepted as proof:

- a birth certificate showing the place of birth to be any of the 50 U.S. states, Puerto Rico, the U.S. Virgin Islands, or Guam
- a valid U.S. passport
- if the birth certificate cannot be obtained, a baptismal certificate with the seal of the church showing the place of birth and date of baptism, which must have occurred within two months after birth
- affidavits of two U.S. citizens who have personal knowledge of the petitioner's birth in the United States, if neither the birth nor the baptismal certificate can be obtained
- a certificate of naturalization

- Department of State Form FS-240, Report of Birth Abroad of a Citizen of the United States, which proves U.S. citizenship for someone born abroad, and
- a certificate of citizenship issued by the INS or USCIS, which is also adequate proof that someone is a U.S. citizen born abroad.

U.S. Passport

4. Proving U.S. Lawful Permanent Residence

As a green card holder, you have the right to petition for your spouse and unmarried children, by submitting proof that you are a permanent resident. Although USCIS has your file and alien registration number in its records, you must still submit a copy of your green card.

The official name of your green card is Permanent Resident Card (also sometimes called Form I-551). The Form I-551 is the best form of proof of lawful permanent residence.

If your green card is lost or not available, your passport—bearing the USCIS rubber stamp showing lawful admission for permanent residence and your alien registration number—is acceptable proof of your permanent resident status.

E. Submitting Photographs for Identification

The immigration authorities are quite strict about photo requirements. The style and specifications for USCIS photos are the same ones used for U.S. passport photos.

While it is not essential to hire a professional photographer to take USCIS photos, it may be tough to comply with the picky requirements for size, lighting, clarity, and digital resolution. If you or a friend attempt to take the photos on your own, be sure to take many pictures and to read the requirements first. Vending machine photos won't be accepted, but many pharmacies offer passport-photo services for around $10.

If, as is normally the case, you're asked to submit more than one photo, the photos must be identical—you can't just take a few photos that look quite similar and submit them.

RESOURCE

Want more detail on the photo requirements? Visit the State Department website at www.travel.state.gov. Click "U.S. Passport," then on the top row, under "Your U.S. Passport," click "Passport Photo."

1. The Photographs

The overall size of the picture, including the background, must be at least 50 mm (2 inches) square.

The photographs must be in color—with no shadows, marks or discolorations on them. The background must be white or off-white; it is not acceptable to be photographed against a patterned or colored background. There must be good lighting; the photo must not appear too light or too dark. And the final image must be original, not retouched in any way.

2. Your Image Within the Photo

The image on the photo—total size of the head—must be 25 to 35 mm (1 inch to 1⅜ inches) from the top of the hair to the bottom of the chin.

Your eyes must be between 1⅛ inches to 1⅜ inches (28 mm and 35 mm) from the bottom of the photo.

Your face should be pictured from the front, with eyes open. Be sure not to wear jewelry or hats—unless the headwear is required by your religion. Your facial expression should be natural—smiling is not necessary. It's okay to wear glasses if you do so every day.

Photos must be taken within six months of submitting them.

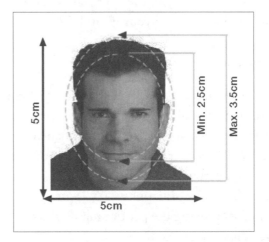

Before You Put Anything in the Mail

Most applications can be filed only by mail. Before mailing any immigration documents, make copies for your own records.

We recommend using U.S. Postal Service Priority Mail, which comes with tracking. This way, you will get confirmation that your papers were received.

F. Fingerprinting Requirements

USCIS requires fingerprinting (also called "biometrics") to accompany a variety of applications, including permanent residence, asylum, and naturalization, among others. Fingerprints are generally reviewed by the FBI and CIA to determine an applicant's actual identity and to determine whether the person has a criminal background that would make him or her inadmissible. USCIS will also check to see whether you've submitted previous applications under a different name.

If the application you are filing requires biometrics, you should include a fee (currently $85) as a check or money order made out to USCIS. This is in addition to any fees for the application itself.

USCIS will usually contact you within 45 days by letter, telling you when you should go to a USCIS-authorized site for fingerprinting. You will be given directions and a specific date and time at which you must appear.

If you cannot make it during your appointed time, you can ask to be rescheduled.

If you live abroad and are filing your application outside the United States, you may be fingerprinted at a U.S. consulate or military installation. The fee is $85. Whether or not you will be fingerprinted abroad depends on the type of application you submit and the particular U.S. consulate.

G. Keep Your Own File

For your own records, make copies of everything that you submit to the U.S. government, including the immigration forms and the supporting documents. Also make a copy of the receipt USCIS issues to you after you pay any filing fee.

Keep your own copies and original documents in a safe place. You will need them again when you are called to receive your immigrant visa at the U.S. embassy or when you attend your personal interview for your green card at USCIS.

Also, like any other bureaucracy, USCIS does sometimes misplace files. It will save you a lot of headache and heartache if you can show that you have already filed the application with USCIS by presenting a copy of the documents filed and the receipt from USCIS.

H. Tips for Filing Applications

USCIS loses a surprising number of applications, or the documents and checks that came with them. To protect yours, and to make sure they get through the system as smoothly as possible, follow the tips below.

1. Submitting Applications by Mail or Courier

After you've filled out your application forms, assembled the needed documents, and written the checks, you'll be eager to submit everything to USCIS. Most applications must be submitted by mail. But don't just pop yours in the nearest mailbox. Take all applications and other immigration papers to the post office, and send them by Priority Mail or certified mail with return receipt requested. Keep complete copies for your files—even copy the checks.

Although USCIS prefers delivery through the U.S. Postal Service, sending your application via couriers such as FedEx or DHL is also a good way to make sure you have proof of its arrival. However, make sure the USCIS office is equipped to accept this form of delivery. A few never do, because a live person has to be there to sign for the package. Most designate a special address for such deliveries, which you can find on the USCIS website (www.uscis.gov/forms).

When your application arrives at a USCIS office, the clerical staff will first examine your papers to see if everything is in order. Your papers will likely be returned to you if you:

- did not enter your full name, including middle name
- did not sign your application or other papers requiring a signature

Moving to a New Place? Take Precautions

When files must be transferred between USCIS field offices, they may get lost, at least for a time. No wonder some people postpone moving until after their cases have finished processing! If you don't want to go to such an extreme, at least keep in touch with the new people living at your place, to see whether anything from USCIS arrives.

Also, you must report any change of address to USCIS within ten days. Use Form AR-11, either the paper form or online; go to www.uscis.gov/ar-11. The online form is easiest for most people. If you have your receipt number, the online system will update your address in the main database as well as with the USCIS office currently processing your application. Select the form that you filed with USCIS and enter the zip code used when filed (if any). Then enter the applicant/petitioner information, citizenship information, old and new addresses, and location and date of your U.S. entry (if any). You can also elect to receive email confirmation of the address change. Keep this email handy in case you have trouble with your address change. You may also want to send a letter to the USCIS office processing your application—just in case. Include your receipt number on the letter.

Applicants in a limited number of visa categories (including self-petitioners under the Violence Against Women Act and serious crime and human trafficking victims) can't use the online address system. They will have to send a letter to the USCIS Vermont Service Center.

If you file a paper AR-11 and have no pending applications, you don't need to do anything else. Otherwise, you also need to call 1-800-375-5283 to update your address.

- signed a name different from that shown on your attached birth certificate
- did not enclose the correct filing fee
- left some questions unanswered, or
- forgot to include some documents.

When your papers are returned, there should be a letter included with them, telling you what information was incorrect or missing. You will usually have a chance to correct what was wrong and send back your documents and check or money order.

When your documents are in order, USCIS will accept your submission and will send you a receipt notice on Form I-797C.

2. Some Applications Can Be Filed Online ("e-Filing")

A handful of petitions and applications can be submitted to USCIS online—but only the form itself. And since every USCIS application requires supporting documents (such as photocopies of birth certificates and passports), it's usually easier to just mail everything together, as a paper application.

As of the date this book went to print, the following forms were available to e-file. Each comes with various restrictions as to who can actually use the form (depending on the reason for filing), so be sure to check the e-filing instructions first (at http://www.uscis.gov/e-filing):

- ☐ I-90—Application to Replace Permanent Residence Card
- ☐ I-131—Application for Travel Document
- ☐ I-140—Immigrant Petition for Alien Worker
- ☐ I-526—Immigrant Petition by Alien Entrepreneur *(via the USCIS Electronic Immigration System or ELIS)*
- ☐ I-539—Application To Extend/Change Nonimmigrant Status *(via USCIS ELIS)*
- ☐ I-765—Application for Employment Authorization
- ☐ I-821—Application for Temporary Protected Status (only if a TPS country is designated for reregistration purposes, not initial applications), and

☐ I-907—Request for Premium Processing Service

The main advantage to e-filing is that you can do so with a credit card or debit card (paper applications still require checks or money orders) and you will receive an instant confirmation.

> **TIP**
>
> **Will faster, "premium" processing become available?** With USCIS's Premium Processing Service, 15-calendar day processing is available to people filing certain applications who are willing to pay the premium processing fee (currently $1,225). Unfortunately, only a few kinds of cases are currently eligible for premium processing, and none of them are covered in this book. (It's mainly available for petitions by companies on behalf of important workers.) However, USCIS may someday make the service more widely available.

3. Always Use Your Alien Number

There are two kinds of numbers by which the Department of Homeland Security identifies every person who comes in contact with it. The first one, an A followed by nine numbers—for example: A093 465 345—is given to those who apply for or receive permanent residence (see Chapter 18) or who have a removal case. It's called an "Alien Registration Number" or "A Number."

Until recently, A numbers were issued with only eight numbers. That means that when USCIS needs to enter an "old" A number into its current system, it automatically adds a zero to the beginning. For example, "A93 465 345" becomes "A093 465 345."

Once you have an A number, it never changes. It is even recorded on your Naturalization Certificate if you become a U.S. citizen.

The second type of number USCIS assigns is the receipt number, which changes with each application you submit. It starts with the initials of your district or Regional Service Center followed by ten numbers— for example: WSC 1422334455 or EAC 9512345678. Such numbers are given to applications submitted to the various service centers, to track them through processing.

Once your immigration papers are accepted by USCIS, its computer system verifies whether you have ever been assigned an alien number or whether the alien number you wrote on your application is the right one for you.

The clerk then checks the computer files, looking for all the names you may have used, your date and place of birth, and your parents' names. The clerk will confirm the alien number you wrote on your application, or if you have other alien numbers previously assigned, will note them on your application so that all your files can be consolidated under one alien number. If you do not have a previous alien number, the clerk will give your file a new one.

Keep a record of your immigration case number, because any time you pose a question to USCIS, it will ask you first for your number. And if you send letters—for example, asking why your case is taking so long—you must include your A number or processing number.

4. Use One Check for Each Filing Fee

Occasionally, you may find yourself submitting more than one petition or application at the same time. For example, in a marriage case where your spouse is here in the U.S., you can file Form I-130 and Form I-485 simultaneously. Or, you may file applications for your spouse and your stepchild in the same envelope. In any of these situations, resist the temptation to combine all the filing fees into a single check.

If you submit separate, individual checks for each filing fee, then if you make a mistake on the check (for example, you forget to sign it, or you make it for the wrong amount), USCIS will reject only the filing that is affected by that check. But if you submit a single check covering all fees, and you've made a mistake, you will ruin all of the filings at once.

It's a pain to have to write more than one check for forms and applications being submitted in the same package, but most of the time it's worth it.

5. Looking at Your USCIS File

If you need to see your immigration records or to have a copy of a document you submitted, you can do so by filing Form G-639, Freedom of Information/Privacy Act Request, downloadable from the USCIS website (www.uscis.gov/g-639). To mail it, mark your envelope "Freedom of Information Request" and send it to the following address: National Records Center, FOIA/PA Office, P.O. Box 648010, Lee's Summit, MO 64064-8010.

Or, you can fax your request to 802-288-1793 or 816-350-5785, or email uscis.foia@dhs.gov.

You can submit this request without using Form G-639, but it will be harder to get right. First, you'll need to be sure to include the same information as requested on that form, such as your full name, mailing address, date of birth, and place of birth. Then, you'll need to have your signature notarized or executed under penalty of perjury (see the form for the appropriate language).

Although USCIS has promised that it will answer a Freedom of Information/Privacy Act Request within ten days, it has interpreted this promise to "answer" to mean that it will send you a letter within ten days, letting you know that it has received your request. USCIS does not post processing times for FOIA requests, and while response times can vary, current processing time is generally more than one year.

Tracking Your Application Through the System

When you submit an application to U.S. Citizenship and Immigration Services, you probably expect to receive an official reply within a week or two. But a month may pass, then two—and still no reply arrives. You would like to find out why your application is delayed, but each time you contact the USCIS office, you are simply told to be patient and wait—that your paperwork is "being processed," or "pending."

There are a number of things you can do to be sure that your dealings with USCIS move as smoothly and efficiently as possible. Those options are explained in this chapter.

A. Understanding the USCIS Culture

USCIS is just one branch of a huge agency, the Department of Homeland Security (DHS). The people working in USCIS reflect the workforce of any other government bureaucracy. These workers can generally be divided into two kinds: those who are earnest and conscientious in doing their jobs, and those who are at their posts in body but not in spirit. You take the luck of the draw as to which kind of bureaucrat will be handling your application or answering your questions.

Although USCIS is governed by law (the Immigration and Nationality Act, Code of Federal Regulations, and Operational Instructions), how these controlling rules and laws are applied depends upon USCIS office workers, who have their own cultural and social biases.

For example, you may be confronted with an immigration officer who is anti-immigrant, and who detests dealing on a daily basis with people who do not speak English, who speak with an accent, or who look, dress, or even smell differently from what he or she thinks of as "ordinary" Americans. This bias may make the worker grumpy, officious, intimidating, unhelpful, unreasonable, discourteous, or downright infuriating.

Furthermore, USCIS is not very phone-accessible, and the people at its national information line aren't well-informed about local office procedures. Some of them may give you wrong information.

Visiting USCIS Offices in Person

The only USCIS offices that you can visit in person are the district or field offices. Each U.S. state usually has one or two such offices (though in a few cases, you'll have to travel to another state). To find the office that serves you, go to www.uscis.gov and click "Find a USCIS Office." Click "Field Offices," and at the bottom of that page, click on your state on the U.S. map.

It used to be a major headache to visit a USCIS field office in person. To ask even a simple question about a form or a pending case, you often had to line up very early in the morning and wait half a day just to be seen by an officer. Nowadays, however, the USCIS InfoPass system allows you to go to http://infopass.uscis.gov and make an appointment. The appointment system is very slick—it can communicate in 12 different languages—and appointments are usually scheduled within a few days or weeks of the request. Best of all, you don't have to show up at USCIS until a few minutes before your appointment, and USCIS says that most visits last less than an hour! But be sure to use a computer with a printer when making the appointment—you'll need a printout of your appointment notice when you go.

B. Where to Go

If you're actually at a USCIS office and you feel an immigration officer is being unreasonable, go up the chain of command and appeal to the worker's supervisor. Insist on speaking with the supervisor personally. You can even do this in the middle of an appointment or interview. If that's not possible, try to obtain the supervisor's telephone number and call and explain what happened—or write a detailed letter. Be clear on what action was taken by the worker and what you want the supervising officer to do.

Because the DHS is a bureaucracy with many departments and branches, it is easy to get mixed up in a game of finger-pointing in which each person with whom you speak claims that the problem is not his or her fault.

The most important bit of knowledge you can learn is the exact section where your application is pending and where you need to be directing your inquiry.

- The USCIS District or Field Office is open to the public for forms and information and also handles green card interviews. Most states have at least one. It is rarely possible for a member of the public to talk to someone at the District or Field Office by telephone, but you can speak to someone face to face by making an InfoPass appointment.

- The USCIS Regional Service Center is a processing facility that you cannot normally visit, but to which you may be required to send certain applications. There are four service centers nationwide. You can check on the status of applications that you've filed with the service centers by telephone (see the phone number on your receipt notice) or online at the USCIS website (www.uscis.gov), where you'll click "Check Your Case Status" and enter your receipt number.

- The National Benefits Center (NBC) was recently created to handle administrative case processing burdens formerly borne by local USCIS district or field offices. Many kinds of petitions and applications that used to be filed directly with local offices are now filed with a lockbox facility located either in Chicago, Illinois or Phoenix, Arizona. The lockbox performs fee deposits, issues receipts, and handles initial data entry. After receiving cases from the lockbox, the NBC completes all necessary pre-interview processing of Form I-485 applications (including conducting background security checks, performing initial evidence review, and other tasks). Then NBC forwards the case files to local field offices for a final interview (if applicable) and a decision.

- The National Visa Center (NVC) is not actually part of USCIS or the Department of Homeland Security. It is an arm of the Department of State, and is an intermediary that steps in after your initial visa petition has been approved. It collects your visa fees and gets your case ready for transfer to a U.S. consulate in your home country. If you will be processing your case in the U.S. rather than abroad, the NVC will transfer your file to a USCIS office upon your request. As NVC is not part of DHS/USCIS, however, it will not accept the adjustment of status fees, and if you send it money for consular processing, those fees will not be transferred to your adjustment case or refunded. Depending upon your basis for green card eligibility, your case file may be kept at the NVC for a number of years. The good news is that, unlike most other immigration-related offices, the NVC is easily accessible—you can ask questions, for example about why your case is delayed, or whether they're waiting for anything from you. They prefer to be contacted by email, at NVCINQUIRY@state.gov, but you can also call, at 603-334-0700.

- Immigration and Customs Enforcement (ICE) is the enforcement arm of the DHS. Its investigators check on whether both employers and employees have complied with the immigration laws. They do surveillance, make arrests, and issue orders to show up for removal hearings—previously called deportation or exclusion hearings—before the Immigration Court.

- The detention section is run by Enforcement and Removal Operations (ERO), which is part of Immigration and Customs Enforcement (ICE), and comes under DHS. Its job is to find removable people, determine whether to hold them in custody, and execute final removal orders. ICE has an online system that allows the public to find out where a particular detainee is being held: Go to www.ice.gov, and at the bottom of the page click "ODLS," then search either by entering the detainee's A number and country of birth, or the detainee's name, birth date, and country of birth.
- The Naturalization Section is part of DHS/USCIS, and is responsible for deciding which aliens are eligible for citizenship and who qualifies as a citizen of the United States.
- The Adjustment of Status Section is part of DHS/USCIS, and is responsible for adjudicating applications for permanent residence.
- The Litigation Section is called the Office of the Chief Counsel. It is under the direction of DHS and Immigration and Customs Enforcement (ICE). It is the legal arm of the DHS and represents the government during hearings involving an alien before the Immigration Court and the federal and state courts. It also counsels the other sections of the DHS on legal matters.
- The Immigration Court (also called the Executive Office of Immigration Review), was part of the INS until 1987. Now separate from DHS, it is under the direction of the Department of Justice.

C. Inquiring About Delays

If you're waiting for an appointment or a decision on an immigration petition or application, you're likely to be frustrated. Action by USCIS and the State Department usually takes longer than anyone thinks it should. The question is, how long is too long? To some extent, this depends on the office you're dealing with.

For U.S. consulates, you'll have to ask other people in your country, or contact the consulate directly, to find out its normal schedule. Some consulates post such information on their websites, which you can locate via www.usembassy.gov.

You can find out just how backed up the various USCIS offices are by going to USCIS's online service at www.uscis.gov, and under "Tools," clicking "See Office Case Processing Times." You'll be able to get information on your own application, if it's with a service center and you have a receipt notice. You can also find out the dates of applications filed by other people like you—and can at least see whether they're still dealing with people who applied before you, or seem to have skipped over you and are dealing with people who applied after you.

In general, however, if you are waiting for an initial receipt, such as one for an I-129F or I-130 visa petition filed with a USCIS Service Center, a month is the longest you should wait. After that, there is a good chance that something is wrong. If you sent your application by Priority or certified mail, or with some other delivery confirmation, you may be able to find it that way. If you sent a check with your application, find out from your bank whether the check cleared. If it did, get a copy of the back of the canceled check, which should be stamped with the USCIS receipt number that will help you track your application.

For live assistance, call the USCIS National Customer Service Center at 800-375-5283 (Monday through Friday, 8:00 a.m. until 6:00 p.m. local time). Have as much information as possible on hand. The USCIS receipt number will make it easier for them to find your application, but they also may be able to find it with the other information contained in the application, which you will provide on the telephone. USCIS also offers automated information via the same phone line, 24 hours a day.

Make a note of the NCSC referral number or the name of the person with whom you speak, as well as the date of the call. It will help to have this information if further inquiries are needed.

Although the National Customer Service Center will rarely answer your question while you are on the telephone, they can usually make sure that your inquiry gets to someone who can answer it, and you will often get a response later. They customarily ask you to wait 45 days for a response, although the response often comes more quickly than that.

The other good way to inquire about a delay in your case is to make an InfoPass appointment. (This assumes that you are in the U.S. legally. People who are in the U.S. without authorization should not go in person to a DHS office.) Make the appointment by going to www.uscis.gov, and indicate that you need to speak with an information officer.

Bring whatever paperwork you have related to your application and your immigration status to your InfoPass appointment. Again, the information officer usually will not be able to "fix" your problem while you wait, but he or she normally can make an inquiry that may lead to processing of your case.

If your application is at a District or Field Office, or at the National Visa Center, you can send that office a letter of inquiry. If your case is at any of the Service Centers, however, the only response you are likely to get to an inquiry letter is a standard form letter recommending that you call the 1-800 number for the National Customer Service Center.

CAUTION

Avoid the temptation to be rude. Be courteous, clear, and to the point. Demonstrate that you're well organized, and that you know exactly when USCIS or the State Department received your materials, and when you should have gotten an answer.

Attorneys can't always get results any faster than you could on your own, but they do—especially if they're members of American Immigration Lawyers Association—have access to inside fax lines or phone numbers, which can help them make inquiries.

D. Speeding Up Processing in Emergencies

An emergency may arise where you need an action expedited or your immigration papers approved very quickly. For example, your wife may still be abroad because your petition for her is not yet approved, when she is stricken with a rare disease for which the only treatment is found in the United States.

In this type of situation, you need to speak with an information officer face to face. Make an InfoPass appointment through the USCIS website. If no appointments are available soon enough to meet your need, go to the USCIS office where your InfoPass appointment would be scheduled and explain that you have an emergency. If it is a true emergency, the information officers will usually make an exception and at least talk with you.

Once you talk with the information officer however, you will find that USCIS is extremely reluctant to bend its rules and act outside the standard operating procedures. But if your case truly deserves an exception from the general rule, and you approach the right USCIS worker in the right way, you may get a satisfactory resolution because there is a humanitarian reason to grant your request. It enables USCIS to show its human side.

Unfortunately, it is sometimes difficult to locate USCIS's human side.

For your best chance of success at your InfoPass appointment, bring a letter that you have written explaining your situation, and documents showing why immediate action is necessary. Where appropriate, bring the originals of documents, as well as copies to leave with USCIS. The letter you have written gives the information officer something to show his or her supervisors in trying to advocate on your behalf. However, do not expect the officer to read the letter before you have explained your urgent situation.

First of all, be resigned to the fact that there are two kinds of USCIS workers: One makes a decision strictly according to the letter of the law, and the other exercises discretion when appropriate and makes a decision according to the spirit of the law.

If the USCIS worker fails to respond to your inquiry or denies your request, try to go up the chain of command and speak with the supervisor.

Sample Letter to Supervisor

Leona Burgett, Supervisor
USCIS Office
Anytown, Anystate 12345

August 12, 20xx

Dear Ms. Burgett:

My file number is A12345678 and I have an adjustment of status application pending in your office.

I received a letter from my mother, with a certification from the hospital, that my father suffered a heart attack and his prognosis is dim. I filed for advance parole two days ago, but my application was denied. The USCIS worker said he believed that the certification from the hospital was fraudulently obtained, and did not accept my mother's letter because it was not translated into English.

Yesterday, I returned with a translation of the letter and my affidavit explaining that in our remote hometown, the most modern equipment available is a manual typewriter, on which some letters may be crooked or spaces may be skipped. The USCIS worker said that my advance parole will still be denied regardless of my explanations that my father is truly very ill.

I am married to a U.S. citizen and have been law-abiding—except for overstaying in this country until submitting my adjustment of status application.

Please help me with my advance parole request.

Sincerely,

Max Haxsim

Max Haxsim

If your request for immediate action is still denied unjustly, you may have to hire a lawyer to help put the pressure on. As a last resort, the lawyer may file a case of mandamus in the federal district court to force USCIS to act on your request.

E. Reporting Wrongdoing

Sometimes, a USCIS worker's actions may be truly reprehensible, involving gross incompetence, immoral conduct, or unlawful behavior—for instance, asking for a bribe, either before or after doing what the worker is supposed to do. In such cases, report the misdeed to the head of the particular USCIS office.

Your letter should specify the name of the USCIS worker, if known. If you did not ask for the name or the USCIS worker refused to answer, describe him or her. You also should indicate the time, date, and manner of misconduct and the names of any witnesses.

Although your complaint may lead to an investigation where you may be asked to repeat your facts in front of an investigator or an administrative judge, do not be afraid or unwilling to get involved. The officer's abusive behavior is not likely to stop, and many more people are likely to be injured by it unless you take action.

Sometimes, They Surprise You

While it's important to make your dissatisfaction known about a USCIS officer's bad or abusive behavior, the contrary should also be true. If you are served by a USCIS worker who goes the extra mile to be helpful, by all means write to the worker's office and let them know that there is an outstanding worker in their midst.

It may encourage more workers to deliver superlative service to the public.

Sample Letter

Department of Homeland Security
USCIS
[use local address]

April 15, 20xx

Dear Investigating Officer:

This is a complaint against a male USCIS officer who refused to give me his name. He is Caucasian of medium build, has gray hair, and wears eyeglasses.

I spoke with this officer on Tuesday, April 5, 20xx, at 10:00 a.m. on the 8th floor of the USCIS office in New York. He demanded a hundred extra dollars in cash before approving my request for advance parole.

When I refused to pay the additional money, he said that although all my paperwork was in order, he would have to deny the request since I wasn't willing to "pay what it took to get the wheels in motion."

Alfred Beiz, a paralegal at the law firm of Dias & Associates, was standing in line behind me, waiting to file some papers, and overheard the officer's remarks. Mr. Beiz is willing to file an affidavit swearing to the conversation he heard.

I request that you promptly investigate my charge against this officer, and inform me about the action taken.

Thank you for your attention.

With my best regards,

Ali Mufti

Ali Mufti

Keeping, Renewing, and Replacing Your Green Card

Now that you have finally obtained that plastic card giving you the right to stay and work in the United States without any hassle, and to leave and return without applying for a visa, make sure you don't you lose the card—or your right to it.

If all goes as it should, your green card will give you the right to live in the United States for as long as you want to. However, you need to protect this right by taking such measures as telling USCIS when you move, not spending too long outside the United States, and not becoming inadmissible or deportable. You should also make sure to renew your green card on time and replace it if it's lost.

 CAUTION

Think about applying for U.S. citizenship. After a certain number of years with a green card (usually five, but less for some people), you can apply for U.S. citizenship. This is a much more secure status—you'll be able to travel for longer periods of time, be safe from deportation, and will gain the right to vote. Start planning now: If you wait until five years go by to start thinking about citizenship, you may discover that there was something you needed to do (or something you did that you shouldn't have done) while you were waiting. For complete guidance, see *Becoming a U.S. Citizen: A Guide to the Law, Exam & Interview,* by Ilona Bray (Nolo).

A. Renewing or Replacing Your Green Card

Whether your green card is lost, or expires and needs to be renewed, U.S. Citizenship and Immigration Services (USCIS) requires that you file Form I-90, Application to Replace Permanent Resident Card. (See the sample at the end of this chapter.)

The filing fee is currently $450, plus $85 for fingerprints. (However, you don't need to pay the filing fee if you're getting a replacement green card because of a mistake by USCIS, for example if it misspelled your name on the card.) Where to file

Form I-90 gets a bit complicated depending on why you are filing it, so the best thing to do is visit USCIS's website at www.uscis.gov for the most up-to-date procedures. Consider e-filing this form in order to avoid any confusion about how to proceed. (See instructions for e-filing in Chapter 21.)

You can also use Form I-90 to get a new green card when:

- your name has been changed, due to marriage or divorce, in which case you must include a copy of your marriage or divorce certificate and your old card
- you turn 14 years of age; USCIS requires that you change your green card for a new one
- you receive an incorrect card with an erroneous name, birth date, photo, or date of entry
- you never received your green card, or
- your green card is blue, Form I-151; these old cards were issued during the 1960s and 1970s and expired on August 2, 1996, because of their lack of security features, giving opportunities for fraud.

You must swear that all the answers you give when applying for a green card are correct. If you knowingly falsify or conceal a material fact, or use any false document in submitting the application, you may be fined up to $10,000, imprisoned for up to five years, or both.

You should receive your new green card (Form I-551) within 30 to 45 days after USCIS receives your paperwork and filing fee.

B. When the Immigration Authorities Can Take Away Your Card

As a green card holder, you are expected to be law-abiding. Because you were not born with the right to stay in the United States and have not yet been naturalized, the immigration laws put certain restrictions on you that do not apply to U.S. citizens.

1. Failing to Report a Change of Address

The immigration law says that an alien who fails to give written notice to USCIS of a change of address can be deported or removed from the United States. Not only that, the alien could be charged with a misdemeanor and if found guilty, fined up to $200, imprisoned up to 30 days, or both.

The alien would have to convince the Immigration Judge during removal hearings that failure to notify USCIS of an address change was reasonably excusable or was not willful.

Therefore, to avoid any possible problem whenever you move to a new address, submit Form AR-11. To submit by mail, get the form from a USCIS office or the USCIS website at www.uscis.gov and send it to:

Department of Homeland Security
U.S. Citizenship and Immigration Services
Attn: Change of Address
1344 Pleasants Drive
Harrisonburg, VA 22801

However, you can also submit the form online, by going to www.uscis.gov/AR-11 and clicking "Online Change of Address." You'll need your:

- USCIS receipt number (if you have a pending case with USCIS)
- A-Number
- new and old addresses
- names and biographical information for any family members for whom you have filed a petition, and
- date and location (port of entry) of your last entry into the United States.

The advantage to submitting online is that you'll receive confirmation that your message got through.

There is no fee for filing this form.

2. Failing to Maintain a Residence in the United States

You become a permanent resident presumably because you intend to live in the United States. Sometimes things happen, however, that require you to spend long periods of time outside the United States. To make sure that you do not unintentionally lose your permanent residence, it's important to keep certain things in mind.

First, if you are outside the U.S. for one year or more without getting advance permission, the law will presume that you abandoned your permanent residence. Like any legal presumption, you can show that it is wrong in your particular case, but it is not easy to make this showing, and you might be required to prove your case in Immigration Court. If you are not successful, your right to U.S. residence and green card will be taken away.

To avoid this situation, if you know that you may be out of the U.S. for one year or more, apply for advance permission before you leave. Do this by filing Form I-131 (available at www.uscis.gov/i-131). This form is used for several different purposes, so you want to check off the box in Part 2 that shows you are a permanent (or conditional) resident applying for a reentry permit. Be sure to include a copy of your permanent resident card. (Only copy the back of the card if you have the old style card with information written on the back.) The filing fee for this is currently $360 (plus an $85 biometrics fee if you are between age 14 and 79). There is a sample Form I-131 at the end of this chapter.

A few weeks after USCIS receives your Form I-131, it will send you a receipt notice, and then a fingerprinting notice. You must attend this fingerprinting appointment (where your photo will also be taken) before you leave the United States. However, once that's taken care of, USCIS doesn't mind if you leave the U.S. before your reentry permit is actually approved and sent to you.

a. Six-Plus-Month Departures and Inadmissibility

Apart from the one-year rule that we just discussed, another important thing to know about traveling as a permanent resident is that an absence from the U.S. of more than six months at a time is treated differently than an absence of less than six months. An absence of less than six months at a time is not considered to be a legally significant departure. What this means is that USCIS will not consider whether any of the grounds of inadmissibility apply to you when you return. (See Chapter 4 for a discussion of the grounds of inadmissibility.)

If you are out of the U.S. for more than six months at a time, however, the immigration authorities consider this a legally significant departure and when you (attempt to) return, they will consider whether any of the grounds of inadmissibility now apply to you. If they think you are inadmissible, you will have a chance to show that they are wrong, but you might be required to prove your case in Immigration Court. If you are not successful, your green card (permanent residence) can be taken away.

b. Residence Can Be "Abandoned" After Departures of Any Length

There is one more thing to keep in mind to make sure that you do not unintentionally abandon your U.S. permanent resident status. It is not enough to be sure that you are never outside the U.S. more than one year at a time; it is not even enough to be sure that you are not outside the U.S. more than six months at a time. Even if you take only short trips outside the U.S., if, over the space of several years, you are spending more time outside the U.S. than inside the U.S., at some point border officials will wonder if you are acting more like a tourist in the U.S. than a permanent resident. In a situation like this, you should be ready to demonstrate your strong ties to the United States. The things that the border official will consider are:

- your purpose in leaving the U.S.
- whether your purpose is consistent with a temporary absence

- whether you still have a job, home, or family in the United States, and
- the duration of your trip.

Even if you are not going to be outside the U.S. for one year or more, if you know that you will be away on so many short trips that you will be outside the U.S. much more than inside over the course of several years, getting a reentry permit may be a good idea. It is good evidence that you intend to continue living in the United States as a permanent resident. It means that the authorities cannot rely solely on the length of your absences to determine whether you have lost your permanent residence status. However, since they can still look at other facts in your life, you should maintain as many ties to the United States as possible—even if you get a reentry permit.

If you have to go abroad before you receive the permit, you can request that the permit be delivered to your address overseas or, if the mail in your country is not reliable, through the United States embassy or consulate in your country.

If a reentry permit is issued, it is good for two years. However, if you have been outside of the U.S. for four out of the past five years, the permit will be issued for only one year. And if you have been out of the U.S. for that amount of time, you can also expect to receive intense questions at the airport about whether you have maintained your legal residence in the United States.

3. Explaining Your Failure to Reenter the United States

If you stay longer than the two years allowed by the reentry permit, or if you stay longer than one year without applying for the reentry permit, you will jeopardize your immigration status.

Upon arriving at the port of entry, the officials will question you on your right to return as a green card holder. You must be ready to present proof of why you did not return to the United States within the time expected.

Illness. A permissible delay could be due to your own serious illness or that of a close relative, especially if the illness started after you left. Convincing evidence of the illness would be copies of a doctor's written diagnosis, medical bills, prescriptions, and letters to you from friends.

Death. A death in the family could be another reason for delay. Bring with you copies of the death certificate, letters from the court or a lawyer on settlement of the estate, life insurance letters concerning distribution of the insurance proceeds, and a court order dividing property of the deceased.

Business reasons. Setting up or closing down a business enterprise could also be a valid reason for delay. Be ready to show bank statements, a contract of sale, invoices, letters from the bank, and letters from your business partners, your lawyer, and your accountant.

In other words, if you are detained at the airport for a more thorough questioning, you must be ready to convince the officer that you had a very good reason for not returning to the United States when expected. If the immigration officer is still not convinced, you will have another chance to explain your case before the Immigration Judge at your hearing.

Insist on your right to a hearing. Too often, the officer acts intimidating, and the scared green card holder signs away all green card rights. Once you do this, it is very difficult to get a second chance to explain your side before the Immigration Court. Your status will most likely automatically revert to that of a nonimmigrant—and you will have to repeat the process of getting a green card all over again.

However, if you were coerced or forced to sign away your rights, contact an immigration attorney, who may be able to help you fight to keep your green card.

4. Becoming Inadmissible

Grounds of inadmissibility are conditions that the immigration authorities can legally use to keep you from entering the United States. You had to prove that you weren't inadmissible (that is, hadn't committed any crimes, didn't have any serious illnesses, and weren't likely to need public assistance) in order to get your green card. But these same grounds apply to you every time you leave the United States for more than six months at a time and try to return. Even with your green card, you could be refused reentry. If one of these grounds applies to you, however, you may be able to get it waived. (See Chapter 4.)

5. Becoming Removable

In addition to the grounds of inadmissibility described above, the immigration laws list grounds of removability. These are actions or circumstances that can cause you to lose your right to the green card and be placed in removal proceedings in the United States. If you lose, you could be deported back to the country you came from.

The grounds of removability are too complex to explain in detail here. We have already discussed one of them, namely your obligation to report your changes of address to USCIS. In general, however, you need to make sure not to violate any immigration or criminal laws and not to get involved with any organizations that the U.S. government believes to be terrorist.

For a complete list of the grounds of removability, see I.N.A. § 237 or 8 U.S.C. § 1227.

C. Planning to Apply for U.S. Citizenship

You can avoid all the hassles and worries about losing your green card by applying for U.S. citizenship as soon as you're eligible. Citizenship is the highest benefit available under the U.S. immigration laws, and once you're a citizen, your status can't be taken away (unless you committed fraud in your citizenship application). You're not eligible for U.S. citizenship just yet—most people must wait between three and five years after getting their green card. But it's not too early to start thinking about citizenship and planning to apply.

The basic requirements for U.S. citizenship include:

- You've had permanent residence (a green card) for the required number of years—usually five, but three years if you've been married to and living with a U.S. citizen all that time. Also, asylees will receive green cards that are backdated one year to give them credit for some of their time spent in the U.S. as an asylee before actually getting approved for permanent residence, so in effect they don't need to wait a full five years after the approval. Similarly, refugees can, after receiving a green card, count all their time in the U.S. since their date of entry toward the required five years of permanent residence.
- You've been "physically present," that is, lived in the U.S., for at least half your required years of permanent residence.
- You've been "continuously present" in the United States since being approved for your green card.

- You've lived in the same U.S. state or USCIS district for three months before applying to the USCIS there.
- You're at least 18 years old at the time of filing the application.
- You've demonstrated good moral character over the years leading up to your application for citizenship—for example, by paying your taxes and child support and not committing any crimes.
- You can speak, read, and write English.
- You pass a brief test covering U.S. history and government.
- You're willing to affirm loyalty to the U.S. and serve in its military if necessary.

For now, the important message is to think twice before taking any long trips outside the U.S., do your best to learn English, and be a responsible member of society. You can start worrying about the details of your eligibility, and start studying for the test, closer to the time when you're allowed to apply.

 **RESOURCE**

Need complete instructions on the eligibility criteria and how to apply for U.S. citizenship? See *Becoming a U.S. Citizen: A Guide to the Law, Exam & Interview,* by Ilona Bray (Nolo).

Sample Form I-90, Application to Replace Permanent Resident Card (page 1)

Application to Replace Permanent Resident Card

Department of Homeland Security
U.S. Citizenship and Immigration Services

USCIS
Form I-90
OMB No. 1615-0082
Expires 12/31/2015

For USCIS Use Only	☐ Applicant Interviewed Date:_____ Class of Admission	Receipt	Action Block
		Remarks	

▶ **START HERE - Type or print in black ink.**

Part 1. Information About You

1. Alien Registration Number (A-Number)

▶ A- `2` `4` `0` `7` `0` `5` `0` `2` `3`

Your Full Name

NOTE: Your card will be issued in this name.

2.a. Family Name
(Last Name)   Cosmin

2.b. Given Name
(First Name)   Mihaita

2.c. Middle Name   Alin

3. Has your name legally changed since the issuance of your Permanent Resident Card?

☐ Yes (Proceed to **number 4.a. - number 4.c.**)

☒ No (Proceed to **number 5.a. - number 5.f.**)

☐ N/A - I never received my previous card.
(Proceed to **number 5.a. - number 5.f.**)

Your name exactly as reflected on your Permanent Resident Card

NOTE: Attach all evidence of your legal name change with this application.

4.a. Family Name
(Last Name)

4.b. Given Name
(First Name)

4.c. Middle Name

Mailing Address

5.a. In Care of Name

5.b. Street Number and Name   8383 Kew Gardens

5.c. Apt. ☒ Ste. ☐ Flr. ☐   401

5.d. City or Town   Queens

5.e. State NY   **5.f.** Zip Code 11415-1212

5.g. Postal Code

5.h. Province

5.i. Country   U.S.A.

U.S. Physical Address

6.a. Street Number and Name   8383 Kew Gardens

6.b. Apt. ☒ Ste. ☐ Flr. ☐   401

6.c. City or Town   Queens

6.d. State NY   **6.e.** Zip Code 11415-1212

Sample Form I-90, Application to Replace Permanent Resident Card (page 2)

Part 1. Information About You *(continued)*

7.   Gender   ☒ Male   ☐ Female

8.   Date of Birth   *(mm/dd/yyyy)* ▶ 10/02/1955

9.   City/Town/Village of Birth
     Bucharest

10. Country of Birth
     Romania

11. Class of Admission
     F1

12. Date of Admission
     (mm/dd/yyyy) ▶ 10/31/2012

13. U.S. Social Security Number (if any)
     ▶ 1 1 2 6 4 5 7 9 3

Part 2. Application Type

NOTE: If your conditional status is expiring within the next 90 days, then do **not** file this application. (See Form I-90 instructions for further information.)

My status is (Select **only one** box):

1.a. ☒ Permanent Resident (Proceed to **Section A**)

1.b. ☐ Permanent Resident - In Commuter Status (Proceed to **Section A**)

1.c. ☐ Conditional Permanent Resident (Proceed to **Section B**)

Reason for Application (select only one box)

Section A. (To be used **only** by a permanent resident or a permanent resident in commuter status.)

2.a. ☒ My previous card has been lost, stolen, or destroyed.

2.b. ☐ My previous card was issued but never received.

2.c. ☐ My existing card has been mutilated.

2.d. ☐ My existing card has incorrect data because of USCIS error. (Attach existing card with incorrect data along with this application.)

2.e. ☐ My name or other biographic information has been legally changed since issuance of my existing card.

2.f. ☐ My existing card will expire in 6 months or has already expired.

2.g1. ☐ I have reached my 14th birthday and am registering as required. My existing card will expire after my 16th birthday. (If you are filing this form before your 14th birthday, or more than 30 days after your 14th birthday, do not select 2.g1. You must select 2.j.)

2.g2. ☐ I have reached my 14th birthday and am registering as required. My existing card will expire before my 16th birthday. (If you are filing this form before your 14th birthday, or more than 30 days after your 14th birthday, do not select 2.g2. You must select 2.j.)

2.h1. ☐ I am a permanent resident who is taking up commuter status.

My port of entry (POE) into the United States will be:

2.h1.1. City and State

2.h2. ☐ I am a commuter who is taking up actual residence in the United States.

2.i. ☐ I have been automatically converted to permanent resident status.

2.j. ☐ I have a prior edition of the Alien Registration Card, or I am applying to replace my current Permanent Resident Card for a reason that is not specified above.

Section B. (To be used only by a conditional permanent resident.)

3.a. ☐ My previous card has been lost, stolen, or destroyed.

3.b. ☐ My previous card was issued but never received.

3.c. ☐ My existing card has been mutilated.

3.d. ☐ My existing card has incorrect data because of USCIS error. (Attach existing permanent resident card with incorrect data along with this application.)

3.e. ☐ My name or other biographical information has been legally changed since the issuance of my existing card.

Sample Form I-90, Application to Replace Permanent Resident Card (page 3)

Part 3. Processing Information

Mother's Name

1. Given Name
   (First Name) | Silvia

Father's Name

2. Given Name
   (First Name) | Claidus

Additional Information

3. Location where you applied for an immigrant visa or adjustment of status:

   Bucharest, Romania

4. Location where immigrant visa was issued or USCIS office where adjustment of status was granted:

   U.S. Consulate, Bucharest, Romania

Did you enter the United States with an immigrant visa? Complete **number 5.a.** and **number 5.a1.** (If you were granted adjustment of status, proceed to **number 6.**)

5.a. Destination in United States at time of admission

   Queens, NY

Port of entry where admitted to United States:

5.a1. City and State

   New York, NY

6. Have you ever been ordered removed from the United States? ☐ Yes ☒ No

7. Since you were granted permanent residence, have you ever filed Form I-407, Abandonment by Alien of Status as Lawful Permanent Resident, or otherwise been judged to have abandoned your status? ☐ Yes ☒ No

NOTE: If you answered **"Yes"** to **number 6** or **number 7** above, provide a detailed explanation on a separate sheet of paper. You must include your Name and A-Number on the top of each sheet.

Part 4. Accommodations for Individuals With Disabilities and Impairments *(Read the information in Form I-90 instructions before completing this Part.)*

1. Are you requesting an accommodation because of a disability and/or impairment? ☐ Yes ☒ No

If you answered **"Yes,"** check any applicable boxes:

1.a. ☐ I am deaf or hard of hearing and request the following accommodation (if requesting a sign-language interpreter, indicate for which language (e.g., American Sign Language)):

   _____

   _____

   _____

1.b. ☐ I am blind or sight-impaired and request the following accommodation:

   _____

   _____

   _____

   _____

1.c. ☐ I have another type of disability and/or impairment (describe the nature of the disability and/or impairment and accommodation you are requesting):

   _____

   _____

   _____

   _____

Sample Form I-90, Application to Replace Permanent Resident Card (page 4)

Part 5. Signature of Applicant *(Read the information on penalties in the Form I-90 instructions before completing this part. You must file Form I-90 while in the United States.)*

I certify, under penalty of perjury under the laws of the United States of America, that this application and the evidence submitted with it is all true and correct. I authorize the release of any information from my records that U.S. Citizenship and Immigration Services needs to determine eligibility for the benefit I am seeking.

1.b. Date of Signature *(mm/dd/yyyy)* ▶ 01/06/2015

2. Daytime Phone Number (718) 675 - 4892

NOTE: If you do not completely fill out this form or fail to submit required documents listed in the instructions, your application may be denied.

1.a. Signature of Applicant

Mihaita Cosmin

Part 6. Signature of Person Preparing This Application, If Other Than the Applicant

NOTE: If you are an attorney or representative, you must submit a completed Form G-28, Notice of Entry of Appearance as Attorney or Accredited Representative, along with this application.

Preparer's Full Name

Provide the following information concerning the preparer:

1.a. Preparer's Family Name *(Last Name)*

1.b. Preparer's Given Name *(First Name)*

2. Preparer's Business or Organization Name

Preparer's Mailing Address

3.a. Street Number and Name

3.b. Apt. ☐ Ste. ☐ Flr. ☐

3.c. City or Town

3.d. State ☐   **3.e.** Zip Code

3.f. Postal Code

3.g. Province

3.h. Country

Preparer's Contact Information

4. Preparer's Daytime Phone Number   Extension

(☐) ☐ - ☐

5. Preparer's E-mail Address *(if any)*

Declaration

To be completed by all preparers, including attorneys and authorized representatives: I declare that I prepared this benefit request at the request of the applicant, that it is based on all the information of which I have knowledge, and that the information is true to the best of my knowledge.

6.a. Signature of Preparer

6.b. Date of Signature *(mm/dd/yyyy)* ▶

NOTE: If you require more space to provide any additional information, use a separate sheet of paper. You must include your Name and A-Number on the top of each sheet.

Sample Form I-131, Application for Travel Document (page 1)

Application for Travel Document
Department of Homeland Security
U.S. Citizenship and Immigration Services

**USCIS
Form I-131**
OMB No. 1615-0013
Expires 03/31/2016

For USCIS Use Only	Receipt	Action Block	To Be Completed by an *Attorney/ Representative,* if any.

☐ **Document Hand Delivered**

By: _____ Date: ___ / ___ / ___

Document Issued

☐ Re-entry Permit *(Update "Mail To" Section)*   ☐ Refugee Travel Document *(Update "Mail To" Section)*

☐ Single Advance Parole   ☐ Multiple Advance Parole *Valid Until:* ___ / ___ / ___

Mail To *(Re-entry & Refugee Only)*
☐ Address in *Part 1*
☐ US Consulate at: _____
☐ Intl DHS Ofc at: _____

☐ Fill in box if G-28 is attached to represent the applicant.

Attorney State License Number:

▶ **Start Here.** Type or Print in Black Ink

Part 1. Information About You

1.a. Family Name *(Last Name)* Cosmin

1.b. Given Name *(First Name)* Mihaita

1.c. Middle Name Alin

Physical Address

2.a. In Care of Name

2.b. Street Number and Name 8383 Kew Gardens

2.c. Apt. ☒ Ste. ☐ Flr. ☐ 101

2.d. City or Town Queens

2.e. State NY   **2.f.** Zip Code 11415-1212

2.g. Postal Code

2.h. Province

2.i. Country USA

Other Information

3. Alien Registration Number (A-Number)

▶ A- | 2 | 4 | 0 | 7 | 0 | 5 | 0 | 2 | 3 |

4. Country of Birth
Romania

5. Country of Citizenship
Romania

6. Class of Admission
F1

7. Gender ☒ Male   ☐ Female

8. Date of Birth   *(mm/dd/yyyy)* ▶ 10/02/1955

9. U.S. Social Security Number *(if any)*
▶ | 1 | 1 | 2 | 6 | 4 | 5 | 7 | 9 | 3 |

Sample Form I-131, Application for Travel Document (page 2)

Part 2. Application Type

1.a. [X] I am a permanent resident or conditional resident of the United States, and I am applying for a reentry permit.

1.b. [ ] I now hold U.S. refugee or asylee status, and I am applying for a Refugee Travel Document.

1.c. [ ] I am a permanent resident as a direct result of refugee or asylee status, and I am applying for a Refugee Travel Document.

1.d. [ ] I am applying for an Advance Parole Document to allow me to return to the United States after temporary foreign travel.

1.e. [ ] I am outside the United States, and I am applying for an Advance Parole Document.

1.f. [ ] I am applying for an Advance Parole Document for a person who is outside the United States.

If you checked box "1.f." provide the following information about that person in 2.a. through 2.p.

2.a. Family Name *(Last Name)* _____

2.b. Given Name *(First Name)* _____

2.c. Middle Name _____

2.d. Date of Birth *(mm/dd/yyyy)* ▶ _____

2.e. Country of Birth
Romania

2.f. Country of Citizenship
Romania

2.g. Daytime Phone Number (718) 675 - 4892

Physical Address (If you checked box 1.f.)

2.h. In Care of Name _____

2.i. Street Number and Name _____

2.j. Apt. [ ] Ste. [ ] Flr. [ ] _____

2.k. City or Town _____

2.l. State _____ **2.m.** Zip Code _____

2.n. Postal Code _____

2.o. Province _____

2.p. Country _____

Part 3. Processing Information

1. Date of Intended Departure
(mm/dd/yyyy) ▶ 12/15/2014

2. Expected Length of Trip *(in days)* 395

3.a. Are you, or any person included in this application, now in exclusion, deportation, removal, or rescission proceedings? [ ] Yes [X] No

3.b. If "Yes", Name of DHS office: _____

4.a. Have you ever before been issued a reentry permit or Refugee Travel Document? *(If "Yes" give the following information for the last document issued to you):*
[ ] Yes [X] No

4.b. Date Issued *(mm/dd/yyyy)* ▶ _____

4.c. Disposition *(attached, lost, etc.)*: _____

If you are applying for a non-DACA related Advance Parole Document, skip to Part 7; *DACA recipients must complete Part 4 before skipping to Part 7.*

Sample Form I-131, Application for Travel Document (page 3)

Part 3. Processing Information *(continued)*

Where do you want this travel document sent? *(Check one)*

5. [X] To the U.S. address shown in **Part 1 (2.a through 2.i.)** of this form.

6. [ ] To a U.S. Embassy or consulate at:

6.a. City or Town

6.b. Country

7. [ ] To a DHS office overseas at:

7.a. City or Town

7.b. Country

If you checked "6" or "7", where should the notice to pick up the travel document be sent?

8. [ ] To the address shown in **Part 2 (2.h. through 2.p.)** of this form.

9. [ ] To the address shown in **Part 3 (10.a. through 10.i.)** of this form.:

10.a. In Care of Name

10.b. Street Number and Name

10.c. Apt. [ ] Ste. [ ] Flr. [ ]

10.d. City or Town

10.e. State [ ]   **10.f.** Zip Code

10.g. Postal Code

10.h. Province

10.i. Country

10.j. Daytime Phone Number ([ ] [ ] [ ]) [ ] [ ] [ ] - [ ] [ ] [ ] [ ]

Part 4. Information About Your Proposed Travel

1.a. Purpose of trip. *(If you need more space, continue on a separate sheet of paper.)*

To care for my terminally ill brother and likely assist with the settlement of his estate.

1.b. List the countries you intend to visit. *(If you need more space, continue on a separate sheet of paper.)*

Part 5. Complete Only If Applying for a Re-entry Permit

Since becoming a permanent resident of the United States (or during the past 5 years, whichever is less) how much total time have you spent outside the United States?

1.a. [X] less than 6 months		**1.d.** [ ] 2 to 3 years		
1.b. [ ] 6 months to 1 year		**1.e.** [ ] 3 to 4 years		
1.c. [ ] 1 to 2 years		**1.f.** [ ] more than 4 years		

2. Since you became a permanent resident of the United States, have you ever filed a Federal income tax return as a nonresident or failed to file a Federal income tax return because you considered yourself to be a nonresident? *(If "Yes" give details on a separate sheet of paper.)*

[ ] Yes   [X] No

Sample Form I-131, Application for Travel Document (page 4)

Part 6. Complete Only If Applying for a Refugee Travel Document

1. Country from which you are a refugee or asylee:

[   ]

If you answer "Yes" to any of the following questions, you must explain on a separate sheet of paper. Include your Name and A-Number on the top of each sheet.

2. Do you plan to travel to the country named above? ☐ Yes ☐ No

Since you were accorded refugee/asylee status, have you ever:

3.a. Returned to the country named above? ☐ Yes ☐ No

3.b. Applied for and/or obtained a national passport, passport renewal, or entry permit of that country? ☐ Yes ☐ No

3.c. Applied for and/or received any benefit from such country (for example, health insurance benefits)? ☐ Yes ☐ No

Since you were accorded refugee/asylee status, have you, by any legal procedure or voluntary act:

4.a. Reacquired the nationality of the country named above? ☐ Yes ☐ No

4.b. Acquired a new nationality? ☐ Yes ☐ No

4.c. Been granted refugee or asylee status in any other country? ☐ Yes ☐ No

Part 7. Complete Only If Applying for Advance Parole

On a separate sheet of paper, explain how you qualify for an Advance Parole Document, and what circumstances warrant issuance of advance parole. Include copies of any documents you wish considered. *(See instructions.)*

1. How many trips do you intend to use this document?
☐ One Trip ☐ More than one trip

If the person intended to receive an Advance Parole Document is outside the United States, provide the location (City or Town and Country) of the U.S. Embassy or consulate or the DHS overseas office that you want us to notify.

2.a. City or Town

[   ]

2.b. Country

[   ]

If the travel document will be delivered to an overseas office, where should the notice to pick up the document be sent?:

3. ☐ To the address shown in **Part 2 (2.h. through 2.p.)** of this form.

4. ☐ To the address shown in **Part 7 (4.a. through 4.i.)** of this form.

4.a. In Care of Name

[   ]

4.b. Street Number and Name [   ]

4.c. Apt. ☐ Ste. ☐ Flr. ☐ [   ]

4.d. City or Town [   ]

4.e. State [   ] **4.f.** Zip Code [   ]

4.g. Postal Code [   ]

4.h. Province [   ]

4.i. Country [   ]

4.j. Daytime Phone Number ([   ]) [   ] - [   ]

Sample Form I-131, Application for Travel Document (page 5)

Part 8. Signature of Applicant *(Read the information on penalties in the Form instructions before completing this Part.)* If you are filing for a Re-entry Permit or Refugee Travel Document, you must be in the United States to file this application.

1.a. I certify, under penalty of perjury under the laws of the United States of America, that this application and the evidence submitted with it is all true and correct. I authorize the release of any information from my records that U.S. Citizenship and Immigration Services needs to determine eligibility for the benefit I am seeking.

Signature of Applicant

Mihaita Cosmin

1.b. Date of Signature *(mm/dd/yyyy)* ▶ 10/04/2014

2. Daytime Phone Number (718) 675 - 4892

NOTE: If you do not completely fill out this form or fail to submit required documents listed in the instructions, your application may be denied.

Part 9. Information About Person Who Prepared This Application, If Other Than the Applicant

NOTE: If you are an attorney or representative, you must submit a completed Form G-28, Notice of Entry of Appearance as Attorney or Accredited Representative, along with this application.

Preparer's Full Name

Provide the following information concerning the preparer:

1.a. Preparer's Family Name *(Last Name)*

1.b. Preparer's Given Name *(First Name)*

2. Preparer's Business or Organization Name

Preparer's Mailing Address

3.a. Street Number and Name

3.b. Apt. ☐ Ste. ☐ Flr. ☐

3.c. City or Town

3.d. State

3.e. Zip Code

3.f. Postal Code

3.g. Province

3.h. Country

Preparer's Contact Information

4. Preparer's Daytime Phone Number   Extension

(☐☐☐) ☐☐☐ - ☐☐☐☐

5. Preparer's E-mail Address *(if any)*

Declaration

To be completed by all preparers, including attorneys and authorized representatives: I declare that I prepared this benefit request at the request of the applicant, that it is based on all the information of which I have knowledge, and that the information is true to the best of my knowledge.

6.a. Signature of Preparer

6.b. Date of Signature *(mm/dd/yyyy)* ▶

NOTE: If you require more space to provide any additional information, use a separate sheet of paper. You must include your Name and A-Number on the top of each sheet.

How to Find and Work With a Lawyer

lthough this book's philosophy is to help you understand the immigration law and procedures, your situation may be too complicated for you to handle on your own—particularly if you've spent time in the U.S. illegally, have a history of drug use or criminal activity, or fit any of the other problem scenarios described in this book. Or you may be unable to get USCIS to respond to a request for action on your application. It may become necessary to hire a lawyer or other immigration professional for help. This chapter gives you valuable tips on where to find help—and what to do once you find that help.

A. Where to Look for a Lawyer

A bad lawyer is worse than a thief. Good lawyers are worth their weight in gold. Look carefully to find a good, competent, honest lawyer who will help you with your immigration problems without charging you a hefty fee up front and a huge hourly fee as your case proceeds.

You can go a long way toward ensuring that you get the best lawyer possible by spending some time and effort before you hire one. There are a number of good places to begin your search.

1. Immigration Groups

Organizations that specialize in helping people with immigration problems may be able to answer your questions, represent you in your case, or refer you to an experienced immigration lawyer if the group does not take on individual cases. Ask your local USCIS office or a church, mosque, or temple whether they know of any such immigration groups.

Many of these organizations are what are called "nonprofits," meaning they exist to help the public, not for anyone's personal gain. They raise money from individuals, businesses, and charitable foundations. Unfortunately, because the U.S. government gives almost no money to nonprofits that help immigrants, and because other funding is rarely enough to meet the community's need, you'll need to be patient with these groups. They may be understaffed and have difficulties returning your phone calls within a reasonable time or spending time with you at all. Also realize that they can charge you market-rate fees for their services, although most try to offer lower fees for low-income immigrants.

> **CAUTION**
> **Don't rely on advice from someone who is not a lawyer, or at least supervised by a lawyer.** For example, some church groups try to have volunteers help immigrants with their legal problems. Though their efforts may be well meant, immigration law is too complex to be puzzled out by nonlawyers.

2. Friends and Relatives

Ask your friends and relatives about their own experiences with their immigration lawyers—whether they were satisfied with the representation, the competency, and the fees charged, and about their personal rapport with their attorney. Never choose a lawyer simply because he or she was the relative or classmate or friend of your brother or sister or best friend, without having an idea of the lawyer's competency or track record.

3. Embassies or Consulates

Your own embassy or consulate may have a list of immigration lawyers to recommend to you. Normally, your country's consular officers have your interests at heart and would not recommend a lawyer who is incompetent, a rogue, or a cheat.

4. Ads in Ethnic Newspapers

Your own ethnic newspapers and journals usually have an array of immigration lawyers offering their services directly through advertisements.

But beware—anyone can buy ad space. Be sure to investigate the lawyer's reputation on your own.

5. Lawyer Referral Groups

Although the local bar association and other lawyer groups may offer referral services, there is often little or no screening of lawyers listed in these services. The only qualification may be that no malpractice case has been filed against the lawyer.

The American Immigration Lawyers Association (www.aila.org) operates a lawyer referral service. The lawyers who participate in the service are usually competent and knowledgeable.

Nolo also offers, for certain parts of the U.S., a lawyer directory where lawyers have a chance to describe their philosophy and services, at www.nolo.com/lawyers. Nolo checks the lawyers' bar memberships and requires each participant to take a pledge to:

- Respect clients' efforts to educate themselves.
- Provide clients with a clear, fair, written agreement as well as detailed and timely bills.
- Perform legal work to the best of the lawyer's ability, regardless of the size or complexity of the legal matter.
- Use their professional skills to meet clients' objectives, and communicate regularly with clients.
- Be loyal to clients, inform clients of any possible conflicts of interest, and give clients honest and complete advice and information.

6. State Bar Associations

You can check with the bar association in your state to see whether it maintains a list of Certified Specialists in Immigration and Nationality Law. This is someone who has passed state requirements demonstrating knowledge of and experience in immigration law, often by taking a written exam, completing extra coursework, and being favorably evaluated by other attorneys and judges. Not all states certify specialists, however.

Beware of the Bad Guys

Nonattorney practitioners, visa consultants, immigration pseudo-experts, travel agents, people posing as attorneys, and nonprofit organizations not authorized by U.S. Citizenship and Immigration Services (USCIS) to represent aliens before USCIS—all of them litter the immigration marketplace.

Some of them provide good advice. But for the most part, be wary—especially if they promise you a green card without any hassle for a certain amount of money. Aside from the fact that it is unlawful to practice immigration law without being admitted by a state bar association, there is no way you can check on these individuals' expertise, and nowhere to complain if their services are poor. Many incompetent consultants prey on immigrants and then simply pack up and move when too many people catch on to them.

Report any wrongdoers to the attorney general's office in your state so that they will be forced to stop victimizing unsuspecting immigrants.

B. Deciding on a Particular Lawyer

Once you have a referral to a lawyer—or even better, several referrals—contact each to see which one you like best.

A law firm may have a good reputation for its immigration practice, but the lawyer assigned to handle your case is the lawyer responsible for the success or failure of your case. Base your decision about whether to hire an individual lawyer on the rapport you feel with him or her—not just on the law firm's reputation.

1. The Initial Interview

Start by asking for an appointment. The office may ask you to first discuss your immigration problem over the phone, because the lawyer may not handle cases such as yours.

When you do find a lawyer who agrees to meet with you, go to the meeting with the thought in mind that you are interviewing him or her—not the other way around. It will be you who decides whether or not you want to hire that particular lawyer to handle your case.

Rely on your instincts when you first interview the lawyer. Does he or she seem competent, knowledgeable, fair, efficient, courteous, and personable? It would be unfortunate and unwise for you to feel uneasy every time you are in contact with your lawyer while paying your hard-earned money.

Find out in which state (or states) the attorney is licensed to practice law. Because immigration law is based on federal law, an attorney is allowed to practice it in any state, as long as he or she is licensed to practice in some state. Then you'll need to check the bar association of the attorney's licensing state to see whether any complaints have been filed against the attorney.

2. Consultation Fees

Some lawyers may not charge you an initial consultation fee, but most immigration lawyers charge between $100 and $200, depending on the city where you live, the expertise of the lawyer, and how long the interview lasts. When you call for an appointment, ask whether a consultation fee is charged and how much it is. Also ask how long the lawyer has been in immigration law practice and how many cases like yours he or she has handled.

If you take a few minutes to get organized beforehand, 30 minutes to an hour should be enough time to explain your situation and get at least a basic opinion of what the lawyer can do for you and what that help is likely to cost. Bring with you:

- your passport
- Form I-94 (if you entered the U.S. legally)
- records of any arrests
- a copy of any immigration forms you may have filled out and correspondence received from the INS or USCIS, and
- documents you may need to prove family relationships, such as husband and wife or parent and child.

3. Dealing With Paralegals and Assistants

Because the practice of immigration law usually involves filling out a great number of forms, the lawyer may hire a paralegal or secretary who interviews you to get many of the answers needed to complete your paperwork.

The paralegal or secretary becomes your contact person. At the initial interview, ask to meet the paralegal who will be working on your case, too, so that you have an idea of how comfortable you will be in dealing with the assistant. Ask whether he or she is supervised and whether the lawyer normally reviews the forms before submitting them to the U.S. government.

C. Paying the Lawyer

Some law firms or organizations specializing in immigration may take your case *pro bono,* meaning they will provide a lawyer to handle your case without asking for any money or for only a small amount to cover expenses. However, due to limited resources and great demand, they may not be able to accept your immigration case and may only be able to tell you what your legal options are and advise you about whether you seem to have a strong case. These groups may refer you to a list of attorneys they feel would be representing you in the same spirit of service as they do and whose fees would be reasonable.

1. Types of Fee Arrangements

Many immigration attorneys charge a "flat fee" for their work. Flat fees must be based on the amount of time that an attorney expects to spend on your case, times their hourly rate. The hourly rate should be specified in their contract, and becomes important if you decide to end the attorney's representation before the work is completed. (See "Firing a Lawyer," below.) Most lawyers are guided by the principle that time is money.

Since you are being charged a flat fee for a specific job, be sure you know what that job is. For example, if you are hiring an attorney for an adjustment of status case, does the flat fee include filling out the forms (including the forms for the work permit and travel document), making sure that USCIS receives the forms, preparing you for the interview, and attending the interview with you? If you are among the few people who get called back for a second or third interview, does the attorney charge for those interviews separately from the quoted flat fee? If USCIS does not decide your case in a timely fashion, are additional inquiries charged for separately? What are the "incidental" charges that you will be expected to pay in addition to the flat fee? For example, you should know whether you will be paying the USCIS filing fees separately from the attorney fee, and whether you will be responsible for mail or courier charges and copying costs.

Many lawyers will agree to let you pay a flat fee in installments during the period it takes to process your immigration papers.

Some immigration lawyers do not charge a flat fee. They will charge for their work based on quarter-hours, so that if you call and spend ten minutes on the telephone, you will be charged for a minimum of 15 minutes of work. Unless you are completely satisfied that your lawyer is honest, you may be opening yourself up to paying into a bottomless money pit when you agree to pay the lawyer according to an hourly charge.

If you agree to the per-hour billing rate—usually unwise unless you are in a removal proceeding due to grave criminal conduct or some other complicated case—request a schedule of legal work to be done and a maximum you will pay for each task.

2. Get It in Writing

Most disagreements between lawyers and clients involve fees, so be sure to get all the details involving money in writing—the per hour billing rate or flat maximum fee, how often you will be billed, and how the attorney will handle any funds you may have deposited in advance to cover expenses.

D. Managing the Lawyer

A great many complaints against lawyers have to do with their failure to communicate with their clients. Your lawyer may be the one with the legal expertise, but the rights that are being pursued are yours—and you are the most important person involved in your case. You have the right to demand that your lawyer be reasonably available to answer your questions and to keep you posted on your case.

You may need to put some energy into managing your lawyer.

1. Carefully Check Every Statement

Each statement or bill should list costs that the lawyer has paid or that you are expected to pay. If any one lacks sufficient detail, call your lawyer and politely demand that a new, more detailed version be sent before you pay it. Don't feel as though you're being too pushy: The laws in many states actually require thorough detail in lawyers' billing statements.

2. Educate Yourself

By learning the most you can about immigration laws and what to expect during the procedure, you'll be able to monitor your lawyer's work and may even be able to do some legwork, make a suggestion, or provide information that will move your case along faster.

Unfortunately, USCIS and the State Department are bureaucracies and oftentimes a case is simply held up until the slow-grinding wheels of procedure get through it. Many people unfairly blame their lawyers for delays that are actually the government's fault—or just a natural result of how the immigration laws are structured. However, if an immigration application is proceeding much more slowly than your lawyer initially told you it would, then ask your lawyer whether it would make sense to contact the appropriate office and find out the reason for the delay.

3. Keep Your Own Calendar

Note when papers and appearances are due in court. If you rely on your lawyer to keep your case on schedule, you may be unpleasantly surprised to find that an important deadline has been missed. This could put your immigration status in jeopardy. Call or write to your lawyer at least a week before any important deadline in your case to inquire about plans to meet it.

Of course, you need to do your part, by showing up for appointments with your lawyer on time, so that your case can be adequately prepared. And you must be especially careful to arrive on time—or better yet, early—for any appointments with immigration officials. If you're not in the room when you're scheduled to be there, your case may be delayed for weeks or months, or, in the case of Immigration Court, you may receive an immediate order of removal (deportation).

Your lawyer will be unable to help you out of this mess, even if he or she was in the courtroom at the time.

4. Maintain Your Own File

Never give away original documents connected with your case; keep the originals for your own files and give only copies to your lawyer. USCIS will, in most cases, accept copies of the original documents. Also, ask for a copy of every letter and application your lawyer sends to USCIS. By having a well-organized file of your own, you'll be able to discuss your case with your lawyer intelligently and efficiently—even over the telephone.

Being well-informed will help keep your lawyer's effectiveness up and your costs down, especially if your lawyer is working on an hourly basis, in which case telephone consultations are less expensive than office visits.

Also, your lawyer cannot hold your immigration files ransom in case you decide to change legal counsel, because you have copies of everything the office file has on your case.

In any event, you have a right to promptly receive a copy of your file. The attorney may ask you to sign or produce a written authorization and transfer request before turning the file over to you.

E. Firing a Lawyer

Change lawyers if you feel that's necessary. If the relationship between you and the lawyer you chose doesn't seem to be working, or if you feel that your case isn't progressing as it should, think about asking another lawyer to take over.

If you get upset every time you talk to your lawyer because he or she does not seem to understand what you are saying about your case, or will not take the time to listen, you will save yourself both money and mental anguish if you look for someone else to represent you.

But be clear with the first lawyer that you are taking your business elsewhere, and immediately put your decision in writing. At that point, your first lawyer should stop working on your case. The lawyer can then give you an accounting of how much time was spent working on your case. If you have paid the lawyer a lot of money up front, and he or she did not yet spend much time on your case, you will probably be due a refund.

If you were paying in installments and the lawyer spent more time working on your case than you have so far paid for, you may still owe money for the work that was performed, even though you are firing the lawyer.

Do not expect your first lawyer to share any of the fee you've paid with your new lawyer. Unless you have a contingency fee arrangement where the lawyer takes a share of the damages won—and very few immigration cases are structured that way—your fee agreement with your new lawyer will be completely separate from your fee agreement with your first lawyer. Between the two lawyers, you may end up paying more than you would have if you had only one lawyer. Both lawyers may claim they handled the lion's share of the work in your case. Do not be embarrassed to negotiate with the lawyers.

> ### What to Do About Bad Legal Advice
>
> Take prompt action against any behavior by a lawyer that appears to be deceptive, unethical, or otherwise illegal. A call to the local bar association, listed in the telephone directory under "Attorneys," should provide you with guidance on what types of lawyer behavior are prohibited and how to file a complaint.
>
> Still, in most states, groups that regulate attorneys are biased toward them. Unless the lawyer's conduct is plainly dishonest or he or she has abandoned your case, you will probably not get much satisfaction. However, sometimes the threat of filing a complaint can move your lawyer into action. And if worst comes to worst, filing a formal complaint will create a document that you'll need should you end up later filing a malpractice lawsuit against a lawyer.

Index